THE REDGRAVES

THE REDGRAVES

A Family Epic

DONALD SPOTO

The Robson Press

7 92. 092
RED

This edition published in Great Britain in 2012 by
The Robson Press (an imprint of Biteback Publishing Ltd)
Westminster Tower
3 Albert Embankment
London SE1 7SP
Copyright © Donald Spoto 2012

This edition published by arrangement with Crown Archetype, an imprint of the
Crown Publishing Group, a division of Random House, Inc.

Donald Spoto has asserted his right under the Copyright, Designs and Patents Act
1988 to be identified as the author of this work.

All insert photographs by British Film Institute, Film Stills Archive,
unless otherwise noted.

ISBN 978-1-84954-394-1

10 9 8 7 6 5 4 3 2 1

A CIP catalogue record for this book is available from the British Library.

Set in Granjon

Printed and bound in Great Britain by
CPI Group (UK) Ltd, Croydon CR0 4YY

For Ole—
again, and always

⸺⟨⟩⸺

"... right next to the right one ..."

TIM CHRISTENSEN, *Danish composer and lyricist*

It takes the pity of God
to get to the bottom of things.

ENID BAGNOLD, *The Chalk Garden*

Contents

Introduction and Acknowledgments

THIS BOOK IS the result of more than thirty years of research; it is also a record of many valued friendships.

The project began when I first met Michael Redgrave in January 1981. At seventy-two, he was suffering greatly from the debilitating effects of the illness that would end his life four years later. He no longer gave interviews, and avoided meeting strangers, but he made an exception when I was living in London and working on my biography of Alfred Hitchcock. In response to my letter, Sir Michael's secretary, Joan Hirst, replied that he would welcome me for a brief chat about *The Lady Vanishes,* the 1938 Hitchcock thriller in which Redgrave had made his movie debut.

At two o'clock on the appointed afternoon, I arrived at his cozy mews house in a quiet, cobbled street of Belgravia. Joan Hirst had asked me to limit my visit to no more than a half hour, but my host would hear none of that. Three hours later, following a lengthy interview and several rounds of drinks, he finally allowed me to depart, but with the promise that we would meet again. Sir Michael's memories of *The Lady Vanishes* that afternoon were precise, witty and richly detailed; he had also confided more of his private life and career than he had perhaps intended.

After his death in 1985, when I was researching the life of Laurence Olivier, I was drawn closer into the family circle by Michael's widow, Rachel Kempson Redgrave, who had been a close confidante of Olivier's second wife, Vivien Leigh. My subsequent years of friendship with Rachel provided even more insight into the long history of her family, for by this time, the three children of Michael and Rachel—Vanessa, Lynn and Corin—had achieved international fame and many accolades for their own career achievements. I treasure the transcripts of my conversations with Rachel and my letters from her, as I do the memories of our many lunches at West End restaurants and late-afternoon cups of strong tea at her flat in Flood Street, Chelsea.

It was clear to both of us that one day, as she hoped, I would undertake this book. In the intervening years, I researched and published other biographies—the lives of Ingrid Bergman and of Alan Bates, for example—but the Redgraves were always on my mind, as they were topics for discussions during interviews. The many people who were forthcoming are acknowledged here; some of them, like Michael and Rachel, also became good friends.

—m—

IN THE TWENTIETH century, the most famous knights of the British theater were John Gielgud, Ralph Richardson, Laurence Olivier, Alec Guinness and Michael Redgrave. Biographies of the first four appeared on both sides of the Atlantic—but no life of Michael Redgrave has been published in the United States, and no Redgrave family history has appeared anywhere, despite their remarkable theatrical lineage that spans centuries and continues to flourish even as I write these words.

Corin Redgrave wrote a brief memoir; he was also the author of his father's autobiography and of books credited to other family members. These he stitched together, from articles and from compilations of Michael's published lectures (*The Actor's Ways and Means* and *Mask or Face,* for example, published in 1953 and 1958); Corin also relied heavily on two outdated, half-century-old sources: Richard Findlater's *Michael Redgrave: Actor* (1956) and a long interview with Michael conducted by Lillian Ross (1962). Corin's book, and the ghostwritten lives of his relatives that he produced, copied identical passages from these sources, and repeated the same unfortunate errors of time, place and circumstance.

Corin was a splendid actor, a person of strong principles and of un-assailable goodwill, but his talents did not extend to careful authorship. The same may be said of Vanessa and Lynn: the former's book is long on political and social history but comes up short as autobiography; the latter's hundred-page reminiscence is but a brief, selective prelude to a massive collection of diet recipes. Like those of their parents, the signal achievements of the Redgrave children and grandchildren have deserved fuller treatment than any of them provided. Their books, sometimes entertaining and provocative, are radically incomplete and unreliable as history, biography or autobiography.

Serious problems arose from the gaps in the Redgrave books. Why, for example, did they all insist that Michael was born illegitimately when the historical record proves otherwise? Why did Lynn Redgrave, despite all written evidence to the contrary, always claim that her father's diaries contained no mention of her birth or accomplishments? I was convinced that these and other critical matters relative to their personal and professional lives—and the tangle of their relations with one another—merited examination and assessment: hence the book you are now reading.

Involved as deeply in the world's reality as in the realms of creative imagination, the Redgraves lived their individual and collective lives in epic dimensions, and in a ceaseless rhythm of activity and accom-plishment unmatched by any other family in theatrical history. They mastered difficult and demanding crafts as actors, producers and di-rectors, and they were triumphant in works from ancient tragedies to contemporary plays, from the classics to experimental theater, from repertory to movies and the lecture hall. It is no exaggeration to assert that the Redgraves defined and extended the possibilities for actors in every medium for over a century, from the days of provincial touring companies to the era of television. They also made their marks on the political and social order of our time.

Charting the course of their work from the last quarter of the nine-teenth century up to 2012, we can tally an astonishing list of appear-ances in more than 2,600 plays, films, television programs and radio entertainments. A discussion of each item would necessarily transform this family biography into a tiresome, multivolume encyclopedia. I have, therefore, decided to offer descriptive comments or brief assessments of only those theatrical works that seem crucial or memorable for each Redgrave's career, and to mention only those film and television appearances readily available in home video formats. Occasionally, I have provided a brief list of titles during a specific time frame, but this is only to indicate the prodigious energies that have characterized every Redgrave. (Because it seems less academic and repetitious, I have most often referred to theaters informally: the Haymarket, the Comedy, the Albery, the National, and so forth, without the word *Theatre* following the name.)

—m—

As ALWAYS, I owe an enormous debt of gratitude to very many people—most of all to Sir Michael Redgrave and to Rachel Kempson, Lady Redgrave, for their trust and confidence; and to Lynn Redgrave, for her gracious endorsement of this project and her encouragement even in the final weeks of her life. But for all their benevolence, this is in no sense an authorized biography.

Over the course of three decades, I interviewed actors with important connections to one or another Redgrave, and I gratefully acknowledge their contributions to this book: Peggy Ashcroft, Hermione Baddeley, Ingrid Bergman, Claire Bloom, Constance Cummings, Denholm Elliott, John Gielgud, Alec Guinness, Katharine Hepburn, Margaret Lockwood, Karl Malden, Siobhan McKenna, Bernard Miles, John Mills, Marian Seldes, Susan Strasberg, Ann Todd, Dorothy Tutin and Josephine Wilson.

Writers, producers and directors were equally helpful: Michelangelo Antonioni, Frith Banbury, Robert Bolt, Jack Cardiff, Cheryl Crawford, Simon Gray, Alfred Hitchcock, Christopher Isherwood, Elia Kazan, Joshua Logan, Joseph Losey, Sidney Lumet, Joseph L. Mankiewicz, Ronald Neame, John Osborne, John Schlesinger, Irene Mayer Selznick and Fred Zinnemann.

I also benefited from the special insights and generous assistance of experts, friends and colleagues: Stella Adler, Katharine Andres, John

Andrews, Elaine Dundy, Mary and Laurence Evans, Lewis Falb, Angela Fox, Sue Jett, Irene Mahoney, Patricia Milbourn, Gerald Pinciss and Maria Piscator.

At the Danish Film Institute, Lars Ølgaard provided me with some important bibliographical materials on the Redgraves, and Madeleine Schlawitz arranged access to photographs in the DFI collection. Similarly, I acknowledge the kind help of Dave McCall, commercial manager at the British Film Institute, who set before me the vast photo collection of the BFI. With her usual friendly alacrity, Stacey Behlmer, at the Academy of Motion Picture Arts and Sciences, Beverly Hills, always had valuable suggestions.

Through the generosity of my good friend Claus Kjær, I was able to hear Michael Redgrave's 1955 recording of Hans Christian Andersen's "The Fir Tree," made in Denmark at an Andersen festival that year.

My many months of research in the Michael Redgrave Archive, in the Theatre Collections at the Victoria and Albert Museum, London, would not have been possible without the assistance of the staff headed by chief archivist Ramona Riedzewski. Suzanne Barker, in the Record Copying Department of the National Archives of the United Kingdom, Kew, responded quickly and efficiently to my calls for help.

John Darretta, an expert on the history of Italian literature, provided important insights into the work of Antonio Fogazzaro, whose novels greatly influenced Vanessa Redgrave's education.

The recollections of cinematographer Paul Elliott, a true artist of the movies, were, as always, valuable and perceptive.

Biographer and film historian Bernard Dick generously shared with me his compelling analysis of the Graham Greene novel *The Quiet American* and the movie version of it, directed by Joseph L. Mankiewicz.

Michael Green has noteworthy credentials in movie productions, and his prodigious memory of projects in which he was involved with various Redgraves contributed to my understanding of key moments in the family's careers.

—ﻌ—

ELAINE MARKSON, MY agent for more than thirty years, has always been my primary professional advocate: I value her counsel as I cherish her abiding friendship. Gary Johnson, also at the Markson Thoma Agency, deserves more than words can describe for his guidance, good humor and endless patience. My support system at the agency includes Geri Thoma and Julia Kenny.

Seven years ago, Elaine introduced me to Julia Pastore at Random House. Julia's warm encouragement, her insights and her extraordinary gifts as editor have made this project a rich and happy experience from day one.

Finally (but never really so), I offer limitless gratitude to Ole Larsen, far beyond the term of a book's production. I owe him more than I can say for his endorsement of my work and, more to the point, his constancy and devotion, and for his commitment to our life together—hence, once again, you see his name on the dedication page.

D.S.
Sjælland, Denmark
Christmas 2011

THE REDGRAVES

One

THEIR WEDDING DAYS

(1894-1991)

DURING THE COLD AFTERNOON OF FRIDAY, MARCH 20, 1908 — IN a modest, poorly heated room above a newspaper shop on Horfield Road, in Bristol, England—a twenty-three-year-old actress named Daisy Scudamore Redgrave gave birth to a plump, blond-haired boy. After the newborn's first cries, a woman who had helped during the delivery asked if Daisy had chosen a name for the baby. "Mother looked across the street and saw St. Michael's Church," said Michael Redgrave years later. Daisy's notebook confirms the choice of name she had made without consulting her husband, an actor who was then in London, a hundred miles away. Recently, he had been absent much of the time.

For the previous three months, obeying her doctor's instructions, Daisy had accepted no roles in the provincial tours that frequently kept her busy but brought neither wealth nor fame. During her confinement, instead of traveling and meeting with theater managers, she paid her rent by working a few hours each day in the shop beneath her rented room. She had met Roy Redgrave the previous summer, when they began a passionate romance that almost at once resulted in her pregnancy. Roy at first hesitated but then proposed marriage, six months before the child's birth. Daisy accepted, but the sequence of surprises was just beginning.

DAISY BERTHA MARY Scudamore was born on November 13, 1884, in Portsmouth, an island-town on the southern coast of England and a major naval port. She was the last of five children born to George Scudamore, who worked for a shipbuilding company, and Clara Linington, who was forty-five at the time of Daisy's birth. The girl's school record was unremarkable, but she had a flair for song, dance and recitation—aptitudes her staid Victorian parents did not encourage.

During a family holiday in Aberdeen at Christmas 1898, fourteen-year-old Daisy appeared in *Aladdin,* a musical pageant for children. She soaked up the applause and clutched the small bouquets friends offered after the performance; with that, the theatrical die was cast. Already a tall, pretty, vivacious teenager with expressive blue eyes, she had (so she was convinced) a fund of talents that guaranteed a successful career.

The following year, Daisy announced that she wanted to work on the stage—news her parents received in mute shock, as if the girl had proclaimed her intention to work on the streets.

At the turn of the twentieth century, the acting profession was only just beginning to enjoy widespread respectability. Since Elizabethan times, most actors were regarded as little more than rogues and vagabonds. The daughter of the actor-manager Samuel Phelps, for example, was expelled from school in the 1850s when it was learned that her father was an actor, and the wife of the great actor Henry Irving ridiculed him about the shame of his profession, and eventually left him for that reason. As recently as 1889, when she was on the verge of international fame, the actress known as Mrs. Patrick Campbell received a letter from her aunt Kate, pitying her as "a poor unfortunate child . . . yet to learn the shame, the humiliation of seeing yourself despised by decent people" precisely because she was of the theater.

Early in her reign, Queen Victoria had begun to reverse this prevalent contemptuous attitude. An avid playgoer, she invited actors to Windsor Castle, to present scenes from respectable dramatic works. Although she denied herself this pleasure for twenty years after the death of her husband, Prince Albert, Victoria later attended command performances and received leading players in her homes. This appreciation was symbolized in 1895, when Victoria bestowed a knighthood on Henry Irving, the first such honor for an actor. Six more actor-managers received the same honor between 1897 and 1913, first from Victoria and then from her son and grandson, Edward VII and George V.

The national census of 1881 had counted 4,565 actors in Britain. Their number had grown to 18,247 by 1911, and during those three decades, twenty-one new theaters were opened in London's West End. At the same time, more actors were coming from respectable backgrounds. An actor's status continued to improve in the public's estimation: higher classes of society were now depicted onstage; amateur theatricals expanded everywhere; and repertory companies multiplied. For the first time since the Middle Ages, the Church also took an eager and sustaining interest in the theater, and actors were no longer regarded as undesirable companions. In London, the founding of the Academy of Dramatic Art in 1904 (granted royal status in 1920 and henceforth known familiarly as RADA) and of the Central School of Speech and Drama (in 1906) also helped to erase the stigma attached to acting by associating it with education.

In light of the loud parental disapproval of her career plans, Daisy bided her time. But then, around the time of her fifteenth birthday, she packed a small bag, slipped away from home without so much as a farewell, and sought out a London theatrical agent whose name she spotted in a newspaper. When she said her name was Scudamore, the agent presumed that she was somehow related to the noted actor-manager-playwright Fortunatus Augustus Scudamore, and he forthwith suggested that she visit that man's home in Barnes, a riverside London suburb.

F. A. Scudamore was actually no Scudamore. Born Frank Davis, he had assumed the classical moniker Fortunatus and the venerable surname of a family that could be traced back before the Norman Conquest and included many nobles and landed gentry on various branches of its tree. When he opened the door to the clear-eyed, ambitious Daisy that afternoon late in 1899—and so met someone he thought was an authentic Scudamore—he improvised a little scene that could have been straight from one of his own sentimental plays. "If you are not my daughter," he cried, welcoming her with a throb in his voice, "then I don't know whose daughter you may be!" He did not investigate, and she did not elaborate.

That was enough for Daisy, who was delighted to be offered a more obliging family than her own, and one better suited to her professional aspirations. (For decades thereafter, the fiction circulated that Michael Redgrave was the grandson of Fortunatus Augustus Scudamore—a canard Daisy did nothing to suppress.*) She had no further contact with her real parents up to the time of her father's death in 1916 and her mother's in 1925.

Taken into the house and welcomed by F.A.'s wife and children, Daisy was thenceforth presented to the world as his long-lost niece, while her true Portsmouth parents faded into oblivion. Over the next two years, "Uncle" Fortunatus created roles for her in several of his provincial productions and at London's Pavilion Theatre, Mile End. After playing small parts in two plays during Sarah Bernhardt's visit to London, Daisy gave (according to one newspaper) "a pleasing represen-tation of the heroine" in Scudamore's four-act melodrama *The Dangers of London,* in which she was required to cry repeatedly to her stage husband, "Kiss me, Percy!" In April 1901 she had better luck with a comedy called *Riding to Win*: as one critic observed, "her grace and buoyancy have been heightened by a capacity for fun that has proved very diverting."

But the press took note of Daisy only rarely, and she began to com-plain that her talents were never fully appreciated. This instilled a cer-tain crusty bitterness that went beyond mere ambition or professional rivalries. Years later her grandson had the impression that Daisy be-lieved in "a charmed circle [that] surrounded the West End theatres, and a kind of freemasonry [that] kept out actresses like herself." It never occurred to her that there might have been other reasons for her disenfranchisement—the absence of a singular talent, for example.

---

* The March 17, 1967, issue of *Time,* detailing the achievements of the Redgraves, took for granted the bogus F. A. Scudamore connection.

—◊—

ONE DAY IN November 1904, Daisy took sides with Scudamore's son Lionel in a dispute with his father. Hastily tossing a feather boa around her neck and lifting her head in mute exasperation, she stormed out, as if rehearsing an actor-proof exit scene in a new play. When she returned the next afternoon for some fence-mending, Daisy found the house unaccountably silent. To her horror, she saw her patron and mentor sprawled on the parlor floor, dead of an apparent heart attack at the age of fifty-six.

Davis/Scudamore had left his house and copyrights to his wife and offspring, but for a time his widow continued to support Daisy with small sums, considering her, as she said, "nearly as dear to me as my own children." This patronage was short-lived, however, for soon the family was overwhelmed with debts and utterly without capital.

But Daisy thrived. By early 1905 she was back in theatrical harness, landing jobs that usually paid one pound a week and scurrying from Cornwall to Scotland, accepting virtually anything on offer. The closest she came to a major role was in a production of Irving's *The Bells* at the Savoy Theatre in June 1906—a production in which she costarred with Irving's son.

In late spring 1907 she appeared in Brighton, in a play called *Their Wedding Day*. Also in the cast was an attractive actor named Roy Redgrave, whose birth name was George Elsworthy Redgrave. He already had at least one wife, several mistresses and a number of children, but soon Daisy thought that she was his favorite, and she foresaw a long and happy future with him once he obtained a divorce. Well might she have encouraged this rosy dream, for she was soon pregnant with Roy's child.

—◊—

FOR MORE THAN a millennium, there have been Redgraves in England—mostly in and around Suffolk, clustered near the historic market town of Bury St. Edmunds. In 1005 there was a Redgravesthorpe Parish, a designation meaning "a family settlement in a grove of reeds." Because variant spellings were common until modern times, the surname eventually took almost as many forms as there were generations, and some of these are still widely scattered over the British Isles—among them Redgriff, Redgrove, Redgrough and Radgrave.

Roy's great-grandfather, Thomas Redgrave, was a prosperous shoemaker in Northampton, where the leather industry flourished. He and his wife, Mary, had twelve children, of whom the seventh, born in 1824, was at least tangentially involved in the entertainment world. As "Cornelius Redgrave, Tobacconist," he set up shop in London near the Theatre Royal, Drury Lane, famous for theatricals since 1663. Sensing a lucrative if somewhat shady means of augmenting his income, Cornelius became one of the first ticket brokers: anonymously, he bought blocks of seats for the nearby spectacles and then sold them at extortionist rates to eager playgoers. "He was one of the first theatrical racketeers," said Michael Redgrave years later.

George Augustus Redgrave, son of Cornelius, moved the clan a step closer to dramatic legitimacy when, in 1872, he married the actress Zoe Beatrice Elsworthy Pym, whose credits included appearances at the Lyceum with the noted Anglo-French classical actor Charles Fechter. George and Zoe's son, George Elsworthy (later Roy) Redgrave, was born in Kennington, South London, on January 11, 1873—the first of five children born in eight years. He and his sister Dolly, with their parents' hearty encouragement, "took to the stage even as youngsters," as Roy recalled, describing their apprenticeship in local amateur dramatics.

His father's death at the age of thirty, in 1881, compelled eight-year-old Roy to work as a barber's assistant to help support the four younger children, while Zoe traveled with an acting company. In 1897 she had enormous success in a revival of Douglas Jerrold's perennially popular comedy *Black-Eyed Susan,* at the Empire, Croydon. She married a second time, and Roy began to pursue a career in acting; one of his brothers, Christopher, became stage manager of the Surrey Theatre.

Roy was a handsome and athletic young man, five feet nine inches tall, with light brown hair, sparkling blue eyes and considerable charm. He became an expert at every kind of theatrical stunt, at fencing, at staged fights that seemed perilously authentic—and, offstage, at the craft of seduction, a talent he practiced with a legion of women. Roy appeared in a West End theater only once, but from the 1890s he was much hailed as a character actor at the Britannia, Hoxton—hence his billing as "The Dramatic Cock of the North," i.e., North London's most popular player.

In 1894 Roy Redgrave married Ellen Maud Pratt, who became an actress and prudently changed her name to Judith Kyrle. Her wealthy father provided a generous dowry and a comfortable home, and between 1895 and 1898 she bore three children. But for Roy, marriage did not mean domesticity: Judith deeply resented his ongoing philandering, which he made little effort to conceal. He was often away from home, acting wherever good roles were available and wherever he could find compliant female companionship.

In 1903 Roy met another actress, Esther Mary Cooke, whose family was part of a successful circus troupe in the English provinces. After descending from the trapeze to the stage, she, too, changed her name, to Ettie Carlisle, and somehow she landed a role in a play starring Roy Redgrave. In short order, two things occurred: Ettie and Roy began to live together as lovers, and Judith Kyrle went on the warpath, breathing scorn and threatening to ruin the careers of both her husband and his mistress. Roy told Ettie he would terminate his marriage so that he could wed her, but she was terrified of being hauled into court as corespondent in a divorce case.

Instead, Ettie signed on with a drama company headed for South Africa, where on November 1, 1903, at St. George's Cathedral, Cape Town, she married the actor William Arthur Parrett, known professionally as Cecil Clayton. Roy, however, was not to be so easily rejected. He followed Ettie, resumed his pursuit, and persuaded her to return with him to England. It took the abandoned Parrett some months to trace his wife and initiate divorce proceedings.

Back home, Roy lost no time finding work. He successfully played the notorious outlaw Captain Starlight in a stage version of the classic Australian novel *Robbery Under Arms,* and soon he had a job at the Standard Theatre, Shoreditch, in *The Girl Who Took the Wrong*

Turning—"an excellent drama with an excellent moral," according to *The Stage*. He earned even more enthusiastic notices in *A Girl's Cross Roads*: "He played the part of Jack Livingstone with much earnestness, depicting a man cursed with a drunken wife." In *Shadows of a Great City,* the positive response continued: Roy effectively portrayed "a dashing sailor hero, giving a touch of true pathos." These performances were much noticed, as were those he undertook when he returned with Mrs. Parrett on his arm.

And what of Ellen Maud Pratt, aka Judith Kyrle? Writers and Redgraves claimed for decades that she and Roy were never divorced, and that therefore his subsequent marriages were bigamous and the children from them were illegitimate. But the National Archives of the United Kingdom contain a divorce record proving the contrary, dated 1905.* The file does not provide the reason for the wife's petition, but Ellen/Judith may have claimed desertion or abandonment in her uncontested divorce petition: Roy was in Australia by this time, performing almost constantly with the prestigious J. C. Williamson Company. In any case, Judith contracted a second marriage in 1907, for which she duly presented her 1905 divorce decree so that, without impediment, she could legally accept the proposal of a respected landowner named Frederick Nettlefold.

———※———

ROY REDGRAVE HAD certainly done a lot of living by the age of thirty, when he signed with Williamson, the most successful theatrical impresario in Australia and the producer of spectacular shows in all its major cities. In addition to the freedom and excitement of acting abroad, and the financial security of a contract, Roy was also, by shipping out, effectively avoiding the responsibilities of his English affairs. And from a professional standpoint, "He preferred to be a big fish in a small pond," as Daisy said many years later.

Success came quickly. "He is already a leading young actor," wrote a Melbourne reporter about Roy's appearance in the play *Sunday.* "He

———

* See the notes.

has a very pleasing, restrained and finished style." His performance as
a high-spirited Greek soldier in *Theodora* earned even more favorable
reviews for his subtle underplaying and refusal to rely on huge gestures
and exaggerated expressions. He also undertook the part of Mercutio,
one of the few classical roles of his career. In these and other productions over the next several years, Roy frequently played opposite the renowned beauty Tittell Brune, an American who had become the most
loved and respected actress in Australia. Happily married, she was no
target for Roy's amorous exploits.

Now it was Ettie's turn to board ship and pursue Roy. She landed
in Australia, where, billed as a soubrette, she performed at least once
in Melbourne, in a Williamson musical. By the following year, she
and Roy were back in England, where (still unmarried to Roy) she
was soon pregnant with his child. Enormously fond of the baby boy,
Papa suggested a postponement of marriage to Ettie until his financial
situation was more secure. To that end, he agreed to work for a summer season at the resort town of Brighton. At his first rehearsal for
Their Wedding Day, Roy met his fellow cast member Daisy Scudamore,
eleven years his junior.

The title of the play was ironic on several levels. Ettie was pressing
Roy to set a date for their nuptials, and now another young woman
had compounded what Roy saw as his "problems." At the end of the
summer, Daisy left Brighton and went to Bristol, where she had a
one-month acting job; there she awaited Roy's arrival. But disappointment came with his first letter, in which, as he protested, "my first duty
is to Miss C[arlisle] and the boy . . . it is the only right thing I can do.
Heaven knows how this other trouble of yours [Daisy's pregnancy]
hurts me, and you know I shall do all I possibly can to straighten
matters."

Daisy replied the same day. Her letter has not survived, but it
must have been a masterpiece of persuasive improvisation, for by
mid-September, Roy had evidently decided in Daisy's favor. "If you say
you will have me, we will be married," he wrote. "I know I love you. I
believe you love me and if you will bear with me, I will do my level best
by you. I know I am not a saint but dear, with the right hand at the

helm I can and will steer straight. I can say no more . . . I *can't* have the boy [i.e., his son by Ettie]. We must have our own." At this point, Ettie Carlisle, summarily abandoned, departs the story.

"I am going to bed tonight the happiest woman in the world," Daisy wrote to Roy in an ecstatic response to his proposal. "It seems all too good to be true that you love me so much and yet I know it is true. I love you and you love me. Dearest, say it again in your letters and whisper it to me when we meet."

Roy and Daisy were married on September 23, 1907, at the Registrar's Office, 4 Minerva Street, Glasgow. He had suggested Scotland because at that time (unlike English municipalities), no term of residency or waiting period was required prior to marriage. Hence, contrary to the suspicions of several Redgraves and their chroniclers, Roy and Daisy's son, Michael, although conceived out of wedlock, was indeed born legitimately, less than six months after his parents married. (Alas, Michael's son, late in life, was still proclaiming, "My father was illegitimate," an assertion his sisters blithely repeated, apparently believing it to be true.) Nor was the marriage bigamous: that irregularity Roy reserved for still another nuptial, nine years later.

The groom returned to his work in London, the bride to hers in Bristol, and he sent her small sums from time to time, pleading inordinate expenses. When their baby was five months old, Daisy rejoined Roy in London. There, she began the custom of placing Michael with nannies or minders for a night or two here, or a week or longer there, while she sought acting jobs. With Roy as her leading man, she performed in a revival of *The Christian* by Hall Caine (based on one of his most popular novels and the first work of British fiction to sell more than one million copies).

This play addressed the so-called Woman Question that exercised writers and politicians in the early years of the twentieth century. In this case, the action focused on the struggles of a young woman named Glory Quayle, who tries to lead an independent life in a large city. "Mr. Roy Redgrave is magnificent as John Storm," ran a typical review, "whilst the work of Miss Daisy Scudamore, as Glory Quayle, approaches very near to perfection." At last, a rave review.

The Christian had a healthy run to the end of 1908. When it closed, Roy told Daisy that he had a splendid offer to return to Australia—this time with an acting company under William Anderson, who had just opened the King's Theatre in Melbourne. "That's where the real money is," he announced. Roy departed at Christmastime; Daisy and their year-old son followed in the summer of 1909. "My mother was determined not to lose my father," said Michael.

Before departing, Daisy appeared in a novelty: a four-minute silent movie. Filmed at a small studio near Brighton and directed by Dave Aylott, the picture (*And Then He Woke Up*) was a two-character comedy starring the popular Ernie Cornford as a tramp who dreams of saving a young woman from danger and then marrying her. For this production and forever after it, Daisy preferred to be known as Margaret Scudamore. Thus she is listed in the archival credits of *And Then He Woke Up,* and thus her name appears in all subsequent English plays and movies.*

—ɯ—

THEATRICAL TOURING IS not the glamorous enterprise it is often imagined to be, and there was certainly nothing privileged about such travel for those making their way across the deserts and outback regions of Australia a century ago. Service on the overcrowded trains was erratic at best; cheap lodgings for actors were uncomfortable and depressing; indoor bathrooms were not routinely available to any but the very wealthy; and theaters were gelid in winter, stifling in summer.

Hoping for better shows as he proceeded, Roy put up with these inconveniences, taking comfort in female companionship and liquor. After six months, his income had dwindled to almost nothing, and so he welcomed Margaret and Michael none too enthusiastically. She, too, had hoped for a good career in the Antipodes, but soon she had

---

* *Marguerite* is the French word for a daisy as well as a proper name, and the English form, Margaret, has always been popular in Britain. Marguerite d'Anjou, wife of England's Henry VI, was one of several historic queens with that name; they all took the daisy as their symbol. Margrethe II, Denmark's queen since 1972, is called Daisy by her family and close friends, and the flower is her emblem, seen ubiquitously all over the country.

to work in this or that town as a laundress or seamstress when there were no acting jobs—which, as it turned out, was alarmingly often. While they were in Melbourne, Michael was baptized in the Church of England.

When she could afford the minimal expense, Margaret left the boy at a boardinghouse while she looked for work; later she recounted colorful details of their experiences. "Australian landladies seem to have been eccentric," Michael recalled. "One kept snakes and a pair of magpies. The birds terrified my mother by darting at my very blue eyes." Another guardian bathed the child by watering him down, fully clothed, with a garden hose, and then putting him out to dry in the afternoon sun.

Up to the end of 1910, Margaret (sometimes with Roy) undertook minor roles in a variety of repertory spectacles. Traveling across Australia, New Zealand and Tasmania, she joined the casts of (among other forgotten plays) *The Bushwoman—A Tale of the Outback* and *The Squatter's Daughter,* melodramas that invariably concerned the hardships of rural life. Margaret's name does not occur in reviews—not even of the occasional one-act plays written by her husband, of which none survives in any form.

During one presentation, two-year-old Michael unofficially and unexpectedly made his theatrical debut. Waiting in the wings with his mother, the child recognized Roy onstage and toddled swiftly and amiably toward him, loudly wailing, "Daddy!" Unflustered, Roy worked the moment into the dialogue, picked up his son and, while both of them stage-whispered some nonsense or other, returned him to his mother's arms. The audience—evidently considering this a sweet, sentimental moment in an otherwise starchy evening—burst into wild applause. Later, Margaret described the event for Michael in storybook detail, and so it entered into family lore.

But amusing family incidents were rare. To his standing as archphilanderer Roy now added the reputation of hard-drinking gambler and man-about-town. Margaret at last became angrily impatient with her irresponsible husband, who was increasingly dissolute and incapable of supporting his family: he was mere "flotsam and jetsam," as she described him. "She gave up the struggle of pursuing him across Australia," wrote her grandson, Corin Redgrave, "all too often arriving at the hotel just after he had left and then being unable to leave until she had paid his bill as well as her own."

Summarizing the time in Australia for an interviewer years later, Michael Redgrave said his mother was "desperately unhappy there, very miserable"—and as for the marriage, "she gave it up as a bad job and brought me home." Mother and son returned to England just before the new year 1911—with no objection from Roy, whom they never saw again. "I don't remember my father. I knew next to nothing about him, and little good."

—※—

BUT MARGARET WAS nothing if not resourceful—and to some men, she was quite irresistible. The harshness and disappointments of her time in Australia had not compromised her good looks, and she was able to affect an appealingly flirtatious manner at opportune moments. One such occurred during her return journey at sea, when she met a man named James Patrick Anderson. Tall and courtly, with the demeanor of an Edwardian gentleman, he sported a neatly trimmed moustache that countered his baldpate; at forty-seven, he was almost twenty years older than Margaret. But he was handsome and charming. And single. And wealthy.

Born in Scotland and raised in England, Anderson was returning after years of successful entrepreneurship with a tea and rubber conglomerate in Ceylon. He found Margaret stimulating as a companion and alluring as a woman, and he arranged for her to join him in the ship's first-class restaurant for dinner. The friendship advanced swiftly: Margaret called him Andy and confided the details of a marriage she now regarded as history, and she encouraged him to recount tales of his colorful experiences in the land of exotica. Andy told her that he had fathered two illegitimate children with (as the designation went) a native girl—offspring whose support and upbringing he had honorably guaranteed with a handsome trust fund.

Andy's enviable financial status obviated the need for him to seek further employment. He was living on investments, the administration of which was his sole occupation, and he had decided to reside at his London club while seeking a suitable Westminster address. Before they disembarked in England, Andy invited Margaret to be his dinner guest a few days later; he then booked tickets to squire her to the theater and to concerts. For almost five years mother and son lived in a series of rooms in various parts of London, Surrey, Kent and Sussex, where she found work in modest theatricals. Andy, meanwhile, lived in respectable bachelorhood at his all-male preserve and then at a home he purchased in Belgravia.

The couple was very much a couple despite the lack of a marriage certificate, and soon Margaret was pregnant with Andy's child. One of Michael's earliest memories was of a tiny flat where he awoke to see Andy quietly leaving his mother's bed. For a moment, before he recognized the man, Michael wondered if this was the father of whom he had heard much. He sensed the absence of the mysterious, mythical Roy—an emptiness he felt even more keenly when he met other children with mothers and fathers. More poignantly, as he wrote in a diary, "I don't remember [my mother] being especially affectionate with me, though [she was] always calm and gracious and beautiful."

But there was a serious obstacle to a marriage between Andy and Margaret, for she and Roy had not been divorced, and her letters to him on the subject went unanswered—perhaps because he was never long enough in one place to receive them. When she bore Andy's daughter in 1911, they named her Peg (the diminutive form of Margaret), but it was decided, for the sake of propriety, that the baby would live with her mother. A woman alone, with a child of apparently unknown paternity, was not the zenith of respectability, but Margaret's situation was not held in such low esteem as it would have been for a wealthy, single gentleman with a baby but no wife in sight. Andy contributed to the support of Michael and Peg, but he did not yet want to live with his mistress.

"When I was very young, as an actress's child," Michael recalled years later, "I was always being left with landladies or being given to total strangers who were introduced as Auntie Dolly This or Uncle

Fred That." His childhood was indeed an uncertain, unstable and peripatetic time of his life—a succession of flats, always dependent on his mother's schedule, never feeling that he belonged anywhere or to anyone, and never accustomed to any warm or even consistent adult guidance or attention. "I didn't know what a home was."

Demanding his mother's attention and fearing to lose her, the boy often begged to accompany her to the theater. "At the age of five, I watched my mother act in an old melodrama. In the last act, she had to clasp her long-lost son to her bosom and cry, 'My son—my son!' I topped her line with one of my own, crying out from my place in the audience: *That's* not your son—*I'm* your son!' The house burst into laughter and I into tears, and I was bribed out of the theatre by an attendant with a box of chocolates."

After another of Margaret's performances (as Lady Gilding in James Barrie's *The Professor's Love Story*), a journalist cornered her and Michael outside the theater. "Miss Scudamore," wrote the reporter, "has a clever small son whose ambition it is to write plays for his mother." This item was apparently a gloss on Margaret's remark a moment earlier, that her son had just written a children's Christmas story which they had sent to none other than Barrie himself—adding that young Michael had already read and reread the *Peter Pan* cycle.

"My dear Michael," Barrie replied in his idiosyncratic orthography, "i like your story very much. I am sending it back to you with many thanks for letting me read it, and some day i expect u will be the author of printed books if there is nothing better for u to do.—Your fellow-scribe, J. M. Barrie." From that time, Michael was a prodigious scribbler of stories—and later of diaries, letters, essays, articles, screenplays, novels and plays. "Being a writer seemed to me far superior to being an actor," he claimed.

—⁓—

DURING THE FIRST two years of the world war, while Peg was still a toddler, Michael attended several schools in neighborhoods that Margaret (perhaps presumptuously) deemed safe from the zeppelins. But security was impossible, and in fact he witnessed some of the most destructive bombings of London. On October 13, 1915, for example, he and his mother witnessed the so-called Theatreland Raid, in which German bombs fell in Charing Cross Road and struck the Lyceum Theatre, causing multiple casualties but leaving them both unhurt.

Despite the anxieties of wartime and his frequent transfer from one school to another, Michael did well in classes. "I got best marks at school," he wrote to his mother while living temporarily with yet another guardian. "She is going to take me to the pantomime. I am in a little play at school on Thursday. With love from your Michael, with kisses.—P.S. The cat walked on my paper."

"The first place where I really learned anything," Michael recalled, "was at this little school in Eaton Gate," just off fashionable Eaton Square. A popular English teacher introduced him to the pleasure of reading the American novelist James Fenimore Cooper, and under the tutelage of an expert musician he excelled with considerable precocity at the piano, for which he had a real talent. On weekends, Margaret occasionally indulged Michael's childhood passion for the "flickers," treating him to silent movie offerings such as Griffith's *Intolerance,* Annette Kellerman's water epics, and Chaplin's comedies. Frequently they met Andy for supper afterward at the Café Royal or at a restaurant near Sloane Square.

But the atmosphere that prevailed between Michael and Andy was chilly at the best of times. Jealous of his mother's attention and affection, the boy was resentful of anyone she liked—particularly this man, who assumed something like the role of husband. For his part, Andy (who had been a father only nominally in Ceylon) had no appreciation of childhood banter or manners. With Michael, he was kind but distant: to him the boy must have seemed part of a package deal. And so the lad was often sullen and mute, even when the conversation turned to congenial topics. "When deeply interested, I frequently say nothing," he later admitted.

Man and boy had to make greater efforts at friendly relations when Andy purchased a house at 9 Chapel Street, Belgrave Square, where Margaret, Michael and Peg finally joined him in 1917. There was still no marriage certificate, but the story was circulated that, somewhere, Mr. Anderson had indeed wed the actress Miss Scudamore and had adopted her two children from an earlier union—an account that was apparently accepted without question.

Margaret saw cohabitation as a pragmatic issue: she rated Andy as a good man who could provide the necessities, but (as she later told her son) she had no great love or enduring passion for him. Nothing can be known for certain of Andy's settled feelings for her, but he had been lonely, and he welcomed a woman who could manage his house and servants and play the role of hostess. It was, in other words, very much a polite, unexceptional arrangement. For the next several years, Margaret accepted fewer theatrical engagements and instead acted the role of a slightly imperious chatelaine in one of London's richest precincts.

Very soon after she arrived, Margaret developed a taste for alcohol—at first a dry sherry or two before dinner, and then gin and lemon at lunch, or gin neat. A carved mahogany bar with lighted glass shelves was always fully stocked with a great variety of apéritifs, whiskeys, cognacs and liqueurs.

Cramped, dusty and cold rented rooms; bathrooms shared with strangers; irregular meals—all these Michael could now count as things of the past, for the house in Chapel Street was something like a temple of luxury, large enough to accommodate maids and a butler in residence. Michael had his own upstairs room overlooking a lovely garden, and below there were parlors and a library, damask curtains, embossed wallpaper, Persian carpets, rows of books, the deep ticking of a massive grandfather clock—and the refuge of a warm kitchen with a ready supply of treats. There were occasional interruptions when everyone had to scurry to the basement during an air raid, but the house remained undamaged throughout the war.

—⁂—

At the time of Michael's thirteenth birthday, in March 1921, Margaret and Andy conferred with a few friends about the best school for the boy. They decided that he would board at Clifton College, Bristol, whose magnificent campus and magisterial buildings Margaret clearly recalled. Since its founding in 1862, Clifton had become much respected for the healthy integration of its arts and sciences curriculum, along with sturdy English athleticism and the requisite dash of polite Anglo-Catholic piety. Just as Andy sent off the first fees for Michael, the press was reporting the formation of Clifton's Dramatic Society and its inaugural performance of *The School for Scandal*—a play perhaps selected with naïve disregard for its incongruous title.

At the dinner table one evening before he left for Bristol, Michael said he would like to join the student drama society when he arrived at Clifton. That was all very well, said Andy, who was paying the bills, but he agreed with Margaret, who at once insisted that Michael should not remotely consider acting as a career. It was, they said almost in chorus, not appropriate for a man. Not long after, Michael learned the reason for their injunction: "she managed to implant in my mind the knowledge of her chief fear: that I might grow up to be like my father."

But Margaret was a bundle of contradictions, for within days, she had provided her son with the opportunity for his professional (if wordless) theatrical debut. William Bridges-Adams, a social acquaintance, was managing director of the Shakespeare Memorial Theatre, Stratford. He invited her to play in a season of repertory, and she brought Michael along during rehearsals. Bridges-Adams, augmenting his list of extras for crowd scenes, told Margaret that her son was tall enough to join them onstage. She could hardly refuse this command performance, and "M. S. Redgrave," as he was billed in the small print, walked on that summer in eight performances of *Henry IV, Part II.*

Until the construction of the new Royal Shakespeare Theatre years later and the advancement of Stratford's reputation, the Memorial Theatre was something of a ragtag company that presented plays after only a few brief rehearsals. Bridges-Adams was an imaginative designer and producer, but he was working with a minuscule budget and little government endorsement; indeed, his seasons were triumphs of improvisation. Unfazed, he insisted that every Shakespearean play be performed in its entirety, without a single line cut—a principle that inspired someone to rechristen him "Mr. Unabridges-Adams."

In addition to his brief assignment, Michael saw two or three performances of every play that season—*Richard III, The Merry Wives of Windsor* (in which Margaret played Mistress Page to good comic effect), *A Midsummer Night's Dream, Macbeth* and *The School for Scandal.* He could not understand why Andy and his mother considered acting "not appropriate" for men.

Two

GHOSTS AND GUILT

(1921–1935)

ROM AGE THIRTEEN TO EIGHTEEN, MICHAEL REDGRAVE supplemented his academic courses at Clifton College with a wide variety of extracurricular activities. He studied mathematics and sciences, literature and history, Latin and French. But his performance in the classroom was mostly unexceptional, never on the honors level and frequently substandard, precisely because of his dedication to athletics, cultural pursuits and an avid social life. He continued his piano study and sang with the Choral Society; and on the fields, he was an energetic rugby player and ran the one-mile race in good time.

Michael also wrote poems, short plays and stories, and he participated in the school's new Dramatic Club. "Whenever it was possible to get up an amateur production, I'd do it." Plays were presented twice annually, and students assumed the female as well as the male roles in them. Acting a woman's character (which had been standard casting procedure in Shakespeare's time) was never considered cause for laughter—much less was it anything like a music hall drag show: on the contrary, a young man's performance as a girl or mature woman was regarded as a serious challenge. In 1922 Michael played the small role of the second niece in Sheridan's eighteenth-century satire *The Critic,* and he undertook female characters in two contemporary (and soon forgotten) comedies, *A Pair of Lunatics* and *The Private Detective.*

While Michael was rehearsing *The Critic,* Margaret learned by cable that Roy had died on May 25, 1922, at a hospice in Sydney; at the age of forty-nine, he had succumbed to tuberculosis complicated by throat cancer. The announcement arrived at Chapel Street through the kindness of Mary Seward Leresche, whom Roy had married in Australia in 1916. Without any attempt to divorce Margaret (or to reply to her requests for the same), he had simply contracted a bigamous marriage, as "Royal Elsworthy Redgrave," to the unwitting divorcée, Mrs. Leresche; this was the invalid union into which Roy entered—not his 1907 wedding to Daisy Scudamore, which had been legal. In his last years, Roy had appeared in several Australian silent movies, and the summer before he died he portrayed, appropriately, a harem keeper in the Rudolf Friml musical *Katinka*.

Shortly before his death, Roy took up a pen and effectively composed his own obituary:

> *One of the best, held his own in a crowd,*
> *Lived like the rest (when finances allowed),*
> *Slapped on the back as a jolly fine sport,*
> *Drank any tack, from bad whiskey to port,*
> *Fool to himself—that's the worst you can say;*
> *Cruel to himself, for the health has to pay.*
> *Months back, he died, and we've only just heard,*
> *No friends by his side just to say the kind word,*
> *No relatives near, and no assets at all,*
> *Quite lonely, I fear, when he answered the call.*
> *One of the best, held his own while he could,*
> *Died like the rest, just when life seemed so good.*

When Margaret told Michael the news, he reacted with predictable indifference: after all, he had no memory of Roy, nothing to arouse feelings of loss or grief. But it is also true that for the rest of his life, he felt increasingly guilty about his emotional diffidence and his refusal to learn anything about the man. As with Hamlet, his father's ghost forever haunted him. For his mother, on the other hand, Roy's death was a passport to marriage respectability at last. On June 26, 1922—one month after she read the telegram from Australia—thirty-seven-year-old Margaret Scudamore Redgrave married James Patrick Anderson, fifty-seven, at St. George's, Hanover Square. Michael had not yet returned to London from his term at Clifton.

—⁓—

FEW DETAILS AND no reviews have survived of his first three appearances in school plays. But the following year, in James M. Barrie's comedy of manners *The Admirable Crichton,* Michael's performance as Lady Mary Lasenby was hailed by the student newspaper as "remarkable: his movements are good, his voice is pleasant to listen to, and he can divest himself of himself and put on a character." Playing the daughter of an aristocrat who falls in love with the family butler, fifteen-year-old Michael somehow found the right comic pathos, weeping real tears in a touching, romantic scene.

A year later, he had reached his full adult height of six feet three inches when he played Mrs. Hardcastle in Goldsmith's *She Stoops to Conquer,* proving that he could switch gears to render with pitch-perfect acuity the role of a venal, imperceptive social climber. "It was no surprise," wrote one reviewer, "that M. S. Redgrave threw himself into the character with verve and gave a very clever presentation of this amusing but unattractive lady. He was especially funny in the garden scene, and kept the audience laughing all the time."

But his great triumph during the Clifton years was certainly his chilling portrait of Lady Macbeth in June 1925. "The part calls for the highest emotional acting," noted a visiting critic, "and it seemed incredible that it could receive such a brilliant interpretation at the hands of a boy. His movements, grace and gestures were entirely feminine, and it is not too much to say that the sleepwalking scene was absolutely thrilling and also the scene of the murder. The chief honours of the production fell to Redgrave." Despite her fear that Michael would turn professional, Margaret had to second the praise. "You not only really seemed to be asleep [in the sleepwalking scene]," she wrote in his scrapbook. "You bowed your head at the end of the scene and your head seemed to drop as if you were tired to death. It was a lovely bit of business."

In the mid-1920s, Margaret was in good humor and seldom ill, despite a prodigious intake of alcohol. As a formidable Lady Bracknell (one of her few major roles), she was "uncommonly good," as one London critic wrote. "She is so seldom given an opportunity to do more than express sweet maturity that she is especially welcome in a character typically Wildean." Margaret also played a disturbing Gertrude in a London *Hamlet,* and the unpleasant Catherine Petkoff in Shaw's *Arms and the Man*—a performance in which, Michael considered, "Mummy overacted a little."

In 1924 Margaret cofounded the Fellowship of Players, a group aiming to offer productions of Elizabethan and Jacobean works. At Christmas that year, they performed *The Merry Wives of Windsor,* in which Margaret again played Mistress Page. Also in the cast, seen for only a moment in a silent role, was a fifteen-year-old boy named Laurence Olivier.

—⁓—

FOR TWO SUMMERS, Andy took the family to France, where Michael met Oliver Baldwin, son of England's prime minister, Stanley Baldwin. Twenty-five in 1924, Oliver took life very seriously indeed: impatient with political hypocrisies, he was also a pacifist, an ardent member of the Labour Party and a champion of liberal causes. He was also quite contentedly homosexual, without a shred of guilt or embarrassment, and he introduced Michael to his partner, John Boyle.

The meeting was doubly significant, and not only because the prime minister's son made no effort to conceal his partner, whom his family completely accepted. In addition, Oliver discussed the thorniest political and social issues of the day. All this was quite new to Michael, who quickly learned that Andy was opposed to just about everything Oliver espoused. "You and I don't talk the same language," Andy told Michael. But the friendship with Oliver flourished.

On his return to Bristol, Michael began to keep a diary. Remarkably self-aware, written in neat but minuscule longhand, this was no mere random record of external events and casual incidents: it was, to the contrary, an astonishingly detailed and frankly confessional account of his inner life, his feelings and fantasies, his romances and hopes, thrills and heartbreaks. The first volume, covering from August 1925 to March 1927, contains no fewer than 190 lined pages, each of them completely filled from top to bottom. In the years to come, Michael added to this intimate testament, writing historically valuable accounts of the development of British theater as well as incisive reflections on the plays and films of his career. The diaries also contain a record of his complicated sexual life, which he described without bravado and often with a sense of searing shame; the pages reveal much about a man who did not readily disclose himself to anyone.

The first entry is dated August 5, 1925: "I dedicate this volume to my friend G. M. H., by whose inspiration it is written." Geoffrey M. Hayward, one year Michael's senior, also acted with the Dramatic Club and, almost from their first meeting, was Michael's first major romantic attachment—although he had already plunged into casual teenage liaisons that cannot really be termed love affairs. "J.D.B., T.E.W., J.S.W., R.J.P. were all selfish friendships. I tried to make G.M.H. love me from a wicked point of view. But he did not love me until I loved him for himself only."

As this entry demonstrates, Michael was caught in a conflict that had as much to do with psychological motive as with physical sex: he had a consuming need for Geoffrey's love, but he wanted to love ardently for Geoffrey's sake—not for the pleasure and the happiness his partner brought him. Disinterested, totally unselfish love, without reference to its rewards, is a very grand (indeed, heroic) aspiration, but perhaps no one can really love without reference to self. Michael's love for Geoffrey in fact became obsessive, and although maturity later altered his ideas about romantic compensations, he longed throughout his life to find one true and perfect love.

Within and away from the walls of Clifton, the two young men exchanged long letters; none survive, but Michael refers to them in his diary. After Geoffrey left Clifton for university in 1925, Michael wondered "if there was anybody who was going to be a 'grande affaire' during my last year." By 1926, as he noted, "All this term, there was no one to fill Hayward's place." But this did not mean that there was in fact "no one" at all: he had several passionate affairs with other schoolmates after Geoffrey. Michael also nourished a deeply amorous but platonic relationship with the assistant chaplain, aptly named David Loveday, who was not yet thirty years old and who responded enthusiastically if not sexually to Michael's amorous feelings. This intelligent, generous cleric greatly impressed Michael to the point that he gladly and gravely prepared for his confirmation on his eighteenth birthday. "I had been very apathetic about it at the beginning of term, but after an interview with D.G. Loveday, I was strongly for it."

Religious devotion, however, did not forestall sexual activity with this or that classmate: "The thought of staying with Cyril [White] was wildly exciting . . . we spent every spare minute together. He was much smaller than myself though older. He was broad and overdeveloped for his size. He had a small mousey face with big dark eyes and fair-ish hair." Eventually, Cyril put a cool distance between them, which Michael thought was due to the "exaggerated attention" he himself had lavished on the other boy.

Their relationship may also have been compromised by wild (and frequently perilous) sexual escapades. During the summer of 1926, on at least six occasions, he and Cyril "amused ourselves at the [Marshall Street] Turkish baths." On July 25 their visit to that steamy place followed, perhaps aptly, their attendance at a performance of *They Knew What They Wanted*. Sometimes Michael went to Marshall Street alone: "I was the only boy there amid a lot of horrible men, some old, some middle-aged, some quite young. But they all stared at me and each tried to get into conversation with me, I knew only too well what for. They stared at my almost naked body until I almost blushed for shame. The openness of their intentions was what was so beastly. Is it to be wondered that I went home with a good-looking young Austrian boy who was there too? I was a fool but I could hardly help myself."

Desire, and a concomitant moral squint, caused enormous guilt for almost Michael's entire lifetime. In addition, his feelings of culpability and remorse were encouraged by the prevailing ethic of both society and church. Only thirty years earlier, Oscar Wilde had been publicly disgraced and thrown into prison, and that which dared not speak its name was still mute in English society. While the law did not address lesbian relationships, which were thought to be virtually nonexistent in any case, men who engaged in sexual activity with other men were set-ups for public humiliation and severe legal penalties that could mean a long prison term. (In this regard, Oliver Baldwin was an exception to the rule, doubtless because of his father.) These sanctions were considered supremely merciful advances over earlier punishments such as torture or even death.

About this time, Michael had one of the few heterosexual relationships of his life. Tall and extravagantly handsome, he was always attracted and attractive to compliant men, but many women also desired him. One such was thirty-nine-year-old Margaret Chute, a London society writer and columnist for *Picture Show* magazine who frequently traveled to Hollywood, where she wrote profiles of Hollywood movie stars—among them, Gloria Swanson, John Gilbert, Pola Negri and Lillian Gish. While Michael was at Chapel Street during a brief school holiday, the redoubtable Miss Chute arrived to interview Margaret about the Fellowship of Players.

The two women established a friendly rapport, and Miss Chute invited Michael to her flat, ostensibly to discuss school dramatics. "What followed, on the carpet in front of the fire, was new to me," he noted. But like the flame in the grate, the ardor quickly died. Margaret Chute returned to her work and to a platoon of men—as did Michael. The experience merited but a few words in his autobiography, and there is no mention of her in the diaries.

—m—

DURING HIS FINAL school term, Michael won several accolades. He received the Gratian Fyffe Prize of three pounds for his expert performance of Chopin piano pieces, and with the money, he bought the scores to Beethoven's symphonies. He was also given the Bernard Hartley Shakespeare Prize for his trio of performances in *The Tempest, Romeo and Juliet* and *Much Ado About Nothing.* "I was immensely proud of myself, and with the one-pound winning, I bought Masefield's poems and Galsworthy's *Forsyte Saga.*" But the honor he most cherished was the T.E. Brown Prize for his poem "The Death of Abel," based on the biblical story. The award "set the stamp on my reputation as a literary man in the school, and I found that on such questions as plays and poems, my opinion ranked high."

Evidently the work of a student who has been introduced to the marmoreal genius of Milton, "The Death of Abel" is noteworthy for its mature construction, dark lyricism and effective use of enjambment. This time, Michael spent the prize money on leather-bound editions of Samuel Pepys and the plays of Barrie and Synge. He had begun to build a significant library.

His final performance at Clifton College was in Sheridan's comedy *The Rivals*—as Captain Jack Absolute, a character with a complex set of motives and shifting loyalties toward both servants and young ladies. Reviewing the production in June 1926, one critic praised Michael's "intelligence, grace of movement and vivid expression." But the young star was somewhat dismayed: "I felt that everyone thought I was ef-feminate [in the role]," he wrote in his diary. "They didn't, really, but I was very sensitive. Besides, Captain Absolute is not an easy part." Nor were the final exercises and examinations before the end of his last term: "My mother and stepfather gave me a good education—but I failed to achieve a school certificate, owing to a violent distaste for mathematics and physics."

At that time, no one in his family, Michael included, thought of him as a candidate for the acting profession. The theater was an indul-gence, said Andy; as for Margaret, she still insisted that the stage was no place for a man. In any case, Michael preferred writing to almost any other possible vocation, and so he went to meet a few publishers and newspaper editors in London. "They said it would be a good thing if I went abroad to learn languages first." Andy, who continued to pro-vide financial support, provided letters of credit and a stipend for sev-eral months on the Continent.

Before he departed, however, Michael received his first compensa-tion (two pounds) for work as an actor. Margaret, implying that this would be a farewell performance, cast him in a nonspeaking role in *The Taming of the Shrew,* which the Fellowship of Players performed twice at the Apollo in October. He surprised the rest of the cast by improvising action for a character not mentioned in the text but invented for the production, as he executed a hilarious pratfall and won from the audience a burst of laughter and loud applause. It was a rare example of Michael Redgrave as shameless scene-stealer.

He departed for Heidelberg on November 5, 1926, eager to learn all he could of the German language and culture, music and literature. After a month of private tutorials under one Professor Wildhagen, Michael was able to write home before Christmas, "I am getting on well with the language, and although I can only speak simply, I can understand nearly all that is said to me." Nor was anything lost on him: his copious diary entries are sophisticated, literate reflections on the history, art and architecture of Heidelberg, Frankfurt, Munich, Berlin and Mannheim. There is no mention of contemporary politics in the diaries, nor of the prevalent spirit of Weimar Germany, a society dancing with wild abandon on a volcano.

The half year abroad was both enriching and exciting. In addition to his lessons, he saw the silent movie masterworks of German filmmakers such as Fritz Lang, G. W. Pabst and Robert Wiene—many of them works of expressionistic horror or futuristic fantasy—and he particularly admired the acting of Conrad Veidt and Elisabeth Bergner. He took to skiing in the Black Forest with a party of new European friends, and he occasionally visited his half sister Peg, who at sixteen was in Germany, consorting with a doctor from Mainz.

At Christmas, David Loveday turned up and, admiring Michael's fluency in German and his impressive appreciation of European culture, urged him to apply for admission to Cambridge. The lack of a Clifton diploma was no hindrance, David said: if Michael passed the required entrance examinations in mathematics, Latin and French, he could win acceptance to the university. There followed, in early 1927, intensive private tutorials in those subjects, with retired professors at Beaugency, on the Loire; and in the spring, he met with teachers in Bristol, who took him through cramming sessions. Finally, with very good test results and a hearty written endorsement from Loveday to colleagues at Magdalene College, Michael was accepted to Cambridge University for the autumn term.

—⁓—

IT IS SOMETIMES taken as given that a fair picture of student life at Oxford or Cambridge in the 1920s and '30s may be found on the pages of Evelyn Waugh's novel *Brideshead Revisited*; in fact, that assumption is justified. At Magdalene, undergraduates could pursue as many extracurricular activities, love affairs and social engagements as they wished, so long as they sat successfully for examinations. For Michael, who had acted at Clifton and was always busy composing this poem or that story between assignments, Cambridge was in every way liberating. He excelled in English literature and modern languages, and the dreaded science and mathematics were now of the past.

From June 1928 to June 1931, he appeared in nine productions with the Amateur Dramatic Club (always called the ADC), a university society founded in 1855 that had earned broad respect. But as Michael often said, "At the time, I felt that being a writer was a much better thing than becoming an actor"—a conviction born from his experience, not from obedience to family injunction. "I wrote stories; I was a drama critic and a film critic; I edited the *Cambridge Review*; and I started a literary magazine that lasted for two years." He also wrote film reviews for *The Granta,* a distinguished university periodical founded in 1889 that was noteworthy for publishing the early work of writers who went on to have important careers, from A. A. Milne to Sylvia Plath.

At Cambridge, Michael agreed with the notion that nothing could be more desirable than living on an intellectual-aesthetic level; equally noteworthy was the general disregard for prevailing sexual mores. Many of the Cambridge esthetes were homosexual or bisexual, for while English society openly scorned anything but heterosexuality, life within the university unofficially condoned and even encouraged anything unconventional.

Julian Bell, Virginia Woolf's nephew, was among the contemporaries in Michael's literary circle. A gifted poet and a political idealist in the mold of Oliver Baldwin, Julian later went off to aid the Republican side during the Spanish Civil War, and while tending the wounded as an ambulance driver, he was killed at the age of twenty-nine. Jacob Bronowski, another contemporary, was a polymath as devoted to literature as he was to his microscope; he earned an international reputation as both a writer and a scientist. T. H. White, later best known as author of *The Once and Future King,* worked with Michael on several literary projects and provided comic-shock relief with his accounts of sadomasochistic sexual practices.

But perhaps most influential was William Empson, by common consent one of the greatest English literary critics, and certainly one of the most eccentric men Michael had ever met. Bisexual, intemperate when drinking, careless of dress and hygiene, Empson nevertheless put his own first-rate mind at the service of a highly imaginative literary criticism. He published important studies in a refined, complex but clear style—evident, for example, in his renowned studies of Milton—and although he was often physically repellent and even downright perverse, Empson was always respected for his insights into the works of famous authors.

The literary magazine Michael cofounded was *The Venture,* which published the early writings of the art historian Anthony Blunt, later a renowned critic and a notorious member of the "Cambridge Five" spy ring. Another of the spies, Guy Burgess, designed the sets for the ADC production of Shaw's *Captain Brassbound's Conversion,* in which Michael played the title role (his only performance in a Shaw play). "Burgess was one of the bright stars of the University scene," Michael recalled, "with a reputation for being able to turn his hand to anything." Unfortunately, Burgess also turned his hand toward countless bottles of whiskey at Cambridge, not to mention astonishingly indiscreet gay liaisons. Michael Redgrave knew the men who were secretly involved in espionage for Russia, but at the time he was unaware that they were in fact spies. He endorsed social principles then considered leftist, but he was never a Marxist; nor was he linked to any political ideology.

Other contributors to *The Venture* included Malcolm Lowry, later known for his 1947 novel *Under the Volcano*; and John Lehmann, a sensualist and poet who later became an important literary editor and London publisher. According to Lehmann, Michael at Cambridge was "tall and slim, with chestnut hair and a romantic profile—an engaging embodiment of the ideal conception of what a young poet should look like and how he should behave." Another contemporary, E. K. Bennett, described Michael as "flower-like and detached," an image perhaps intended to convey a somewhat unflattering notion of Redgrave's often fey and remote deportment. "I was very highly conceited," Michael admitted later. "I thought I could do anything." Some of his friends thought he could, too.

—ɯ—

AT THE END of his first year, Michael portrayed the romantic Florindo in Goldoni's eighteenth-century Italian comedy *Servant of Two Masters*. Writing in *The Cambridge Review* that summer, I. M. Parsons praised his "freedom of gesture, his elegance and his charm of manner, [which] were so polished as to reveal his versatility." Similar encomia followed his performances in a variety of roles: the critic Francis Birrell, for example, wrote that Michael's performance as Edgar in *King Lear* was spoken "with an exquisite sensibility that we rarely, if ever, hear—even in London."

A part of London society got its chance to hear him when Julian Bell arranged for Michael and others to appear in scenes from Milton's *Comus* at the Gordon Square home of the renowned economist John Maynard Keynes and his wife, the Russian ballerina Lydia Lopokova. Julian had persuaded his mother, Vanessa Bell, and her sometime lover Duncan Grant to design the scenery and costumes. Grant, in the fashion of the so-called Bloomsbury Group, was also the sometime lover of John Maynard Keynes; aptly, the production celebrated a confusion of genders, with men playing women who were disguised as men.

At the Keynes residence that December evening in 1929 were (among other notables) George Bernard Shaw, Lytton Strachey, Walter Sickert—and Vanessa Bell's sister, Virginia Woolf, who asked Michael if he was nervous during performances. "I replied, 'Yes, hideously,' but I don't know why, for as an amateur, I was seldom, if ever, nervous on the stage." In the presence of so august an audience, perhaps he felt that that youthful modesty required a protestation of anxiety.

The producer Hilda Matheson was also present at Gordon Square that evening, and after hearing Michael, she invited him to audition for the radio, thus inaugurating decades of his frequent readings for the BBC. When ADC student players were invited to present scenes from *Comus* and from Shakespeare at the Arts Theatre in London the following year, Michael Redgrave's voice was heard for the first time on a West End stage.

His four years at Cambridge were characterized by a ceaseless rhythm of activities and impressive achievements: stage performances, musical recitals, writing and editing, radio broadcasts and, of course, attention to matters academic. He also found time to star in, direct, and contribute the libretto for a comic operetta called *The Battle of the Book* (about, of all things, the work of the diarist Samuel Pepys). There were also long conversations during study sessions with scholars and directors—especially George Rylands, always known by his nickname Dadie (mischievously pronounced to rhyme with "lady," not "daddy"). Sad but genial, a repressed homosexual and a heavy tippler, Rylands, who sometimes acted with the students and had assumed the title role in *Comus,* evoked Michael's lifelong gratitude as "one of the best teachers of how to speak verse. He speaks it wonderfully himself, and he has got several generations of young undergraduates to speak it and understand it."

—⁂—

IN MARCH 1929 Michael marked his twenty-first birthday. That year, he was in the midst of an intense, two-year romance with a popular and handsome university scholar and athlete named Michael Garrett. "The Two M's," as friends and classmates called them, spent the following summer touring Normandy and Brittany, but complications (mostly caused by Redgrave's guilt and fear) followed their return to Cambridge. By 1930, *l'affaire Garrett* was history.

"The two years I have been loving Michael G. have not been wasted," Redgrave wrote in his diary. "They strengthened me for this most perfect love"—by which he meant a romance he quixotically formed with Mary Coss, a young American on a European holiday with her sister.

"My life has been so unbalanced sexually," he continued. "This is now righted [with Mary], I am certain. This purely physical sex, which I have so often enjoyed in my life, mostly with men, once with a woman [Margaret Chute], seems no trouble now, and, moreover, I trace it all to my failings."

However, as he wrote to Rylands and Lehmann, the Coss interval was chaste but for a few fumblings in the moonlight. "I love you more than anything in the world," he wrote to her, "as much as my life, since you cannot be separated from it." But if Michael could so easily delude himself with such aromatic letters, Mary was the wiser: when she learned about Garrett, she gently but firmly extricated herself, and Michael came more or less to his senses. "The two of us found ourselves out of love," he wrote later, "and not in the least missing it." Returning to America, Mary Coss eventually married, divorced and became an ardent member of the Communist Party. Such were the vagaries of mercurial, youthful ardor.

Michael received his baccalaureate degree in English literature and modern languages from Cambridge University on June 24, 1930. His certificate, with "second-class honours, upper division," entitled him to pursue postgraduate studies, which he completed in 1931.

But what would he do with these commendable scholarly achievements? When he gently raised the possibility of a career in the theater, the response from Andy and Margaret was again swift and negative. His stepfather muttered disapproval—"he just didn't want me to go on the stage"—adding that such a step would, sooner rather than later, bring Michael to a state of penury. His mother began by saying, apparently with a straight face, "You are too tall." She then said, "Too many people go into the theatre for what they can get out of it, and not enough go for what they can put into it." For this remark she cannot be faulted.

In other words, Margaret implied that her son was unprepared and very likely unworthy of the acting profession. Occasionally she had praised one or another of his school performances, but now, and throughout Michael's career, he could not look to his mother for professional encouragement. Her own aspirations had been compromised by the comforts of her second marriage, which made work unnecessary, and alcohol had diluted ambition. Perhaps Margaret was also afflicted with more than a mild case of professional jealousy, based on the fear that he would have greater success than she had known.

Jobs everywhere were scarce, and tens of thousands were starving as the Great Depression took a terrible toll worldwide. Michael did not want to be a teacher, as he wrote to his mother in October 1931, but he saw no alternative. "The only commercial asset I had was a university degree, and because I wanted to earn my own living, I decided to take a temporary job as a schoolmaster." Years later, he was quite frank: "I never intended to become a teacher. I just did it to get enough money to become independent of my stepfather."

By this time, David Loveday had become headmaster at the distinguished Cranleigh School in Surrey, thirty-eight miles southwest of London. Loveday needed an additional teacher in the Department of Modern Languages, and Michael was quickly engaged to teach English, French and German. His salary was a very modest £220 annually ($16,000 in 2012 valuation), but he was given free bed and board.

When Michael arrived in January 1932, he found that Cranleigh had no active drama club—a lacuna he filled within months, encouraging talented students to participate and winning their respect for the sense of enjoyment and seriousness he brought to the staging of elaborate and imaginative productions. Michael became the Drama Club's managing director, production designer and leading actor.

He had to begin, however, by training boys simply to stand straight, not to fidget and to be audible from the stage; from there, he could move on to describe the subtler dimensions of the craft, encouraging the young actors not merely to imitate life but to interpret it, to understand emotions rather than simply to copy examples of them. In this he was remarkably coherent and effective, as both a practical director and a teacher discussing the theory and philosophy of drama.

From winter 1932 to summer 1934, Michael directed and acted in six plays at Cranleigh, each successively more demanding, more professional and more widely noted by the press. In addition, he frequently took students to plays in London; to begin, he escorted his French class to performances directed by Michel Saint-Denis.

Trained by his uncle, the critic and director Jacques Copeau, Saint-Denis had founded La Compagnie des Quinze, and their London visit was but one stop during a successful European tour. "I suddenly became fired with what it means to be a director," Michael recalled, "and to have a company that really does express a point of view. The Compagnie had a near-perfection of style, the like of which you didn't often see in the English theatre, especially at that time."

The French troupe of players was noted for ensemble acting, simple sets and an intense physicality in their modern productions of new and classic plays. Saint-Denis insisted on an organic approach to acting, unifying the crafts of movement, dance, acrobatics, singing, speech, wrestling and working with masks—all of it done with a fair amount of improvisation.* These elements complemented Michael's study of the techniques of popular actors such as Henry Ainley and Godfrey Tearle. But the most celebrated among Redgrave's idols was John Gielgud, whose *Hamlet* Michael had seen several times during the 1929/1930 season of the Old Vic Company. "When I first performed the part as an amateur [at Cranleigh in June 1933], my memory of Gielgud was so strong that I must have seemed like Gielgud's understudy."

All these men of the theater had distinct acting styles, and Michael ensured that his classes studied the differences. Still in his twenties, M. S. Redgrave (as he was always billed at school) in many ways made a significant contribution to the life of the theater even within the context of amateur school productions. His performances at Cranleigh earned highest marks from the London critics, who now hurried down to see what was going on in Cranleigh's Drama Club. His Hamlet was considered ferociously regal and better than most of those recently seen in the West End, and his Lear was "compelling . . . unimaginably beautiful." At the age of twenty-six, Michael played the aged, tragic king with rueful pathos.

He also accepted five roles with the semiprofessional Guildford Repertory Company, a few miles from Cranleigh; and he adapted a

---

* While visiting the film set of *Secret Agent* in early 1936, Saint-Denis was persuaded by the director Alfred Hitchcock and the star John Gielgud to appear in a brief, improvised comic scene—as a Swiss coachman unable to understand even elementary English.

mystical short story by Arthur Quiller-Couch called *The Seventh Man,* which he transformed into a haunting one-act play.* Written in 1933 and performed two years later, it told of six men, shipwrecked and near despair in the frozen north but saved at last when one of them sees a mysterious figure—the seventh man, who brings them saving sunlight.

Students excelled under Michael's direction, and several went on to successful careers in the arts. Paul Jacklin became stage manager for the Croydon Repertory, acted in contemporary plays and was later a producer in Australia. Vivian Cox performed in three of Michael's six productions at the school (*Samson Agonistes, King Lear* and *Hamlet*); after studying at Cambridge, he produced major works for stage, screen and television.

Michael's "temporary job" at Cranleigh extended to eight terms, the better part of three years. "Teaching provided me with a very comfortable life, even though I was certain that I had no vocation for it. But I enjoyed myself during my time at Cranleigh, for we did six productions—one Milton [*Samson Agonistes*], one Gilbert and Sullivan [*Pinafore*] and four Shakespeares [*As You Like It, Hamlet, The Tempest* and *King Lear*]. The success of these, and my enthusiasm for what I saw in the Saint-Denis productions in London, led me to make up my mind. My true vocation was in the professional theatre." Perhaps presuming that he could commence that vocation in London with a high-level company, he auditioned for London's most important theater manager, Lilian Baylis, at the Old Vic, during the Easter holidays 1934. "I thought I could do anything—I was still very, very conceited."

But Michael's audition that April morning went awkwardly. "I can't see anything but hands!" cried out the formidable Miss Baylis, referring to his exaggerated gestures during the recitation of lines from Shakespeare and Milton. About employing him, she was evasive, and he left the stage convinced he would not be invited to join the Old Vic. He then fixed an appointment with William Armstrong, the respected

---

* At Guildford in 1933 and 1934, he played Menelaus in *The Trojan Women* (Euripides); Young Marlow in *She Stoops to Conquer* (Goldsmith); John Worthing in *The Importance of Being Earnest* (Wilde); Robert Browning in *The Barretts of Wimpole Street* (Besier); and Clive in *The Circle* (Maugham).

and successful managing director of the Liverpool Repertory. Noël Coward and Gertrude Lawrence had appeared there as teenagers, and Rex Harrison and Robert Donat had begun their careers at Liverpool, which was rated by most professionals as the finest repertory company in England.

Before Michael traveled north for the meeting with Armstrong, however, he was surprised to receive a letter from Baylis, offering him a contract for the 1934/1935 season at the Vic, at a salary of three pounds a week; the roles were still to be determined. With that offer in hand, Michael submitted his resignation from the Cranleigh School, effective at the end of June.

Armstrong, a warm and congenial Scotsman, reacted favorably to Michael's audition. "We'd like to have you here," he said. "You're nice looking and the photographs are interesting."

Michael was grateful but said, "I've been offered a contract with the Vic."

"How much are they offering you?"

"Three pounds a week," he replied—and later regretted his candor: "I should have said eight."

"I'll give you four," said Armstrong.

On May 21, Michael received Armstrong's formal letter, offering him a contract from the end of August to Christmas—"but you are almost certain to go on with us till next summer. You will have to take your chance of parts like everybody else [and] we do not pay big salaries in Repertory." He added that Michael seemed to him "full of promise," and that, in light of the plays he had staged at Cranleigh, the period of employment in Liverpool "might lead to something in the way of Assistant Producer [i.e., assistant director] as well as actor."

Michael replied at once, accepting Armstrong's terms and confirming that he would arrive on the appointed day in August, to begin rehearsals for his small role in *Counsellor-at-Law,* by the American playwright Elmer Rice.* As for his choice of Armstrong's offer over

* The 1931 Rice play and the 1933 film of it sometimes appear with a hyphenated title (as Rice, once a lawyer, wrote it) and sometimes not.

that of Baylis, this was not merely a matter of one pound sterling. Michael wanted to broaden his range and refine his vocal technique—not by restricting himself to speaking Elizabethan verse in minor Shakespearean roles at the Old Vic, but by appearing in a variety of modern plays in contemporary language, which was Liverpool's stock-in-trade. The role of Roy Darwin in the Rice play—a smooth, adulterous New York character pursuing the leading character's wife—was a good place to start.

Very soon after opening night (August 30, 1934), Michael saw that the Liverpool company was "really wonderful, and Armstrong was a great encourager. He had a flair for finding people, and he had a great love for the work at hand. One of the most beloved people in the English theatre, he had made a reputation for the Liverpool Playhouse which was at that time outstanding. At the end of a scene in rehearsal, his voice could be heard from the back of the [auditorium], 'Oh! It's so beautiful—so moving!'"

The venue and the productions were equally memorable. "It was a very lovely theater, we had enthusiastic audiences, and we were always packed, every night, for whatever play we did. They were nearly all modern [plays]. We never did anything like Ibsen. Once a year we did a Shakespeare." Notable names in the company that season were Robert Flemyng, James Stephenson and Ena Burrill, all of whom advanced to major careers. Hyperbolically, Michael was described in a local newspaper as "a promising member [from] an old theatrical family." He had had no formal training, but his performances at Cambridge and Cranleigh had been based on serious academic study of the dramas and their historic contexts. Those plays were presented only two or three times each year; now the repertory system kept him busy forty weeks annually, with rehearsals by day and performances at night.

As he admitted later, he was "an ambitious, arrogant and conceited young man. I wanted to play everything, and I took it for granted that people should offer me everything." Which is effectively what Armstrong did—casting him, in less than two years at Liverpool, in twenty-three modern plays (all of them soon consigned to oblivion, and none produced later in any standard repertory) and in two by

Shakespeare. The company also presented a Christmas play Michael wrote for children.

In early 1935, Armstrong raised Michael's salary to six pounds a week. The first play under the new contract was to be John van Druten's *Flowers of the Forest,* scheduled for late March (in advance of its Broadway premiere). Michael was cast in a secondary but crucial role, and for the leading lady he campaigned for Ruth Lodge, an actress in the company. "Oh, dear!" said Armstrong on hearing this recommendation. "I've already cast the part—with Rachel Kempson." Michael had seen Miss Kempson in several Shakespearean roles at Stratford, where her elegance, beauty and talent dazzled audiences and critics. "But she's much too short," Michael countered, adding, "I shall have to go down on my knees to kiss her!"

Three
FAITHFUL, IN A FASHION
(1935–1937)

OH, GOOD — YOU'RE TALL," SAID MICHAEL REDGRAVE WHEN HE
was introduced to Rachel Kempson. "I thought you were
going to be tiny." Shoeless, she stood at a height of five feet
eight inches, capable of a commanding presence and, more to the
point, of not making the six-foot-three-inch Michael appear unnatu-
rally gigantic.

With significant classical experience behind her and eager to join a
new company for roles in contemporary plays, Rachel was nevertheless
a profoundly insecure young woman. Although she impressed others
with her patrician deportment, genteel loveliness and apparent confidence onstage, she had a lifelong sense that (as she said) she "never quite
belonged anywhere," a feeling caused by the lack of "a tough ego." Her
deep sense of displacement in the world was also owed, most recently,
to the arrival at Stratford of a new director—a man who for some odd
reason advised her to recommence her career with less important roles
than those Shakespearean parts she had so successfully undertaken
(Juliet, Ophelia, Ariel, Olivia, Titania and Virgilia, among others).

The reason given for this de facto demotion was management's sense
that Rachel was not, in her heart, entirely of the theater world—that
she did not have the kind of intense ambition essential for success on
the stage. "I do not believe that the theatre is her home," wrote her
father, agreeing with the new executive team at the Shakespeare Memorial Theatre. But this was a wildly flawed judgment. Rachel was
certainly not a cauldron of burning ambition, nor did she ruthlessly

pursue celebrity, but she loved the theater and showed obvious talent in a wide range of roles.

—⚭—

SHE WAS BORN at Dartmouth, to Beatrice and Eric Kempson, who had met in Devon during the late autumn of 1907 when he was twenty-nine and she, twenty-three. A distinguished, courtly gentleman, Eric was at once smitten by the pre-Raphaelite nimbus that seemed to hover around Beatrice Ashwell—by her crimson hair, pellucid blue eyes and an irresistible remoteness that at first he took for a mystic calm. The couple married in June 1908.

Whereas Eric, in his twenties, developed modern liberal ideas about social equality, Beatrice was virtually a cliché of the proper Victorian lady with conservative values. Convinced of the rightness of class distinctions, she was also something of a melancholic who, according to Rachel, "like most young women of the day, was entirely ignorant of the facts of life. In addition, I have often wondered whether her father was homosexual or bisexual. Sex was apparently never mentioned in my mother's home, and later she said that my grandfather 'simply adored' young men, and the house was always filled with them. If his sexual life was in fact so repressed, that would go a long way to explaining his heavy drinking and violent temper."

Although marriage was an escape for Beatrice, she regarded it with a sense of dread and humiliation when it came to her wedding night. Completely oblivious about the mechanics of lovemaking, she almost collapsed in fright when Eric said, "I'm afraid I have to ask you to do the most awful thing"—not the sort of tender obliquity she had read in contemporary romance novels. But she did her duty. Rachel arrived on May 28, 1910, and her brothers, Nicholas and Robin, followed in 1914 and 1916.

Alas, Beatrice had no gift for warm maternity. "She had a habit of pushing me away," Rachel confided years later—"and of saying no to just about everything." Indeed, Beatrice's attitude and manner contributed greatly to her daughter's lifelong sense of insecurity. This may also partly explain Rachel's desire for the compensatory approval of an audience's applause. Emotionally barren, Beatrice apparently demonstrated maternal affection only for her youngest child, Robin, on whom she lavished the devotion she had denied the first two. Rachel tried to rise above this lack of maternal love and turned to her father, who was more attentive when at home but was absent several years during the war. Accordingly, a deep and lasting wound was inflicted on the girl. In some silent inner place, perhaps predictably, she never considered herself worthy of anyone's wholehearted affection, and she was astonished when it was offered.

The Kempson union was, for many decades, strained and essentially loveless—"they were in an impasse of sexual frustration," according to Rachel. A sad, cold woman who was difficult to love, Beatrice at some point attracted the attention of a farmer named Joey Stock, for whom she harbored an intense, pathetic passion that remained chaste and led to nothing but bitterness and guilt.

—⁊⁊—

EARLY IN THE marriage, Eric Kempson was employed as a science teacher, a vocation inspired by his father's work as a homeopathic pharmacist. But after he returned from military service in the Great War, Eric found his academic position cancelled because of budget cutbacks. He then took a poorly paid job as a school inspector, and family life—which involved frequent relocations to Rugby and Kew, among other places—was frugal to the point of deprivation until he was engaged as headmaster of the Royal Naval College at Dartmouth, in 1927, a position he held until 1942.

While attending a variety of academies—at Kew; at a gloomy Anglo-Catholic convent in Sussex; and at the Colchester County School—Rachel developed a keen interest in poetry recitations and student plays. At Dartmouth, the respected actor-manager Cyril Maude was a neighbor and family friend; he noted her talent and arranged for a qualifying test that would admit her to the Royal Academy of Dramatic Art, where she won a place on September 30, 1931. During her two years at RADA, Rachel advanced quickly, winning the Kendal Prize for elocution and a citation for writing monologues and dialogues; she also shone as a Shakespearean heroine.

For her final school performance, she was awarded the prestigious Anmer Hall Award for her Rosalind in *As You Like It,* in a student production open to the public (on March 7, 1933, at the Haymarket). "Only Rachel Kempson and [actor] Mervyn Blake were at all impressive," wrote the critic W. A. Darlington in *The Telegraph,* while another reviewer praised her as "an actress of the utmost charm and freshness—the most captivating heroine I can remember." Her English rose beauty, clear and expressive diction and graceful gestures made her one of RADA's most admired young performers when she graduated on her twenty-third birthday in 1933.

By that time, Rachel had been engaged by W. Bridges-Adams at Stratford, where she appeared to great effect in eight performances weekly during the summer festival. Following her debut, as Hero in *Much Ado About Nothing,* she played ten additional roles during the 1933 and 1934 seasons—notably a passionate Juliet (always her favorite role); a heartbreaking Ophelia; a lively, gilded Ariel; and a coercively loving Titania. For her efforts, she was paid eight pounds a week, the typically modest Stratford compensation.

Local and provincial newspapers invariably carried favorable reviews of her acting. Of her Juliet, for example, the critic for *The Times* wrote, "Miss Rachel Kempson, who has youth and grace, brings to Juliet a pale, cool beauty which seems at first too faint in hue for its purpose, but then puts on a glorious intensity of its own. Her delivery of the lines might be more musical, but it is unaffected, and besides giving freshness and spontaneity to familiar passages, it has the emotional power that belongs to sincerity. Whether ecstatic on the wings of happiness or distractedly rushing to death, her feeling is deep and true." The *Birmingham Mail* called her performance "a triumph—she lived, never acted, the part." Of her Romeo, however, most reviewers were bluntly dismissive: "John Wyse's performance was a distinguished failure," sniffed *The Times.*

In almost every production in which she participated at Stratford,

Rachel was cast alongside John Wyse. With his movie star attractiveness, he played Ferdinand to her Ariel and Oberon to her Titania; "golden and handsome, he looked glorious," Rachel recalled. And when Wyse was Romeo to her Juliet—*pace* the critics—she seemed indeed to be living, not merely acting the part, and there was a good explanation for her credibility: "I believed myself to be in love with John Wyse—but he was homosexual, like many men in the company."

Replacing Bridges-Adams at Stratford in 1934, Ben Iden Payne presumed that Rachel was fundamentally without a strong professional drive, however much she pleased audiences and critics. Hence he offered to retain her, but in smaller roles that were effectively beneath her experience and abilities. With that, she rejected the security of the familiar and struck out on her own. Perhaps also to escape the ubiquitous but unavailable John Wyse, Rachel left Stratford and went to London, where she had a few modern roles. Then, in early February 1935, she performed at the Oxford Playhouse in John Masefield's *The Witch* and, most affectingly, in Somerset Maugham's *The Sacred Flame,* as a devoted young wife caring for a man crippled in an automobile accident. William Armstrong attended these performances and invited her to Liverpool to act with Michael Redgrave in the John van Druten play.

—◊—

AT THE END of February, the Liverpool Repertory began rehearsals for *Flowers of the Forest.* This was a nobly conceived but dramatically weak thesis-play against war; its first and third acts, set in the postwar era, enclose a second-act flashback to wartime, but this interesting conceit failed. Rachel bore the emotional burden of the drama as Naomi, a woman forty years old in the first and last acts and twenty in the flashback. Not yet twenty-five herself, she required a convincing wardrobe and skillful aging makeup; the role—soon undertaken in the Broadway premiere by no less a seasoned actress than Katharine Cornell—demanded much of the actress.

Michael had the brief but significant part, in the second act, of Richard, a young army officer who is Naomi's lover before he goes off to war and she marries another. The first of their two scenes together concerned their declaration of mutual love; in the second, Richard returns from combat, disillusioned and bitter, to learn that Naomi is pregnant. He resumes his military duties only to die in battle, and she aborts their child.

"I fell more in love with Michael every day during rehearsals," Rachel said years later. "In fact, I think I fell in love with him even before we met, when I saw his photo outside the theater on the day I arrived for the first reading . . . [and by opening night] I was more in love than ever." As one of her daughters later said, "She was the most romantic person I ever knew—always full of romance."

Michael regarded Rachel as a mature and gifted colleague, and he liked her humor and her adoration of him. She is first mentioned in his diary on March 12: "Rehearse Act II—Rachel Kempson [as] Naomi. To lunch with her at the Bon Marché [department store]." He also jotted down a list of minor physical complaints he endured ("I am an awful hypochondriac and keep taking things"). Rachel suffered from a nervous stomach due to occasional bouts of spastic colitis, and during their luncheons that month she often apologized as she rummaged in her handbag for this tablet or that digestive powder. "It's wonderful to find someone else who takes things [for various indispositions]," Michael told her cheerfully. This she took as an expression of profound compatibility between them: it was, she felt, virtually a proposal of marriage, which she now intended to secure.

On his side, Michael's attraction to Rachel was a tangle of desires and feelings. He liked her; they were both dedicated to the theater; they read plays together; they found they had similar tastes and aspirations; and he enjoyed being seen with one so attractive, articulate, presentable—and worshipful.

One afternoon, her intentions became more serious as she discussed her ideas about a lifelong commitment. Michael had never discounted marriage for himself: he wanted to be a father, and he foresaw the condition of wedded life as both a check on his homosexual escapades and an effective public statement of heterosexuality. He may also have considered the public's warm admiration for married couples working together in the theater, even those whose relationship was one of professional companionship more than great passion—so much was true of the marriage of Katharine Cornell with Guthrie McClintic, for example, and of Alfred Lunt with Lynn Fontanne.

For the present, the *amitié particulière* of Rachel and Michael remained chaste because, to Michael's credit, he was unwilling to stage a seduction scene by taking advantage of a woman he genuinely liked—and because, as she said, "I was very fearful, especially as I was still a virgin. I loved him passionately, but I did not *dare* to be his with my body; I ached with longing, but I still had no knowledge and didn't know how to prevent a baby. I couldn't bring myself to go to a doctor to find out what to do before marriage. Indeed, who would have told me in those days? I was Michael's first close experience of a virgin in love."

They shared an inexpensive lunch every day before the premiere, and by the end of March, Rachel was lost in a haze of romantic self-abnegation. Just before the final dress rehearsal of *Flowers of the Forest,* one evening in Michael's rented rooms in Falkner Street, they were reading lines and trying bits of business. During the love scene, as she recalled, the words "were so real to me that I dared not look at Michael but gazed out the window, so that he shouldn't see the truth in my eyes."

On opening night, March 27, a technical blunder jeopardized their second-act love scene. As the forlorn young hero, Michael was to switch off a lamp, a bit of stage business designed to provide a romantic glow for their embraces and promises of fidelity—a scene illuminated only by artificial stage firelight. But his gesture with the lamp failed to plunge the stage into the expected darkness, for the lighting director had fallen asleep at the offstage switch. "So I left the wretched light and continued the scene as best I could—and at the very moment when I took Rachel in my arms, the lamp went out. Big laugh from the audience." The technician, though embarrassed and apologetic, repeated his gaffe on the second night.

The critics were cool to the play but warm toward the leading lady. "Miss Kempson, who gave infinite pleasure to the eye in the part of Naomi, was perhaps a little too restrained and equable in the second

act, though her statuesque style suited the older Naomi to perfection."
Michael was mentioned only briefly, as "an admirable player [who] focuses the theme of the play."

Although they had been acquainted for only a few weeks, Rachel
took the initiative a few days after the premiere. "Couldn't we get married?" she asked him. Michael was troubled: "He said that there were
difficulties in his nature," she recalled, "and that he felt he ought not
to marry."

Rachel had no experience of sex, but she was aware of its variet-
ies. "I knew what Michael meant by 'difficulties,' and so I said, 'I understand. It doesn't matter to me—I love you so.'" There was a long
pause before he replied, "Very well, if you are sure—then we will." On
April 7 they told William Armstrong of their engagement, and a press
announcement was published on May 8. At least in Liverpool, their
stars were ascending: they acted together in half a dozen productions
during the next year, in pleasant but unmemorable plays.

"It was his enormous sensitivity, coupled with a certain gentle elegance, that made me love Michael so very much," said Rachel. "I was
sure I could overcome his difficulties—I would have done anything for
him. Besides, I was very scared of the macho type of man. Of course,
it was partly his great beauty that attracted me, and he didn't speak or
behave like so many actors, who peppered their conversations with 'My
dear,' and 'Darling' this and 'Luvvie' that, to any and every stranger.
The fact that he had happily consented to marry convinced me that
he and I would be forever faithful—and that my love for him would
change him." But as she admitted years later, "the truth was that neither of us knew the other at all, [and] I swept Michael into marriage
against his doubts." Michael's diary entries for that year contain remarkably little about his fiancée. "R. reassures me" was his most extravagant written statement (on June 29).

A midsummer marriage was planned, during the Liverpool Rep's
seasonal hiatus. At first, the families reacted with sublime indifference,
his mother and her father especially. To Margaret's thinking, clouded
by jealousy and alcoholism, Rachel was simply unsuitable. For Eric,
a practically insolvent actor made a poor candidate for marriage; as

Michael recalled, the prospective father-in-law said frequently during May and June that it was not too late to cancel the wedding, set for July 18 in the chapel of the Royal Naval College. Over time, both families accepted the couple more gracefully, but there was never any great love between Margaret and Rachel, although the latter tried valiantly to be-friend her mother-in-law.

Margaret's coolness, which occasionally flared into open, fiery re-sentment of Rachel, may have been at least partially based on the un-pleasant fact that her own career had declined into a disappointing list of smaller roles, while Rachel—beautiful, young, energetic—seemed to go from strength to strength onstage and off, usually without enor-mous effort. Not one of the plays in which Margaret appeared after 1930 is remembered today; of her eight film roles between 1909 and 1947, only *A Canterbury Tale* and *Black Narcissus* have survived, but in these she is seen only for a half moment and to no significant effect. Perhaps her most famous theatrical costar was Greer Garson, with whom she appeared in *The Visitor,* staged at Finsbury in July 1936. "It folded after three weeks," recalled its author, Nicholas Monsarrat. "We said it was the hot weather—actually, it was a bad play." In any case, Margaret's career may have been brighter without the dimming effect of drink.

"There were moments when I would have been only too glad to hear that the wedding had been called off," Michael recalled. "But I flunked the role of the jilter." Rachel took note of his feelings: "He was far from happy—indeed, he was very frightened." But plans had been made, wedding presents had arrived, invitations had been mailed, gowns and dress suits ordered: cancellation was quite out of the ques-tion. Nor did the engaged couple wish to give their families any kind of Pyrrhic victory. The wedding ceremony was duly held on July 18, and Mr. and Mrs. Michael Redgrave set off for a brief honeymoon at a seaside resort in Exeter.

Each remembered rather differently the consummation of the mar-riage. According to Rachel, this occurred on the wedding night, al-though her description is not rapturous: "I was feeling pretty carefree, and due to his knowledge and my determination, it was a moderate success. Whether I'd enjoyed it or not, I was, for better or worse, no longer a virgin. I was a married woman."

Michael's account of that summer night varies significantly from hers. "Rachel seemed rather nervous, so I volunteered to go down to the bar and have a drink while she changed clothes upstairs in the hotel room. The wedding champagne and two dry sherries somehow failed to produce the amorous, seductive character I was hoping to become. We were both eager to get into bed, yet I knew for a certainty that when we did, I, for one, would fall asleep"—which he did: as he told it, the consummation was postponed until the following morning. Perhaps because neither of them expected to register or report high marks on the scale of physical ecstasy, the union was from day one not founded on shared sexual passion. "My father," said his daughter Lynn Redgrave years later, "can be called either bisexual or gay—but he couldn't ever be called my mother's Romeo. She was so in love with him, and in his way, he loved her. But he had this longing in his nature for something else."

—⁓—

In August they returned to Liverpool, and when they could, they traveled to London that autumn. Nineteen thirty-five was the year of a legendary production of Rachel's favorite play, *Romeo and Juliet,* starring John Gielgud, Laurence Olivier, Peggy Ashcroft and Edith Evans. Each of these four eminent actors was to become significant in the lives of the Redgraves.

Then thirty-one, Gielgud was London's preeminent Shakespearean actor and director, having earned enormous critical and popular acclaim as Romeo, Richard II, Macbeth and Hamlet. Successful in roles requiring both outer strength and interior reflection, he was admired for an aristocratic poise and a mellifluous voice that turned ordinary speech into sublime poetry. That year, Gielgud realized that he would soon be too old to repeat his portrayal of Romeo, and this frank self-assessment gave him an idea.

Since the nineteenth century, it was not unusual for actors to exchange or alternate roles in the same production: Samuel Phelps and

William Macready, and later Henry Irving and Edwin Booth, had alternated Othello and Iago, and now it was Gielgud's intention to do the same with Romeo and Mercutio that autumn. "I had seen Larry [Olivier] quite often on the stage," recalled Gielgud. "At first [Olivier] demurred, saying he was hoping to mount the play for himself and [his wife at that time] Jill Esmond. But finding I was already determined to have Edith Evans as the Nurse and Peggy Ashcroft as Juliet, he immediately agreed to join us."

This was as wise a decision on Olivier's part as it was generous and judicious on Gielgud's. Except for one or two failed modern productions, the last in 1928, Larry had not played Shakespearean roles since drama school. In 1935 he was regarded as an appealing but lightweight performer in mostly comic modern plays: he was, for example, the second lead in the premiere production of Noël Coward's *Private Lives*. Michael and Rachel were but two of many theater folk who wanted to see how Olivier—a year older than Redgrave—would manage the transfer to major classical roles. In October the play opened at the New Theatre, with Olivier as Romeo and Gielgud as Mercutio, and six weeks later the two exchanged roles. During the run of the play, Michael and Rachel saw them in both roles: "a fine clear statement of the play," he noted in his diary, "always full of interest, but never moving."

The received tradition for reciting Shakespeare, of which Gielgud was prime guardian, was to stress the poetic lyricism of the verse. But from the first rehearsal, Olivier spoke his lines as if they sprang from blunt, spontaneous feeling and were not lines of venerable iambic pentameter. He played Romeo as a hot-blooded adolescent seething with erotic energy, and so the words sounded like a rush of passionate desire. At first, Gielgud tried to restrain him, and the atmosphere during rehearsals was frequently charged with tension, but then Gielgud gave Olivier complete freedom.

"He felt that I was too verse-conscious and exhibitionist in my acting of Shakespeare," Gielgud said years later. "Of course, he was a great exhibitionist himself, but in quite a different way—daring, flamboyant and iconoclastic." Gielgud was well bred, literate, the grandnephew of the great actress Ellen Terry, and familiar with all the classics—as

Olivier was not, and he knew it. (As late as the 1940s and '50s, during his marriage to Vivien Leigh, Olivier depended on her literary sophistication for advice concerning which plays were most suitable for him.)

Since his school days, Olivier had wanted to "knock their bloody eyes out" with his acting, and in 1935 his attitude was still, as he said later, one of defiance: "I will show them, I will show them, I will show them. I'm going to be a simply smashing actor." In some important ways, he succeeded—but not that year. The London critics savaged his Romeo as "inexpert" and "gabbling," adding that he was "temperamentally ill at ease" and lacked both a lyrical voice and a sense of poetic diction. On the other hand, there was rousing praise for Gielgud, Ashcroft and Evans.

"He was deeply hurt," Gielgud recalled, "and he went on, all his life, about the way he resented this early critical rejection." This was the first sign of Olivier's lifelong hypersensitivity to negative criticism. Forever after, he presented himself as a benighted victim, as if the critics had demolished his career at the outset. A pungent, churlish envy characterized his subsequent relationship with John Gielgud—and eventually his collaboration with Michael Redgrave, too.

—⁓—

ACCORDING TO RACHEL, the first months of her marriage would have been intolerable without their careers and trips to London for the theater. "A very important facet of marriage is the sharing of a bed—with its warmth and nightly companionship [that] can draw you closer. For us, there was the work." She could not have found encouragement when Michael frequently slipped away alone, leaving her in their rented rooms at Falkner Street as he went to the local Turkish baths in Liverpool—visits he marked in his diary on November 17 and 24, 1935, and again on January 6 and 28, 1936, with the curious notation "I went to the Turkish baths after some debate with R." Precisely why he felt it necessary to rub salt in the wound of abandonment by "debating" the rightness of such conduct is difficult to understand.

Before the end of 1935 the five-month-old marriage had become severely compromised by Michael's escapades, and he could not have been surprised by his wife's bouts of anxiety. "Rachel does not sleep well," he noted in his diary on January 9, 1936, and six days later: "Rachel seems vaguely put out," which could not have been past his comprehension. Still, she adored him, and he counted on her endless patience and understanding—even as he seemed to have demonstrated a sanguine attitude that essentially said, "I warned you." Nor could his adventures have improved her self-confidence as woman and wife: her emotional vulnerability and natural longing for the normal signs of affection and marital love were being denied by a man she respected and loved—and whom, she wrongly assumed, she could change.

All this was unknown to the Liverpool staff and audiences, who virtually idealized the young married couple, especially when they performed roles as husband and wife or lovers. At Christmastime, the Redgraves produced and acted in *Circus Boy,* Michael's full-length play for children, a touching fable about the abandoned son of gypsies; after inheriting ownership of a circus from his father, the boy loses it to the machinations of a villainous ringmaster before regaining it with the help of other children (chosen from the audience). Michael understood and loved youngsters, and he had not given up his dream of fatherhood—hence, in 1936, he and his wife decided to have a child.

—∞—

JUST WHEN RACHEL received confirmation of her pregnancy, the director Tyrone Guthrie returned from staging two plays on Broadway; even taller than Michael, intellectual and imposing, Guthrie was about to take up the post of resident director at the Old Vic. Passing through Liverpool, he first saw Michael as Richard II and Rachel as his queen, Anne of Bohemia, in Gordon Daviot's *Richard of Bordeaux.* Guthrie shared the critical reaction: "Michael Redgrave possessed the looks, the dignity, the voice and the emotional capacity for so strenuous a part. And Rachel Kempson is ideally cast as his queen."

Also in the audience was Frith Banbury, a young actor who had appeared in the West End production of *Richard of Bordeaux* the previous year and later became a busy and respected director. He had been among Rachel's friends and classmates at RADA and wanted to meet

Michael. "He had all the graces," said Banbury, who admired Redgrave's intelligence and theatrical scholarship. "Michael was an attractive chap who could be sweet and forthcoming, but you never quite knew—you might do or say something he considered inappropriate, and then . . . " Banbury's minatory conclusion hung in the air.

Guthrie remained several nights, to see the Redgraves again—this time in James Bridie's *Storm in a Teacup,* a pleasant trifle about an eccentric Irishwoman whose beloved dog is impounded after she fails to pay a license fee, a lapse that causes local trouble. The comedy was negligible, but Guthrie again regarded the performances by Rachel and Michael as first-rate, and he left a letter for them: "I don't suppose there is much likelihood in being able to persuade you and your wife to come to the Old Vic with me next autumn. The money we can offer you will *not* compare favourably with a West End salary, but the work would, I think, be more interesting." Laurence Olivier and Edith Evans were also about to join the Old Vic.

"He offered us several young character roles, commencing that autumn," recalled Michael, "and so our cup of happiness was full." By the time they prepared to leave for London, Rachel had performed in a total of eight Liverpool productions, Michael in twenty. In their last play with the company that June, she was an admirably lively Viola to his richly inventive Malvolio in *Twelfth Night.*

Audiences were filling West End theaters as usual that year, but the offerings were mostly inferior and insubstantial fare—except for a few plays by Noël Coward (*Tonight at 8:30*), a high comedy by Terence Rattigan (*French Without Tears*) and a thriller by Emlyn Williams (*Night Must Fall*). But at the Old Vic, Lilian Baylis (for whom Michael had auditioned before he went to Liverpool) was the most important theater manager in London and she succeeded where most mainstream producers did not: in the realm of quality.

Renowned for having staged the full canon of Shakespeare's works, Baylis also opened the Sadler's Wells opera and ballet companies and engaged an extraordinary roster of talent that eventually included John Gielgud, Laurence Olivier, Peggy Ashcroft, Sybil Thorndike, Alec Guinness, Maurice Evans, Ralph Richardson, Edith Evans, Michael

Redgrave and Rachel Kempson. Her influence continued long after her death: the Old Vic became the first locus of the nascent National Theatre, and the Sadler's Wells Opera was renamed the English National Opera. All this Baylis achieved with a set design budget of no more than twenty-five pounds per production (with recycled costumes) and with actor salaries not exceeding ten pounds weekly.

Built on reclaimed marshland south of the Thames near Waterloo Bridge, the Old Vic was opened in 1818 as the Royal Coburg, a hall promising "entirely new entertainment on a scale of magnitude and great expense." That was certainly true of the first night, which offered a long melodrama followed by an Asian ballet. In 1831 the great tragedian Edmund Kean took on the roles of Richard III, Othello, Macbeth and King Lear during a six-night engagement. "In my life," he told a rowdy audience following one performance, "I have never acted to such a set of ignorant, unmitigated brutes as I have before me now." Apparently he was not exaggerating: the neighborhood remained seedy and dangerous, and many of the patrons were locals who simply rushed into the theater without the formality of buying a ticket. After sleeping, snoring, boozing or brawling during performances, some of them hunkered down there for the night.

Despite the change of name to the Royal Victoria (honoring the theater-loving princess who had visited in 1833), the place went into major decline: the historian Charles Kingsley, for example, described it as "a licensed pit of darkness, a trap of temptation, profligacy and ruin." But in 1880 a social worker named Emma Cons began the transformation of the Royal Victoria by rechristening it the Victoria Coffee and Music Hall, "a cheap and decent place of amusement along strict temperance lines," as she announced. She dropped the word *Theatre* because she reckoned that the public still attached to it a negative and decadent connotation.

In 1898 Emma's niece, Lilian Baylis, then twenty-four, became acting manager, and so began the golden era of the Old Vic (which was an affectionate nickname before it became a legal title). Operas were staged from 1912, and a great cycle of Shakespeare's plays began two years later. Before long, no one hoping for a serious theatrical career would think of declining the opportunity to work cheerfully for Baylis, notwithstanding the absurdly low salaries she paid, which were little more than a charity token. But she was a fearless soul. As bombs fell during the Great War and audiences looked for escape or shelter, Baylis called to them from the stage, "What's a raid when my curtain's up?"

"She was an extraordinary person, rather like a devout old landlady," according to John Gielgud, who recalled the short, dumpy and untidy woman with gentle eyes and a slightly crooked mouth. The actress Sybil Thorndike added that Baylis "ran the place like parish rooms and looked like a church worker. She had two smelly dogs, Scamp and Snoo, of whom it was said that you never knew which end you were patting.

"All the stories about her are quite true," Gielgud continued—"her scruffy, spoilt dogs; the slightly Cockney accent; the directness in her approach; her thrift; and her deep godliness. Her presence seemed to pervade the whole theatre as she wandered about, peering into rehearsal rooms or watching bits of performances from her box, where she would often sit and deal with her correspondence, occasionally peeking out and then jotting down a note. She loved her end-of-season festivities, making speeches to the audiences, wearing her cap and gown and medals. She was, I suppose, a bit of a genius and also a bit of a saint and was suitably mysterious and dedicated."

When Queen Mary, wife of King George V, arrived late for the Vic's centenary gala in 1918, Baylis escorted her on a tour of the theater's picture gallery. "I'm glad you've turned up at last, dear," she said airily to Her Majesty while the Board of Governors blanched. "I know it's not your fault being late, as I hear that your dear husband, going to the Union Jack Club, has held up traffic in the road. But we've got a long program to get through, and so we had to make a start without you." The queen's reaction has not been recorded, but she was surely unaccustomed to such democratic informality. Finally, the two women came to a painting of the king: "It's not as large as my Aunt Emmie's—but then of course your dear husband has not done so much for the Old Vic as she did."

Impervious to criticism and innocently eccentric, Baylis once told an actress that her wig was unsatisfactory and would have to be returned to Berts, the theatrical wigmaker.

"But Miss Baylis," protested the actress, "this is my own hair!"

"I don't care," replied the manager. "It will have to go back to Berts."

On another occasion, Laurence Olivier approached Baylis to request a raise. He enjoyed working with her, he said, but other offers were coming in, and he wanted more money. She replied that she would pray over the matter and give him an answer the next day. She did: "Sorry, Larry—God said no." And that was that. "The place had the atmosphere of a parish hall," according to Olivier. "There was a smell of hard-boiled eggs and stale tea, plus a hint of something I could only describe as dead cats. But I adored her," as perhaps everyone did.

—⁓—

DURING THE TORRID summer of 1936, the Redgraves took a small, dark flat in Greycoat Gardens, Westminster. Michael engaged a part-time secretary named Edith Hargreaves, whose love for all things theatrical was soon matched by her devotion to all things Redgrave; she gradually took on countless duties and remained with the family for many years. Among her early achievements was finding a more spacious residence for the Redgraves—a six-room, two-bathroom apartment in Pembridge Mansions, Moscow Road, Bayswater. Their joint salary of £20 weekly enabled them to afford the rent of £180 annually, as well as a nanny and a cook-housekeeper. (The former was typically paid twenty-five shillings a week, the latter about a pound.)

On September 14, the Vic presented *Love's Labour's Lost,* with Michael as Ferdinand, king of Navarre, and Rachel as the princess of France. (Alec Guinness was also in the cast.) To the delight of Lilian Baylis and perhaps to their own surprise, the new players easily adapted their performances to the new acting space that was twice the size of the Liverpool Playhouse. In her billowing, voluminous costumes, Rachel could hide her pregnancy, and she acted with elegance and freedom. Although Michael delivered the verse brilliantly, he could not find the elusive key to Ferdinand, an idealist who falls in love with a princess and promises her a year of chaste living in order to win her confidence.

During rehearsals, Guthrie frequently challenged Michael in private: Did he not understand Ferdinand's dilemma? Did he not appreciate the penitential sacrifice the character was making to win his beloved? Behind the scenes, Rachel understood. "Michael always had to present *himself* in a character, but he knew he had to comprehend the character first. In this case, there was a problem, precisely because he was not quite sure who 'he himself' was at this point in his life. He had always had a chameleon quality, and he changed according to whom he was with, even to altering his intonation of voice and his pronunciation."

Her use of the chameleon metaphor was on the mark, for Michael was many people that season. To the public, he was the handsome and devoted actor and husband, playing onstage what he was in real life. To colleagues and friends, he was a polite but somewhat aloof and inscrutable gentleman. And to his wife, he was an enigma, a man who protested his devotion even as he left the flat for dangerous nighttime excursions.

There was another problem during these early performances at the Vic, for Michael was self-conscious about the gap in the center of his irregular upper teeth and had developed the habit of speaking clearly and even smiling without parting his lips—an ability that nearly equaled that of an expert ventriloquist. This was an awkward limitation until he could afford to have his teeth straightened and capped.

His debut at the Vic evoked mixed reviews, as did his second leading role, that of the randy Mr. Horner in Wycherley's bawdy Restoration comedy *The Country Wife,* a major revival that went into the repertory on October 6. Horner circulates the rumor that he is impotent in order to gain access to countless married women whose husbands wrongly presume they can trust him alone in female company. Here was graceful, attractive Redgrave of the mellow voice, "neither old enough nor sardonic enough," as one critic wrote, "and altogether too nice a youth" to play so reprobate (if comic) a character. Guthrie knew that the censors were alert and eager to make cuts in this broadly sexual romp, and Michael was responsible for toning it down.

"I should have played it dirty, but I was being obedient. I kept wanting to leer and make all sorts of noises that sounded lascivious," Michael recalled. "But Guthrie said, 'No, no, just play it straight.' And so I was playing against the text." Whereas he could not find sympathy for Ferdinand because of the play's motif of enforced chastity, he resented having to play the lustful Horner as an essentially decent fop, all tidied up for the conventions of 1936. He was fortunate, however, in his two leading ladies: the American stage star Ruth Gordon, in the title role of Margery Pinchwife; and Edith Evans, as Lady Fidget.

Almost at once, Evans was an enormous help to Michael in preparing this difficult role. "I remember her saying to me, 'When you hear me say that line—just four words, *"perfectly, perfectly, Mr. Horner"*—put your hand on my diaphragm.' And I did, and she said the four words—but so that you could hear it through the whole house. And then she said, 'Do you realize that I'm using more strength of voice just to say those whispered words than I need when I'm speaking out loud?' That was a subtle way of telling me that I was occasionally dropping my voice—and that when I wanted to talk quietly, I actually had to use more force, and not less, to raise my voice when I wanted to lower it."

There was, therefore, an odd web of circumstances responsible for Michael's dissatisfaction during that autumn at the Old Vic. He felt outside the roles, for one thing—and he placed the blame on Tyrone Guthrie, who directed the first two productions. "Guthrie made me very nervous," Michael recalled. "I had the impression he felt he had made a mistake in choosing me [for the Vic]—that I wasn't as good as he hoped I would be." But the most glaring reason for his discomfort was due to his own conduct. Although he was married just over a year, and his wife was in the late stages of pregnancy, he believed himself to be hopelessly in love with another cast member—this time, a woman.

As Rachel was ever more confined at home, she had become accustomed to relying on the company of the faithful, middle-aged Edith Hargreaves, in whom she did not confide but who seemed to be aware of tension between the Redgraves. Michael, meanwhile, began to spend ever more time with the other Edith, Miss Evans. For the time being, Michael and Edith rehearsed privately and shared a casual luncheon or post-theater supper. There were no indications of any romantic inclinations on either side until one evening, when Michael, hastening down the backstage staircase, impetuously kissed Edith full on the lips. No word was exchanged between them, but she caught his long, imploring gaze.

Four

LOST LADIES

(1937–1939)

E DITH EVANS HELPED ME ENORMOUSLY," MICHAEL REDGRAVE SAID three decades after he had begun a theatrical collaboration with her. "She was one of the very greatest influences on me, and I owe a very, very great deal to her."

"Find the life in the part" was Edith's motto. Born in London in 1888, she had been widowed some years when she first appeared on-stage with Michael. Long-boned, large of feature and never conventionally pretty, Edith somehow projected an unusual kind of radiance and an aristocratic but warm authority; she was never less than brilliantly effective in a remarkable variety of classic and modern roles in theater, film and television during a career that spanned seven decades.

"There was no doubt," said John Gielgud, "that she was among the two or three finest actresses of the twentieth century. She was not always easy, and there was something rather aloof about her, but I think that had to do with shyness and an intense dedication to her art. Throughout her lifetime she tried to take up the things that ordinary people do: farming, dancing, driving a car, ice-skating. But she really had only one talent—for the theater—and it was an enormous gift." Her voice, as Edith herself said, "runs up and down more or less naturally, and I let it. But it has to be controlled, like a singer's voice." Control was the essential element of her technique.

By the time she performed with Michael in *The Country Wife,* Edith had played more than one hundred roles in England and America; she was never unemployed for long, and that was the way she liked it. Her rendering of the Nurse in *Romeo and Juliet* had been a triumph in London and New York—"the highly distinguished performance of a highly distinguished performer," ran a typical review. "She played a guileful, temperamental bawdy Nurse that was as fresh as if the part had never been acted before," according to another.

Essentially a character actress and not a romantic leading lady, she was, as the critic James Agate said, "a great artist who possessed the gift of observation along with a fine sense of both comedy and pathos." Audiences never forgot the experience of seeing her onstage, and in movies there was no one remotely like her.*

—m—

ON RUTH GORDON's recommendation, the American producer Gilbert Miller invited Michael to New York to repeat his role in *The Country Wife,* scheduled for Broadway at the end of the year. At the same time, Michael had been offered the leading role of Orlando in the Vic's production of *As You Like It,* with Edith as his Rosalind. Temporizing, he sought her advice.

"What sort of actor do you want to be, Michael?" she asked.

"How do you mean? I'd like to play all sorts of parts."

"No, no—I don't mean that. I mean, do you want to be like John [Gielgud] or Larry [Olivier], or do you want to be like Peggy [Ashcroft] or me? What sorts of standards are you aiming at?"

He realized, as he said later, "that she was suggesting that if I applied myself and put thought and passion into it, I might find my place in just such august company. It took my breath away."

She then addressed the matter of the American production of the Wycherley comedy. "You don't want to go to *New York*," she said, as if no grown-up could ever contemplate something so ridiculous. "You'd rather stay *here* and play Orlando with me." And with that, the matter

---

* Fortunately, her film roles provide enduring witness to her talents—among them, her hilariously haughty Lady Bracknell in *The Importance of Being Earnest* (1952); the wise, compassionate Reverend Mother Emmanuel in *The Nun's Story* (1959); the comically befuddled Miss Western in *Tom Jones* (1963); the possessive grandmother, Mrs. St. Maugham, in *The Chalk Garden* (1964); and the heartbreaking Mrs. Ross of *The Whisperers* (1967).

was settled: Michael would not see New York for several more years, and under very different circumstances.

Their romance began at her London flat in West Halkin Street, Belgravia, during final preparations for *As You Like It* in early November 1936. "I fell head over heels in love with Edith," he recalled, "and she with me." Married for only a year, he was now transported with passion for a woman who was both mentor and mother *manquée*—a reading of the relationship that was articulated by Michael himself: "Acting with Edith Evans is like being in your mother's arms. You're safe."

As for Rachel, she was in a way fading into the background of her husband's life. "At first," she recalled, "I didn't realize that they were in love. By then I was used to Michael having a wandering eye, and being out a great deal. This new relationship, therefore, surprising as it may seem, didn't upset me too much." That calm consideration was made a half-century later, after Michael's death, and she may indeed have accepted the revelation without "too much upset." But her statement is difficult to take at face value, for at the time, Michael was effectively treating Rachel the way his father had treated his mother, and the way his mother had treated her own father: by simply absenting himself, as if the other had ceased to exist. There was a difference: Michael eventually returned home after a visit to Edith. But he was, alarmingly often, abandoning the mother Rachel was about to be, and ignoring his responsibilities to her just when she had a proper claim on his attention.

Michael had turned to a great actress who was both lonely and lavish in her affections. Hence Rachel had more to confront than the anxieties of pregnancy and her husband's tearful expressions of regret about this or that assignation with a stranger. As the princess of France said to the king of Navarre in *Love's Labour's Lost,* so could Rachel have said to Michael, "I understand you not: my griefs are double."

—ɷ—

"MICHAEL AND EDITH became lovers for a time," according to Edith's confidant and biographer, Bryan Forbes; in fact, the affair was explicitly documented in letters, notes and telegrams. "I hope we can love each other and find some honourable way and not hurt anyone else or each other," Edith wrote to Michael, signing "with my dear, dear love." A few days later, she was ending her notes with phrases such as "I love you shamelessly."

The relationship was particularly intense during the run of *As You Like It*—first at the Vic and then during a West End run in February 1937, when both of them received reviews of which most actors just dream. "Charm . . . virility . . . power" were the words most often employed to praise Michael, while Edith's Rosalind "set a standard for our time: she was young love incarnate."

They were not so fortunate in the next production. In early December they collaborated again at the Vic, on a production by Michel Saint-Denis of an obscure and difficult Restoration tragedy, *The Witch of Edmonton.* The director had been one of Redgrave's heroes from afar five years earlier, when Michael brought Cranleigh students to see the London tour of La Compagnie des Quinze. In the *Witch,* however—cast in an indifferent supporting role and with no connection to the leading character played by Edith—Michael made no impression on Saint-Denis: "He decided that I was just another young man." No one was helped by the surrealistic production Saint-Denis had created, which reviewers found self-consciously arty and inappropriate for British audiences.

But privately the lovers thrived that season. Controlled and sometimes aloof in public, Edith was no shy mistress: "I do hope that you have no notion whatever of living your life without me," she wrote to Michael. "You simply *can't* do it. We have such beautiful things in common: rice pudding on the hearthrug [*sic*] and coats over the back of the chair. Darling, please don't alter." Proud of her share in his life, she also regretted that "nobody knows [about us]. Mike, why am I always the secret person? I want to come out into the open and say everything to everyone . . . My heart's love to you always always always." She became (thus Forbes) "as one obsessed and, according to close friends, could think and talk of nothing else."

Michael's few surviving letters to her are deeply affectionate but not quite so elaborate: "My darling Edith, how I love you!" and similar exclamations were supposed to say everything. Reflecting years later, however, he admitted that he felt "immeasurably strengthened by Edith's love." But the affair had a term date. The role of potential home wrecker was inconsistent with Edith's profound moral sensibility, and (thus Michael) "it was Edith who ended it. She was incapable of jealousy and hated deception—and she was very fond of Rachel. She always wrote, at the end of her letters, 'My love to your two ladies.'"

The second lady was the child Rachel bore during the evening of Saturday, January 30, 1937. From the Stonefield Nursing Home, Blackheath, the news came to Michael at the Vic, while he was performing Laertes to Laurence Olivier's Hamlet. "Ladies and gentlemen," said Olivier, stepping before the curtain at the finale and speaking as more of a forecaster than he knew, "tonight a great actress has been born—Laertes has a daughter." Mr. and Mrs. Redgrave had already decided on the child's name, after Michael had leafed through a book and found the name of Virginia Woolf's sister, whom he knew and who was the mother of his friend Julian Bell. The Redgrave daughter was therefore named Vanessa.

Backstage, Michael sprang to a telephone and rang Edith. "Nothing could have made me happier," she wrote to him an hour later, "than that you should have rung me up to tell me that Vanessa had arrived. I wanted to cry with joy and pain and everything. God bless Rachel and Vanessa always."

—ɯ—

MICHAEL HAD A variety of supporting roles during late winter and early spring 1937, and his accumulated work evoked increasing praise. The critic A. E. Wilson, for example, wrote, "Among the young actors who have recently attracted notice, few, I think, are more certain to be heard of in the future than Michael Redgrave." But with Vanessa's presence in his life, he became more a doting father than Rachel perhaps anticipated, and he spent his free time strolling in Kensington Gardens with Rachel and the baby, pushing the pram, spreading a blanket for them, singing happily to Vanessa and (as Rachel recalled) "nuzzling her tummy to make her laugh."

When Vanessa was five months old, Rachel left her in the care of a nanny and appeared in several plays. "But I soon felt private life to be the more important. I loved the work, but it took second place, and human relationships first place." Henceforth Rachel Kempson would have a distinguished but sporadic career. "She wanted to dedicate herself totally to the stage," according to her second daughter, Lynn. "But with my father's very, very rapid rise to stardom, and having children, she felt she had to take second place. She always said there wasn't room for two big careers in the life of one couple."

Another aspect of the absorbing theater world to which Rachel referred was Michael's continuing education: that year, for example, he discovered the writings of the Russian actor and director Konstantin Stanislavski. "But I misappropriated what I read, in much the same way as the later disciples of what is called the Method have misused it . . . because it's the job of the actor to present the character created by the playwright, not his own character or personality or life history. The actress who can weep onstage when she thinks of the death of her dog, or an actor who can start crying when he thinks of his mother dying: this may sometimes be effective, but it's awfully dangerous and tricky, because such actors merely communicate themselves, not the characters in the plays. I don't think much of this sort of thing—it makes me laugh—as when an actor said to a friend who complained of a stomach ache, 'Use it!' "

His "misappropriation" of Stanislavski's technique was evident while he performed in a minor comedy called *A Ship Comes Home*, which ran for twenty-five performances in the West End that spring. Playing a doctor visiting the extremely untidy room of another character, he felt that the clutter would offend the doctor's sense of order—as it offended his own sense of order—and so he proceeded, onstage during the action, to tidy things up, tuck stray items into cupboards and generally put things right.

"I hadn't warned any of the other actors that I was going to do these bits of business, and they thought I had gone quite mad, right then and there. My gestures represented a total misunderstanding of Stanislavski's teachings. What I was doing communicated nothing to the audience: it was just irrelevant, slightly comedic scene-stealing on my part. And it just threw the actors. After all, the visiting doctor wouldn't tidy up people's rooms for them—unless his actions were directly related to the action of the play, which they weren't. I was making the mistake of certain so-called Method actors who say, 'If it's true for yourself, it's true,' which is utter nonsense."

These statements point toward the worst excesses of the Method, and they are based on some of the weaknesses in the Stanislavski "system" itself. The Russian actor and theorist tended to stress the actor over the playwright (which meant that the text was often diluted and even muddied). He required extreme self-analysis and self-assertion (which italicized a constant danger to an actor's ego); he constantly emphasized a mystery he called Nature (which led to a penumbra of confusion); and he insisted on a certain perfectionism that led him (as one theater historian has said) "into a delirium of moral fervour and rhetorical phrase-making."

The unfortunate emphasis on self-analysis led some self-styled disciples—the American actor and teacher Lee Strasberg perhaps primary among them—to counsel such extremes of self-analysis that he was known to send students off to a psychiatrist's couch. This, of course, can quickly put the breaks on dramatic inspiration and increase the peril of self-absorption; in this regard, Michael Redgrave was not alone in denouncing such egoism. The American actor Karl Malden expressed a common sentiment when he famously observed that Strasberg "set back for fifty years the cause of good acting and sensible technique in America."

—m—

DURING THE AUTUMN of 1937, John Gielgud invited Michael to appear in three plays he was producing at the Queen's, along with a stellar cast—Peggy Ashcroft, Alec Guinness, Harry Andrews, Anthony Quayle, Glen Byam Shaw, George Devine and Rachel (who had agreed to play only minor roles).

It turned out to be a difficult year for Rachel, even after she made a swift recovery following Vanessa's birth. Gielgud invited her to assume the small but challenging role of Maria in Sheridan's *The School for Scandal* (in which Michael played Charles Surface). This she accepted, although she was understudying the leading lady in J. B. Priestley's *I Have Been Here Before.* Then, during the run of the Sheridan, she was asked to play Celia in Ben Jonson's *Volpone,* at the Westminster. "I found myself in the unique [not to say exhausting] position of under-studying at one theatre, playing in a second and rehearsing in a third."

The strain rapidly accumulated, and one evening during her perfor-mance as Maria, Rachel had a panic attack onstage: she was suddenly unable to remember her lines and, for a few moments, was unaware of her surroundings. Eventually, she carried on, but as she recalled, "this was another blow to my self-confidence, and it was severe. Lack of confidence has always been my Achilles heel."

To his credit, Michael looked after Rachel, providing calm encour-agement during an anxious time that lasted several weeks. He was also coping on his own with his mother's emotional instability, for Andy was at a loss and invariably relied on Michael.

For one thing, Margaret could be unaccountably snappish: in a let-ter she posted to her son and daughter-in-law on May 16, 1938, she accused them of ingratitude and a lack of caring—consequently, she "did not wish to see or hear from [him and Rachel] again," an assertion she immediately regretted and reversed. Contrariwise, on a rare occa-sion, she could appreciate her son's success: "That was a grand perfor-mance yesterday," she wrote to him after attending a rehearsal at the Queen's. "It places you definitely in the top rank." But praise did not forestall criticism when she thought that was called for: "You speak too quickly," she wrote that autumn after attending a screening of his first film appearance, "and at the ends of sentences, your words faded. I think you might see to it. You have nothing to be afraid of and it would be a help in future films."

—∽—

AFTER PLAYING BOLINGBROKE in *Richard II* and Charles Surface in *The School for Scandal,* Michael was assigned one of the most impor-tant parts in his career: Chekhov's rueful Baron Tusenbach, in *The*

Three Sisters, a man who finally cherishes life only when he sees its imminent end. (Lilian Baylis died suddenly, at the age of sixty-three, on November 25, 1937. Honoring the tradition that "the show must go on," the opening night of the revival of *The School for Scandal* went ahead hours later.)

The director of the Chekhov was Michel Saint-Denis, working this time more successfully with Redgrave than during the production of *The Witch of Edmonton.* "He was the greatest possible help to me," Michael recalled. "For instance, when I came to a big speech of Tusenbach's, which starts, 'Cranes and migratory birds . . . ,' I began to spout it off with a great flourish. Michel interrupted me, gesturing impatiently with his pipe and saying, 'No, no, no, my friend! This man is a bore, and he has no personality. You are playing this as if he had personality. You are trying to make sense of his speech—as if it were something important.'

"Rather aggrieved, I replied, 'Well, isn't it the actor's job to try and make sense of the speech?'

"And he said, 'In this case, no. Nobody should be listening to him—he's just an old bore.'

"I was rather upset, especially as this took place in front of the entire company, and I felt I'd made a fool of myself. So I began again, thinking oh, to hell with it, and I just threw away the lines, almost muttering them, without thinking. At once the speech came to life—and when I was finished, Michel said, 'Ah! Do you hear? That is it—it's perfect!'

"I replied, 'Well, if that's what you want, it's easy.' And from that moment, my performance started to grow. I had something to work on—the fact that I was playing a bore, which is one of the most difficult things to make interesting."

A week after the premiere, Saint-Denis took Michael aside. "It's wonderful, my friend," he said. "But now you are aware that you are moving the audience, and whenever you underline certain effects, it is bad—it's not art." And so Michael also learned the great lesson that *less is more.* The result was a deluge of critical raves and a general consensus that he was now in the league of major stage actors: "Mr. Michael Redgrave, who has given many good performances in his time, gives his greatest," wrote the dramatist and critic St. John Ervine. Another review observed how "his very bones seemed to shape themselves differently, and his physical habits [seemed] to adapt themselves to the mental habits he took on with the character."

—ɯ—

DURING THE RUN of *The Three Sisters,* Michael's agent, Bill Linnet, arranged for him to test for a movie contract with the Gainsborough Pictures division of the Gaumont-British Corporation. At that time, most British actors considered film acting something like professional prostitution. Occasionally they succumbed to the blandishments and offers of studio producers—mostly for the handsome compensation, which, at many times the salaries for stage acting, enabled them to continue working in plays. But only a few serious actors, such as Charles Laughton and Laurence Olivier, had absolutely no compunction about working in London or Hollywood movie studios and were even proud of their cinematic credits.

Michael's test was made in Gainsborough's cold and drafty soundstage in late January 1938: with Rachel as his leading lady, Michael performed two scenes from Noël Coward's *Private Lives*. Soon after, Linnet rang with the news that a five-year contract had been offered, with six months freedom each year for theatrical performances. Several hundred pounds sterling annually was too attractive to turn down, and so Michael signed—without knowing what his initial film assignment might be.

That information was forthcoming in early March: he was to appear in something called *Lost Lady,* to be directed by Alfred Hitchcock.* Peggy Ashcroft, John Gielgud and even Michel Saint-Denis

---

* It is often wrongly asserted that Michael Redgrave had previously played a bit part in Hitchcock's *Secret Agent* (1936). But the actor with whom he is confused in that film was Tom Helmore, who at the time bore a striking resemblance to Michael Redgrave. (Helmore appeared in three Hitchcock pictures, most notably in *Vertigo*.)

had already acted for Hitchcock—she briefly but unforgettably as the crofter's wistful, lonely wife in *The 39 Steps*; Gielgud as the reluctant, eponymous *Secret Agent*; and in that same film, Saint-Denis, heavily made up, in a cameo as a Swiss coachman. They did not particularly enjoy their movie experiences, but with good wishes they sent Michael off to the studio. The picture, ultimately retitled *The Lady Vanishes,* turned out to be a huge success; it also made Michael Redgrave's name internationally known and firmly established his stardom.

—m—

THE LADY VANISHES was on several counts anomalous in Hitchcock's career. At the time, he had a contractual obligation to direct one more picture for producer Edward Black, even as Hitchcock's agents were busy negotiating for him to go to Hollywood. With nothing suitable to fulfill his obligation to Black, Hitchcock then found himself in the awkward position of appearing in the producer's office asking if there might be a script already prepared, something another filmmaker had perhaps been forced to abandon. After more than a dozen years of making successful and popular pictures, this was an egregious exception to Hitchcock's ordinary working method: he was accustomed to having creative involvement on each of his pictures from the start, beginning with the outline and creation of the script and proceeding through every stage of preproduction, design, shooting, postproduction and final editing.

Black informed Hitchcock that there was indeed a project available, carefully prepared but jettisoned the previous year: a screenplay by Frank Launder and Sidney Gilliat, based on *The Wheel Spins,* a novel by Ethel Lina White. The original director was Roy William Neill, but when a crew went to Yugoslavia in late summer 1936 to film background material, the authorities flipped through the script and forthwith denied permission for any work to continue. Their main objection was to a swift cut indicated in the screenplay—from strutting soldiers to one of waddling geese (a shot that never made it into Hitchcock's film). While revisions were hurriedly attempted, an assistant director broke his ankle; Neill went down with a protracted respiratory virus; and despite the substantial cash investment, the crew returned to London and the picture was shelved.

Hitchcock read the screenplay, made one or two suggestions to Launder and Gilliat about the opening and conclusion, and announced that he could make the picture in four weeks. But there were more delays: virtually all British studios were shut down for almost six months from the autumn of 1937 as politicians and producers fought over the financial and trade details of a new Films Act. During that time, the writers worked on revisions to *The Lady Vanishes* at Hitchcock's flat in Cromwell Road, in the constant presence of the director's wife and frequent collaborator, Alma Reville. "The difference between the new opening we wrote for Hitch and the one in the original script was that the pace became faster [in the finished film]," Launder recalled. "And the new ending was certainly more exciting as Hitch directed it, with more twists and turns." Filming finally began on March 20, 1938, Michael's thirtieth birthday.

One of very many movies set entirely or partly on a train, *The Lady Vanishes* begins in an unnamed (apparently Balkan) inn, nestled in the snow-covered countryside.* Iris Henderson, a young Englishwoman heading home to be married, meets a charming old woman named Miss Froy, and they both depart by train for London. Miss Froy mysteriously disappears during the journey, but everyone denies having seen her. Iris turns for help to Gilbert Redman, a handsome young musicologist she met at the inn.

At first, he does not believe her—especially when a doctor on board explains that the missing lady is obviously a figment of Iris's imagination, the result of a disorienting concussion. Suspicions are aroused, however, with the appearance of a nun in full habit but wearing high-heeled shoes. Miss Froy is at last found, and it turns out that she is a spy for England, trying to deliver a secret back to London—a vital

---

* Among many pictures exploiting the dramatic motion and romance of the rails: *Santa Fe Colorado Express* (1903), *Shanghai Express* (1932), *Twentieth Century* (1934), *Union Pacific* (1939), *Night Train to Munich* (1940), *Sleeping Car to Trieste* (1948), *Strangers on a Train* (1951), *North by Northwest* (1959), *Von Ryan's Express* (1965), *Murder on the Orient Express* (1975), *Silver Streak* (1976) and *Julia* (1977).

code contained in a folk tune. The doctor, the false nun and several others on board are part of an enemy plot against Miss Froy, who escapes and is finally reunited with Iris and Gilbert in London.

Casting was completed quickly, with the addition of Dame May Whitty in the role of Miss Froy; Margaret Lockwood, already under contract at Gainsborough, as Iris; Paul Lukas as the sinister brain surgeon Dr. Hartz; and Michael as the amiably raffish Gilbert. The production schedule meant that Michael worked days at the studio and then hurried to the theater for evening performances.

"At first, I couldn't summon much enthusiasm for the project, which I thought was silly and shallow," he recalled in 1981. "To be honest, I was something of an intellectual snob at the time, and of course film acting was not regarded very highly by British stage actors. Hitchcock sensed that I preferred the theatre, and so he decided to cut me down to size. The first day of shooting my scenes, he came over to me and said, 'You know, don't you, that Robert Donat [who had starred in Hitchcock's *The 39 Steps*] wanted to play this part in the worst way?' I suppose that remark was meant to remind me that I was Hitchcock's second choice and therefore a little unwelcome, but it didn't—I really wasn't making much of an effort in any case. In fact, I just didn't give a damn, and I was nearly half-way through the picture before I started to try."

Paul Lukas, who already had two decades of major acting credits in European and American films and on Broadway, saw Michael's diffidence and offered advice. "You're a great actor, my friend," said Lukas. "But here, you're not really doing much of anything."

"I find it all intensely boring," replied Michael.

"Listen, my dear boy, once the director has made the last shot of a scene, it's too late to wish you could do it again. This is your first picture—and whether you realize it or not, your future in films depends on how well you do now." In Michael's next scene, the entire cast and crew noted a fresh liveliness in his acting. And his insouciant manner and casual way of reciting lines—laced with a young man's sense of superiority, which was so right for Gilbert's character—reflected his ability to seem as if he were not acting at all.

The sequence that first day of shooting, Michael's introductory scene with Margaret Lockwood, required him to perform a variety of complicated actions and gestures while making them seem both natural and amusing. As Gilbert, he entered Iris's hotel bedroom, stood smugly in the doorway and greeted her cynically. Then he removed his coat and rucksack, stashing them, along with his walking stick, in various places around the room. He then approached Lockwood, sat on her bed and unpacked a suitcase—and then, still in a single take, he left the room, tipping his hat and muttering, "Confidentially, I think you're a bit of a stinker, too."

All this Michael deftly accomplished, completing the various stages of the sequence while progressing from one precise spot on the set to another—to the points where his lights were meticulously set up. This aspect of movie acting can be a nightmare for any performer.

"Hitchcock wasn't really an actor's director," Michael recalled—an assertion echoed by Margaret Lockwood, who said, "I found him most disconcerting. Having worked out the whole picture in script and sketch form, Hitchcock didn't seem to direct us at all, and in fact he rarely spoke to us. He was a dozing, nodding Buddha with an enigmatic smile on his face."

"Maggie was right," Michael added. "Everyone knew that Hitch's reputation in England was more for preparation and technique than for working with his cast. He hired actors he thought knew their craft and would give him no trouble or cause delays, and the film didn't depend on any single performance. Strangely enough, this put us all at our ease, and his nonchalance made it rather easy for us. He knew where he wanted to put his camera; he knew what mood he wanted. He had the whole thing visualized ahead of time, and once we got to the set, it could all be done very quickly and painlessly."

Notwithstanding Hitchcock's apparent indifference to his cast, Michael learned far more than he could have expected during his motion picture debut. The small bits and pieces of which a film is composed may seem at first exasperating to an actor accustomed to going through long, uninterrupted scenes onstage, but these separate components are the basics of cinematic grammar. Masters of the form, Hitchcock among the best of them, knew what to include and exclude in a scene—what to extract, what to stress by close-up or isolation—and from which angle and for what length of time the audience must be guided to regard something or someone. Everything was chosen for an emotional purpose and effect—for telling stories primarily with pictures, not words.

All of this was very different from the audience's view of a stage, and all of it worked toward a language that was essentially wordless, or at least for which words were secondary to action and glance. Every thing, every position, was foreseen and measured, planned and executed, and all of it conspired to evoke a reaction from the audience.

"I learned that in films you can do something that you cannot onstage," Michael added. "For one thing, there is a spontaneity that the camera can catch when you're feeling your way in a part, before it becomes too polished. On the stage, you can work for weeks in rehearsal to achieve something, but the movie camera can catch something early that is more effective than the polished, practiced thing."

David Hare, the British playwright, director and filmmaker, put the matter succinctly. The movie actor, according to Hare, "has a far better chance than in the theatre of offering an original performance, which springs straight from his own imagination, and which has not been mediated through a long process of discussion and repetition [in the theater]. There is very little rehearsal on most films. The actor appears on the set at eight in the morning and offers something of his own to which the director, if he has any sense, reacts. The director may build, but his starting point is what the actor offers. In the theatre, an actor's original impulse is just the starting point for a four-week-long attritional process of modification. Sometimes by the time opening night arrives the actor's performance resembles a trampled field. In the movies there's a much higher chance of the actor's spontaneity retaining its vitality for all time."

Michael's education in the art of film advanced significantly during the weeks it took to complete *The Lady Vanishes*. As he said years later, his brief period with Alfred Hitchcock gave him the equivalent of years of professional training before and behind the camera. Hitchcock was nothing like a buddy to his players, but he taught everyone a great deal by the simple act of brilliantly and methodically composing each moment of his films. "What did I learn from Hitchcock? To do as I was told and not to worry too much. But later I realized that there was much more that I took away from the experience."

—⁓—

ONE OF THE script elements Hitchcock chose to emphasize in both the narrative and on the soundtrack was the motif of music, and this much intrigued Michael the music lover. As in Hitchcock's *The 39 Steps* and, later, in his *Shadow of a Doubt,* a melody is the carrier of something significant; in this case, it's "the secret clause of a peace treaty between two countries," as tweedy Miss Froy says in a triumph of obfuscation. As always, Hitchcock has no interest in specific politics; nor should his audience entertain any such concern: his focus is universal, timeless, not subject to shifting circumstances. Thus the controlling elements of every sequence and the links for the relationships of *The Lady Vanishes* are music and sleep. At the inn, Iris cannot sleep because of Gilbert's music and the dancing of the peasants. On the train, her troubles begin (and Miss Froy is abducted) when Iris falls asleep. Later, she and Gilbert feign sleep. But there is more. Miss Froy is a music teacher who plays the piano. Gilbert is also a musician, studying complex tunes indigenous to Middle Europe.

Appearances in the world of international espionage are deceptive, of course. The frumpy, comfy British nanny is a fearless spy, able to dash across the European countryside. The polite, urbane Dr. Hartz is actually a murderous enemy, a deadly brain surgeon. A woman wearing a nun's habit is no nun at all, but an enemy accomplice who then shifts her loyalty when she learns that Dr. Hartz plans to do away with nice old Miss Froy. ("I didn't know she was English!") Several images stick in the mind long after first viewing: Miss Froy's handwriting on the train window, which disappears just when Iris needs to prove the old lady's presence; the eerie appearance of a completely bandaged and unrecognizable surgical patient; Gilbert spotting a telltale tea label sticking to the train window; and, perhaps most famously, the shot of a character who seems to be a nun in full habit—but who wears fashionable high-heeled shoes.

As always with Hitchcock, the secret contained in the tune is finally meaningless, and we care only about the safety and the budding romance between Iris and Gilbert, two handsome, plucky people whose charm reverses the pathetic situation of the adulterous couple, Mr. Todhunter (Cecil Parker) and his anxious, angry mistress (Linden Travers). Hence, with Hitchcock up front stoking the cinematic engines, *The Lady Vanishes* chugs merrily along from first frame to last.

—w—

WHEN THE PICTURE was released at the end of 1938—first in Britain and America, and then worldwide—it was an instant success. Hitchcock won the New York Film Critics Circle Award for directing, and Michael Redgrave achieved the kind of instant, universal stardom never bestowed by theatrical work alone.

Positive advance word about *The Lady Vanishes* circulated round London, and at once Michael's agents swung into action. During the summer of 1938 he completed two more pictures, but they set no records for charm or success. For both, Gainsborough loaned him out to other production companies, charging high fees for his participation, pocketing huge profits—over £1,000 a week—and paying Michael only his £180 contracted weekly salary.

His first post-Hitchcock assignment was billed as a comedy for the singer and dancer Jessie Matthews, but the producers ran out of money for such extravagances, and the script for *Climbing High,* as it was called, allowed Matthews no chance to demonstrate her talents. Michael was cast in the dreadfully stereotyped and underwritten role of an American millionaire playboy; as he admitted, "my presence didn't help much," and the movie sank into obscurity almost at once. The only benefit from this fiasco was working with director Carol Reed, with whom Michael formed an agreeable collaboration resulting in two far better pictures to come.

The second movie was *Stolen Life,* a romantic melodrama directed by Paul Czinner that starred his wife, Elisabeth Bergner. But this was not anyone's cup of Earl Grey that year: with hysterical dialogue and bizarre, irrelevant sequences, its tortuous narrative about identical twin sisters—with Michael the confused lover of one, or the other, or both—failed to attract audiences.

"I agreed to do many pictures just because of the money, which helped me to choose in the theater only those parts I liked." The movie income also enabled the Redgraves to purchase a kind of folly: a derelict windmill above a cottage that could be turned into a weekend retreat. The family sometimes escaped to White Roding Windmill, but only infrequently before selling it in 1946.

An even greater outlay of cash was made within the year, when they took a long lease on a large house at 102 Clifton Hill, St. Johns Wood, and spent lavishly—as if ignoring the costs—on refurbishing and repainting, and then on new furnishings, carpets, draperies and chandeliers; they finally moved in during the spring of 1939, when Rachel was pregnant again. By that time, a new minder had been found for eighteen-month-old Vanessa, who (as Rachel recalled) "became happy at last, where before she had been irritable and difficult" because of her first, indifferent nanny.

In the autumn of 1938, Michael was back at the Phoenix under the direction of Saint-Denis. In *The White Guard,* set during the Russian Civil War, Michael played a kindly hero, but the play, direct in its denunciation of Stalinist communism, was withdrawn from the repertory after the Munich Pact: British censors forbade the presentation of plays that concerned any controversial political issue. When the closing notice was posted, Michael told a writer from *Theatre World* that he very much "wanted to go on experimenting and learning, playing character parts as often as straight, and gradually growing into the big parts." *Twelfth Night* replaced *The White Guard* in the repertory, and the role of Andrew Aguecheek provided Michael with opportunities for richly inventive comic business. He exploited his height, becoming a gangling overgrown boy and winning critical praise for "magnificent clowning" and for bringing flair and "uncommon freshness to the character."

Despite favorable reviews for the superb talents in these two productions at the Phoenix, the plays were performed to half-empty houses. By the end of 1938 there were widespread rumors of war, and audiences were avoiding serious and even classic plays in favor of lightweight modern comedies and music hall variety shows. But despite a broad consensus that most people did not want to see Shakespeare, the BBC scheduled a live television broadcast of *Twelfth Night* from the Phoenix, on January 2, 1939. There were approximately fourteen thousand television sets in English homes at the time, and most were turned on that evening as viewers watched *Twelfth Night.* This may have been at least partly due to the success of *The Lady Vanishes,* which had just been widely released: people were eager to see, live onstage, the matinee idol whose photo could be found on magazine covers, in newspaper stories and on movie marquees all over London.

"The first thing that happened on that television broadcast was that all the actors spoke louder," Michael recalled, "acting in a broader style and projecting their performances with a great deal more vigor. There was twice as much laughter [than usual] from the audience at the comedy scene and this was because the comedy passages were twice as funny that night." As it turned out, this was Michael's last performance, for the next nine years, in a play from the classical repertory.

—᙮᙮᙮—

IN LATE WINTER 1939, Rachel was forced to withdraw after a few weeks of performance in the Elizabethan comedy *The Shoemaker's Holiday.* "It was a hard struggle against the daily nausea of pregnancy," she recalled, adding that she was mostly confined to Clifton Hill for several months. During much of that entire year, she added, "Michael was out a great deal."

There were two reasons for his continuing absences. The first was a series of intense rehearsals and then the brief run of a play that turned out to be one of the greatest disappointments in his career: the premiere of T. S. Eliot's second full-length work for the theater, *The Family Reunion.* Rehearsals began in February 1939, and the play opened at the Westminster on March 21, only to close a month later. Written in an odd conjunction of blank verse and allusive, often obscure prose, the play exploited elements of Greek drama and mythology in a modern setting. This was a noble attempt at high-toned modern theater; alas, as drama, it lacked tension and fully developed characters. (Eliot himself soon acknowledged that it suffered from serious flaws in construction.)

Michael was cast in the leading role of Lord Harry Monchensey, a man consumed with guilt over his wife's death—not because he killed her (which may or may not be the case), but because he wished her dead. One critic saw Harry as "an unresolved amalgam of Orestes and Hamlet," and in some ways the text supports this. In any case, the play needed both clarity and pacing, but Eliot could not or would not improve the text, even after long, mutually respectful discussions with Michael (who received good notices for "a new flexibility of emotion and neurotic imagination").

When he first read the play, it was with "tears of fright pouring down my cheeks," as Michael recalled—especially when he came to the lines addressed to his character:

> *It is possible*
> *You are the consciousness of your unhappy family,*
> *Its bird sent flying through the purgatorial flame . . .*

"I am cowardly about my own personal unhappiness," he wrote in his diary on May 12. "I like to pretend that it [i.e., the unhappiness] isn't there. I get nothing from being unhappy and seek fretfully to distract myself. I have a vague feeling of guilt and sin."

This was almost a summary of Lord Harry and his spiritual dilemma. But in Michael's case, the "vague feeling of guilt and sin" was itself the second reason for his protracted absences from home: his ongoing search for a male lover. One soon arrived, only to become a player in a real-life drama as byzantine as *The Family Reunion*.

five

THE STARS LOOK UP AND DOWN

(1939–1941)

RACHEL'S SECOND PREGNANCY WAS DIFFICULT, AND AS HER DELIVery date drew near in the summer of 1939, Michael spent as much time with her as his schedule permitted. That season, he was working six days a week on a new picture, but he was at home on Sunday morning, July 16, when his wife gave birth to their second child, a boy they called Corin William. The first name was that of the shepherd in *As You Like It;* the second was chosen because Michael considered it "the most euphonious of all masculine names." On August 13 the child was christened, with Elisabeth Bergner standing as godmother and, as godfather, the actor Max Adrian, who had appeared onstage with Michael in *The Bat* at the Embassy in 1937 and quickly became a good friend and confidant. Corin was "big and fine and placid," Michael wrote to Edith Evans, "and Vanessa grows more and more enchanting. She talks a great deal now and seems to forget nothing she has ever heard."

THE FILM THAT occupied Michael that summer—his fourth, and his second under Carol Reed's direction—was based on A. J. Cronin's 1935 novel *The Stars Look Down,* a serious treatment of poor miners and their dangerous working conditions.

Michael had top billing in the picture, which also featured several actors from *The Lady Vanishes* (Margaret Lockwood, Cecil Parker and Linden Travers) and the actor-playwright Emlyn Williams. First seen as a weary, begrimed worker emerging from a long day in the mines, Michael played the part of Davey Fenwick, a multifaceted character, the loyal elder son of a dirt-poor family but also a bright young man who competes successfully for a university scholarship. Davey marries a coldly calculating social climber (Lockwood) and becomes a teacher, but his income and status do not satisfy his wife's expensive demands. After he loses her to a scheming rival, he returns to his roots, mobilizing the miners into a union that strikes for better working conditions—a goal promised but not achieved even after his father and brother are killed in a dreadful accident caused by the venality and negligence of the mine's owners and the corruption of local politicians.

Michael prepared for the part by walking London's streets wearing tattered and soiled workman's clothes, to see if a poor laborer was regarded differently from a well-dressed, solvent wage earner. The unpleasant result of his experiment confirmed his suspicion. His social consciousness—indeed, his increasingly left-wing outlook—was deepened further when the production traveled north on location to Cumberland, where Michael insisted on accompanying workmen a thousand feet into a mine, walking two miles along a dank underground shaft and then crawling one hundred yards along a tunnel only twenty inches high—all of this to experience for himself the grim and painful life of a miner before filming began at Twickenham. He and his young costar, Desmond Tester (as his brother) agreed that they were "conscious of the whole business of exploited work, at the [coal] pits and elsewhere . . . and of those terrible sorts of houses [the miners] had."

In light of this experience, Michael jotted some notes on "the theory of artistic temperament as a disease of actors, whose nature demands that they lose themselves—or rather, find themselves—in other characters. To live happily, it would seem that I must concentrate on the portrayal of romantic, upright, simple men [like Davey Fenwick] who in any case—next to the childishness of Baron Tusenbach or Sir Andrew Aguecheek—is [sic] what I do best." This was a rather naïve (not to say limited) appreciation of his talents: in fact, in the years to come, he rarely played "romantic, upright, simple men." But at the time he seems to have been afraid of more complex roles, at least in the movies, and of characters that "frighteningly altered [his] private life," an observation he left tantalizingly vague and unexamined. Still, Michael rendered Davey Fenwick as appealing, deeply vulnerable and optimistic—a working-class man suddenly thrown into a middle-class life—and he did not dilute the role with any bogus sentiment.

"Movie-making was in his blood," he said of Carol Reed, "and I think he was in a kind of movie dream-world during every waking moment, thinking of stories and of how actors might play them. He had a rare kind of generosity insofar as he was able to give his cast the feeling that everything was really our doing, and that he was just there to make sure we were seen to our best advantage." When the picture was released early in 1940, critics unanimously praised Michael's performance in his first serious and thought-provoking movie role.

The Stars Look Down was completed on September 2, 1939—the day before Britain and France declared war on Germany. The bombing of London was expected at any moment; for a time, theaters were closed because of blackout restrictions; and repertory seasons were cancelled. (Eventually, the Blitz destroyed the Shaftesbury, the Queen's and the Little, while the Old Vic, the Duke of York's and the Sadler's Wells were badly damaged.) The Redgraves moved temporarily to the mill house, but Michael soon returned to London to confer with his agent about work: after all, apart from any psychological or patriotic considerations, he had a family to support. When it became clear that the anticipated German terror campaign against Britain was not to occur immediately, he began to look for a popular play, simple to stage and easy to perform for provincial audiences eager for pleasant diversion.

For ten weeks beginning that October, Michael and Rachel—along with another married acting couple, Roger Livesey and Ursula Jeans—toured in a production of *Springtime for Henry,* Benn Levy's 1931 farce about marital infidelity and the fine art of seduction among the upper classes. With daffy charm, Michael played an amoral roué, and Rachel portrayed his amusing secretary, a nervous woman with a past and an eye on him.

At first their collaboration was uneasy. "I was terribly nervous during rehearsals," Rachel recalled, "because I felt I couldn't convey the comedy. And Michael, who was directing, was awfully anxious for me and continually gave me notes to the point that I was confused and almost sick with anxiety. Only after a visit from the playwright Benn Levy, who said I was doing everything splendidly, was I able to calm down and go on as scheduled."

Levy's wife was the actress Constance Cummings, who had a distinguished career lasting seven decades onstage and in films, both in her native America and in England, where she lived following her marriage. The Levys often collaborated professionally and were involved in humanitarian causes; later, Benn was a Labour Member of Parliament.

Their friendship with the Redgraves began with long dinnertime conversations that greatly influenced Michael's thinking. The Levys were acutely aware of the critical social and political issues of the day and expressed them without hysteria, hyperbole or anything like intimidation tactics. Articulate advocates of the National Council for Civil Liberties and ardent antifascists, they were active later in the Campaign for Nuclear Disarmament and throughout their lifetime worked on behalf of all forms of civil rights. Under their benevolent influence, Michael became (as his son later wrote), "a convinced and very public socialist." Now he began to consider more deeply the issues to which Oliver Baldwin had introduced him years earlier.

Years later, Michael's name turned up on a government list of those who had engaged in unspecified "left-wing cultural activities" and so were suspected by the government of being foreign agents working against Britain. But not a shred of evidence was ever found, and no charges were ever brought against him.

—m—

BY THE END OF 1939, the tour of *Springtime for Henry* had ended. Rachel went home to her two children, while Michael hastened to rejoin his new lover.

Three years younger than Michael, Thomas Arthur Rowett Hynd-man (who preferred to be called Tony) was born in Wales on June 26, 1911. At eighteen, he left his unhappy family life and went to London, where he joined the Coldstream Guards, the primary ceremonial regiment of the British Army. Two years later, he left that service and, aware that his good looks and easy virtue could provide him with a comfortable life, made himself agreeable and sexually available to generous men—among them, the writers T. C. Worsley, John Lehmann and J. R. Ackerley.

"His appearance was attractive: curly red-brown hair, sparkling yellow brown eyes, big smiling teeth," recalled Christopher Isherwood, with whom Tony had traveled briefly. "He was full of fun and the love of argument—left-wing politics, or just argument for its own sake. He used the jargon of an intellectual, but his own kind of intelligence was intuitive and emotional."

Eager to be well connected, Tony managed an introduction to the poet and novelist Stephen Spender in 1933. "He was pleasant-looking, friendly, quickly intelligent in certain ways, and capable of learning," according to Spender. "He read a good deal and had a response to poetry which often astonished me." For two years the pair lived together in Spender's flat, where Tony worked as his assistant. They often traveled together, their affair blazing intensely until 1936, when Spender married the novelist Inez Pearn.

Tony then became an ardent Communist, joined the International Brigade and fought on the Republican side during the Spanish Civil War. "His relaxed, pleasure-loving nature seemed ill suited to Communist puritanism," Spender recalled. So it was. Disillusioned, Tony soon abandoned politics and the Spanish Civil War, deserted his unit, was captured and spent time in prison. Spender then traveled to Barcelona on a rescue mission and obtained his release on the basis of poor health. Back in London, Tony began drinking excessively and became proprietary toward anyone who showed romantic interest in him. He also became a skilled petty thief.

This was the troublesome but charming, improvident but witty, dazzlingly attractive, sexually audacious and compliant man whom

Michael Redgrave met late in 1939 through Stephen Spender, and to whom he at once felt passionately drawn. Tony responded fully to Michael's advances, and they often met in grand hotel suites (at the Savoy, for example) or in a seedy furnished room (booked anonymously and at the last moment), for a few hours.

Tony was no merely passive favorite: he knew how to court, and he sent Michael poetry excerpts by, for example, W. H. Auden: ". . . the word is love / Surely one fearless kiss would cure / The million fevers." Michael ("by now fathoms deep in love," as Corin said years later) may well have thought of a line applicable to himself, from *Love's Labour's Lost:* "And I, forsooth, in love!—I, that have been love's whip." The intrigue endured from the last quarter of 1939 through much of the following year, Michael effectively replacing Stephen Spender.

By the spring of 1940, Tony was working as a model at an art school directed by Cedric Morris. "The knowledge that I shall certainly see T[ony] again this week makes all the difference, of course," Michael wrote in his diary on April 29. "When he went away, I was lost and wild and couldn't bring myself to come home in good time." They took long walks in the countryside, Michael writing in his diary a few days later that he was "blissfully happy and cannot and shall not try to describe the happiness beyond noting that at one moment I said to myself: tomorrow you will be in London, but if you are wise, you can still be happy and think of this walk, and not [be] sad and greedy."

Returning home, he was frank with Rachel. "She asked me about Stephen S[pender], his wife . . . etc. I always reply to her questions as fully as I can. She understands so much, but there is so much for her to understand."

Rachel did her best to comprehend Michael's wanderings, which she accepted with almost incomprehensible tolerance. She never threatened him with divorce; she became resigned when he found affection and sexual satisfaction elsewhere; she welcomed him home when he returned—indeed, she became the prototype of a submissive and complaisant wife. Her behavior in the face of what many other married women might have found intolerable may be explained partly by the fact that it was she who had insisted that they marry despite the "difficulties in his nature," and she who had been determined to "change him." In addition, as she admitted to herself and others, she lacked fundamental self-confidence and had no strong sense that her own assessment of people, and of her husband, was fair or valid.

But there were other reasons for her forbearance. For one thing, Rachel genuinely loved, admired and respected Michael, and not every day or season of her life with him was painful or frustrating. They had a good and comfortable existence; they socialized with the most celebrated theater people; their names carried a certain cachet that she would have lost had she pursued a life on her own—indeed, where and to whom would she have gone? The Redgraves had a favorable public image as a theatrical couple; they were a growing family; and at that time, divorce was not the commonplace it later became. In addition, Rachel derived her greatest satisfaction from her children, whom she attended with unfailing devotion and whose love she earned in return.

Three-year-old Vanessa knew how to amuse herself when the nanny was busy and her parents were otherwise engaged: she played with dolls in the garden, sang and danced around a tree and bounced a ball. There was perhaps something a little forlorn about these solitary scenes, and she often tapped at the dining room window and asked to come in and rejoin the elders. "She wanted to go to the nursery," Michael noted one day, "and cried a little at being told to stay in the garden. Any attempt to compromise brings on a real temperamental fit of tears."

But the child was also touching and resourceful: "Vanessa called on me in bed this morning," Michael wrote in his diary on March 19, "and she sang long verses of a hymn she had learned." Next day, a few friends arrived with good wishes for his birthday, "and Vanessa leads the conversation and dresses up as someone she calls Queen Pretoria." For his part, Corin was (thus Michael) "always cheerful—it is pleasant to watch him living a life of pure sensation: the noise of the birds, the leaves of the pear tree, the colour of the sky, the friendly, loving sounds we make at him . . ."

SOMETIMES MICHAEL AND Rachel argued violently, and once, he picked up a vase and hurled it. "I jumped up and down, shouting at him, 'Missed! Missed!'" recalled Rachel. "I flung another one back, also missing him. These rows ended in laughter or tears or both. I was apt to give way too easily and leave the problem unresolved. I even had the feeling that our homes were really his, not mine. I felt embarrassed to have my parents stay, whereas his mother could come whenever she wanted to." After five years together, the Redgraves had two children and he was an internationally famous actor. But Michael had deeply compromised the marriage.

"For two nights I have not been home," Michael wrote in his diary on May 4, "and though I imagined that R[achel] knew where I was and accepted it, it appears that I have caused her two days of agony. I felt in despair with myself at my cruelty. Tried to explain the feeling of guilt I have towards her. Always it returns to this question of the split personality, and I cannot feel that it would be right, even if I had the will-power, which I have not, to cut off or starve the one side of my nature . . . I feel as I felt last night and have obscurely [felt] before: that [in the words of *The Family Reunion*] I am the conscience of my unhappy family—its bird, sent flying through the purgatorial flame."

"This was a difficult time in our marriage," Rachel recalled years later. "Michael was busy with work and other people, and I was spending my time with the children. He made many new friends, and I rather dropped out of his social life. I was still a young woman in love, with my heart on my sleeve. I think he and some of his friends thought I was possessive about him. Maybe I was, but it was a lonely period for me." Michael had companionship elsewhere, but it came with a high burden of fearful anxiety and considerable guilt.

—⁓—

BEGINNING IN SEPTEMBER 1939 and continuing for almost thirty years, the number of recorded offenses for homosexual activity increased fiftyfold. In wartime, there was a certain amount of quiet tolerance for private, casual sexual contact between men, but no one dared admit that he was homosexual or engaged in same-sex activity. As the conflict progressed, however, hundreds of men were court-martialed for what was called "indecency between males"; in fact, more British men were brought to military tribunals for homosexual acts than for treason.

But in civilian life, gay and bisexual men found even less quiet tolerance. The theater had more than its complement of notable homosexuals, but everyone was mighty tight-lipped. In government, the situation was similar. Sir Paul Latham, a wealthy Conservative Member of Parliament who served in the Royal Artillery during the war, was tried and convicted of sexual congress with three men over a period of time. Dishonorably discharged, he went to prison and was forced to quit his seat in Parliament.

Pubs and cafés known to welcome gay men were closed or forced to deny such men entrance for fear of police action. Life became even more difficult for gay civilians when Theobald Mathew was appointed director of public prosecution: the primary goal of his administration was the suppression of homosexuality, which was of course an impossible agenda, as any sensible person knew. Nevertheless, entrapment became common, and men were frequently arrested after having sex with policemen who agreed to cooperate in the sting.

In this atmosphere of hysteria and hypocrisy, men like Michael Redgrave lived in constant terror of exposure. Their intimate lives had to be conducted with the utmost discretion lest their careers and families be summarily destroyed, and their celebrity was no guarantee of immunity. It was a mark of Michael's loyal friendship, therefore, that he frequently visited Max Adrian during Max's three-month imprisonment for attempting to solicit sex at Victoria Station. He openly condemned Max's jail term and tried, without success, to have a judge reduce the sentence. As Frith Banbury recalled, "Redgrave was wonderful in this crisis, visiting [Max] in prison and helping him financially on his release. For a man who was himself vulnerable to similar suspicions, his actions must be seen as courageous."

—◦◦—

THE EXPENSES OF his love affair with Tony and the support of his family required Michael to work constantly in 1940. First, he appeared in an unusual, taut and effective movie thriller, *A Window in London,* the story of a man traveling by train who may or may not have witnessed a murder. The resolution of the mystery, involving a magician and his assistant, alternates illusion with reality and ordinary London settings with expressionistic music hall episodes.

From this job Michael went directly into rehearsals and voice training to play the dashing highwayman Macheath in a new Glyndebourne Festival production of the eighteenth-century play *The Beggar's Opera,* which included popular songs from the same era. John Gielgud, the show's director at the Haymarket, heard Michael vocalize and said he was perfect for the role, but Rudolf Bing, the festival's general manager, had to be convinced. He engaged the renowned singing coach Jani Strasser to work long hours rehearsing with Michael.

The Beggar's Opera is an aggressively satirical work, ridiculing not only social and moral degradation but political ineptitude as well, and from start to finish, a powerful and sustained musical-dramatic style is required of the actor playing Macheath. Some critics praised Michael's energy, but most felt that although he looked both debonair and dangerous and sang more than adequately, he did not wholly inhabit the role—something was missing. He admitted that he was "not properly prepared," as he wrote in his diary. "I never laid the foundations of the character. I was lucky to pull it off as well as I did, but there was much bad work." The show closed on May 25, after ninety-six performances.

By that time, he was rehearsing his next role, that of a cynical British war correspondent who has withdrawn from the busy world to a lighthouse on a tiny island in Lake Michigan. Michael had been deeply moved when he read Robert Ardrey's anti-isolationist play *Thunder Rock,* which had failed the previous year after three weeks on Broadway. He believed that the play would appeal to London audiences in the dark days of the Battle of Britain, and he understood the potential emotional power of the drama's fantasy element, in which ghosts of the past visit the virtual hermit and force him to resume his sense of commitment. The play opened in a small theater on June 18 and was so successful that it transferred to the West End, where it ran all summer long; the leading part, ran a typical review, was "better played by Michael Redgrave than it was by Luther Adler in the U.S."

In fact, the character was very like Michael—"probably the closest character to the father I knew," said Corin years later. "It's an enormously veiled performance—very dark, very brooding, very hollow-cheeked, rather remote and inaccessible. That was the father that for long periods of time I knew." Michael Redgrave's children often felt that their father was "cold" or "remote" or "inaccessible" or "distant" from them; he frequently gave that impression to others, too. Much of this had to do with the fact that he had no experience of parental warmth during childhood—no memory of his father; and of his mother, as he said, he had no recollection of demonstrative affection. Michael had, therefore, very little on which to draw for his dealings with his children; indeed, he knew only what he saw in Rachel's conduct with them.

For the next five years, until June 1945, Michael was seen in eight more plays—none of them from the classical repertory—and five films, one of which was a movie of *Thunder Rock*. But for all his quiet intensity and the picture's earnest idealism and haunting special effects, the final cut lacked both focus and tension.

—m—

THE TONY HYNDMAN affair continued, but the earlier, intense level of romantic fantasy was beginning to fade. "Yesterday T. came to lunch," Michael wrote in his diary early that summer. "He is a lonely, muddled creature [who] cannot bring himself to work." On her side, Rachel found Tony "an undesirable friend who was always asking for loans of money [that] were never repaid."

Heavy air raids began during the late summer and early autumn, and Michael had to find safe haven for his family, while Tony fled to friends in the countryside. Vanessa, though not yet four years old, experienced the bombings of the Battle of Britain firsthand and could never shake the recollection of that summer of 1940. "The earliest memory I can recall in sharp focus, with sounds and smells, is of an early summer morning in August 1940." Eating a bowl of cereal alone in the garden at Clifton Hill, she suddenly noticed "a vast wailing" in the sky—and then her nanny called out to her from a top-floor window, "Vanessa! Come indoors. Come indoors at once!" It was the first air-raid warning the child had heard.

Rachel herded the children and servants down to the basement, which had been shored up with beams. "We put down old mattresses on the floor while the bombings continued," she recalled. "While the bombs fell," Vanessa added, "our parents sang songs and played games with us—anything to keep our spirits up, at any hour of the night." But as the strafing of London intensified, Michael insisted that Rachel and the children leave in late August and take refuge at the country home of Rachel's aunt Lucy Kempson—a wealthy widow who had been among the first women to study at London University. Lucy offered protection at her home in Bromyard, Herefordshire. Michael, working in London, put his family on the train at Paddington and moved into rooms at the Athenaeum Court apartments in Piccadilly (later redesigned as the Athenaeum Hotel).

One hundred miles from London and thirty-three from Birmingham, Bromyard was at first far safer and quieter than 102 Clifton Hill. But Coventry was sixty miles distant, and it was almost entirely destroyed by German attacks on the night of November 14, 1940, when 515 German bombers leveled homes, businesses, factories and the nine-hundred-year-old cathedral. Thousands of civilians were killed and countless more injured. "I saw a fierce red glow on the southeast horizon," Vanessa remembered. "I had never felt fear of the war until that night. For years afterward I had nightmares."

Lucy and her staff of five provided the daily afternoon ritual of hot tea and freshly baked scones, along with whatever distractions they could devise for the children—reading to them, teaching them card games and tricks and gathering them around the wireless for the nightly weather forecasts and news headlines. "She was mother and godmother to us all," according to Rachel. "She had a big shelf full of her old childhood books, which Vanessa gradually got to know." But with the onset of late autumn and early winter, the comforts gradually diminished. From late afternoon to morning, there was virtually no heat, the electricity was weak, and the taps provided only cold water.

As it did for countless families, the war came closer to home than the destruction in a neighboring town. Rachel's brothers, Nicholas and Robin, arrived on leave from navy service, and the sight of Robin was a terrible blow. Serving on a torpedo boat that had been badly hit, Robin was haggard, all but mute and in the throes of a dangerous nervous breakdown. After a long recuperation, he finally returned to duty, but he was later killed in action in the South China Sea at the age of twenty-five.

On hearing the news of Robin's death, Rachel at once went to her parents in Dartmouth. "Looking back, I realize what a maternal love I had for Robin," she said. "It had always fallen to me to look after him if he was unwell. Robin resembled mother, [with his] curly red-gold hair and brilliant blue eyes, the difference being his thick eyelashes and his rosy complexion. His death was a tragedy for us all."

At year's end, Rachel returned to London, joining Michael in the cast of a movie called *Jeannie,* in which he played the inventor of a new type of washing machine—and again revealed a light but sure hand at comedy; Rachel assumed the small supporting role of the title character's sister. "Captivating and enchanting, with the gleam of real gold," wrote the *New York Times* critic when the picture was finally exported three years later. That same season, Michael was considered for a role in an Alexander Korda film, but Korda told him, "No actor is worth all the money your agent is asking"—to which Michael at once replied with a smile, "And no film is intrinsically worth its cost."

Michael then worked a third time under Carol Reed's direction, in a film of H. G. Wells's 1905 novel, *Kipps,* the story of a poor draper's apprentice who finds sudden wealth and is pitchforked into the life of a gentleman. The movie benevolently satirized rigid class distinctions, a social angle frequently seen in wartime British movies, as men in uniform came from all levels of society. Before production began, Michael successfully arranged for his friend Max Adrian to be cast in *Kipps,* as he had for him to be included in *Jeannie*—gestures of kindness Max especially appreciated because his recent imprisonment had made it difficult for him to find work at movie studios.

Much of the filming at Shepherds Bush occurred during the heaviest nightly attacks over London. "In the evenings we left the studio ten minutes before blackout, and as we drove home in the dusk the sirens would start. [Reed and Redgrave were both in residence at the Athenaeum Court.] And to face the cameras each morning [in the role of] a younger man, I was obliged to take heavy sleeping pills each night in order to sleep through the noise of the bombardment." After *Kipps,* Michael worked on a picture called *Atlantic Ferry,* which reached American shores as *Sons of the Sea.* This was not, as some moviegoers presumed, a Laurel and Hardy two-reeler: it was based on the historic account of the competition to control maritime cargo service between Britain and the United States. It was also an undisguised plea for America to join England in the war effort.

—m—

IRONICALLY, MICHAEL'S LOYALTY to his country was briefly but loudly questioned in early 1941—a matter eventually settled only by the direct influence of the highest officeholder in the land, and by Michael's entry into wartime service. "My father was a very idealistic man," Vanessa said many years later. "But he withdrew from the front lines of political action after a bitter experience."

The issue was in fact not complicated. Since the days of his friendship with Oliver Baldwin, Michael had allied himself with principles that were fundamentally socialist and based on humanitarian ideals—ideals that had been reinforced by association with Benn Levy and Constance Cummings. "I am a red-hot socialist," he told a reporter from the *Liverpool Echo* during his first year at the Old Vic. "I believe in everything to do with socialism." Such assertions were common in 1937, when the Spanish Civil War was raging and the Communist Party seemed to some, for a while, to be the great hope for the workers of the world. "He embraced socialism wholeheartedly, trustingly," according to Corin.

Which explains what went wrong in 1941.

Sitting in the shade of a pear tree in the garden at Clifton Hill, Michael found among the day's mail a manifesto calling for people to sign up in support of a People's Convention to work for a People's Peace. Michael was not a pacifist: at thirty-three, he wanted and expected to be called up for service and had expressed his eagerness to join the navy. But the notion of a peace movement seemed right and proper, and he signed the vaguely stated declaration of principles. Thus began a season of embarrassing and troublesome negative publicity.

Members of the British Communist Party were attempting to gather people from the arts and the political left wing to join them in an obscure program that campaigned for a higher standard of living and more secure bomb shelters. So far, so good. But the People's Convention did not expressly oppose Hitler's Germany. The real enemy, the Communists insisted, was Prime Minister Winston Churchill and his coalition wartime cabinet, because they were "as bad as Nazi Germany." On orders from Moscow, the British Communist Party collaborated toward the achievement of a Stalin-Hitler alliance. This was the agenda that went forth under the guise of the rather more innocent socialist program for improved working conditions and broader public safety. It was deception, neither pure nor simple, but clergymen, trade unionists and celebrities signed on—Michael among the most famous of them.

Nazis at home and abroad were predictably delighted, for the People's Convention, which had seemed so idealistic, was poised to aid the Führer in his most extreme goals. Completely ignorant of the Convention's unstated agenda, Redgrave was vilified in the press for having signed what he saw as a peace manifesto. On March 4 the BBC forbade him and a dozen other actors to be heard over the airwaves. "BBC Gives Stars an Ultimatum," blared the newspaper headlines above Michael's photo. "Quit People's Convention, or You Don't Broadcast." A BBC official added that this ultimatum was consistent with the banning of Sir Hugh Roberton from conducting a radio music program "because of his pacifist views" which were seen as "opposed to the national war effort."

The ban was lifted on direct orders from Prime Minister Winston Churchill, who stated that such a censure was beyond the BBC's authority. Soon it was acknowledged that the notion of Michael Redgrave as either a Communist or a fascist, or as supporting either Stalin or Hitler, was utterly without basis. To underscore his position as a loyal Englishman with no foreign allegiance, Michael at once resigned from the People's Convention and asked that his name be removed from its program. "The careers of those of us who signed the People's Convention were, so far as I know, unaffected by all the fuss and consternation," he said forty years later.

His direct involvement on behalf of any political issue or cause ended forever in 1941. "My political development stopped with the People's Convention. The fear that I had been used by people and by a party I did not wholly trust, for a cause I did not fully understand, made me cautious, and in time my caution turned to conservatism, though with a small 'c.'"

But Michael's children were to pick up his cues. "The reasons for his silence and his fears," according to Vanessa, "were of central importance in shaping his life—and mine. But Michael never spoke on a public platform for socialism again."

—\m—

IN JUNE 1941, Michael was at last summoned to military service. As his father-in-law was headmaster at the Royal Naval College and his brothers-in-law were in the navy, he expressed his preference to serve in that branch and was assigned to training in Plymouth in July. Just when his papers arrived, Michael heard from a former school friend in Wales who had contracted tuberculosis and was morbidly ill. Hurrying to visit the patient, Michael stopped overnight to change trains in Manchester. There he saw the premiere of Noël Coward's new comedy *Blithe Spirit* before its London opening.

Michael and Noël had met socially several times during the 1930s, and the Redgraves regularly attended performances of Coward's plays, which eventually numbered more than fifty. The preeminent man of the British stage during the 1920s and '30s, Coward was now, at forty-one, an accomplished playwright, director, composer, actor, lyricist, poet and author of memoirs, stories and a novel.

Celebrated for his wit and high style, Coward was known by many in the theater circles as discreetly homosexual, which was of course neither publicly acknowledged nor openly discussed. ("There are still a few old ladies in Worthing who don't know," he said wryly in the more liberal 1960s.) He did, however, have several long-term partners—among them, the stockbroker and producer John C. Wilson; playwright Keith Winter; actors Louis Hayward, Alan Webb and Graham Payn; and Prince George, the Duke of Kent and a brother of King George VI—a royal intimacy that placed Noël right in the social precincts of Buckingham Palace.

A small platoon of transient partners also made appearances in Coward's life. For all that, he was both friend and confidant to many in high places, most notably Queen Elizabeth, consort of George VI and hence Prince George's sister-in-law; Coward's friendship with Elizabeth endured throughout her fifteen-year tenure as queen of England, and then during her long term as Queen Mother.

So it happened in Manchester, just before Michael departed for naval service, that he and Noël Coward began an intense romance that lasted several years and eventually became an abiding friendship. Both men were of the theater to the core of their being; both were highly intelligent, cultivated and sophisticated; and both were devout sensualists. "Noël's nickname for Michael was 'Dear China,'" recalled Rachel, who caught the allusion to sex from Wycherley's *The Country Wife*: "I'll have some china, too, Mr. Horner," cries Lady Fidget. "Don't think to give other people china, and me none."

But Rachel was denied any such comfort when the time came for her husband to leave for the Royal Navy. "I had of course wanted to spend the last night with Michael before he went down to Plymouth to join up. But he spent that night with Noël instead."

The pattern was becoming clearer each season, with Tony, Noël and others. A part of Michael wanted to be married and a father, and another part of him did not want either of these roles. On the one hand, he needed the social and public image Rachel and the children provided, and in his own way he loved them and was proud of them.

But if the occasional backstage whispers about his other life were to have become shouts, the consequences would have been disastrous both professionally and personally, for him and the family. His wife and children were inevitably impingements on the freedom to live that other life—and so he began to resent the very people he needed and loved, precisely because they represented a nagging responsibility.

As Michael's younger daughter, Lynn, said of her parents many years later, "They had a long marriage, but they had a difficult marriage. The difficulty"—which had been Michael's term for the conflict in his divided sexual orientation—"finally took over, and it shut my mother out."

Six

A GARDEN OF EARTHLY
DELIGHTS

(1941-1946)

ROM JULY 1941 TO NOVEMBER 1942, MICHAEL SCUDAMORE RED-
grave served in the Royal Navy, where his superiors invariably
rated him as "very good" in character and "superior" in efficiency.
His duties as an ordinary seaman mostly involved helping and often
supervising the crews maintaining the interior and exterior condition
of ships. He was also asked to direct musical entertainments. Far from
wartime action, Michael spent most of his service at ease in America,
where the English vessels on which he worked were repaired and renovated.* These assignments were facilitated by none other than Lord
Louis Mountbatten, captain of the *Illustrious* (on which Michael served
for three months), who happened to be a close friend of Noël Coward.

Because his name and photograph were often in the press, Michael
was welcomed in grand style by Broadway and Hollywood stars when
he landed in Manhattan. Among those who hosted parties in his honor
were Ruth Gordon (the eponymous country wife at the Old Vic), Paul
Lukas (from *The Lady Vanishes* and *A Window in London*), Helen
Hayes, Ronald Colman, Tyrone Power, Lillian Gish, and Thornton
Wilder.

---

* Redgrave was on the *Raleigh* from July 2 to September 8, 1941; on the *Drake* from September
9 to October 15; on the *Illustrious* from October 16 to January 20, 1942; and again on the *Drake*
from January 21 to March 3.

"I'd always heard that in England you have to fight to get publicity, and in America fight harder to avoid it," Michael wrote to Rachel, "and I guess it's true. The fans! It started the first evening!" *The Lady Vanishes* and *The Stars Look Down* were being screened to capacity crowds, and when his guest appearances on live radio shows were announced in the press, "there were the faithful, massed across the street [from the studio]." His signature was prized by celebrity seekers whenever he was recognized—and Michael traveled with an autograph book of his own, first used that season when he asked Ethel Barrymore to sign her name after a performance in *The Corn Is Green*. "I thought she was marvelous," he recalled, "and I was stage-struck."

During at least one of his furloughs, he was reunited with Noël Coward, who was in New York for the American premiere of *Blithe Spirit*. After registering in two separate suites at the same hotel, they slept in only one, spending (as Michael later wrote to Noël) "a wild and wonderful dream of a weekend."

Only Noël and Rachel knew that Michael's term of service was likely to be curtailed for a legitimate medical reason. "I am waiting for the doctor to discharge me for my crooked arm," he wrote to Coward, "which hasn't been right since ammunitioning ship in October. I trek off to hospital each morning. The new X-rays have been sent to some specialist for his opinion." Meanwhile, in March 1942 he was given a long leave at home and was transferred to the Naval Reserve, while doctors hoped that time would heal the worsening pain and limpness and enable him to return to duty. Eight months later he was honorably discharged from the navy. "You will be more use making films for the public than giving ship's concerts for the Navy," said the surgeon admiral, surveying the final X-rays.

—⁂—

THAT SPRING, MICHAEL hastened to Bromyard, where his wife and children still resided with Lucy Kempson. Rachel urged Vanessa and Corin to perform one of the little skits devised in Michael's absence by his daughter and a playmate. "We acted in little plays," Vanessa recalled, "charged people a half-penny and sent the money to merchant seamen."

In midyear, Michael and Rachel attempted to put their marital troubles behind them, and soon she was pregnant again, but the harmony was fragile and impermanent. "I really didn't know my father at all during my childhood," Vanessa said later. "Mother was there, and she was with us, teaching, singing, looking after us with the nannies." Corin agreed: "He observed his children fondly, but from a distance, untroubled by any particular responsibility for their nurture. What with the war, his service in the Navy, and after the Navy his work in theatre and films, I have very few memories of my father at this early stage of my childhood."

Very soon, Michael was back onstage for the first time in two years. Because of his recent naval activities, his agents and the authors of a play called *Lifeline* invited him to rewrite and direct this unlikely stage drama about the trek of an oil tanker across the Atlantic during the war. "It closed within a fortnight," he wrote (incorrectly) years later; *Lifeline* was not compelling theater, but it was highly patriotic fare, and after its premiere on July 2, the play ran for more than two months and was still listed on the Official Theatre Guide of London for the week of September 7 to 12, after logging eighty-five performances. Michael's much-publicized status as a Reserve seaman and the release of an episodic propaganda movie called *The Big Blockade* (in which he had a small role) worked together with the good reviews for *Lifeline,* and so he rediscovered his celebrity status.

But he was no hero to his family, for whom he once again became something of a phantom. For three months he lived alone in a London hotel because, as he said, "Rachel was on tour," which she was not. She had accompanied him back to London and after learning of her pregnancy, quietly returned to Bromyard. Alone in London, Michael sallied forth and met a new companion at a place like The White Room, a bar and café that did not cater exclusively to gay men and women (no place could), but where it was possible to find lonely servicemen and "the seedier West End chorus boys," as Noël Coward recalled. "I have no doubt that a good deal of the wanderer in Roy rubbed off on his son," said Corin.

"It wasn't a very good time to be pregnant," Rachel said, recalling her husband's absences as well as the hardships of the time. "Food rationing was still mandated, and pregnant women were not yet given extra provisions. I was really very concerned about the health of the unborn baby, and I relied a great deal on the help of Cousin Lucy." Eventually, Rachel raised with her husband the notion of a formal marital separation after the birth of their third child. "But she never persisted," continued Corin, "because the mere mention of it brought such a storm of grief [from my father] that she had to spend the rest of the week comforting him."

—⁂—

ANOTHER TWO-MONTH RUN followed that autumn of 1942, with Michael (again) directing and starring in *The Duke in Darkness,* a controversial drama by Patrick Hamilton. This elaborate costume play set in sixteenth-century France is a complex moral fable in which the release from capture of a long-imprisoned duke is compromised by the incipient madness of his loyal servant (portrayed by Michael), who has to be sacrificed so that his master may be freed. At the conclusion, the servant's dead body is thrown from a parapet—a stage action Michael had to explain for his daughter's peace of mind. Considering that it was time for five-year-old Vanessa to see her father at work, he wisely prepared her for the final scene by taking her backstage before the performance and pointing to the pile of mattresses breaking his fall.

There were some critical doubts about the play's apparent parallels to the situation of war-torn Europe, but none about the leading performer: "Redgrave gave the finest performance of his career as the crazed servant," ran a typical notice. Apart from his eccentric character in *Thunder Rock,* this was the first time Michael undertook the role of a neurotic slipping into total psychosis—a type of character to which he frequently returned, and in which he always found the telling combination of terror and pathos.

—⁓—

MICHAEL WAS HAUNTED by the character of Rakitin, the honorable, unhappy suitor frustrated by desire in *A Month in the Country,* and during his career he was involved three times in various productions. The first opened after *The Duke in Darkness,* in February 1943, when he began almost a year's run of Turgenev's play at the St. James's and on tour. He felt particular affinity for Rakitin (as he did for the play, which he later directed twice). As Michael understood, the playwright "had orchestrated an entrancing cotillion of love, no less endearing because it is desperate." Rakitin was also a spiritual kin to himself: a man of muted passion driven by a need for a forbidden love he suspects will forever elude him.

The press and audiences from London to Liverpool responded enthusiastically to the play and the actor: "His performance is exemplary," wrote the critic T. C. Worsley. "His Rakitin stands at just that distance from himself that the ironist commonly keeps, and when he moves into passion, it is with an admirably restrained intensity." Passion with restraint—hence all the more effective and recognizable as a human passion—was becoming one of the primary colors on Michael Redgrave's theatrical palette, and one he used ever more frequently in the decades to come, to shade or brighten a complex character.

—⁓—

WHILE PLAYING RAKITIN no fewer than 313 times during 1943, Michael was occupied with several other activities.

First, the imminent birth of their third child led the Redgraves to seek larger quarters. After Clifton Hill and the windmill cottage were sold, they found a bright, spacious flat near Putney Bridge in Rivermead Court, commanding a wide view over the Thames. The relocation chores were completed none too soon, for on March 8, Rachel was taken to the London Clinic, where she gave birth to a daughter they named Lynn Rachel. The first name was bestowed in honor of the English actress Lynn Fontanne. At the height of the Blitz, she and her American husband Alfred Lunt, by then well established as Broadway stars, had offered to bring Vanessa and Corin to the United States for safekeeping. But secure travel arrangements had been impossible, and Michael and Rachel were not keen on a family separation. "It's a very good thing your parents turned us down," Fontanne told Lynn Redgrave years later, "because Alfred and I know absolutely nothing about children."

In times to come, Lynn Redgrave frequently mentioned a shocking discovery she made at the age of forty. Reading her father's journals, she came upon a startling omission: "Here . . . 1943 . . . that's the year of my birth! Apprehensively, I turn to my day, March 8. But no birth. No Lynn. I feel overwhelmed and sad." But if she indeed turned the pages of her father's diary on that gloomy day in 1983, she must have done so quickly or read carelessly, for her father clearly noted her entrance into the world on the page dedicated to March 8: "Our second daughter was born about 8.15. Lynn very podgy, R[achel] well."

Michael incurred considerable expenses as his family grew along with his celebrity, and so he accepted several theater jobs during the busy months of 1943. While fulfilling his commitment to all performances of the Turgenev play, he directed and starred in six afternoon performances of *Parisienne* at the St. James's that June. First performed in Paris in 1885, Henri Becque's comedy had been considered scandalous because of its casual treatment of a woman balancing several lovers who mean no more to her than her dull husband. "He was amusingly over-intense," Frith Banbury said of Michael, who then rushed into rehearsals as the director of *Blow Your Own Trumpet,* by twenty-two-year-old Peter Ustinov.

Set in a seedy Italian restaurant during wartime, the Ustinov play survived for only thirteen performances; audiences and critics were bewildered by its tone and unsure of its intent, as comic dialogues alternated uneasily with philosophical diatribes. "With all its faults, it had ambition," insisted Michael, who wrote an impassioned (and imprudent) essay for the *New Statesman,* attacking critics who cried out for new talent and fresh dramatic styles and then denounced every young playwright who had a unique voice. His article ("An Actor to the Critics") evoked a stormy reaction that lasted longer than the hapless play, as Michael was pilloried for his arrogant hypersensitivity and for daring "to defy the superstition that the actor must never answer back." The problem with the piece was not Michael's plea for better critical standards but his haughty and professorial tone.

Duplicating the fate of *Blow Your Own Trumpet,* Michael's next directorial venture also ran for thirteen performances, that September. Maxwell Anderson's verse drama *The Wingless Victory* had been moderately successful during the 1936/37 Broadway season, thanks to the drawing power of Katharine Cornell. But in London its fatal flaws were at once evident, for the play (concerning racial intolerance and religious bigotry in nineteenth-century Massachusetts) offered no equivalent actress to compensate for its prolix text and, as Michael later admitted, its "thin high-mindedness."

Perhaps because he relished the chance to attempt some sort of salvific theatrical alchemy, Michael could not correct the bankruptcy of Anderson's dramatic sensibility until it was too late and the play was well into a pre-London tryout. (Katharine Cornell, who had received good notices in New York, was more than merely clever when she observed that an actress of her stature "cannot afford to appear in a good play.") The London critics disliked this arid verse drama: "Mr. Redgrave's production, so portentously slow, emphasizes the pretentiousness of the writing," according to a typical notice.

Rachel had a minor role in *The Wingless Victory*—and then returned happily to Vanessa, Corin and Lynn, whose full-time care she had, with misgivings, entrusted to a pair of nannies. "She didn't play down her career," as Frith Banbury put it; "it was to a certain extent played down for her. She had three children to bring up." Rachel hoped for a quiet life with her husband and children during late 1943 and the winter of 1944, and this she had rather more than she anticipated. Apart from Christmas and Boxing Day, the family's time at Rivermead Court passed without Michael, who was pursuing a new lover.

—⚭—

ONE EVENING IN January 1944, at The White Room in Denman Street, Michael met an American serviceman billeted to London as a member of a multilanguage communications team. His name was Norris Houghton, and he was thirty-three, with flawless, Byronic features and bright gray eyes. Born in Indianapolis in 1910, he had decided as a schoolboy to be a man of the theater in the broadest sense of the word. At Princeton he met and worked on amateur theatricals with the young James Stewart and Joshua Logan and, with the University Players on Cape Cod, with Henry Fonda and Margaret Sullavan.

In 1934 Houghton won a Guggenheim Fellowship and traveled to Russia, where he became fluent in the language and was championed by Stanislavski and Meyerhold. Houghton subsequently published *Moscow Rehearsals,* an account of production methods he observed during the last great years of the Russian theater. Returning to New York in 1937, he designed sets for several Broadway shows until he enlisted in the war effort, where his expertise in Russian was put to good use. During his military service, Houghton was separated for long periods from his lifetime partner, the stage manager Robert Woods—"a relationship I cherished for almost forty-five years," he said, until the death of Woods in 1978.

Houghton did not at once recognize the famous Michael Redgrave at The White Room, but he was impressed by the "tall, broad-shouldered, powerfully built man who conveyed the image of the medieval warrior . . . but with a vulnerability and nervous instability . . . and a combination of power and weakness." He found this fellow "fascinating" and never forgot their first conversation. Houghton introduced himself to Redgrave, who at once exclaimed, "You're the author of *Moscow Rehearsals*! It's a marvelous book—one of the best!"

"Who are you?" Houghton asked.

"My name is Michael Redgrave."

"I can't believe it! Why, you're a great star—I know all about you!"

What he may not have known Norris Houghton quickly learned, for almost at once, as he said, "we were together as often as our schedules permitted." By the end of January, Tony Hyndman and Noël Coward were almost (but not quite) of the romantic past, whereas Norris Houghton was entirely of the present. "Michael introduced me to half the theatre folk of London," Norris recalled, "and to Rachel, who welcomed me cordially. Their close friends became mine. He took me to galleries and museums, showed me his favorite paintings and sketches; took me to grand restaurants, where he was ushered to the best tables, and to little holes-in-the wall, where he described their specialties. As spring blossomed, he showed me out-of-the-way little squares and favorite mews and small hidden public gardens."

Norris had benefited from a superb education, and he found Michael "more than literate—he was erudite. Deeply versed in history and literature and in theatre lore, he was also a linguist. He talked easily and wittily, [and] I never wearied of listening to him." Michael was flattered by the admiration of this extraordinarily attractive, bright, energetic and gifted young man who aspired to produce and direct (which he eventually did, and with historic success); it was also stimulating for Michael to hear firsthand about the Russian theater and about Houghton's friendships with the great directors.

The new relationship preoccupied Michael in the early weeks of 1944, but this time his distance from the family pitched Rachel into a dangerous state of clinical depression. On the advice of a friend, she began sessions with a popular psychiatrist named Charlotte Wolff, a politically outspoken lesbian who had fled Nazi Germany and, after settling in England, become an authority on two marginal subjects: Wolff published several books on psychological diagnosis by a careful study of the human hand, and on the history of lesbianism. Eventually, Michael also paid a few visits to Wolff's office.

But there was one serious problem. Dr. Wolff thought it was a good idea to tell Rachel what Michael had said in therapy sessions, and to relay to Michael what Rachel had confided—a procedure that of course directly breached every principle of professional ethics. On May 23, for example, Michael recorded in his diary that Wolff told him, "Rachel's longing for certainties is a natural result of her fear, and her refuge in commonplace ideas will pass, along with her need of feeling that I am not watching her critically. But my conflict is independent of Rachel."

The Redgraves chose to ignore Charlotte Wolff's extraordinary malpractice in this regard—which, had it been disclosed to the

British Psychological Society, would have been sufficient to warrant censure. Perhaps Rachel and Michael accepted that each psychiatrist had unique methods—at least that was Charlotte Wolff's stated creed.

—ɯ—

MICHAEL'S JOURNAL FOR 1944 was one of the most detailed he kept. On February 7, he wrote: "R[achel] comes in and sits on bed and I cannot go on without telling her about N[orris]. R says, 'It's silly, but I feel quite happy about it.'" She then told her husband about a dream in which they and Norris "are all living together, as if I had two husbands." In dreams and fantasies, at least, things were becoming more and more curious.

"I mean to wear you, Norris, in my heart's core," Michael wrote in a letter on March 7. "I am so grateful for this wonderful luck which has brought us together." When Norris had to leave London for a month-long military assignment abroad, Michael wrote in his diary, "I gave him my gold naval cufflinks. He gave me some books [and] chocolate, and loaned me a desk pen, calendar and what-not. There is no one [who has] stimulated me more than N." But in the absence of Norris, Michael turned to Tony Hyndman on several occasions, as he recorded in April and May.

This erotic intensity and confusion of realms affected Michael's mood, for he was often testy and impatient that spring. "I have been existing too long on R's green sleeping pills and having too many colonic irrigations," the last of which he was demanding with increasing frequency, evidently believing that such a procedure would immunize him against every bacterium and virus on the planet. But despite every physical remedy he attempted, his spirit was not lightened: "R wheels in breakfast and already it has started—this thing which makes me resent her so and hate myself for resenting her."

Michael's resentments and repressions were paradoxically used to good effect that year in his first great commercial success. Thomas Job's *Uncle Harry* had been an enormous Broadway hit of the 1942/43 season, when it ran for 430 performances. With chilling, quiet power, the play spun an unusual and sinister tale of recrimination, jealousy,

murder and guilt. Michael directed the London production, took
the title role and cast Rachel in a small but important supporting
part. After opening at the Garrick on March 29, it played 121 performances before closing on July 8 for three weeks, and then it resumed
on a road tour.

The title role, Harry Quincey, is a nervous, mild-mannered bach-
elor living with his two possessive, domineering sisters, Lettie and
Hester, who conspire to prevent him from leaving them to marry.
Harry then prepares a cup of poisoned cocoa, which he arranges for
the unknowing Lettie to serve to Hester. Lettie is wrongly sentenced
to death for the crime of killing her sister, and Harry expects that at
last he will be free of his sisters' meddling control and can marry his
fiancée. But she rejects him. Torn by remorse and a sense of utter fu-
tility, Harry confesses to Hester's murder. The police refuse to believe
him, and Lettie will not cooperate to exonerate herself: with the death
of Hester and the revelation of her brother's crime, life no longer has
meaning for her and she prefers to die—and to leave Harry to ever-
lasting isolation and remorse. He is thus left to live a haunted, outcast
life of loneliness and guilt.

Michael prepared and delivered his role with no attempt to soften
the character of Uncle Harry. Here was another in his rogue's gallery
of neurotics—a murderous milquetoast, awkward and bespectacled,
his words tentative, his voice thick with sadness and cunning. In a curious way, this unsympathetic role established both Redgrave's wide
theatrical popularity in London and the gravity with which his stage
acting and directing would henceforth be assessed. That season, he at
once gained a level of critical respect thus far denied him.

"He has given no better performance than this subtle exposure of
moral cowardice," according to *The Times,* "and when the curtain falls
on his confession, the mind follows him forward into the deepening
shadow of eventual madness." In the role, wrote critic W. A. Darlington, Redgrave was "greater than [in] anything he has hitherto been able
to show us, and it has done very much to enhance his reputation. Nor
does any pretentiousness spoil the evening." Perhaps because she appeared in only two scenes, Rachel's performance—unsentimental yet

touching, according to those who remembered it—was all but ignored in the press. The reviews highlighted the acting of Michael and of Beatrix Lehmann and Ena Burrill, who played the two sisters.

But Michael's success came at a price. Halfway through the run of the play, the part affected his emotional stability. "It was getting me down. In simulating hysteria, you're bound to experience it a little yourself." He began to arrive at the theater just fifteen minutes before the curtain rose and then hurriedly applied his makeup and dashed onto the stage. "By the end of the evening, I was good for nothing, and when the final week of performances came, I was very close to a complete nervous collapse. Harry was a dangerous part for an actor—frightening, really—and I wasn't at all confident that I could reach the end of the run with my health intact." It was a period, he recalled, of ailments real and imagined, "of [the strong stimulant drug] Benzedrine and colonic irrigations . . . of nearly personal disintegration."

"I fail myself," he wrote in his journal on June 1, "because of my too well-known private life [and] my liking of a drink too many." Indeed, he was taking far too much alcohol that year, although as yet it did not affect his performances. In mid-June he decided on "reform week," as he wrote in his journal. But it became "retrench week," as he admitted after noting his drinks for just one day: "1 small gin before lunch, 1-1/2 big gins before the show, 2 Pimms [a gin-based drink] at supper and a nightcap in bed." Inevitably, he became depressed, and when he marked his ninth wedding anniversary on July 18, he wrote, "I understand the meaning of Keats's 'Ode to Melancholy' as perhaps never before."

—⁓—

AFTER THE LONDON closing of *Uncle Harry,* a hiatus prior to the provincial tour allowed Michael a much-needed rest and the time to dispatch roles in two memorable films. "He was tired and fed up," according to Rachel, "and said he must have some time on his own. He went to stay at the Savoy Hotel for a month, and my father stayed with me [at Bromyard]." But Michael was not alone at the Savoy, thanks to the return of Norris or the occasional presence of a substitute companion for the night. (The American ceramicist and art professor Grover Cole was one such.)

An anxious episode occurred that summer. At the Garrick, Michael received an anonymous letter threatening public exposure of his sexual life if he did not turn over a considerable sum of cash to a blackmailer he was to meet in Trafalgar Square. But Michael ingeniously foiled the plot. He asked a friend to take a reply on the night specified and hand it over in lieu of cash. In the note, typed and unsigned, Michael acknowledged that everything the blackmailer said was true; that he had repented of his past and that it was now the past; and that if there was any disclosure about Michael's private life, he would initiate a lawsuit and see that the blackmailer was put away for twenty years. Nothing further happened, but Michael and Rachel were rattled for several weeks and wondered if this might be but the first incident in a developing pattern.

The Houghton affair was also troubling that summer, after Norris discussed Robert Woods—a man "whose existence I had either not known or had forgotten," as Michael said. Hearing about the other man, Michael was suddenly, unaccountably and quite unfairly pitched into a jealous rage. "It hurt my vanity," he admitted in his diary. He dismissed Norris for the evening and hastened to a party at Noël Coward's home in Gerald Road. "Waking up there next morning reminds me too vividly of the last time I did so," he noted wistfully in his diary on August 31.

Two days later he regretted his behavior: "I miss N. very much and at times wish I had gone with him. Seeing U.S. naval uniforms in streets reminds me constantly of him." But two days after that, his mercurial temperament was revived: on September 4 he accepted an invitation to a party at Norris's flat. "The sad thing is, I got very tight. Norris said later that I spent the evening not looking at him. What a pity to spoil it so." Impatient as much with himself as with others, he then went to Bromyard to visit the family, now staying with another of Rachel's cousins, who lived closer to a school for Vanessa. "Don't let us drift apart so soon," Norris wrote to Michael soon after leaving London.

During this time, the family read Shakespeare aloud, taking all the parts in *The Tempest, Measure for Measure* and *The Comedy of Errors.* "What an amazing child Vanessa is," said Rachel, "and Lynn grows more adorable and attractive." As Michael wrote in his diary, "The children scramble onto my bed as soon as I am awake. They are the dearest things, and Corin is [growing up] in a surprising manner."

—◊◊—

IN MID-AUGUST, MICHAEL traveled to North Yorkshire, where he appeared in airfield scenes for a brief but important part in Anthony Asquith's film *The Way to the Stars,* based on a screenplay by Terence Rattigan about British and American flyers during the war. Michael portrayed a poetic, brave flight lieutenant who marries, has a child, and—thirty-five minutes into the picture—dies piloting his bomber over Germany. In the role, he had little more to do than encourage his compatriots and gaze lovingly at his on-screen wife (Rosamund John), but he established a tone that Asquith, shooting in sequence, sustained in every ensuing scene of the picture.

During the filming in Yorkshire and London, Michael and Rachel became friends with his costar John Mills and his wife, the playwright Mary Hayley Bell. Mary needed a title for her new play, and after reading it, Michael suggested *Duet for Two Hands.* Mary thought this was inspired, and so the play was known when it was staged in London and New York.

On September 19, after completing *The Way to the Stars,* Michael hurried to the Ealing Studios, where he appeared in "The Ventriloquist's Dummy," the best-known episode of the splendidly creepy anthology movie *Dead of Night.* He agreed to the role not because it was a modern type of Gothic horror character, but because the ventriloquist is a case study of a psychotic, the extreme of men he had represented to great effect in *The Duke in Darkness* and *Uncle Harry.* In addition, *Dead of Night* provided a marvelous opportunity to portray on-screen someone very different from lightweight Gilbert (in *The Lady Vanishes*), idealistic Davey (in *The Stars Look Down*) and noble Archdale (in *The Way to the Stars*).

The story was straightforward, but with a certain tragic inevitability. The ventriloquist regards his dummy as a separate, living personality he must own and control, but the tables are turned with a vengeance. His obsession eventually leads to madness after he tries to kill a rival performer, and finally his identity is completely obliterated, overcome by the spirit of the dummy he has smashed to bits.

This was not a novel idea. Medieval myths and German fairy tales contain many examples of inanimate creatures or artworks that come to malevolent life and subordinate human beings. In 1929 Erich von Stroheim played a similarly obsessed ventriloquist in the movie *The Great Gabbo,* and by 1944 the American radio entertainer Edgar Bergen was well established onstage and in films as a ventriloquist with a fractious, sarcastic dummy named Charlie McCarthy (famously outfitted in white tie and tails, which was the direct inspiration for the dummy's getup in *Dead of Night*).

The script was short and the episode timed for a half hour, and Michael prepared with unusual attention to detail. He had long discussions with the director, Alberto Cavalcanti; he studied with the popular ventriloquist Peter Brough; and he read several books about the incidence of schizophrenia among artists and performers. Seen decades later, his performance in *Dead of Night* remains both chilling and deeply disturbing, for Michael portrayed the ventriloquist as a charming, amiable comedian who becomes an anxious, antisocial neurotic and then a terrifying madman.

—⚒—

REQUIRING A CHANGE of tone and a return to the theater in his next project, he decided (unwisely, as it turned out) to direct and star in the London premiere of *Jacobowsky and the Colonel*. Written as a comedy, *Jacobowsky* dramatized the experience of novelist Franz Werfel when he escaped from the German police in Paris. But the fall of France and the terrors of the occupation are not easy to transmute into a light entertainment with elements of farce, which S. N. Behrman's adaptation tried to insert with almost manic desperation. Heavy with unclear satire and fuzzy symbolism, the play failed to aim for what might have been the witty and poignant theme of stoic vitality in the face of annihilation.

Jacobowsky and the Colonel opened at the Piccadilly on June 6, 1945. Critics and playgoers were not amused, especially with Rachel's portrayal of a winsome French girl balancing two suitors. "At rehearsals, it became evident that she was gravely miscast," recalled Frith Banbury, who was also in the cast, "and Redgrave bullied her unmercifully, to the intense embarrassment of us all." Just when Charlotte Wolff urged her to return to work after a period of dark depression, the press now pilloried Rachel. *The Times,* for example, was venomous: "Miss Rachel Kempson drenched France with the authentic perfume of Wimbledon."

She all but dismissed this experience from memory, but Corin did not. Just as Vanessa had been introduced to her father's work during the run of *The Duke in Darkness,* so Michael took six-year-old Corin to a performance of *Jacobowsky and the Colonel.* "I remember nothing except a pistol shot, which frightened the life out of me," he wrote later, "along with the dull dissatisfaction that during the entire afternoon, I failed to recognize my father."

Michael foresaw critical disaster and a poor audience response from the start of the run, and for some inexplicable reason he chose Banbury as a whipping boy for his own disappointment—perhaps because Banbury was living happily with a male partner, an arrangement Redgrave coveted. Onstage, Michael turned his back to the audience and tried to distract Banbury with comic faces—"surprising in an actor who ostensibly took his work so seriously," as Frith recalled. Years later he reflected that Michael wanted to be a major film star with a vast fan base but he also longed to be regarded as a serious stage actor, the equal of Olivier and Gielgud; more to the point, Frith felt that Michael had to deal with a lifelong conflict of desires that "made him both so tortured a man and so exciting an artist." *Jacobowsky* closed after sixty-one performances, and from then to December 18, 1947, Michael was absent from the stage.

During this period, he accepted roles in four important films. At the top of the agenda was an adaptation of Graham Greene's first novel,

The Man Within—a production Michael very much wanted to join and which he fitted into his congested schedule that year. His first appearance in a color film, this was a strange tale of misplaced affection, torture and betrayal—all of it told in flashback, the story of a young sailor and a smuggler attracted to the boy. (For the picture's American release, it was much edited, its title changed to *The Smugglers* and all implications of a homoerotic subtext removed.*)

The Captive Heart, set during the recent worldwide conflict, was the second project, much of it shot at a grim former prisoner-of-war camp in Germany. Michael took the role of a Czech soldier who assumes the name of a dead British officer in order to escape capture by the Gestapo, who want to arrest him because of his anti-Nazi activities. In captivity—to help prove his new identity—he replies to letters from the slain man's wife, who is unaware of her husband's death. The story moves inexorably toward the end of the war, the meeting of the couple, and the predictable romantic ending.

Michael had the opportunity to use his idiomatic, fluent German in *The Captive Heart,* and he infused the role with gentle melancholy and a muted intensity—not as a madman this time, but as someone emotionally lost who tries to find meaning in a strange act of kindness. At the invitation of producer Michael Balcon and director Basil Dearden, Rachel made a test for the part of the dead man's wife who, not knowing the truth, waits for his return and must then cope with the fact that her correspondent was not her husband but a well-meaning fraud. Rachel's beauty, all the more impressive for her expressive stillness, made the character more than a cliché, and she earned glowing reviews for her dignified restraint and affecting communication of love lost and rediscovered.

Michael's third picture during this period offered a similar kind of narrative, but with some even more unlikely twists. In *The Years Between,* based on Daphne du Maurier's play, he first appears halfway

---

* Greene's novel bears a striking resemblance to George Crabbe's nineteenth-century poem "The Borough," which became the basis for Benjamin Britten's opera *Peter Grimes* (first performed in June 1945). Redgrave regarded the opera as a splendidly subversive work, a judgment widely shared by critics and later vindicated by its place in the standard repertory.

through the movie, as a colonel believed to have been killed in the war. He suddenly turns up, just in time to cause his wife (who thinks she is his widow) more headaches than happiness. Played by Valerie Hobson, she has assumed his seat in Parliament and is on the verge of remarrying, and the return of her husband is like the sudden intrusion of a stranger to her and their teenage son.

Michael's character proves to be an impatient and unsympathetic sort of fellow, and this augurs poorly—until we recall that, after all, this is a movie about stouthearted, loyal folks during and after the war. Hence love is reborn for the couple on VE Day, just as the British are cheering in Trafalgar Square and in front of Buckingham Palace. Michael's calmly modulated performance (filmed in two weeks) reflected the sensibility of a man who comes home perhaps to nothing, and Valerie Hobson's understated portrayal of a woman with an odd dilemma remains a highlight of her career. Otherwise, *The Years Between* dilutes with sublime indifference a severe psychological problem and merely substitutes (as one contemporary critic wrote) "genteel reverence [for] a poor and empty adaptation of a poor and empty play."

The fourth movie Michael completed during his theatrical hiatus was *Fame Is the Spur,* offered to him by the producing-directing team of the Boulting Brothers, with whom he had collaborated on *Thunder Rock.* Clearly based on the life and career of former British prime minister Ramsay MacDonald, the picture also mirrors Michael's own ambivalence about the harmful effects of fame and fortune on moral and social principles.

In the film, he offers a taut, intense portrait of a committed socialist agitator longing to eradicate poverty and injustice. But the character's unfortunate transformation, from a humble servant of the people into a powerful politician, compromises his former high ideals and turns him into an Establishment puppet. Michael's performance was widely praised as "grand, and wholly credible." The final half hour of the picture contains some of his finest film acting, in sequences detailing the politician's remorse in his advanced age and his lonely grief as he remembers the youthful days of promise and goodwill. For these scenes, Michael perfected an old man's bent and quivering gait; he spoke with a tentative, thin voice; and he beheld the present with a gaze both rueful and guilty. Director Roy Boulting felt that Michael had "played immaculately, [emerging] as a sad, rather than unsympathetic character, reluctant to face his gradual abandonment of early principles."

In fact, Michael had not forgotten the fracas over the People's Convention. "We children, growing up after the war in a very privileged household," recalled Corin, "were unthinking, flag-waving little conservatives. When my father noticed our conservatism, he tried to counteract it, but feebly. He entered our nursery one morning, where the only newspaper to be seen was our nanny's newspaper, the [conservative] *Daily Mail*. Waving a copy of [the more liberal] *News Chronicle* at us, he said, 'Read this for a change.' He meant us to see that a person's choice of newspaper is a political act—in Michael's case, the sole remaining political act, [for by 1946] he played no part in politics. I'm certain it caused him some regret and disappointment, [which are] wonderfully conveyed in his performance in *Fame Is the Spur*." But the picture, as Roy Boulting added, "received a mixed press. After five years of death, destruction and austerity, the movie was far too grim for an audience now seeking escapism and peace. It flopped."

—⁂—

MICHAEL UNDERTOOK THESE roles mostly to alleviate the sorry state of his finances, which were in complete disarray in 1945 and 1946. His problems arose from the combination of a heavy overdue tax burden, a substantial bank overdraft, and a lavish way of life that included frequent parties; an expensive car; a secretary; a bar at home, fully stocked with the finest whiskies, wines, cognacs and liqueurs; a nanny for Lynn; weekly visits to fashionable restaurants; a wardrobe augmented seasonally; Vanessa's after-school dance lessons—and the purchase of an impressive new residence.

Michael also paid for a holiday to Italy that autumn, which he arranged as a tonic for Rachel. Before the two departed, she bought Lynn a cuddly teddy bear that squeaked when embraced and sported several changes of wardrobe. Sixty years later—after receiving several new eyes, much darning, re-stuffing and cleaning—the bear was still the favorite relic of Lynn's childhood, a talisman she brought to her dressing room for each of her theater performances.

After visits to Milan and Venice, the Redgraves returned to London. Rachel felt refreshed and encouraged by this rare gift of a holiday alone with her husband, and over the next three years she accepted supporting parts in several West End plays. But she preferred her role as full-time mother at home and had domestic tasks in full complement over the next year—as did Michael, after he bought Bedford House, an eighteenth-century residence on Chiswick Mall, backing onto the Thames. Financial problems notwithstanding, he wanted to own a great home at last, and he regarded Bedford House as too valuable an investment to ignore, a place worthy of his reputation.

The neighborhood was home to many people in the arts, to writers, designers, composers and museum curators. The price of £12,000 was at first daunting, but Michael easily obtained a mortgage on the strength of film work under contract. The deed of sale was completed in autumn 1945, but before he could move the family from Rivermead Court, major structural repairs were needed at Bedford House after the heavy bombings.

The former mansion home of the dukes of Bedford had three floors and a basement, was built of brick and mortar, and boasted eight bedrooms and three baths, a library and a spacious living room with a vast fireplace. There were three gardens sloping down to the river, all with paved paths and climbing rosebushes, to which Rachel soon added rows of her favorite flowers, blue hyacinths, and a riot of irises, delphiniums, herbaceous plants, a hothouse for tomatoes and vegetables and even a chicken coop. Bedford House was considered one of the most desirable homes in London.

After months of refurbishment and redesign, supervised by the renowned decorator John Fowler, the place was finally ready for the family. Michael, however, was not prepared for the sudden and substantial bills that seemed to arrive daily, and he was forced to ask several vendors and workmen to await payment until he received the first checks from his movie contracts that year. Still, the family's standard of living remained high. There was a chauffeur to drive the Rolls-Royce, a cook and two housemaids, and a gardener—most of them residing in staff quarters at Bedford House.

The arrival of the Redgraves at their new address in March 1946 coincided with a major London social event, the Oxford and Cambridge Boat race on the Thames. Invitations to a lavish party celebrating the race and the opening of Bedford House were sent to a guest list that included the likes of Laurence Olivier and his second wife, Vivien Leigh; John Gielgud; Noël Coward; John and Mary Mills; the theatrical producer Hugh Beaumont; Norris Houghton; and more celebrities from the world of theater, film and the arts. "John and Mary [Mills] are amusing and pleasant," Michael noted in his diary, "and Mary is having another baby." (Born in April, that baby grew up to become the actress Hayley Mills; her older sister, Juliet, was also to have a successful acting career; and her younger brother, Jonathan, became a writer and producer.)

The Redgrave calendar was full of social activities and the gala premieres of Michael's movies. Introduced at one of them to Princess Mary, the forty-nine-year-old sister of the reigning King George VI, Michael noted in his diary that she arrived "looking a little mad, in ermine if not white satin—ermine is surely the stuff to go mad in—and she shook our hands in a distrait, solemn manner."

There were also invitations from friends. No summons was more prized than one from the Oliviers for a weekend at Notley Abbey, their thirteenth-century, twenty-two-room manor house in Buckinghamshire, where Rachel and Michael were frequent guests. On their arrival at the appointed hour of Friday midnight, they found that Vivien had arranged everything to perfection. Servants had laid a fire in each bedroom, where guests found books by their favorite authors, a bottle of Malvern water and a single perfect rose. Cocktails were served at one in the morning in the paneled library, and sometime after two o'clock, a four-course dinner with appropriate wines was offered in the baronial dining room.

Michael was duly impressed, while Rachel was concerned for the physical and emotional health of her friend Vivien, who, in a breathless whirl of activity, worked feverishly at her career and at confirming the public image of the Oliviers as England's most romantic acting duo. At that time, not many people were aware that the six-year-old marriage was deeply troubled and destined for a miserable finale. Still regarded as the theater's golden twosome, Larry and Vivien were attempting to finesse the concomitant demands of private and public life; an extravagant lifestyle made precarious by the uncertainties of compensation; Larry's insecurity; and Vivien's incipient mental illness.

In the matter of an unstable marriage, the Redgraves were like the Oliviers, but few outside Bedford House had any notion that there were marital difficulties. "Rachel is justifiably angry," Michael wrote in his journal after he returned from a weekend with Norris, "and she says many true things and one or two which hurt a great deal. I promise to try to do better." Years later he confided the reason for the parental discord to Corin, who wrote, "About this time, my father no longer shared my mother's bed." Michael regarded this new arrangement as welcome; Rachel did not. His needs were being met elsewhere, while she had no such comfort or compensation and felt lonely, unattractive and unloved. But that was about to change.

Seven

A TERM IN HOLLYWOOD

(1947)

Mᴄʜᴀᴇʟ ᴄᴏᴍᴘʟᴇᴛᴇᴅ ʜɪs ʟᴀsᴛ sᴄᴇɴᴇs ɪɴ *Fame Is the Spur* ᴅᴜʀ-ing the first days of 1947—just as his London agents concluded negotiations with two American film companies eager to land him before his price became too high. By mid-January he was in Los Angeles, where the director Fritz Lang welcomed him and, as flash-bulbs popped, shuttled him off in a limousine to a lavish bungalow at the Hotel Bel-Air.

From the earliest days of the motion picture industry, there was no shortage of British actors in Hollywood, and by 1947 a legion of English, Irish, Welsh and Scots players was in residence. Among the many were Charlie Chaplin, who first landed in 1910; Cary Grant, who arrived in 1931; and Charles Laughton, who went to Hollywood in 1932. Laurence Olivier, Ronald Colman and Ray Milland had already appeared in American movies, and James Mason and Michael Rennie were among those who soon joined them. Alfred Hitchcock, Gladys Cooper, Basil Rathbone, Ann Todd, Nigel Bruce and Claude Rains were famously in residence that year, for English accents, training and talent were always welcome. It was also patently true, as Hitchcock said, that many Brits were delighted to escape their country's weather and relocate to sunny Southern California. And if their agents could obtain handsome Hollywood salaries for them, so much the better.

Michael expected to begin full-time work at once. The two films on his agenda were a psychological thriller called *Secret Beyond the Door,* directed by Lang and starring Joan Bennett; and a movie based on

Eugene O'Neill's play *Mourning Becomes Electra,* with Rosalind Russell. He was summoned for costume fittings and lighting and makeup
tests for the first production, but then Michael spent his early weeks in
a whirlwind of luncheons, dinners and cocktail parties because of the
usual studio delays. The arbiters of Hollywood social life stepped in to
fill the empty days.

After he settled in at the Bel-Air (courtesy of the producers of *Secret
Beyond the Door*), Katharine Hepburn collected him and they drove
out to a reception at the home of Ethel Barrymore in Pacific Palisades.
Later that day, the director George Cukor drove Michael back to the
hotel, and with them in the car was Greta Garbo—who suddenly
turned to Michael and asked (à propos of nothing), "Is there much
Buddhism in England?"

"Not a great deal," Michael replied. "What little we had, we exported to the States."

"The great blue eyes turned to ice," he recalled, "and she returned
her gaze to the California landscape. I should think from that reaction
that her sense of humor is somewhat limited." There was no further
conversation during the journey.

"I have met quite a few luminous people," Michael wrote to Norris
Houghton four weeks later, dropping a short list of stellar names—
Olivia de Havilland, Gene Kelly, Judy Garland, Loretta Young, Fanny
Brice and Beatrice Lillie. "My general impression is that everyone here
is exactly as you'd expect them to be, only more so. The most startling
of all is Mickey Rooney, who gives a remarkable imitation of his screen
self, with the slight difference that I happened to be introduced to him
when he was stark naked, which is something I don't happen to have
seen on the screen.

"The introduction took place in the steam room of the Beverly Hills
Club, and within two minutes, it was just Mickey and Mike, and he
had invited me up to his house that night to see a coupla [*sic*] pictures
he was running. I declined with acute regret, but strictly between ourselves, I think I need the protection of the silver screen where that far-
ceur is concerned. As I was leaving, some time later, he was re-entering
the steam room and observing, in his celebrated tones, 'There's three

things that never hurt anyone—to eat, drink and fuck.' He got his laughs, all right."

By the time he left California months later, Michael had sent a series of long letters to Norris, for the more he saw of Hollywood, the more he longed to perform again on the London stage in the great classical roles. He aspired most of all to undertake the role of Macbeth, as he reminded Norris, and producer Hugh "Binkie" Beaumont was warm to the idea. This is certainly one of the most difficult parts in the Shakespearean canon, and although Beaumont was eager to present it as soon as Michael returned, they could not agree on a director. Redgrave then told Houghton that he wanted "an original mind watching and directing—so I ask you."

At first, the offer caused Houghton considerable anxiety, for it would not only be his first time directing Shakespeare—it would be his first professional assignment as a director. After some worry over the potentially disastrous reaction of London critics and audiences to the presence of an unknown American directing a hallowed British drama, Houghton accepted Michael's offer and began intensive preparations. The plan was to open in December, and so Beaumont swung into action.

—⁓—

MICHAEL HOPED TO bring Rachel over for a holiday in Los Angeles, either during the interval between his two pictures or after he had completed both. Accordingly, she asked her agent to scout a potential Hollywood movie role for her so that a production company would underwrite her travel expenses. The good news came in a letter she wrote from Bedford House to Michael on February 12: after director Zoltan Korda had looked at her scenes in *The Captive Heart,* he offered her a brief but good supporting role in *A Woman's Vengeance,* starring Charles Boyer, to be produced at Universal Studios that spring.

In the same letter, Rachel detailed the austerities of life in postwar Britain during that very harsh winter. In a population of forty million, five million people were unemployed, and food, clothes and fuel were strictly rationed. Between nine o'clock in the morning and four

in the afternoon, electricity was provided only to hospitals and critical national industries, while homes, shops and hotels were without
power. Candles and oil lamps were difficult to obtain as substitutes for
electrical lighting, no heating coal was available and bakery ovens were
closed. Bus routes were curtailed or cancelled because of job cutbacks
and fuel shortages.

At the ages of eight and ten, the older Redgrave children were
remarkably alert to the problems of the day: "Corin and Vanessa now
rail against [Prime Minister] Atlee," Rachel wrote to Michael, "and
come out with streams of statistics and generally appear to know almost more than any of us about the whole situation. They read all
the news and retain it all." She concluded her letter with the request
that Michael send them some bars of soap, "as the soap factories are
closing down."

During their father's absence from Bedford House, Vanessa and
Corin occasionally invented evening and weekend entertainments
for their mother and her friends. Corin frequently acted the role of
a movie director arriving in a helicopter—"for which he made the
sound effects," as Rachel recalled. Vanessa played a dancer or a poet,
while four-year-old Lynn sat attentively in the audience. "My sister and
brother were outgoing, healthy and opinionated," according to Lynn.
"In contrast, I was desperately shy, anemic, and always sick." Vanessa
remembered Lynn's bouts of bronchitis, "which made her breathless
and unable to walk far. Her frailty, combined with the gap between
our ages, meant that she could not share in the games Corin and I
played together, or more truthfully, that we seldom wanted her to. My
most abiding memory of Lynny as a child is of the little girl who trailed
behind us crying, 'Wait for me!' "

But Lynn recalled her older sister's attentiveness and affection during their childhood. "Vanessa was the dream sister. She looked like
Tenniel's [drawings of] Alice [in Wonderland], only prettier. Once she
took a shoebox and made me a little house for my dolls, with tiny windows, and then she illustrated books for me. In her room there was a
little platform, just like a stage—[her room was] full of books and il-
lustrations, because she was a very good artist and drew beautifully. If I

asked her for anything that belonged to her, she gave it to me with such generosity and sweetness."

Vanessa and Corin at first attended a primary school a mile from Bedford House, in Sutton Court Road, but they were soon bored and therefore inattentive; Vanessa, especially, felt like "a fish out of water," as she remembered. Rachel then conferred with their neighbor Alec Guinness and other nearby parents, and soon her two older children joined Alec's son Matthew, the local rector's sons and a few other youngsters for lessons at the local vicarage with a private tutor named Miss Glascot. She taught them English, French, history, mathematics, natural history, art and Bible study, supplementing the classes with visits to museums and nature walks along the riverbank and in Chiswick Park. Of all these activities, Vanessa preferred reading: farsighted though she was, and hesitant to ask for eyeglasses during austere times, she was rarely without a book. "I was hungry for reading so much . . . [that I read] often in bad light [or] by torchlight under my blankets at night and in the early mornings."

Vanessa was also passionate for the ballet, and she attended dance lessons several times each week after Miss Glascot's classes. "I knew at an early age that I absolutely wanted to be a dancer, but at the age of nine, it was a bit too late to start. My parents knew perfectly well that I was going to be far too tall to be a ballerina, but they didn't tell me. And I cherished this illusion for quite long time. But then one day I discovered that, yes indeed, I was definitely way, way too tall—even taller than my mother. I had a good cry about that, and then I realized, 'Well, I could become an actress, and maybe I could dance in some of the future acting roles that might come my way.'"

—⁂—

RACHEL ARRIVED IN Los Angeles on a warm, sunny afternoon in March and was whisked away by Michael to their poolside bungalow at the Bel-Air. On the evening of March 20—his thirty-ninth birthday—they were hosts for a celebration at the hotel; among the guests were Michael's former costar Dame May Whitty ("Miss Froy" in *The Lady Vanishes*) and Ivor Novello with his romantic and professional partner, Bobby Andrews. Also present was a handsome man named Robert Michell. The next day, Rachel learned from her husband what she had probably guessed: that Bob was Michael's new lover. According to his diary, she took the news "very generously but is clearly very hurt."

Michael had met Bob at a Sunday luncheon at George Cukor's home. Because his father was a former policeman turned convicted crook, Bob had changed his birth name from Leroy Meyers after his mother took a boyfriend named Jack Michell. Bob had served in the army during World War II, and although he had little education, he was a quick study, eager to learn from those he regarded as his betters. When he met Michael, he was working at a telegraph office in Hollywood and sharing an apartment with his sometime girlfriend in the San Fernando Valley. Sociable and polite, Bob Michell was familiar with gay men in the movie world.

As tall as Michael and a decade younger, he was dark-haired, with a deep olive complexion that (he said) partly reflected his Native American ancestry; and he made himself agreeable as much by his respectful manners as by his startling good looks. "He had a dazzling smile," recalled Corin, "with the whitest teeth I had ever seen." Michael's diary from February 1947 through the next several months includes a mention of Bob on virtually every page—typically, "Out with Bob, who stays the night" (or words to that effect), for Michael, as usual, gave little thought to expenses and booked a pro forma room for Bob at the Bel-Air.

Another guest soon arrived in the person of none other than Michael's mother, who was widowed when Andy died on March 18 at the age of eighty-three, after a long battle with cardiovascular disease and years of blindness. Over the years, Andy had taken an interest in Michael's career only from a distance and with the mildest enthusiasm. They had always been strangers to each other, and the announcement of Andy's death did not reduce Michael to tears of grief. But later he spoke with gratitude and admiration of the man who had subsidized his education, his European studies and holidays, his early years on his own—and his mother's very comfortable life, none of which Roy

Redgrave could have provided. When Michael heard from Margaret the news of Andy's death over a crackly transatlantic telephone connection, she sounded so pathetic and fueled by alcohol that he offered to bring her to California for a rest—an invitation she at once accepted.

On May 8, Margaret stepped off the train in Los Angeles after a stopover in New York, and Michael took her not to a hotel but to a four-bedroom, fully furnished home with a pool and guest quarters, rented for him by the studio producing his next picture, *Mourning Becomes Electra.* The house was located on Angelo Drive, off Benedict Canyon in Beverly Hills; neighbors included Humphrey Bogart and his wife, Lauren Bacall; Hedy Lamarr; Jack L. Warner; Lana Turner; and Katharine Hepburn.

Margaret's arrival inaugurated a time of more domestic friction than the presence of Bob Michell, who frequently visited for a day or three, as Michael's diary attests. (The fate of Bob's reputed Valley girlfriend has not been determined.) Rachel, hoping to be a comfort to Margaret after Andy's death, seemed in her mother-in-law's eyes to do nothing correctly. "She thought I was not much good compared to her son," Rachel recalled, "and it took every atom of my patience to look past her bitterness and jealousy and see the lonely and frightened woman who came to live with us for a few weeks."

—m—

THE TENSE HOUSEHOLD atmosphere continued during Michael's work on his first Hollywood picture that March, while Rachel's project was postponed for several months because of script problems.

*Secret Beyond the Door** was produced in direct imitation of much that was successful in Hitchcock's *Rebecca* and *Spellbound.* Produced by Walter Wanger, directed by Fritz Lang and drenched in the sort of facile Freudianism popular in the 1940s, *Secret Beyond the Door* exploited another common postwar movie motif: women reunited with husbands they now feared were strangers to them. Films such as *The*

---

* The film was never entitled *The Secret Beyond the Door,* which remains the common but incorrectly used identification.

Man I Married, Jane Eyre, Gaslight, My Name Is Julia Ross and *Undercurrent* were typical of this popular psychological suspense genre, and to it Lang added his neo-Gothic visual sensibility and a lifelong obsession with Teutonic myths and romances. Composer Miklós Rózsa was engaged; perhaps because his score for *Spellbound* had just won an Oscar, Wanger and Lang chose not to tone down the ubiquitous hysteria of the music—one of the reasons audiences ultimately reacted with more laughter than terror. (Seen muted, without music and dialogue, the picture is in fact immensely rich, thanks to the artistic cinematography by Stanley Cortez.)

In its final form—with a confusing voiceover and severe cuts that render almost everything incomprehensible or absurd—the movie attempts to tell the disjointed story of a wealthy but naïve and somewhat self-deluded young woman (played by Wanger's wife, Joan Bennett). While on holiday, she meets and precipitously marries a handsome stranger (Redgrave) and then discovers he is pretty close to certifiable lunacy—more like a potential Bluebeard than the successful architect he claims to be. She moves to his family's estate, a creepy place with locked doors, weird relatives, a chillingly precocious teenager and elaborate rooms with artifacts depicting the gruesome murders of women.

The poor wife encounters a dozen warning signals and plenty of red herrings before her twenty-minute sprint along shadowy corridors while outfitted in the most glamorous costumes Universal Studios could afford. She then sits calmly in a room she rightly thinks has been designated for her murder. By this time, her husband is in a psychotic rage and about to kill her, but she talks him out of it, releasing his long-repressed memories and averting his compulsion to repeat the nefarious deeds of history with which he is so obsessed. It turns out that the man's funny habits and lifelong resentment of all women can be traced back to the night his mother failed to read him a bedtime story when he was just a toddler. There remain only a few minutes in which to insert an upbeat ending: the couple, it is implied in an idyllic final scene, will live and love happily ever after.

Joan Bennett and Walter Wanger had previously collaborated with Fritz Lang on successful movies (*Woman in the Window* and *Scarlet*

Street), with her in the leading roles—hence she was greatly disappointed when the director acted like "a real Jekyll and Hyde character, calm and purposeful one moment, and off on a tirade the next." This was no exaggeration, for the cast was subjected to the director's famously sadistic treatment. Actress Natalie Schafer was placed close to a roaring fire for numerous takes of an uncomfortable scene. Lang also bullied Barbara O'Neil, whose performance was unintentionally reduced to a terrified monotone. And for the final sequence, as Bennett and Redgrave performed the flight from a burning house, the director "wouldn't use doubles for Michael Redgrave and me," as Bennett recalled. "We fled, terrified, through scorching flames, time and again."

As for Michael, he had accepted the part (after James Mason had read the script and promptly turned it down) for the opportunity to work with the respected director of *M, Metropolis, Fury* and *You Only Live Once.* There was also the attraction of Michael's $47,000 salary, which far exceeded his English income over several years.

Before filming began, the atmosphere was cheerfully optimistic. Michael dined almost every evening with the Wangers, and they were often joined by Lang, who was gravid with ideas for representing visually the complex psychology of *Secret Beyond the Door.* But everyone's anticipation was unmet by the reality. "I have never seen the film," Michael said years later. "It had a silly story, pseudo-psychological and pretentious. I thought I could learn something from him." In this he was disappointed, especially when Lang insisted, during the early filming of the honeymoon sequence, that Michael tumble out of a hammock and fall to a cement floor. This action Lang ordered to be painfully repeated six times. "I knew before we finished making [the picture] that it wasn't going to be up to much," Michael concluded.

"Michael Redgrave was a mess," recalled Joan's daughter Diana, nineteen at the time and a frequent visitor to the soundstage. "He was nervous and uptight, and Fritz was being very naughty, diabolical and cruel. Maybe he thought he was going to get a performance that way."

When Universal-International released *Secret Beyond the Door* in January 1948, after eight months of serious surgery in the editing and dubbing rooms, the film was dismissed by critics, ignored by moviegoers and eventually rated as the biggest financial failure on the studio's ledgers. It was also a searing disappointment for Michael, who had attempted, with only moderate success, a flat American accent; had lost weight and dyed his hair blond.

Once again, he played a most unsympathetic and disturbed character. In *Thunder Rock*, he had been a neurotic hermit, and in *The Duke in Darkness*, a mad servant; his Uncle Harry was a vengeful killer; in *Dead of Night*, he had portrayed a raving psychotic, and in *The Man Within*, a sadist. These can be called inspired examples of casting against type, but in fact Michael Redgrave was not known for playing what is termed straight roles, or romantic leading men. His strength was his unexpectedness: audiences could never be quite certain if that handsome, likeable character on the stage or the screen, with his appealing good looks and his evident need of help, just might turn into a dangerous lunatic.

—⁊⁊—

THERE WAS A month's interval between the completion of *Secret Beyond the Door* and the commencement of *Mourning Becomes Electra*, and Michael spent virtually every day with Bob, as his diary entries confirm.* And so it went that year, a minor-key rondo of marital and extramarital intrigues, with themes and episodes of deepening intensity and only the slightest variations.

—⁊⁊—

WHEN MICHAEL RETURNED to work for his next picture, it was to one with prestige written all over it.

Eugene O'Neill had already won three Pulitzer Prizes for drama when his six-hour play *Mourning Becomes Electra* opened on Broadway in 1931; five years later, he was awarded the Nobel Prize for literature. "He has never before fulfilled himself so completely," wrote the critic

---

* Michael again remembered Lynn's birthday, marking his diary on March 8 that year after sending her a present and putting through a call to her at Bedford House.

for the *New York Times* about *Electra,* adding that the play was "an occasion for great rejoicing . . . it is his masterpiece." In the decades since then, critics and O'Neill biographers have claimed that this play marked the high point of O'Neill's career, unequaled until the posthumous production of *Long Day's Journey into Night.*

O'Neill had hesitated to sell the film rights to *Mourning Becomes Electra* because, after the Broadway premiere, he felt that the language of his play did not equal the great classical themes and the theatrical style he had chosen. He also feared that Hollywood could not improve it. In this estimation, he was off the mark (as he later admitted): when O'Neill read the screen adaptation by writer and director Dudley Nichols, he felt it could be done.

The film went into production in the spring of 1947 with high expectations of critical and popular success. Nichols had assembled an impressive cast: Rosalind Russell, Raymond Massey, Katina Paxinou, Leo Genn, Kirk Douglas—and Michael Redgrave, who had read the play and the screenplay with enormous appreciation for O'Neill and was eager to be associated with a film that boasted a literary pedigree. The finished picture offers one of his finest, most complex and deeply realized performances.

The ancient Oresteian drama by Aeschylus that inspired O'Neill and Nichols was comprised of a unified trilogy—*Agamemnon, The Libation Bearers* and *The Eumenides; Mourning Becomes Electra* retained this structure as "Homecoming," "The Hunted" and "The Haunted." Updated from the Trojan War to the end of the American Civil War, *Electra* reworks the classical drama as the sorry saga of the Mannons, a wealthy and respected New England family with a tortured past and a demented present. With the help of her lover Adam (based on Aegisthus), Christine Mannon (Clytemnestra) poisons her husband, Ezra Mannon (Agamemnon). At the instigation of their daughter Lavinia (Electra), her brother Orin (Orestes) murders Adam and Christine then kills herself, an action that pitches the frail Orin into madness and finally suicide. Hovering over everything is Lavinia, left alone at the conclusion in the empty, ghost-haunted house.

In O'Neill's New England, the emphasis is not on the forces separating men from gods but rather on the kind of twisted Puritan sexual repression that results in derailed and deranged passion. This was preserved in the movie version, which presents the Oedipus and Electra complexes in all their dark ferocity, dramatized in an epic tale of adultery, murder, guilt, revenge, suicide and incestuous affections. To underscore the ritual, timeless aspects, many critical scenes on Broadway and in the film were enacted in front of a nineteenth-century Greek revival mansion that suggests the ritual temple of classical drama.

Cast in the movie as Orin Mannon, Michael first appears in the second of the film's three parts, halfway into the three-hour running time. With his head bandaged from a war wound, Orin returns home frail and highly strung. He is welcomed by his ferociously devoted mother Christine (played by the Greek actress Katina Paxinou), whose incestuous attraction to him is represented by an excess of language, embraces and kisses: "My boy, my baby," she cries several times, and he replies, "Oh, Mother, I don't want anyone else—you're my only girl!" Lavinia (Rosalind Russell), seeking revenge on her mother for their father's murder and jealous of her mother's affair with her own former suitor Adam (Leo Genn), goads Orin to murder him.

At this point, Michael's performance becomes the most fully realized portrait thus far in his gallery of madmen: his New England accent was flawless, and he organically constructed the character so that the wounded, mother-dominated youth logically becomes the tool of his sister, the killer of the man who would replace him in his mother's affection—and finally he becomes the new Ezra, unable to endure the guilt and thus compelled to take his own life.

During the last days of a production for which every scene was shot in strict continuity, Michael conveyed Orin's terrifying madness, a heartrending breakdown leading to suicide. Using aspects of all his previous, unhinged characters, he created a portrait of remorse converging into the soul of a weak man who has been irredeemably wounded by battle and scarred by a family legacy of hatred and greed—a once-good man destroyed by the corruption of his own best instincts. In long and difficult speeches, by means of manic laughter and hysterical sobs, he was not a case study, or only a theatrical exaggeration. He was recognizably human, and so evoked the terror, pity and catharsis that characterize authentic tragedy.

—⁓—

ALMOST ALONE AMONG major reviews, *Life* magazine was enthusiastic when the picture was released in late 1947: "The movie sustains an assault on the emotions as no other movie has ever done. It is an artistic triumph and a landmark in the development of cinema artistry." But *Mourning Becomes Electra* was excoriated by most critics. "A static and tiresome show, a millstone upon the screen," yawned the *New York Times,* which praised only the performance of Michael, "who turns in a good job as the weak, confused, Oedipean [*sic*] and hysterically-inclined Mannon son." Even the normally high-minded *New Yorker* dismissed the movie as unworthy of moviegoer's time or money.

Nor did the picture have any appeal to a public eager for uplifting amusement after the war, when the most popular pictures were cozy productions such as *Miracle on 34th Street, Life with Father, The Farmer's Daughter* and *The Egg and I;* audiences did not want to see men returning from battle broken and suicidal. The movie lost more than $2 million, virtually bankrupting RKO Studios just as *Secret Beyond the Door* had impoverished Universal. After a New York premiere in a legitimate Broadway playhouse, the picture was sent out on the countrywide circuit, renamed *This Strange Love.* It was then returned to the editing room several times until it lost more than an hour, but no strategies brought people to the box office.

Michael Redgrave and Rosalind Russell were nominated as best actor and actress of the year by the Academy of Motion Picture Arts and Sciences. They did not take home the statuettes, but Russell won the Golden Globe for her performance; *Life* magazine named her performer of the year; and the prestigious National Board of Review named Michael best actor of 1947.*

---

* The Oscars for best performances by an actor and actress that year went to Ronald Colman, for *A Double Life,* and to Loretta Young, for *The Farmer's Daughter.*

The National Board citation surprised him, for he regarded the film as a failure "because the camera remained fixed on the face of whichever actor was speaking, often in very long close-ups, as if hardly daring to look beyond for fear that the audience might not concentrate on the speech." He also thought that Rosalind Russell, elsewhere an expert comedienne and an effective dramatic actress, was "easy to act with" but wrongly cast, although this was a role she had long coveted and for which she had painstakingly prepared. The qualities of pragmatic good humor and healthy optimism that illuminated many of her movie roles "worked against her as Lavinia/Electra," according to Michael. Russell, forever rankled by her loss of the Oscar that rumor and goodwill had virtually guaranteed, reduced her important achievement to a few negative words in her autobiography, complaining that the production was "murder, [and] Michael Redgrave, a hell of a good actor, [was] nervous, taking pills to calm himself." That, and a sideswipe at Katina Paxinou, was the extent of her comment on *Mourning Becomes Electra*.

When the picture was finally released in England five years later, audiences queued up for months and critics were mostly enthusiastic. In London, Birmingham and Manchester, the movie was a surprising success, and its long run provided a generous income for the British distributors, who promoted it—misleadingly—as "the movie they didn't want you to see" (*they,* of course, referring to the British distributors of 1947, who had turned down the movie for exhibition).

—⁓—

LATE ONE EVENING that spring, as a studio driver was delivering Michael back to Beverly Hills after a day's work at RKO, a man stepped into a car in front of the house on Angelo Drive and headed quickly downhill toward Benedict Canyon. Moments later, Rachel, replying to her husband's question, said that she had come home several hours earlier in that same car, and with the same man. They had shared lunch and driven along the crest of the Santa Monica Mountains before returning to Angelo Drive for an intimate late afternoon. She then

admitted that she was involved in an affair with none other than Leo
Genn, Michael's co-star in *Electra,* "a dark, handsome man with a
charming deep voice," as she accurately described him.

A respected actor in London, New York and Hollywood, Genn
had been introduced to the Redgraves at a Sunday luncheon in Malibu,
at the home of the English actors Eileen Erskine and her husband,
Philip Friend. Leo's rendezvous with Rachel began soon after that—at
the instigation and with the hearty encouragement of his wife, Marguerite, "whose affections lay elsewhere," as Rachel knew. "It was a
wonderful feeling for me," she added, "for I began to feel beautiful,
desirable and loved. We continued to meet where and when we could,
and we were very happy together." That season, he gave Rachel a book
of poetry, inscribed "with love from Leo, from the city of love which
knows so little about it."

According to Rachel, Michael accepted this news with equanimity, perhaps even relief, "for problems remained between us, and, as in
England, he was often out late" with Bob, with whom he sometimes
disappeared for days. Michael understood and accepted the situation,
in other words, precisely because he had to understand and accept it:
he could hardly have assumed the role of aggrieved husband, outraged
at his wife's infidelity. Besides, as Rachel said later, "Michael didn't admire Leo much as an actor, though he liked him well enough. I exaggerated my admiration for him as an actor, because of my infatuation."
Collaborating on *Mourning Becomes Electra* was not awkward for the
two men: they appeared in only two brief scenes together and behaved
with friendly professionalism. In effect, Michael seems to have cared
little about Rachel's affair, so long as there was no talk of divorce: "Rachel and I had reached a turning point in our marriage, and all things
seemed aggravated by being in Hollywood."

On June 20, Margaret departed for London after a six-week holiday that Michael described as "rather a dull time" for his mother and
a period when he found himself "snapping at her." She left Los Angeles surprisingly healthy and refreshed, although her drinking was
more than ever a source of worry for Michael and Rachel. Three days
later, he concluded his scenes in *Electra.* The two American films to

which he had so looked forward had turned out to be profound disappointments, and Michael never had a good thing to say about his five months in Hollywood. Nor did he work there again.

Immediately after his last day at RKO, the Redgraves left the house on Angelo Drive, as his contract required. Michael had planned a holiday with Bob before returning to England, and Rachel moved into a rented apartment and leased a car while waiting to begin her movie role. Leo Genn forestalled any possibility that she would be lonely.

Michael and Bob headed north to San Francisco and then continued across the country to Niagara Falls and Montreal before arriving in Manhattan. After two weeks of theatergoing and fine dining, they boarded the *Queen Mary* for London, where they collected Vanessa, Corin, Lynn and the nanny and hastened down to register for rooms at the Wilton Court Hotel in Bexhill-on-Sea, a resort town on the Channel, east of Brighton.

Tony Hyndman never made it into Michael's ghosted memoir; Noël Coward was mentioned indifferently, without reference to their personal relationship; and Norris Houghton's name occurred, parenthetically, as "a great friend." Without the slightest allusion to the true nature of their intimacy, Michael wrote in his published book about his time and travels with Bob only once, and briefly: "I was accompanied by a young American, Bob Michell, who offered to come to England with me in the hopes of working there. Try as we might, a work permit couldn't be arranged. But Bob stayed with us, a dear friend to me and to the whole family, for nearly twelve years." And that was that. (In fact, another man replaced Bob in Michael's affections after eight years.) Later, Corin recalled that his father returned with recordings of Broadway shows, American candy bars—"and he brought a friend with him, Bob Michell." According to Corin, Bob was also a friend to the children, playing with them and never appearing bored with childish games and pranks.

—⁂—

FROM HOLLYWOOD, RACHEL wrote postcards and notes to the three children every week that summer, when she finally began studio work on *A Woman's Vengeance,* adapted by Aldous Huxley from his own story, "The Gioconda Smile." She portrayed Emily Maurier, the invalid wife of a man (Charles Boyer) who is in love with a much younger woman (Ann Blyth); he is the prime suspect when Emily dies of poison. Rachel brought a bitter, sad and lonely woman fully to life as she foresees death, but director Zoltan Korda severely edited her scenes and reviewers ignored her brief appearance. She was still working on the picture in early autumn, when Michael and the children returned to London from Bexhill-on-Sea.

—⁂—

AFTER RACHEL AND Michael exchanged letters about ten-year-old Vanessa, they agreed that she should be transferred from the insular atmosphere of private lessons in Chiswick to the Queen's Gate School for Girls, near the Natural History Museum in South Kensington. (At the age of four, Lynn was still too young for school.)

During her seven years at Queen's Gate, Vanessa excelled in English, French, Italian and history but took no interest in science and mathematics. The headmistress at this private academy, a certain Miss Spalding, recognized the theatrical talent of the new girl who, since an early age, had acted in impromptu skits. Joining the school's drama club shortly after her arrival, Vanessa earned the applause of her Queen's Gate classmates when she wore a shiny outfit to play the Tin Man in a school production of *The Wizard of Oz* and a heavy disguise as Mole in *Toad of Toad Hall,* a dramatization of Kenneth Grahame's *The Wind in the Willows.*

With classmates, she was asked to read aloud portions of *War and Peace* and *Anna Karenina* during recitations that were in effect dramatic readings: for these as for English novels, Vanessa's ability to assume accents was the talk of the school. "Dad had taken us to David Lean's film of *Oliver Twist,*" she recalled, "and I could copy Robert Newton's accent as Bill Sykes, or Kay Walsh's as Nancy."

She also continued her ballet lessons, although one afternoon, after gazing at her own reflection in a mirror at home, she broke down weeping and telephoned Rachel: "I just looked in your mirror and I can't see my head!" Hearing her sobs, Michael rushed into the room: "Don't worry about being tall, Van—hold yourself up and be severe, demanding, splendid!" That was perhaps the first time he gave her a note (a direction or suggestion) as her drama coach, and from that day, a new pride and poise was added to her obvious talents. In addition to her height, she was (like many other teenagers) embarrassed by the eruption of facial acne. But she prudently chose not to smother her face in ointments and instead relied on cold-water compresses and let the condition take its course; by the time she was twenty, her skin had mostly healed.

Accustomed to devising her own amusements and coping with parental absences, Vanessa Redgrave as a teenager was both independent and gregarious, capable of reading in solitude for long hours and of contributing to school activities with original ideas and a contagious sense of fun. Eager to make her own mark, she never exploited the family name to advance her social standing or her place in school dramatics. She was, in other words, very much her own person.

When it came to selecting a school for Corin, his parents thought he would benefit by attending a residential academy for boys. Several friends of the Redgraves had attended a Church of England primary school named for the town of Malvern Wells, almost three hours by train from London. In September 1947, Corin arrived there as a boarding student—greeted, as he recalled, with "a buzz of excitement" because his father was a famous movie star. Did Corin know Deanna Durbin or Jane Russell? Could he persuade Stewart Granger or Errol Flynn to sign autographs? He didn't and he couldn't, but at the age of eight he had a knack for friendship and was, at first, reasonably content.

—m—

So WAS RACHEL, when she completed her scenes in *A Woman's Vengeance*—an apt title for a movie at this time of her life. Leo and his wife had returned to England while she was working, but then he returned to Hollywood alone, to assume an important role in *The Snake Pit* with Olivia de Havilland. "As soon as he arrived, he sent me a message asking me to meet him," Rachel recalled. "From then on, for the rest of my time in Hollywood, we met every evening, and at weekends we stayed in his apartment at the Chateau Marmont [Hotel]."

With the children settled in school, Rachel in Hollywood and Lynn at home in the nanny's care, Michael worked intensively with Norris on their *Macbeth*.

First, Michael spent long hours with the text. "If you come to play Macbeth," he said later, "to study it and to say to yourself, as an actor should say, 'What does the text mean?' you will find yourself appalled at how little the text says in Macbeth's own lines that will enable you to build up this great and terrifying figure." To resolve this conundrum, Michael then worked with Norris, analyzing every line of every scene, discussing every gesture and posture, selecting the cast members, working with the set and costume designers and testing various lighting patterns. Nothing was left to chance or accident. But chance and accident, errors of creative judgment and perhaps a resentful attitude among some churlish critics conspired to evoke a mixed reception from the press when the Redgrave-Houghton production opened at the Aldwych on December 18.

Eight-year-old Corin, home for the Christmas holidays, attended the premiere and recalled it years later. "Now and again [my father] seemed to have difficulty pronouncing the words—and when he had to walk backwards up a staircase, he suddenly tripped and fell." This accident occurred at the start of a sword fight, and at once the theatrical spell was broken. Then there was the matter of Michael's diction. In stressing Macbeth's atavistic fury, Michael recited the verse in a coarse, sometimes inaudible tone. In addition, he was weighed down by the elaborate and heavy costumes, and overwhelmed by the scenery he and Norris had devised, with its multiple steps, towering mountains, glowering parapets and distracting painted backdrops. The play was effectively drowned by a kind of stagecraft that dwarfed the actors.

One critic found Michael's performance "lacking poetry and tragic emotion"; while another objected, "Speeches and phrases of incomparable beauty [were] hurled out in martial rage"; and a third observed bluntly, "While Macbeth is constantly on the rack, Mr. Redgrave too often seems merely in the dumps." These notices stung, for this was

Michael's return to the theater for the first time in two and a half years, and he ardently hoped for a better reception.

In this regard, it was not beyond reason to suspect that there was some shortsighted critical prejudice against a popular, successful and admired actor who had absented himself from the London stage for two years; who had only just returned from *Hollywood,* of all places; and who now swept back into town and donned the garments of a major Shakespearean character. In fact, there was an accusatory tone to some of the reviews, rather as if Michael Redgrave ought to be ashamed of his incautious bravado: *Macbeth,* indeed!

There was one important positive response, from T. C. Worsley. He insisted that Redgrave offered a performance "that commands our respect, with the gradations [of character] exactly marked and movingly rendered . . . [in] a production that is sustained on an extraordinarily high level. For this, we have to thank [Houghton] and also Mr. Michael Redgrave, who chooses to plot his course beautifully within the proportions of the whole."

But critical controversy can sell seats: people queued for tickets, and *Macbeth* sold out its limited run of seventy-six performances. Michael made no reference to it in his memoir, however, and the production stifled any talk of a future collaboration with Norris, with whom he remained on friendly but distant terms. "I wasn't very good on the first night," Michael recalled years later, "but I'm not in the least ashamed of some of my later performances." When asked why he thought most critics had treated him and the production so harshly, he was forthright: "It may have been that we were all wrong and I was just not very good. There is something about Macbeth which rather appalls me."

During the six weeks before the premiere, Michael and Bob often stayed at the Savoy Hotel or at the Berkeley, as his diary for November and December confirms. Spending lavishly on himself and Bob, Michael squandered the cash he should have been saving for the children's schools, the maintenance of Bedford House, and British taxes. "I do not like being called decadent, but that is what I am," he wrote in an undated diary entry; the identity of his accusers is not recorded.

Rachel was home by Christmastime. "Leo asked me to meet him," she recalled, "but somehow the magic had gone out of it. It was never the same again." Magic or no, the affair was not suddenly discontinued; the couple continued to rendezvous for more than a year, and then they parted as lovers but remained friends. Also as the year ended, Bob, with no job prospects, returned temporarily to Los Angeles, promising to return or to meet Michael soon, somewhere in the United States. And then, as if on cue, Tony Hyndman turned up, eager to resume his former place. But Michael, too, found that "the magic had gone out of it."

Eight

A THUNDERBOLT

(1948–1953)

T HE YEAR 1948 BEGAN WITH A FAMILY CELEBRATION AT BEDFORD
House: the five Redgraves gathered around a festive dinner table,
and a hearty songfest followed. "Michael was a brilliant pianist,"
Vanessa remembered, "and not only playing the classics—he was also
crazy about American musicals. There were always song sheets lying
about, and we all sang together around the piano—when he was
home." That winter, her father was in residence until the conclusion of
the run of *Macbeth,* at the end of February. He then departed immediately, for the same production was scheduled to open on Broadway
four weeks later.

Bob Michell was waiting for him in New York, and together they
moved into an apartment on East Sixty-fourth Street. Bob had abandoned his Hollywood life and set his sights on an acting career, a goal
Michael, rightly, did nothing to encourage. Bob soon discovered that,
with no training or experience, his prospects were very dim indeed;
instead, he became Michael's personal assistant. When rehearsals for
Macbeth began, the production company employed Bob as Michael's
dresser, at the handsome salary of fifty dollars a week.

The curtain of the National Theatre on West Forty-first Street
rose on March 31, and the critical response was rapturous, perhaps at
least partly because Michael had modified the technique that was held
against him in London. Redgrave and Houghton were suddenly the
stars of Broadway, their *Macbeth* commanding superlative reviews. Michael, wrote the senior *New York Times* drama critic, was "personally

vigorous, with a resonant voice he is not afraid to use with all the stops out, [in] a lusty characterization that has size and depth. He has given us the most stirring Macbeth we have ever had."

Michael's energy and good spirits were severely taxed that month, for he was afflicted with gout and had to rely on a cane everywhere but onstage. Following his first entrance, he scaled the complicated steps of the set and, especially during the fight scene, had to shift his weight from one leg to the other—"but when it came to Macbeth's death fall, I could not 'save myself,' because I knew it was a good fall, and my actor's vanity overcame any desire to protect myself." The painful limping continued throughout the run of the play, and the walking stick became a constant accessory.

Rave reviews notwithstanding, patrons did not come to the box office in great numbers that season, and the production closed four weeks later, after twenty-nine performances. During an expensive Bermuda holiday with Bob at the end of April, the gout disappeared, as did the income Michael had earned in New York. Together, the men returned to London, where Bob moved into a studio Michael had bought on Church Street, a few steps around the corner from Bedford House. From that time, he was Michael's London assistant and chauffeur as well as his lover. "I noticed that he looked more and more like my father," Corin added. "He went to the same tailor"—courtesy of Michael—"and he took to smoking a pipe, again like my father, though he never looked comfortable with it."

At that time, the children knew only that Bob was a family friend attached to the household, but years later Corin recalled that Michael seemed to go about with "quite a heavy burden of guilt vis-à-vis my mother and us children. My father was gay, or bisexual, at a time when you would be ashamed, humiliated, penalized and possibly put in prison—and that affected him deeply. He was greatly worried, for us as much as for himself." Rachel had come to accept what she knew she could never alter in Michael's life, but there were unavoidable tensions in this unconventional ménage, and the compromise was never easy.

Rachel's father died of heart failure that spring, and while Michael supervised the funeral and the legal details, Bob was enormously comforting and attentive to her and her mother—qualities that forever earned Rachel's gratitude. Eric Kempson's death occurred during her rehearsal period for *The Paragon,* by Roland and Michael Pertwee, in which she played the wife of a man obsessed with the memory of his son, believed heroically killed in the war. But the young man returns, healthy and nothing like a paragon: he was a deserter in the army and then turned to blackmail and murder.

Rachel's role was written without color or consistency—she seemed to exist only for the sake of dramatic exposition—but she deftly projected an aura of strength amid the play's thorny unpleasantness. Reviews stressed the male actors, citing Rachel only parenthetically, and despite a respectable run of 152 performances, *The Paragon* did not advance her career. At thirty-eight, she was not a leading lady, nor would she ever be. But she was as much of the theater as Michael, and her instincts were sharp—both for what she could and could not do onstage and for how she wanted to parcel her time.

That summer, Michael, Bob and the children again retreated from London to Bexhill-on-Sea; with her schedule at the Fortune Theatre, Rachel was able to join them only on weekends. "I didn't remember Daddy very well when he came back—he'd been away so much in America," Lynn recalled, "and I didn't really know him. I was in awe of him and I adored him, and I was terrified of him and I hated him and loved him, all in one go. My father must have found me maddening." He did not, but he had no interest in ingratiating himself with a five-year-old who drew back from him, and so a certain distance between Michael and his younger daughter prevailed, right through the coming decade.

"My father must have seemed a stranger to Lynn, and she was perhaps frightened or shy of him," said Corin. "He seemed to give up the challenge of winning her affection." Instead, Bob drew Lynn into the circle of entertainments and pastimes he supervised for Vanessa and Corin, looking after them all while they swam in the surf and went foraging for seashells and live shrimp in the rock pools. Bob also took Lynn for pony rides, which she loved.

While Bob amused the children, Michael worked several hours

each day, transforming a Henry James novella into a play. For some
time, he had been intrigued by *The Aspern Papers* and its theme of a
public person's right to privacy—an issue that had special relevance
for Michael, who had been seen in America, in London and at Bex-
hill without Rachel but with Bob. The James novella thus gripped his
imagination with its dramatic conflict between a biographer's legitimate need to know everything about his deceased subject (in this case
an American poet) and the man's survivors, who insist that the subject's letters remain private. It took twelve years of hard effort before
Michael was able to produce what was essentially an intellectual thesis,
but it is easy to understand why he persevered. He, too, had to cope
with a public career and the fear of exposing a private life that could
destroy that career.

—∞—

ALONE IN LONDON during the long days of summertime, Rachel felt,
as she said later, "isolated, insignificant and cold, like a figure one
shakes in a glass ball, with snow swirling all around." She returned
to Charlotte Wolff for therapy sessions and began to see herself "as an
individual, rather than just as an appendage to Michael, who was a
deeply troubled man, often moody and unpredictable with both me
and the children, and with friends who paid scant heed to me. Even
if he got drunk, behaved badly, left me alone, I allowed my husband
to do what he liked." This, Rachel now realized, was a "very unwise"
course of action.

Bedford House was full again that autumn, when both Redgraves
were rehearsing new productions. The London theater was realizing
its highest profits in a decade, thanks partly to the influx of tourists for
the Summer Olympics. As it happened, John Gielgud was about to
direct and star in a revival of *The Return of the Prodigal,* and he chose
Rachel for a supporting role.

First staged in 1905, St. John Hankin's cynical morality play concerned not the forgiveness of a wayward son (as in the Bible) but the
family that privately supports a man's louche life. Dressed by Cecil
Beaton in glorious white gowns, Rachel was cast as a young woman

who dreams of high romance but must adjust her aspirations. When she uttered one of the play's key lines—"The great people won't marry me, and I mustn't marry the little people"—the audience responded with rueful laughter, as the critics noted. Reviewers disdained the play—"the best dressed and best acted bad play in London," whined *The Times*—but Rachel was praised for her charm as the straightforward, plainspoken sister of the title character. Alas, once again a comprimario part in a badly received revival did not encourage producers to race to their telephones with offers for her to work. When the play closed on January 22, 1949, she had missed none of the sixty-eight performances.[*]

Six nights after Rachel's debut in *Prodigal,* Michael took the stage of the Embassy, playing the title character in *The Father,* August Strindberg's darkest, angriest (and most autobiographical) tragedy. In taut, suspenseful dialogue, the play concerns a man and wife who disagree on the specifics of their daughter's education. He believes she would benefit by leaving home to study abroad, but the mother wants her child to remain. This apparently undramatic premise is only the pretext for the couple's bitter struggle for power. The wife insists that the final decision must be hers alone, because (she now reveals) her husband may not actually be the girl's father. Confronted with this news, he becomes violent, is forcibly restrained, and then succumbs to a massive stroke. Thus concludes what one critic called "a thunderbolt of wrath and hatred."

The play had not been on Michael's schedule, but when the actor preparing the role withdrew during rehearsals, he stepped in, for this was a play and a part he had long coveted—for reasons he may not have wanted fully to recognize. The title character in this domestic battle of wits has lived within a doomed marriage for years, and now he finally feels the loss of his paternal prerogatives because of his wife's influence and his own weakness. Once again, Michael had assumed a character unable to cope with outer circumstances and inner demons and so, unwittingly, he precipitates his own flight from reality.

---

[*] Except for the Gielgud production, *The Return of the Prodigal* was ignored for over a century after its 1905 premiere. Since 2007, however, it has been staged several times in England and America to critical and popular acclaim.

This thesis was powerful on the page, but Michael lost dramatic steam toward the end of his performances. "He failed to convey the full macabre intensity, the feeling of one possessed," according to *The Times*. "The fuse was laid, but there was no explosion," wrote one of his most admiring critics; the character's "intelligence was still conspicuously in command, when reason should have been dissolved." Perhaps Michael's theatrical exculpation of the character, by tone and gesture, was meant to humanize both the father and, in a way, himself—a trap into which Robert Loraine, the most famous English actor to inhabit the role, had also fallen. That interpretation runs counter to Strindberg's text: the father is not merely misunderstood or henpecked; he is thoroughly misogynistic. Realizing later that he had miscalculated, Michael admitted that his performance had been "another half-successful assault on a great part."

There was another problem in addition to the final scene of the play. Tony Hyndman had fallen on hard times and into what seemed serious depression, and Michael responded not by resuming their affair, but by offering him a job as stage manager for *The Father.** After an angry disagreement over some detail of the production, Tony found a box of metal tacks backstage and sprinkled them on the sofa onto which Michael had to collapse during the last act. Irate and suffering multiple tiny stab wounds, Michael required a physician's care later that evening. Tony was dismissed at once.

From that time, Hyndman went into a sad decline. Dependent on alcohol and drugs, he forged Peggy Ashcroft's signature on a blank check; he stole cash from E. M. Forster; he pilfered pocket money from Spender's children and removed art and artifacts from the Spender home. From 1954 to 1956 he spent several long periods in rehabilitation clinics to cure a heroin habit. This seemed to have been successful, but

---

* Stephen Spender had recommended Tony, who was credited as the play's "stage director," which meant not the play's director but one responsible for supervising the backstage activities of the crew at each performance. In the United States, this job is traditionally designated "stage manager." Theatrical job descriptions on each side of the Atlantic are further confused by the title "producer" in England, which until recently meant the director, not (as in America) the person who arranges the financing and assembles a creative team.

he was never again psychologically sound. In 1982, while living alone in Cardiff after a long period of unemployment, he died of emphysema at the age of seventy-one. Among the many lives that intersected Michael's, few were as full of youthful promise as Tony Hyndman's, and none ended so pitiably.

—⁂—

CORIN, THEN NINE years old, returned to Bedford House for Christmas 1948—"with his cello, which he plays beautifully," Michael noted in his diary. But the family noticed the boy's gloomy silence. When he complained of aches and pains, no ailment could be diagnosed; when he went to bed and shivered with cold, he registered no fever. His parents took him to Charlotte Wolff, who gave him weak tea and chocolate biscuits before taking ink prints of his hands and then saying in her thick Viennese accent, "*Ach!* So *in*-te-res-ting!*" No one ever quite knew what she meant, but soon after, Corin told his parents that he wanted to leave Malvern Wells, that he was unbearably lonely, frightened of the headmaster and homesick. Michael reassured his son that if he found the spring term intolerable, he would be transferred to another school.

With that promise, Corin boarded the train at Paddington for the return to Malvern Wells. During the coming months, Rachel made a few telephone calls to parents of other Malvern boys. The headmaster, as it turned out, "was a crank and a sadist," as Corin said truthfully. "It didn't surprise him that I wanted to leave, because, he said, I was clearly neurasthenic and educationally subnormal."* At the end of term, Michael honored his word: Corin was enrolled—again as a boarder but much nearer home—at the Westminster School, adjacent to the Abbey. Granted a royal charter by Queen Elizabeth I, the school boasted an impressive alumni list that included George Herbert, John Dryden, Christopher Wren and, in modern times, A. A. Milne, John Gielgud and Peter Ustinov. Winning friends easily and able to go

---

* Later, when Corin won a scholarship to Cambridge and subsequently graduated with honors, his parents sent the good news to the headmaster of Malvern Wells, who replied that this was no reason to modify his low estimation of Corin's intelligence and abilities.

home on weekends, Corin was much happier at Westminster, where he remained until leaving for university studies.

At the age of twelve, Vanessa knew that her height precluded a career in ballet: no male dancer could partner her 5-foot, 11-inch, 135-pound body. But she continued Saturday lessons with the renowned teacher Marie Rambert, becoming more aware "of the significance of physical movement and physical space," as she recalled. "In my daily life I was round-shouldered and stooping, much taller than my friends and self-conscious about my height." But these attributes were no hindrance to acting in school plays.

Lynn was virtually alone at home, kept from school enrollment until she was eight years old because of pernicious anemia and recurrent asthma attacks. "In those days, I just didn't see my parents much at all," she recalled. "I lived in the nursery. My nanny made my breakfast and lunch, and later dressed me up to go downstairs for tea with my parents—if they were home, which wasn't often." With Vanessa's help, Lynn learned to read before attending school.

—◊—

AFTER THE DARK demands imposed by *Macbeth* and *The Father,* Michael began work on a translation of Georges de Porto-Riche's French play *Amoureuse;* his collaborator was a family friend named Diana Gould (a dancer who soon married violinist Yehudi Menuhin). *A Woman in Love,* as they called it, dated from 1891, but its comic treatment of a love triangle compromised by differing sexual needs was timeless and uproarious. Portraying a doctor whose bedside manner is more than merely professional, Michael strode the Embassy stage with hilarious gusto, "as though farce were his spiritual home," as one critic wrote after the April 26 premiere. "At the same time, he brings to it an intellectual tang that makes his performance very rewarding."

Meanwhile, Laurence Olivier had invited Rachel to join his new production company at the St. James's, where his first task was to act in and direct a new verse play: Christopher Fry's fey romantic comedy *Venus Observed* (a sly reference to Otway's *Venice Preserv'd,* perhaps the most famous Restoration tragedy). But Fry, rushing to meet his deadline for Olivier, was unable to resolve significant script problems in his play about a debonair modern duke who learns that his son is courting one of his mistresses. The play was a maddeningly florid exercise in free verse, with orotund speeches that left some in the audiences glancing at their watches rather too frequently; nevertheless, it somehow ran for ten months. Of Rachel's subordinate role, a typical review noted that she was "not asked to be more than a decorative ducal appendage."

She played the role for all 230 performances and then also appeared, with John Mills, in a second play on which Olivier lost a small fortune: Tyrone Guthrie's *Top of the Ladder,* a gloomy affair about a boy emotionally suffocated by his mother and intimidated by his father. This survived just four weeks, and then Rachel vanished from public life for over a year. Depressed about her stalled career, left alone during Michael's frequent absences and convinced that her life was of little account, she returned to Bedford House, avoiding a complete breakdown only with the help of Charlotte Wolff.

"She was a great help to me over the years," said Rachel, "and I began to realize that the possibility of other relationships would not be out of the question." At the age of forty, she was in an emotional turmoil requiring months of rest and therapy. Wolff's none-too-subtle suggestion that she consider an extramarital affair (again) at first struck Rachel as the height of improbability. "She seemed quite unaware of her physical loveliness," Corin's first wife later said of Rachel. "Few photographs do her justice. Her fine-boned face, with its dazzling blue eyes, took my breath away. She had the firm slim body of a teenager, and her smile lit up her whole face." For all that, Rachel considered herself something of an ugly duckling.

In the spring of 1949, Michael had learned from his accountants that his finances were dangerously precarious: for years he had been spending far more than he earned, and now his projected income was, to say the least, not encouraging. Although he had signed to rejoin the Old Vic at the New Theatre beginning that autumn, he also knew that his salary would not go far toward alleviating his debts and supporting his standard of living. Hence, at Noël Coward's suggestion, he accepted a role in a movie based on Coward's play *The Astonished Heart;* again, the character was a deeply disturbed man—in this case, an eminent psychiatrist who, in a fit of madness over a love affair gone sour, throws himself down from the roof of the Dorchester Hotel. After production began, Michael asked for some script changes that Coward rejected; polite disagreements followed; and finally both men agreed to say that Redgrave was leaving the picture for personal reasons. Noël assumed the part, and Michael departed with his entire contracted salary. (The film turned out to be a dismal failure—"though there was not much joy in that for me," said Michael.)

During his brief time at the film studio, Michael met Noël's new part-time secretary, Joan Sparks (later Hirst). Bob continued to dispatch efficiently his chores as Michael's assistant and driver, but the fine points of scheduling, typing, bookkeeping and managing correspondence eluded him. Michael hired Joan to work several mornings weekly at Bedford House, and from there she went along to Coward's home in Belgravia. Passionate about and familiar with theater history and production, and devoted to what she called intellectual integrity, Joan became virtually a member of the Redgrave family from 1949 until her death in 2002, just as she was an indispensable confidant to Coward and his heirs. According to Noël's biographer, "Redgrave, perhaps more than Coward, represented for Joan her true love of the theatre."

—⚬—

A NEW ASSISTANT was certainly welcome that autumn of 1949, when Michael, now forty-one, began one of the most remarkable periods of his theatrical career, performing four difficult and demanding stage parts—each of which brought him great acclaim, profound exhaustion, little income, and the kinds of reviews that usually emerge only in actors' fantasies. From September 1949 through the spring of 1950 he memorized a quartet of challenging leading roles, a feat that would have deterred or even vanquished many seasoned actors. In Michael's case, this requirement seemed, almost miraculously, to pose no difficulties. That the first three plays were performed in repertory was all the more astonishing. .

First, in *Love's Labour's Lost,* he took on the role of Berowne—the most important character in the play, and the one with the most lines, comprising a rich web of language at its most complex. Forty-eight performances as Berowne alternated with fifty-seven as Young Marlow in *She Stoops to Conquer,* Goldsmith's merry and durable eighteenth-century romp. Hesitant, stammering, callow but amorous, the role suited him ideally, and—like those for his Berowne—the reviews were ecstatic. To the stated surprise of London critics (most of whom had not seen *A Woman in Love*), Michael Redgrave proved himself a master of character-driven comedy.

During the run of the Goldsmith, he successfully revived his Rakitin in *A Month in the Country* for seventeen performances, and following this taxing trilogy, he dared to scale the summit as Hamlet, which was proclaimed as nothing less than triumphant. "He moves with a new grace and certainty," wrote Worsley in a long essay for *New Statesman,* summarizing not only the critical response but also detailing the elements in the actor's craft that made the achievement possible. "His voice, musical and flexible, has a new richness [with] an absolute mastery of the vocal line. He is beautifully sensitive to the words as poetry, [to] every nuance of every phrase. It is an exemplary performance, without tricks, mannerisms or affectations—absolutely true in every scene. This is a performance not to be missed."

Rachel certainly didn't miss the *Hamlet:* she and Olivier leaped into a taxi after the final curtain of *Venus Observed* and managed to see the last hour of Michael's opening night, an experience that left both of them profoundly moved. "Even my mother, who was not a great admirer of Michael, was in floods of tears at the end of his Hamlet," according to Rachel, who saw yet another hue on Michael's acting palette. "He allowed audiences to glimpse the real insecurities and confusions that bedeviled him. He was really very brave in disclosing through his acting his own personal frailty, and this had nothing to do with indecisiveness—he was not indecisive, and he didn't think Hamlet was indecisive, which is the traditional way of describing the character. No, the frailty was connected to a very deep turmoil in his spirit. Sometimes I felt it would drive me mad, but I saw that he, too, suffered, and I loved him for that."

In June 1950, Michael took his Hamlet to the windy parapets of Elsinore's Kronborg Castle, the play's setting: this was the first of many professional visits to Denmark over the years. Always warmly received, he was ultimately honored by King Frederik IX with the prestigious Order of the Dannebrog, for his celebrations of *Hamlet* and (among other Danes) Hans Christian Andersen, some of whose tales he eventually recorded.

—⁓—

BEFORE HER THIRTEENTH birthday that same year, Vanessa, receiving public attention for her student performances at Queen's Gate, was invited to appear in a photo shoot. Wearing a vintage nineteenth-century schoolgirl's costume—a tall bonnet and a long white dress over pantaloons—she stood patiently for hours under bright lights on a studio set in front of French windows. The picture was published in Doris Langley Moore's bestselling book *The Woman in Fashion.*

By this time, Vanessa had firmly shifted her professional sight from ballet to the theater, a decision confirmed in December 1950, a month before her fourteenth birthday. As the heroine of Shaw's *Saint Joan,* she seemed much more than a talented teenager. "I suppose I connected with the visions, hearing the angels and the church bells and their messages to Joan—that was what struck me." After her plaintive cry "How long, O Lord, how long . . ."—as stage light pinpointed Vanessa's large blue eyes and pale features—the mother of another student turned to Rachel: "I don't believe what I have seen." The applause in the school auditorium was thunderous, but Vanessa scarcely heard it: she considered only what she thought had been miscalculated in her performance.

After three evenings of her Joan, there was so much talk about Vanessa at school that *Queen* magazine dispatched the renowned celebrity photographer Angus McBean to take pictures of the eldest in the Redgrave family's next generation of actors. "Vanessa Redgrave already shows signs of possessing considerable acting ability, and she wishes to follow a stage career," ran the accompanying text.

"After that, the whole school revolved around Vanessa's personality," said Michael with little hyperbole as he dashed off to the Netherlands for a series of dramatic readings. "Having a father who is an actor has its disadvantages," Vanessa told a reporter. "It means we do not see much of him. We like it when he's making a film, because then he's home by tea-time."

In the late autumn of 1950, Michael was indeed making a film, but he was rarely home for afternoon tea. The picture—his second of three under the direction of Anthony Asquith—remains one of his signature movie roles and was certainly one of the decade's most acclaimed performances by any film actor. Terence Rattigan's one-act play *The Browning Version* had a good London run in 1948 and early 1949. For the movie version, Eric Portman was to have repeated his success in the leading role, but Michael stepped in on short notice when Portman had to honor other commitments. The leading role is potentially a star-making part; it can also be the downfall of an actor too intent on calculating every nuance in order to win the sympathy of the audience.

The narrative of *The Browning Version* is simple, the emotions complex. Forced into early retirement, mocked by his students, ignored by his headmaster and betrayed by his wife, the classics instructor Andrew Crocker-Harris has long suppressed his feelings of failure as a teacher, scholar and husband. His hard exterior, that of a narrow-minded martinet, is finally breached by the kindness of one boy, a student who gives him, as a farewell present, a translation of the *Agamemnon* of Aeschylus by the poet Robert Browning. That scene provides a deeply wrenching catharsis, for the teacher and the audience, when the apparently rigid, unfeeling Crocker-Harris breaks down weeping after reading what the boy has written (in the original Greek) as a dedication in the book: "God from afar looks graciously upon a gentle master."

Although preproduction time was short and the shooting schedule abbreviated to four weeks, Michael applied his usual meticulous methods of preparation. He tried different styles of eyeglasses without finding the right pair, and so he supervised the design of rimless lenses. Insisting that he had to affect precisely the right pinched vocal tone for a nervous, repressed academic whom time and life have diminished, he requested multiple screen tests with sound. He then chose carefully the blond tint for his hair, which the black-and-white film would represent as dull gray.

After this expert planning, his performance for Asquith was a marvel of tragic sensitivity, free of arch sentiment and yet pitiable in its depiction of a man who has been sidetracked from his early idealism. Acting with delicately shaded feelings precisely right for camera close-ups, Michael provided glimpses of (as the character says) "a certain sickness of the soul" even as he made Crocker-Harris recognizably human and finally sympathetic—not at all a case study in mere stony repression. Brian Smith had played the role of a page in the recent *Love's Labour's Lost,* and Michael wisely recommended him for the part of the kindly pupil, Taplow. Looking younger than his eighteen years and acting with an admirable lack of coyness, Smith gave Redgrave the proper subtle timing for the deeply felt scene in which Michael had to choke back his sobs. ("I've got a headache," Michael told Corin on returning to Bedford House from Pinewood Studios that evening. "I had to cry so much.")

When it was released early in 1951, *The Browning Version* brought Michael a level of international honor he had not known since *The Lady Vanishes.* The words *faultless* and *masterful* were frequently used to describe this performance, and many critics pointed out that Redgrave was a rare kind of artist: a handsome star who is also a character actor capable of evoking shudders, anger, sympathy and even tears of pity from a cinema audience. At the Cannes Film Festival in 1951, Terence Rattigan won the award for the best screenplay of the year, and Michael Redgrave was named best actor. If there were no other permanent record of his career than this one picture, it would be sufficient to prove that he was a great artist, able to indicate with his eyes, with small gestures and with slight shifts of tone the contours of a shattered soul—and the potential for redemption.

—m—

THE AGREEABLE AND skilled Anthony Asquith completed his direction of *The Browning Version* after a tight shooting schedule, one week of it spent on location at a school in North Devon. Michael finished the necessary post-dubbing in late January 1951 and prepared to move for several months to Stratford, where, as part of the Festival of Britain, the history plays of Shakespeare were to be presented as a unified tetralogy. From March through September, he played Richard II, Hotspur in *Henry IV, Part I,* the Chorus in *Henry V* and directed *Henry IV, Part II.* As if his work in the historical plays had not been sufficiently challenging and arduous, he was also a poetic and imposing Prospero in *The Tempest*—"a performance of extraordinary human warmth and a dominating largeness of heart [that is] neither forced nor condescending nor priggish," wrote a critic, summarizing the consensus.

That spring at Stratford, reviewers also wrote in reverential tones about the acting of twenty-five-year-old Richard Burton as Prince Hal in *Henry IV, Part I,* an achievement that provided evidence of his talent as a classical actor and greatly contributed to his popularity and drawing power in theater and films. "It was apparent to all of us even then that Burton was destined to become a great star," recalled Rachel, who was not acting with the company but remained to help as Michael's dresser.

At one point, Michael dashed up to London for three days, to film a cameo appearance in the all-star movie *The Magic Box,* about the early days of motion pictures in Britain. That quick trip included an unhappy visit with his mother. In recent years, Margaret had made occasional forays onto the stage, always in minor roles. But her alcoholism was now so advanced that Michael had to arrange for her to be admitted to a clinic—a confinement she terminated by simply quitting her room and walking out the nearest door to a waiting taxi. She was sixty-seven but looked over eighty and was now a constant anxiety to her son, who subsequently brought her to Stratford, paid her hotel bills and then included her in a late summer family holiday at the seaside, where her grandchildren scarcely recognized her. Once again, Margaret virtually ignored Rachel but was expansively friendly toward Bob, despite his refusal to supply her with gin. But Margaret was resourceful and somehow obtained what she wanted.

At the same time, it was clear—to Rachel, at least—that Michael was drinking excessively, too. His performance schedule was never affected, although he occasionally dropped a few lines, and too many boozy evenings caused predictably bad mornings. In addition, he began to monitor every nuance of his physical, emotional and psychological states: in his diary, he noted in obsessive detail that he slept badly or well . . . that he felt worse or better . . . that he had drunk too much or not too much . . . that he felt happier on this day or depressed on that day. This may have been simply an extreme form of the actor's self-awareness, the consequence of having to be constantly in peak condition every evening. The burnished tools of the trade, after all, often include a terror of losing one's voice, of illness, of forgetting lines or of transposing a scene.

He also experienced bouts of stage fright, especially if he knew that important colleagues were present. On the premiere night of *Richard II,* for example, Michael felt that his first act was "never better." But during the interval, he saw the Oliviers in the audience, "and their presence throws me for a loop, and I am defeated for Act 2 . . . Act 3 better but I am miserable about [my] performance." Part of his discomfiture may also have come from his interpretation of the role, which he chose to play, unevenly, as the most extreme parody of a mincing dandy—"a dainty, feline homosexual," as one of his most supportive critics wrote of a performance evaluated by many as widely off the mark. This exaggeratedly fey performance may have been Michael's way of distracting himself: the day before, he had broken the big toe of his left foot at dress rehearsal, and on opening night he felt considerable pain as he walked and pranced about.

Vanessa, Corin and Lynn, spending the summer holiday at Stratford, attended the first performance of Michael's Richard, and Lynn held her mother's hand for the duration of the play, crying quietly, "It's so sad, Mummy—it is so sad." There were happier moments: "Every afternoon we played tennis," Vanessa recalled, "or hired a boat to row on the Avon. We played endless sets of tennis with the actors William Peacock, David King and Robert Shaw, who befriended us." And every evening, Rachel and the children went to the theater, where Vanessa was particularly captivated by Richard Burton's performances.

—⁂—

DURING THAT STRATFORD season, Bob remained in Chiswick. "He still has hopes of a job," Michael noted in his diary. "But we are unconstrained with each other, and very happy"—to which he added, "It is five years for me and B," and in 1954: "B and I celebrate seven years."

That autumn of 1951, they were extremely discreet, and usually Michael invited Rachel to accompany them to a restaurant or social event to silence any wagging tongues. In addition, Michael also enlisted Bob, whom the children loved, as a kind of companion for them or even, it was sometimes implied, their uncle. "With Vanessa, Corin and B to see [the film] Samson and Delilah," Michael noted in his diary. There were many such occasions, some of them to better movies.

In June, Guy Burgess and Donald MacLean defected to the Soviet Union, an event that led many to make the outrageous claim that being gay was tantamount to treason. As spies, Burgess and MacLean thus confirmed the belief that homosexuals were by definition destructive of the nation's welfare. In light of that, the British government instituted a virtual witch hunt to find and dismiss gays from important posts; entrapment became common; and men were routinely arrested after consorting sexually with other men who—voilà!—at once revealed that they were policemen. "Homosexuals in general," said the Tory home secretary David Maxwell-Fyfe, "are exhibitionists and proselytizers and are a danger to others, especially the young." Homosexuality was therefore regarded as a contagious virus, spread by a secret society of sex addicts aiming to corrupt the good youth of Britain.

This campaign of antihomosexual hysteria destroyed the lives of many, including the eminent scientist Alan Turing, who had broken the Enigma code, been a hero of World War II and was a primary contributor to the invention and development of the computer. Arrested and prosecuted for homosexual activity in the privacy of his home—under the same Sexual Offences Act that ended Oscar Wilde's career and left him a broken man after hard labor—Turing was subjected to chemical castration, was disallowed entry into the United States and finally committed suicide at the age of forty-one.

William Field, a popular Labour Member of Parliament, was also arrested and prosecuted; Ian Harvey, a Tory junior minister, met the same fate; the writer Rupert Croft-Cooke was sent to prison for nine months for having committed "acts of gross indecency"; and John Gielgud was the target of a police sting. Between 1940 and 1955 the number of arrests for homosexual behavior increased by 600 percent. Before 1950, British newspapers made almost no reference to homosexuality, but in that year, the reporting began. "Evil Men" was one of the most alarming stories, and the November 1953 issue of *News of the World* enthusiastically supported a Metropolitan Police plan to abolish "vice" in the capital lest there be an increase in homosexuality itself. That would have been a hilarious notion were it not patently, pathetically ignorant.*

The decriminalization of same-sex relations among consenting adults was still more than a decade away, and gay men and women had to lead secret lives or risk ostracism. The result was a furtive and often dangerous subculture, ringed with fear and a great deal of self-denial, especially by young people not yet established in significant careers. In such a climate, the number of miserable, forced marriages was past counting. The Redgrave marriage had not been forced; nor was it undilutedly miserable. Michael and Rachel loved each other in their fashion, but the union was clearly characterized by a lifelong series of unconventional compromises and crises. Neither of them was adept at self-denial, and Michael, especially, pitched himself into a subculture that had dark and dangerous venues.

—⁓—

AS A WAY of supplementing his income that year, Michael considered writing a memoir. The idea began with Nicolas Bentley, at the publishing firm owned by André Deutsch; beginning in December 1951, a casual correspondence began. There was no contract, and Bentley made no demands about a final submission date for the manuscript, but for unknown reasons, Michael did not like André Deutsch personally.

---

* The official silence about lesbianism was not broken until 1956, when any sexual assault committed by one woman against another was added to the Sexual Offences Act. But this statute did not criminalize female homosexuality: it was simply designed to put heterosexual women on guard against possible threats from other women. (The British government insisted that all women in the military were "very feminine and interested in men"—see the note.)

When a better offer came from Williams Collins Publishers, he signed with them.

In August 1952 Michael informed the editor F. T. Smith at Collins that he had begun writing the first chapter, but a year later he admitted that he had not. The "stumbling block," as he called it, was his mother, then still alive. By 1960 Margaret had been dead for two years, and that September, Michael informed Smith that he had begun the book and was making good progress. But by 1962 he had nothing to show, and ten years after that, there were still no pages. Finally, on June 5, 1981—thirty years after Deutsch and Collins broached the subject—Michael Redgrave made a deal with Weidenfeld and Nicolson (and, in the United States, with Viking Penguin) and was paid a $70,000 advance. The book was finally published in 1983, but Michael had almost nothing to do with the writing of the book that bore his name as author. That function was fulfilled by his son, Corin.

—∞—

RACHEL BEGAN 1952 in good spirits, back in the West End on January 30 in the appealing supporting role of the warm but disapproving "Maman" in the London premiere of Samuel Taylor's Broadway comedy *The Happy Time.* Among the other actors in the play about an eccentric French Canadian family in the 1920s was Peter Finch, who had been imported from Australia in 1949 to appear in a play with Edith Evans and was now deeply involved in a romance with Vivien Leigh.

Olivier had been the producer of *Venus Observed* and, delighted with Rachel's performance, had engaged her for *The Happy Time* (which had only a modest four-week run). Vivien then swung craftily into action, ignoring protocol and effectively losing all discretion. Aware of the unorthodox marital situation at Bedford House, she asked Rachel for a key to the guest studio for her assignations with Finch. "Her request put me in an extremely awkward position," said Rachel years later, "but what could I say?" Michael, who was spending part or all of most weeknights around the corner with Bob, could hardly object, for Vivien knew of his double life—Rachel had confided everything—and Michael knew that she knew. Had everyone been less anxious, this might have played out like a scene from a Fey-deau farce. In any case, Vivien soon had her trysting place, but they were all on the lookout for an unannounced visit from Sir Laurence.

Adding a further arabesque to this byzantine pattern, Olivier was still the managing producer at the St. James's, and he asked director Sam Wanamaker to cast Michael in *Winter Journey.* This American play by Clifford Odets was actually *The Country Girl,* a prize-winning success with a long Broadway run. (The title was changed for the English premiere in order to avoid confusing audiences, who, it was feared, might mistake it for *The Country Wife.*)

Before a contract was signed, Michael dispatched the most energetic and inspired comic performance of his career, in Asquith's brilliant Technicolor film of Oscar Wilde's *The Importance of Being Earnest.* His costar was none other than Edith Evans, as the redoubtable Lady Bracknell; none in the cast had any notion of her past history with Michael.

At that precise time, as his diaries indicate, Rachel spoke to her husband about his drinking, and immediately he thought it would be fascinating and perhaps salutary for him to accept the part in *Winter Journey* of a once-popular actor in alcoholic decline. Marinated in guilt, completely lacking self-confidence and entirely dependent on his wife after the accidental death of their son, he is supported by this "country girl" who was once a vibrant and attractive woman but is now both weary and cheerless.

"Michael Redgrave shows us how very perceptive he can be," wrote Darlington. "He is always a good actor, but when he is given a chance to make a study of a human misfit he is apt to give performances with a special quality of rightness. Here, his picture of weakness and failure is so true to life that it exposes the falsity of Odets' last act, in which Odets pretends that the failure can redeem himself and climb back to the position he held before drink got him. But Redgrave's acting blows this convenient fable to smithereens."

Before resigning from the role after thirty weeks, Michael convinced audiences and critics that this ruined character was indeed once a man who touched greatness—it was "the best serious performance he has given us for years," as Kenneth Tynan wrote. Apparently, the cultural advisers to Her Majesty agreed, for that season Michael was awarded the CBE (Commander of the Order of the British Empire) by Queen Elizabeth II—not a knighthood, but an honor signifying royal recognition of significant service to the nation.

The reason for Michael's withdrawal from *Winter Journey* was an academic commitment he honored that autumn at Bristol University, where he had been engaged to deliver four lectures and then to revise them as a book. For a modest fee but guaranteed publication, he was a scholar in residence in his hometown, warmly received by students and the general public.

Early the following year, the lectures were published to favorable notices as *The Actor's Ways and Means*. Discursive, erudite, witty and occasionally a trifle pedantic, the book reveals the enormous breadth of Redgrave's scholarship, his relaxed familiarity with the history of worldwide drama, and his ability to select examples from his own experience to illustrate important points. His central theme is a paradox expressed in the final lines of the last lecture, and it reveals as much about Michael Redgrave the man as it does about Michael Redgrave the theorist of acting: "For the real actor, the only place where he is truly at home is on the stage—whatever kind of stage it may be . . . In the spiritual sense, he is only at home when he is not himself. To be at his real home, he will tear himself away from loved ones, lover, life itself."

On December 17 he and Bob arrived in New York, where Michael granted interviews to promote the American release of *The Importance of Being Earnest*. After three days, the couple then went to the Caribbean. At home in London, Rachel and the children coped with a bitterly cold winter.

Nine

TOM

(1953-1956)

⎯⎯⎯∞∞∞⎯⎯⎯

ECALLING HER FATHER'S FREQUENT ABSENCES DURING HER CHILD-
hood, Lynn Redgrave was frankly bitter for many years: "Our
lives revolved around our father's work, [and] he was never there
when I wanted him to be. He did not take into account my presence in
the world."

Vanessa understood her sister's resentment, but she had a different
perspective on Michael's coldness: "When he had a large part to play
in the evening, Michael seldom enjoyed company or talked much." He
did not live the part during the day, but "he kept himself in readi-
ness mentally, like a boxer before a big fight, or an athlete before the
race. And because he was never satisfied to repeat what he had done
the night before, he was often distracted and sometimes irritable." At
home, then, Michael was perhaps not so different from countless others whose careers depend on presenting themselves in top form outside the house, performing or singing or playing musical instruments,
with virtually no possibility of stopping suddenly to rectify an error (as
movie actors can). Some manage better than others the intensity of live
performances, and some are more attentive and generous to others in
their social orbit.

Whereas Vanessa was exposed to the theater from an early age,
Lynn, perhaps inevitably and logically, developed a pastime that was
unique in her family. Once she was free from the cycle of childhood
ailments, she kept a pony in Wimbledon, rode with a trainer when she

could and dreamt of the Olympics. "I was an equestrian—that was my absolute passion." For about seven years, she "lived for riding," as she put it. "I trained and trained, went to horse shows in the summer and fox hunts in the winter. Being a Redgrave didn't get in the way—it wasn't a horse-world name, and I was already sick of the effect my name had on people." Her horse was "my one and only real friend." In this regard, her achievements were hers alone, "not attributable to my family."

Before the end of February 1953, Bob and Michael returned from their Caribbean holiday, for the Redgraves were soon to begin rehearsals at Stratford, where they remained for much of the year; the children joined them during the summer.

Rachel was delighted to return, for the first time in almost twenty years, to the place where she had so memorably launched her career. Just as much, she relished the collaboration with Michael. "She loved acting and especially loved acting with Michael," Vanessa remembered. "She taught us to punt [on the Avon], which she had learned from Grandpa Eric, showing us how to trail the pole behind in the water so it would act as a rudder and stop the boat careering helplessly from bank to bank. She took us to tea at the Lygon Arms in Broadway, told us about the deer in Charlecote Park which Shakespeare is said to have poached, and seemed as happy as I had ever seen her."

One of the great seasons in the history of Stratford, the 1953 repertory included three plays each for Michael and Rachel.

His leading roles in *The Merchant of Venice, Antony and Cleopatra* and *King Lear* again required prodigious feats of memory. First, his Shylock, exhausting and impressive, was judged lukewarmly: "Some things he did superbly," wrote Kenneth Tynan in a representative review, "but he simply could not fuse the villainy of the part with its sardonic comedy." Most critics offered similarly faint praise, interlaced with serious reservations about his overplaying. Vanessa had read and studied the text with her father, and she had asked about the charge of the play's anti-Semitism, which Michael rejected. "His speech 'Hath not a Jew eyes?' was a furious denunciation of anti-Semitism," she recalled, "and he wore the Star of David—'the badge of all our tribe'—on his cloak [i.e., his costume] with defiant pride." The critics gave this scant attention.

Michael had more difficulties during the April preparations for *Antony and Cleopatra.* "It's a very curious leading part," he said years later, "because it has all the appearances of nobility and strength, when in fact Antony is a weak man—and except for what Enobarbus says about him, he's not a very noble man; at least you never see him doing anything noble. You have to create convincingly the image of a man who held part of the world in thrall, and you have very little to do it with. All you have is his voluptuousness."

At the last rehearsal, Michael suddenly forgot major portions of the text. Corin and Vanessa were present, and as he recalled, "I saw my father stop over and over again to ask for a prompt. He was wearing his costume, of course—wig, beard, makeup and so on, and yet he hardly seemed to be there." Overcome by what seems to have been a panic or anxiety attack, Michael retreated to his dressing room. Rachel was rehearsing elsewhere, and it was left to Peggy Ashcroft, his Cleopatra, to sit with him quietly for a half hour and then to guide him gently and firmly back to work. The crisis soon passed; as Vanessa recalled, "the next night, he was triumphant."

Whereas reviewers had detailed their disappointment over his Shylock, there was little disagreement about Michael's Antony. "With this performance, Redgrave's place among the great is sealed," insisted Richard Findlater, who never hesitated to criticize. "There is no time to think about the actor's skill: this is Antony."

Rachel had the role of the hapless Octavia—Antony's wife, betrayed by his obsession for Cleopatra. She found the sadness and strength in this character and conveyed a kind of transcendent nobility in Octavia's suffering, and although she spoke only a dozen times in the play, Rachel seemed to make the character present even when she was offstage. Similarly, as Elizabeth, wife of Edward IV in *Richard III,* she was, according to one reviewer, "all urgent concern and compassion."

But it was Rachel's Regan to Michael's Lear that earned the kind of praise she had enjoyed many years earlier. "Rachel Kempson is the most impressive of Lear's three daughters," wrote Alan Dent in the *News Chronicle,* "with her acute and surprising study of a pale and handsome lady who has turned from sweetness to sadism and enjoys it."

Perhaps to no one's surprise, the press covered her husband's performance in greater detail—and in the most glowing terms. "Michael Redgrave has played King Lear and won," Tynan wrote, and almost every drama critic agreed. Reflecting on his father's performance many years later, Corin felt that Michael played the role "in a very large way, like an Epstein sculpture, which doesn't have a great deal of detail, but it imposes itself by its mass and contour. It was something monumental, huge."

—————

FOR RACHEL, LIFE offered more than professional endorsements that summer of 1953. After her recent sessions with Charlotte Wolff, she had begun to see "that other relationships would not be out of the question," and now that possibility became actual.

Glen Byam Shaw was co-manager of the Shakespeare Memorial Theatre, and he directed *Richard III* and *Antony and Cleopatra.* Tall and aristocratic, intelligent and articulate, Glen fell in love with Rachel, and she responded passionately. He was also a man who had seen and experienced a good deal of life and who certainly understood Michael: before he married, Byam Shaw had enjoyed long affairs with the poet Siegfried Sassoon and then with the actor, playwright and composer Ivor Novello. "He was a great charmer with a crazy, almost lecherous passion and a wild, gleeful humor," recalled the director Tony Richardson. By 1953 Glen had been married for over twenty years to the actress Angela Baddeley; they had two children and were believed to be a happy, ideal couple in the theater.

In August Glen and Rachel went farther than their usual walks along the banks of the Avon and began a romance that lasted for decades. "The relationship took place during my father's lifetime," Corin recalled, "and everyone knew of it"—even (as Rachel added) Michael, "who was relieved," and Angela, "who loved [Glen] so much that she would put up with anything."

"If only married partners would generously allow each other a little latitude, how much more easily marriages could stay together," Rachel said years later. "A person *may* only ever love one man or woman in the world; that is fortunate. But it seems to me that if a husband and wife can be generous and understanding to each other in this respect, they can love each other even more deeply." For some, that is as it may be—it certainly was so for these two couples.

The rest of Rachel's long life demonstrated that she was nothing like the shy English rose she was commonly thought to be. Her career in the theater and her marriage to Michael; her long periods of sexual frustration and the nagging ache she must have felt seeing her husband repeatedly in love with men; Vivien Leigh's "joyful" affair (as she described it) with Peter Finch—all these elements led her, from that year, to reply to life with spirited and unconventional answers.

"The only thing that bothered me," said Vanessa forty-five years later, "was when my mother and father made each other unhappy. Their relationships with their respective partners didn't matter—that was immaterial. What mattered was that sometimes they made one another unhappy." Corin also believed that Michael was "frightened that he would be 'outed,' and he dreaded the consequences for us children." At the same time, his father and Bob continued to be known euphemistically as "very close" in theater circles, where strong gay relationships have never been unusual.

In her published memoir, Rachel disguised her long romance with Glen Byam Shaw, referring to him briefly and obliquely only as "Tom." Of her marriage at that time, she said simply, "It was not totally fulfilling for either of us. And so I met a member of the company who was to change my life for many years. We knew of course that we would never be able to marry because of our commitments. This realization was extremely painful." She and Glen were rarely separated for more than a few weeks from 1953 until 1980.

—⁂—

THE SEASON AT Stratford was exhilarating and gratifying, intense and arduous—but it paid no one a living wage, for the Memorial Theatre was not a subsidized institution at that time. Returning to Bedford House in mid-autumn, Michael's anxiety increased, and the reason for his panic attack at Stratford now became clear. Bailiffs had been hounding him there, and now, back home, he received an alarming telephone call from his new accountant, a man named Walter Smee. This just had to be Captain Hook's chubby right-hand man, "Mr. Smee," said Corin gleefully, having recently seen the Disney animated version of *Peter Pan* at a London cinema.

But the real-life Mr. Smee amused no one that day, and Corin's joke failed to lift the gloom that descended on Bedford House. Most solemnly, the accountant informed Michael that his failure to rein in expenditures and to pay an overdue tax bill of £16,000 had rendered him, according to Corin, "nearly bankrupt. He was highly imprudent in everything to do with his finances, and his notions of economy were bizarre—like raging about the house, switching off lights." Money had to be found quickly, or the government would impound the family's home and possessions for the taxes Michael owed.

Nil desperandum, Mr. Smee then intoned learnedly: there was no reason to despair, for a ready source of good cash could be found in film work. Within weeks, Michael had signed contracts to appear in eight pictures, made almost back-to-back, between January 1954 and May 1955. His new agent, Cecil Tennant (who also represented the Oliviers), quickly collected sufficient funds as down payments, and with that, the Inland Revenue was dissuaded from knocking on the door. Before Michael began work on his movie schedule, however, the Redgraves rejoined the Stratford troupe for a tour of *Antony and Cleopatra* in London, The Hague, Antwerp, Brussels and Paris.

Then Michael undertook his marathon of movie roles: in *The Green Scarf, The Sea Shall Not Have Them, The Night My Number Came Up, The Happy Road, The Dam Busters, Oh...Rosalinda!! [sic], Confidential Report* and *1984.* Except for *The Dam Busters* (the true story of the so-called bouncing bombs Britain used against the Nazis), none of these pictures had the prestige of *Mourning Becomes Electra* or *The Browning Version;* Michael always insisted that he dispatched these jobs only for the income: "There is the rent to pay, and the children's school bills."

—⁂—

AS HER HUSBAND moved from this studio to that, Rachel—perhaps finding new confidence from her relationship with Glen Byam Shaw—achieved fresh successes onstage. In April 1954 she portrayed a thoroughly affecting peasant martyr, at once rude, devout, fearful and yet rooted in faith, as George Bernard Shaw's *Saint Joan,* at the venerable Q Theatre. (Corin, during his spring holiday, had a wordless cameo as a court page.)

In September, Rachel followed with a memorable performance as Thea Elvsted in *Hedda Gabler,* with Peggy Ashcroft in the title role. In their memoirs, none of the Redgraves had a word to say about this—a curious lacuna considering the high esteem in which Rachel was held for this play. Contrasted pointedly in wardrobe, gesture, tone and manner to Ashcroft's savage Hedda, Rachel's selfless Thea was a study in quiet, loyal devotion. As a woman who risks everything to help the man she loves, knowing that she will not be cherished in return, Rachel found the lineaments of a character that suited her perhaps more than any other. She played it to perfection, and those who saw the production always remembered her poignancy and radiant credibility. Peggy, whose Hedda was one of her greatest achievements, considered Rachel the finest actress ever to portray Thea.

The production was first seen at the Lyric, Hammersmith, where it was quietly and respectfully (if not enthusiastically) received. The reason for the lukewarm response became clear when the company went on tour to Dublin before returning for a West End engagement. The Irish audiences reacted to the play as if it were a farce, for the director, Peter Ashmore, had imposed on the production a tone and a misplaced sensibility that had turned a tragic drama into drawing room comedy. "Peggy and George [Devine, also in the cast] were worried about the production, which we all felt had been unsatisfactorily directed," Rachel recalled. Near despair, they decided to ask for help from none other than Glen Byam Shaw, who met with them as the show's unofficial doctor, supervising additional rehearsals before the London opening and giving the players notes; he effectively saved the show.

Until March 1955, *Hedda Gabler* continued perhaps the longest and surely the most admired run in its history. From Westminster, the company proceeded to the Netherlands and Denmark, a tour Rachel remembered as "enormous fun." Finally, they arrived in Norway, Ibsen's birthplace, where King Haakon VII warmly greeted the cast and arranged for them to meet one of the playwright's cousins.

—⁂—

WHILE RACHEL WAS finding new depths and fresh rewards in her career, seventeen-year-old Vanessa experienced a political awakening. In May 1954 she read a long news item about the Vietnamese effort to overthrow the American-backed French occupation of the country. "I was ignorant of the history of French imperialism in Indochina, but I knew immediately that I was very glad to read that the Viet Minh had won." When the war was officially declared to have ended on July 21 and the country was divided into North and South Vietnam, "I thought it was the end of that cruel period." Of course it was not an end at all, and for Vanessa, this was only the beginning of a lifelong hatred of imperialism and war.

In 1952 she and five classmates had traveled for three weeks by train to Florence, Rome and Bologna. Now, during the summer of 1954, Michael gave his daughter a present to celebrate her graduation from Queen's Gate: two months in Italy, where she studied in Tuscany, lived with an Italian family and again traveled widely. As her father had quickly learned German and French, so Vanessa returned to London in September virtually fluent in Italian and more than acquainted with the works of Dante and Machiavelli, among other writers.

She was impressed most of all by Antonio Fogazzaro's novels, particularly *Piccolo mondo antico,* written in 1896. A historical romance with the interconnected themes of family problems, political betrayals and social renewal, the book treats of the Risorgimento, seen through the moving chronicle of the Maironi family. "The 'little ancient world' became as real to me as the hot sun," Vanessa recalled, writing long and detailed letters to Michael and Rachel, full of literate observations about Fogazzaro's cries for social, religious and political reform. It is perhaps not at all surprising that this novel would appeal to her, for it was "an artful, romantic story about two strong-willed lovers caught in political conflict," as one scholar has succinctly said.

After that, she read the Italian diaries of the Russian exile Alexander Herzen, the accounts of Garibaldi and Mazzini, and the story of Mazzini's retirement in London. "An Italian novel, some black-and-white photographs, some phonograph records, a porcelain figure and the diaries in Italian of a Russian exile—these few and varied mementoes of history guided my attitude to the political struggles of the 1950s." Vanessa also passed an advanced qualifying examination in Italian language and literature, which would have served her brilliantly had she chosen to seek employment as an interpreter.

Returning to London that autumn, she met Michael during one of his few intervals from filming. When she spoke of her political education, "my father did not wish to talk . . . but he glowed with pride when I told him about the oral [examinations in Italian]" and the offer of an interpreter's job. Instead, she resumed dance instruction—tap dancing this time, and voice lessons with Jani Strasser, who had coached Michael during preparations for *The Beggar's Opera*. Her father encouraged a career in musical comedy, but Vanessa was "yearning for the lights of Stratford-upon-Avon, the plays of Shakespeare, and [a career like that of] Peggy Ashcroft . . . so I told my father I wanted to go to drama school."

At the December holidays, Rachel was still performing in *Hedda Gabler* and preparing for its European tour. "Bob gives me dinner," Michael wrote in his diary on New Year's Eve. "I go home to go to bed but instead play duets with Corin and so am awake when R[achel] comes back [from the theater]. Vanessa out at party . . . She and Corin have a lot of invites, and she is often off to dance parties. . . Lynn starts to cry about some pain in her neck and says she gets it twice a year. This makes me cross and intolerant. R says 'There is no freedom in this house,' which should make me laugh—and does, to a limited extent. Lynn in tears to bed. Row with Rachel and then it suddenly seems silly to both of us and we begin the New Year again in comparative peace and happiness."

—⚏—

NINETEEN-FIFTY-FIVE BEGAN WITH snowfall and a flurry of activities. Michael left for Vienna, to record songs for the movie *Oh!... Rosalinda!,* a reworking of *Die Fledermaus;* from there he sent a telegram congratulating Vanessa on her eighteenth birthday. Armed with a collection of acting manuals and a long article her father had published that month, she had just emerged from a week's study in her room before beginning a three-year program at the Central School of Speech and Drama.*

Since its founding in 1906 by Elsie Fogerty, the CSSD had become one of the finest academies in the world for the study of theater arts, and Fogerty's methods influenced many teacher-training programs. Bishops sent young clerics to her, and she opened a clinic of speech pathology at St. Thomas's Hospital, where she treated patients whose voices had been compromised by congenital malformation, illness or trauma. The school emphasized speech training above everything, and that focus remained unchanged even after Fogerty's death in 1945. All courses supported the primacy of proper elocution: physical training and dance were aimed at correct breathing; fencing was taught to develop rhythmic movement as an aid to coherent speech; and even the classes on costume design and deportment were linked to a study of speech patterns in the history of English drama.

At the Central School, Vanessa was following an impressive list of alumni, among them Laurence Olivier, Peggy Ashcroft, Claire Bloom and Harold Pinter. That year, Judi Dench was one of her classmates; she recalled Vanessa as a shambling, awkward, disorganized figure—too tall, too dependent on eyeglasses, too outspoken in her criticism of old-fashioned teaching methods, and one who gave scant evidence of the treasure buried within. "The only class at which she then excelled was Restoration Monologue," according to one of her directors. "But it

---

* On August 24, 1954, Michael was given time off from filming *The Dam Busters* to deliver an address at the British Film Institute's Summer School, held that season at the Edinburgh Festival. His lecture, about his movie work, was published in the BFI's magazine *Sight and Sound* in January 1955; Michael expanded it for his 1958 book *Mask or Face.* See the note.

astonished everybody in the school that this chaotic young actor was the only one who could pick her way through this notoriously difficult discipline and make perfect sense."

On the morning of March 20, Michael's forty-seventh birthday, Vanessa, Lynn and Corin awakened him with songs and presents. Bob gave him a Dunhill lighter at breakfast, and then Michael went to the airport to meet Rachel, who had concluded the tour of *Hedda Gabler.* "A very happy day," he noted in his diary. "R looks well!" Ten days later, Michael was at the airport again, departing for Denmark, where he attended a celebration of the 150th anniversary of Hans Christian Andersen's birth and read Andersen's famous story "Grantræet—The Fir Tree," the tale of a little tree that constantly dreams of future glory but fails to appreciate each happy moment that blooms in its life.

At Michael's request, R. P. Keigwin, once his house master at Clifton College and then a lifelong friend, translated the tale from Danish to English. Michael's sixteen-minute reading (preserved in a fine recording) began with a rush of youthful cheer before slowly descending into dark foreboding—a light, clipped, allegro baritone gradually retarding to a bass whisper. In yet another instance of his careful scholarship, Michael worked for two weeks with Keigwin, a scholar and writer internationally famous for his renderings of Danish literature into English. Michael prodded him for hours on just the right choice of words to express Andersen's richly idiosyncratic Danish, and then rehearsed the words, returning to Keigwin for careful work on the memorable final words: ". . . nu var den forbi, og træet var forbi og historien med; forbi, forbi, og det bliver alle historier . . . Now all that was over, and it was all over for the tree—as it is with the story. That's what happens at last to every story—all over, all over."

The final effect of Michael's reading was profoundly elegiac, and the audience that day, before standing to applaud, was silent for a full minute when he sat down. The conclusion to the story was a calm proclamation of death come too soon, after everything and everyone had gone unappreciated.

Sir Michael Redgrave
(circa 1946)

Rachel Kempson
Redgrave (1936)

Edith Evans with Michael Redgrave in
The Country Wife (1936)

Michael Redgrave, Dame May Whitty and
Margaret Lockwood in *The Lady Vanishes* (1938)

Noël Coward (1940)

Michael Redgrave as Orin Mannon
in *Mourning Becomes Electra* (1947)

Margaret Scudamore Redgrave
(circa 1950)

Michael Redgrave and Jean Kent in *The Browning Version* (1951)

Vanessa Redgrave
(circa 1961)

Vanessa Redgrave and
Tony Richardson (1962)

Vanessa Redgrave in
Blow-Up (1966)

Corin Redgrave (1966)

Lynn Redgrave (circa 1977)

Vanessa Redgrave and
Franco Nero in *Camelot* (1967)

Tony Richardson
(circa 1970)

Lynn Redgrave and Geoffrey Rush in *Shine* (1996)

Natasha Richardson (circa 1991)

Joely Richardson (circa 1998)

THAT YEAR, MICHAEL joined Peggy Ashcroft, Benjamin Britten, E. M. Forster, Edith Sitwell, John Masefield and others in calling for an end to the death penalty in Britain. And he did not discourage Vanessa when she joined Benn Levy and Constance Cummings in the campaign against the proliferation of nuclear weapons by the superpowers. In fact, he shared her viewpoint, and this conviction was reflected in his next choice of role.

Immediately after his return from Denmark in April, Michael began rehearsals for the Christopher Fry adaptation of Jean Giraudoux's antiwar play *Tiger at the Gates* (originally *La guerre de Troie n'aura pas lieu*), which was now twenty years old but had lost none of its sting; in fact, the play was perhaps more powerful than it had been in 1935. It was a pointed satire not only on the great Homeric characters but also on the recurrent follies of human nature and its inclination to wage war. Michael assumed the role of Hector precisely because Giraudoux presented the character as battle-weary and determined to avoid a disastrous conflict.

Under the sure hand of the American director Harold Clurman, the run of *Tiger at the Gates* began at the Apollo on June 2 and received overwhelmingly favorable reviews, which was no surprise to Clurman: "Michael Redgrave is so intelligent that he destroys all by himself the silly notion that actors are or ought to be stupid."*

"This is a monumental piece of acting," wrote Tynan about Redgrave in *The Observer,* "immensely moving, intelligent in action, and in repose never less than a demi-god." But on opening night, Michael fell from a stage platform—an accident that alarmed everyone in the theater, for it took a moment for the star to recover. "What did you think of when you were down?" Clurman asked during the interval after rushing backstage. Michael took only a moment before replying puckishly, "Well, I thought I'd better get up!" The production played to full houses for thirteen weeks all summer long.

This fresh acclaim, so welcome a tonic after the long and exhausting

---

* For the sake of *Tiger,* which had been long in the planning, Michael rejected an offer to play Professor Henry Higgins in a new musical titled *My Fair Lady,* which opened in New York the following March (and was a boon to Rex Harrison's career).

cycle of movie assignments, should have carried Michael through the summer in high spirits. But there were problems with Bob Michell, who had compounded Michael's financial crisis by constantly borrowing cash, promising to repay the loans—and then offering lame excuses for defaulting. Michael was unable to force the matter, which had the predictable result of a new and serious strain on the relationship, but when Bob asked to accompany him to New York for the American run of *Tiger,* Michael refused him.

Before the end of the year, Bob returned to the United States—a departure unmentioned in Michael's diaries. He resumed his old job in California, and his separation from Redgrave lasted for several years, marked only by Bob's occasional greeting card at Christmas.

Tiger at the Gates, after a healthy Broadway run of 217 performances, was named the best foreign play of 1955/1956 by the New York Drama Critics' Circle, and Michael's performance was called "towering, in the loftiest play of the season," as Brooks Atkinson wrote in *The New York Times.* "Mr. Redgrave is one of England's two or three most eminent actors. He has an imposing figure, which is an asset to any classical actor, and he uses it magnificently. An actor of wide experience in many kinds of parts, [and] a conscious artist who has studied his craft, he plays Hector with skill, passion and intelligence and grandeur. Mr. Redgrave not only cries peace but also gives peace a mind and heart. To Giraudoux's brilliance and sagacity, he adds the power of a superb piece of acting."*

Harold Clurman echoed the assessment: "He combines intelligence with instinct, diligence with inspiration [and] his surface effects are impeccable, his feeling profound." But Clurman had to step in once, advising Michael that he was pushing the play's jokes too hard, and that his makeup and hair were becoming more and more flattering. "He is shy and easily hurt," Clurman recalled, "and eager to be loved. But it was just these childlike qualities that endeared him to me."

---

* In January, Michael suffered a damaged eardrum during a fight scene onstage and required a physician's care for several weeks.

At forty-seven, Michael was beyond the threshold of talent and achievement: he had entered fully prepared into the realm of authentic greatness as a man of the theater. But his status and reputation made no impression on the U.S. Department of State. One morning that autumn, not long after his triumphant opening night, he received a summons from the State Department. At an interview in Manhattan, authorities inquired about his political opinions and the strength of his loyalty to the United Kingdom—questions whose legality he rightly suspected, but to which he replied, fearful of possible deportation. To the inquiries about his political ideologies—questions no doubt occasioned by his antiwar convictions—he answered with a question: "Is it likely—is it *really likely*—that Her Majesty the Queen would have conferred on me the honor of Commander of the Order of the British Empire, the CBE, if I were in fact an untrustworthy subject?" As he later commented, "This statement, delivered in a voice full of hurt and moral indignation, ended the interview." The American government did not trouble him again.

―ᴍ―

For the New York engagement of *Tiger,* Michael received a net income of $30,910 over seven months. He reported the amount to Walter Smee, who replied that this was very welcome news, but that Bedford House would have to be sold the following year in any case: such a grand residence would be impossible to maintain on an uncertain annual income. Michael disguised his disappointment over this development during a three-week Christmas holiday with Vanessa, who arrived in New York on December 17 and stayed with her father at his sublet apartment on East Fifty-second Street. In a marathon of theatergoing, she saw, among other memorable plays, *A View from the Bridge, Cat on a Hot Tin Roof, The Lark, A Hatful of Rain* and *The Diary of Anne Frank.*

Vanessa was also invited to observe for a week at the Actors Studio, on West Forty-fourth Street, where she saw both established and apprentice actors improvise, work on scenes and then submit to criticism from the guru in charge, Lee Strasberg. Vanessa had understood from Michael, and from her own reading and her own experience, that actors must always proceed from the meaning of the text to any analysis of a play and their part in it. But Strasberg insisted that the starting point must be the actor's personal experience, inner life and present feelings about that inner life. At eighteen, Vanessa was fearless when voicing opinions, even when others might think them inappropriate to the moment—and so she raised her hand, asking Strasberg to elaborate. He replied that the character's situation and place in a play were irrelevant—the truth of the actor's feelings and his own convictions were primary.

"I was not convinced," Vanessa told her father, and so he attended a session at the Studio, too. "It may be an excellent workshop," he said not long after, during a lecture at Harvard University, "but some of the methods and exercises are paralyzing and destructive—and, not to put too fine a point on it, a damn nuisance in the theatre. The Method as it's practiced here [at the Actors Studio] is laborious, slow and heavy. A person seems to need to think for forty seconds before he answers a question! But you don't have to *feel* something before you perform it—that's a corruption of Stanislavski."

Redgrave insisted that Stanislavski maintained what all good actors of instinct have always assumed: that the truth of a role is found by doing it—and that an actor need not stop to discover the analog of a personal feeling before attempting to play it; in fact, the subjective emotion ought to be sought only in very rare cases. "The essence of Stanislavski's teaching is that it helps you to know what to do when your instinct tells you that something is false," Michael insisted. He rejected out of hand Strasberg's doctrine that the actor's only raw material is personal experience: "Too many of Mr. Strasberg's pupils seem to believe that the actor's work begins and ends in himself."

In this regard, Michael was much closer to the principles of the actress and teacher Stella Adler, who had broken with Strasberg over this same issue: "Don't use your own past when you approach a role," she insisted. "Use your creative imagination to create a past that belongs to your character. I don't want to see actors self-consciously sticking with their own past histories. That's too small, and your own life is too little—you have to get to the character's life. The actor's job is to communicate the play, not himself."

Adler agreed entirely with Redgrave: "Stanislavski [with whom she had studied in Paris] instructed his actors to be prepared to act and to discover the truth of their acting through the doing of it—not to 'feel everything' before they do it." The injunction made by Strasberg—"to turn ever inwards onto their own personal problems"—as Michael saw from his own observation, was potentially fatal for success as an actor. In the final analysis, the profoundest theories are sometimes rooted in the deepest common sense.

Just past noon on the day he left Vanessa at the Actors Studio— because he had to perform at a matinee of *Tiger*—Michael was approached by one of Strasberg's students, a sometime actor and aspiring director named Fred Sadoff.

Eighteen years younger than Michael, Frederick Edward Sadoff was slim, dark-eyed, good-humored despite unfortunate financial circumstances, and bounding with energy, with plans for his future as a writer and director—and with ideas, some of them interesting. He had appeared in the choruses of musicals and in small roles on Broadway and had recently directed a new play at the Phoenix Theatre, under the management of Norris Houghton. That play, *The Terrible Swift Sword,* by Arthur Steuer, had had a run of eight performances; worthy of the Theatre of Cruelty, it concerned the staff of a military school who commit appalling acts of sadism that were graphically simulated onstage. (A review described the work as "horrifying, brutish, blood-curdling and generally abominable.")

According to one of Michael Redgrave's directors (who was also a friend of Corin), some mutual friends regarded twenty-nine-year-old Fred as "self-serving, pushy and undoubtedly out for what he could get." The actor Peter Eyre knew Fred and noticed "a slightly sinister trait" consistent with *Swift Sword,* "and he was a demanding and needy friend." Acquaintances judged that Fred actually had very little talent and no sense of what worked in the theater—but there was no question that he loved everything to do with the stage, and he was fierce with ambition to succeed. All the caveats notwithstanding, Michael was doomed from the first hour of meeting: days later, Fred Sadoff became the latest grand passion in Michael's life, and the third American. When Vanessa departed for home in January, Fred moved at once into Michael's rented East Side apartment and secured the position of his new assistant.

The run of *Tiger* continued until early April. Michael then traveled to Harvard University, where he delivered the Theodore Spencer Memorial Lecture on April 22. T. S. Eliot had been the inaugural speaker in 1950, and Arthur Miller had ascended to the same dais in the Sanders Theatre. But Michael was the first actor to address the university in this prestigious series. His presentation was titled "Mask or Face: Reflections in an Actor's Mirror." He spoke wittily but seriously; his remarks were scholarly as well as entertaining; and his unorthodox survey of performance history was enlivened by a polite but pointed critique of the Actors Studio, which made his lecture both timely and controversial. He left the theater that evening to prolonged applause.*

Also in April, *A Month in the Country* opened at Norris Houghton's Phoenix Theatre. Michael directed but was not in the cast of the production, for which he was paid $500 a week for the five weeks of the run. He also negotiated a contract for Fred to receive half that amount, a very high salary indeed, "to assist in directing and rehearsing the play," with the additional clause "that Fred Sadoff shall perform his duties under your sole supervision and direction, and shall not receive any billing credit whatsoever."

Meantime, Rachel received a telephone call in March, informing her that bankruptcy would very soon have to be declared—with all the consequent problems then and later—unless Bedford House were sold at once. Coincidentally, the previous owners were willing to repurchase it; the details of transfer were quickly resolved; and Rachel found a large flat for the family in Hans Crescent, Knightsbridge, just behind

---

* This lecture was slightly expanded and became the first chapter in Michael's book *Mask or Face,* published two years later in London. The remainder of the volume contains his essays or other transcribed lectures that appeared in periodicals (*New Theatre, Sight and Sound, World Theatre*) or in compilations by others (*Talking of Shakespeare, Actors on Acting*).

the vast precincts of Harrods department store. The new home was a sprawling, high-ceilinged four-bedroom residence they decorated with damask draperies, rich carpeting, antiques, a grand piano and photographs and posters from plays and movies in the Redgrave-Kempson history.

—⁂—

CONTINUING HER DISCREET rendezvous with Glen Byam Shaw, Rachel also performed in television dramas, just as they were beginning to be more frequently broadcast in England. At the same time, Vanessa was in her last year at the Central School, performing in scenes from Shakespeare, Beaumont and Fletcher, Wycherley, Congreve and Farquhar, George Bernard Shaw, Ibsen and J. B. Priestley. Corin, meanwhile, had become a brilliant young scholar at the Westminster School, achieving highest marks in literature, history and languages, attending West End plays when he could—and sharing with Vanessa his aspirations to be a teacher, a writer or perhaps an actor. He also won the All-England Sabre Championship in the youth division and was told by his fencing master that if he dedicated himself, he might represent Britain in the 1960 Olympics.

Later, Corin's first wife recalled the "charmed relationship and tight bond" between brother and sister, who complemented each other so ideally—"Corin the intellect, Vanessa the romantic; Corin the teacher, Vanessa the pupil; Vanessa the magnetic, Corin the competitor. Both tall, blond, handsome, with charismatic presence and flashing blue eyes." People sometimes felt that neither gave precedence to any other person. "I will never find for myself a man like Corin," Vanessa once said.

At thirteen, Lynn felt outside the circle her older siblings had created for each other, although there was never any sign of conscious exclusion, much less of unkindness. Rachel recognized Lynn's feelings of marginality and made time to be with her at riding exhibitions and special school events.

On May 8, Michael returned to London from New York, with Fred replacing Bob. "As children, none of us knew about our father's lovers,"

Lynn said years later in a filmed documentary. "Bob Michell and Fred Sadoff were brought in as part of the family, but we didn't know just how much family they really were." In Lynn's published memoir, Fred is not mentioned; in Vanessa's autobiography he is described in passing as "a close friend of Dad's"; in Rachel's book he is mentioned once as Michael's producing partner; and Fred's name is nowhere to be found in Michael's autobiography. Otherwise, there seems to be only one extant written reference to Fred by a Redgrave—when Rachel, writing to Michael, described Fred *tout court* as "your lover."

This collective silence about Sadoff after the passage of so many years and after his death can be explained only by the fact that generally the Redgraves did not warm to him. "Some people thought he used my father," Corin said, "and in a way he did. But I think he got no more from their relationship than he gave. Though he could never replace Bob in my father's life, he gave a great deal, [and he was] indomitably cheerful, funny and loyal after a fashion."

Days after their arrival, Michael and Fred attended Lynn's second performance in a school production of *A Midsummer Night's Dream* at Queen's Gate. "Daddy never comes to concerts or school recitals," Lynn wrote in a memoir styled like a running chronicle. "I'm sure he'll think I'm good as Theseus, I've worked very hard at it. I fantasize about his comments: 'Brilliant, Lynny! . . . I never knew you were so talented . . . You spoke so well . . . You looked just like a duke.' Then my teacher whispers, 'Your father has arrived. Middle of the fifth row' . . . During the first Titania scene, I peek through the curtains to see how Daddy is reacting. His seats are empty." For Lynn, that evening had the dimensions of a youthful trauma, resentfully nurtured as the major source of antipathy she felt toward her father for years to come.

—⁂—

WHEN THE FAMILY relocated from Chiswick Mall to Hans Crescent, quarters had to be found for Fred. But he could not immediately secure a work permit and (like Bob) had to depend on Michael for everything. A small but adequate flat was found for him a few minutes away, just across Brompton Road in Rutland Street. And concurrent with this flurry of activities—school examinations, end-of-term plays, packing and moving, Rachel's television schedule and Michael's preparation for two more movie roles—along came a momentous development in London's theatrical life, and Rachel Kempson was part of it.

At the suggestion of the director and actor George Devine, the designer Jocelyn Herbert, a young playwright named John Osborne, and a twenty-eight-year-old Oxford graduate named Tony Richardson, Rachel was invited to be a founding member of the English Stage Company. She valued teamwork and appreciated new writers with fresh ideas, and so this enterprise inaugurated the most stimulating time of her career. (Michael, who would otherwise have been asked to join, too, had commitments for the next three years.)

Some months before, the ESC had been the joint inspiration of playwright Ronald Duncan, producer Oscar Lewenstein, composer Benjamin Britten and the Earl of Harewood, the queen's cousin and a scholarly patron of the arts. As artistic administrator, they chose forty-six-year-old Devine, who had just worked with Richardson on a television drama. The goal of the ESC was to produce new British and foreign plays in repertory (with the occasional revival of a classic), and to present a theater of and for writers of serious contemporary and, if necessary, controversial works.

Their first task was to find a professional home, and they settled on the intimate Royal Court Theatre, on the east side of Sloane Square in Chelsea. Its distance from the West End soon became the symbol of a new and independent theatrical identity and of fresh artistic goals. The aim was not to be iconoclastic or overtly activist, or to be associated with a political agenda, but rather to be a popular company mounting plays that had been rejected for production by the less adventurous commercial theater. The ESC also wanted to appeal to a younger audience less interested in stars and glamour than the typical patrons of the West End were, and they hoped to draw playwrights and actors from all classes in society.

This was a risky endeavor, for in and around Shaftesbury Avenue (London's Broadway) the commercial theater survived by offering standard thrillers such as Agatha Christie's *The Mousetrap,* light-hearted musicals such as Sandy Wilson's *The Boy Friend,* American imports (there were fourteen in 1955) and an endless series of breezy, impossibly artificial drawing room comedies. The West End, in other words, was very much a venue for those who preferred mostly unde-manding and polite fare: the exceptions, such as *Tiger at the Gates,* proved the rule. The ESC, on the other hand, did not want to offer plays with dinner-jacketed characters raising champagne glasses and cigarette holders, cavorting in penthouses or country estates. American playwrights such as Arthur Miller, Tennessee Williams and William Inge had tackled unconventional social issues on Broadway, but En-glish producers were generally hesitant to offer anything controversial.

When Rachel arrived at the Royal Court in March for rehearsals, she joined an impressive list of repertory players, among them Kenneth Haigh, Mary Ure, Nigel Davenport, Rosalie Crutchley, Joan Plow-right, Alan Bates and Gwen Ffrangcon Davies. "We all felt that we were part of something important—even historic," Rachel said later. "We rehearsed one play during the day and performed another that evening, and we were paid next to nothing—a few pounds a week, as I recall—but it was very stimulating because it was more than just a theatrical company, it was a repertory company with a plan and a purpose."

Under Devine's direction, the English Stage Company's first two plays opened on April 2 and 9, and Rachel appeared in both—first, a comedy of manners, Angus Wilson's *The Mulberry Bush*; and then Arthur Miller's *The Crucible.* Most critics complained that the Wilson play was not a premiere (it had been performed at the Bristol Old Vic) and that the Miller was neither British nor new. But the third offering, John Osborne's *Look Back in Anger,* caused an uproar of critical controversy and established a new tone and fresh concerns in the English theater. The world premiere of that play was given on May 8, just as Michael and Fred were arriving on the *Queen Elizabeth* from New York.

Vanessa attended as many ESC rehearsals as she could. Coinciden-tally, at the Central School, she, too, was preparing to act in scenes from *The Mulberry Bush.* This play concerned a family of socialists, and Vanessa was to play one of them—a woman based on the reformer Beatrice Webb, who cofounded the London School of Economics. She had also read the Miller play and was "enthralled" by its treatment of hypocrisy and political expediency, although at the time, she did not recognize "its greatness, nor its contemporary significance." But important notions were now coming into the orbit of her consciousness concerning the nexus between society and the theater.

Pitching herself into the inaugural season of the ESC, Rachel was working close to exhaustion that spring and summer: after *The Crucible,* she portrayed a very old woman with an ear trumpet in *Cards of Identity,* a satire about a conspiracy; and then she was a cigar-smoking Asian in *The Good Woman of Setzuan,* a role that made her physically ill each evening. Then Rachel began to suffer from abdominal pains, and that autumn, a peptic ulcer was diagnosed, forcing her to withdraw from the demanding ESC schedule.

The pressures of work, the stresses in her marriage, the sudden arrival of Fred Sadoff, whom Michael had pitchforked into the family, and even the thorny logistics of arranging her trysts with Glen Byam Shaw had finally brought Rachel to the point that she needed "a place for myself, where I could get away from London." Her mother and a cousin offered cash gifts enabling her to purchase a pair of ramshackle gamekeeper cottages in the middle of a dense forest on the edge of Odiham Common near Basingstoke, Hampshire. Rachel supervised the conversion of the cottages into one two-story house, but the interiors had to be completely modernized.

With great enthusiasm, she also oversaw the reconstruction of a wooden bridge over a small ornamental lake, Wilks Water (which gave the new house its name). She also replanted the English gardens with climbing roses, clematis and honeysuckle, and she planted pots of her favorite flower, blue hyacinth. Wilks Water became the Redgrave family's weekend retreat, although Michael always preferred London.

That summer, Michael and Fred toured the French countryside on their way to meet the actor-director Gene Kelly, who had engaged Michael for a brief role as a blundering general in a film called *The Happy*

Road, produced in Paris and Provence. On their return to London, there was a darker part waiting, in Joseph Losey's confusing and somewhat hysterical movie *Time Without Pity.* Michael portrayed a trembling alcoholic, released from a sanitarium to visit his estranged son, wrongly accused of murder and about to be executed. This was perhaps Michael's only embarrassing appearance on-screen, as he repeatedly pinched the bridge of his nose, apparently confusing acute anxiety with a sinus headache.

Ironically, this was one of only two leading film roles Michael had for the rest of his career, and it was sadly appropriate to his life at the time. "I like him immensely," Losey said, "and his gifts are more than acting—he's an intellectual, a poet, a literary man and an innovator in the theatre. But he's being completely destroyed by alcohol."

Ten

GHOSTS

(1956–1960)

I N THE AUTUMN OF 1956, NINETEEN-YEAR-OLD VANESSA REDGRAVE suddenly felt that her training to be an actress was utterly meaning-less. Appalled by the crisis in Hungary and the futile democratic up-rising that was being brutally crushed by Soviet intervention, she wrote to her father in America, asking permission to travel to European refu-gee camps as a humanitarian volunteer. He admired her goodwill but, concerned for her safety, urged her to do what she could from home; hence she worked late hours after classes, collecting clothes and funds to be sent abroad and learning about the long arm of imperialism.

Michael was in New York that season, directing and performing on Broadway in *The Sleeping Prince;* Fred Sadoff, living with him in genteel comfort, was listed in the Playbill as his assistant. The plot of Terence Rattigan's Ruritanian trifle was gossamer thin: in London on the eve of the coronation of King George V in 1911, the philan-dering prince regent of Carpathia meets an American chorus girl. Reluctant to be seduced by a man for whom love is so perfunctory, she demands royal treatment. The prince yields to her request for gypsy violins, recites verses from *Antony and Cleopatra* and pleads for her ennobling love. Taking all this seriously, the girl refuses to leave the prince, and her sunny common sense brings him down to earth and up to love.

The Sleeping Prince was handsomely designed and the actors splendidly costumed; Rattigan, however, correctly judged his own play as "mucky and trivial." The public's curiosity to see Laurence

Olivier and Vivien Leigh together onstage had sustained it for eight months in London three years earlier, but the New York production had no such good fortune: it opened on November 1 and closed before Christmas. (Rattigan was buoyed, however, by the enormous success of his concurrently running play *Separate Tables,* a superior drama that opened on Broadway a week before *The Sleeping Prince* and ran for a year.) "Michael Redgrave squanders his talents in this insipid parlor charade," according to a major review that also criticized his direction as "tiresome" and "lacking in ironic gaiety." He wholeheartedly agreed with this judgment—and received no better reviews for his American television debut, in a musical version of *Ruggles of Red Gap,* broadcast live from New York on February 3, 1957. Miscast, he admitted that he got through rehearsals without much food "but on too much vodka."

Four days later, Michael and Fred arrived in Saigon to begin work on the movie version of Graham Greene's novel *The Quiet American,* under the direction of Joseph L. Mankiewicz. Audie Murphy, the most decorated and celebrated American soldier of World War II, was now diffidently pursuing a movie career for which he lacked both temperament and talent: he was cast as the Yankee of the title, while Michael had the difficult leading part of a jaded reporter. Thanks to Michael, Fred had a small role and was also paid as Michael's personal assistant.

After four weeks location shooting in Vietnam and six in Rome for studio interiors, Michael was no happier with the result than Mankiewicz, who was under pressure to soften the novel's critique of American imperialism in Southeast Asia. A romantic triangle substituted for political intrigue and arid dialogue for action; later, the director agreed that the picture was essentially a failure: "I wrote the adaptation and directed the picture during a very unhappy time in my life, and it turned out to be one of the worst films I ever made." Michael had feared this outcome when script changes were distributed to the cast daily during the shooting. He also felt that Mankiewicz was attempting, with Murphy, "to get a performance out of an amateur." Of the entire project, Michael was later frank in his resentment: "What could have been a great picture has missed its mark by a mile. It was one of the biggest disappointments of my life."*

After the picture was completed in May, Fred returned to London, where Michael had arranged a lease on a flat for him in Egerton Gardens Mews (quite close to Hans Crescent) and had set up a nominal company to expedite Fred's work permit: FES Productions, named for his initials. He also agreed to guarantee Fred's income as his assistant.

———

WHEN MICHAEL RETURNED to London early that summer after an extended holiday in Italy with Rachel, he had been away for a total of ten months. At once, there was bad news along with the good. The latter came with Vanessa's graduation from the Central School of Speech and Drama on June 4, when she was awarded the esteemed Sybil Thorndike Prize for her acting achievements. The following day, impresario Peter Hoar invited her to join his professional summer theater company at the coastal town of Frinton-on-Sea. Until her scheduled arrival a month later, she worked at a Chelsea coffee bar (one pound daily, plus tips) to augment the guarantee of seven pounds weekly at Frinton that summer.

The bad news for Michael took the form of a detailed report from Mr. Smee that, after the Inland Revenue had taken 80 percent of his salary for *The Quiet American* to pay back taxes, the Redgrave bank account had a total balance of £2,000. He and Rachel had firm offers from Glen Byam Shaw to return to Stratford in 1958, for a combined salary of £100 per week plus housing. But that would not be forthcoming for a year, and in any case would certainly be insufficient income. Consequently, Michael had to "get back on the treadmill," as he said, which meant returning to film acting, radio dramas and documentary narrations to supplement his income. Very gently, Rachel asked about a reduction in the monies going out to Fred, but that topic was not open for negotiation.

———

* When Rachel came down to Rome for a visit during studio filming, Mankiewicz hired her to record the voice of Michael's wife, heard off-camera while he reads her letters.

At Frinton, Vanessa performed in ten plays over ten weeks. Her debut role was a small one in the comedy *The Reluctant Debutante,* but then she had the lead in *Look Back in Anger.* (There were few reviews of the Frinton season, and none of Vanessa's performances.)

"More than anything else in the world, I wanted to show [Michael] what I could do," Vanessa recalled, but as they sat in a pub after her performance, "he said very little, and I began to fear that he had not been impressed. For what seemed a quarter of an hour, my father looked out of the window, or at the space above my head, and drank whisky." He then said that he had been offered a part in a movie, and that he wanted to suggest her for the role of his daughter; that evidently signaled his approval of her professional debut.

"For Vanessa, he was much the most important influence upon her life as an artist," according to Corin, "and he worshiped her talent as if it had nothing to do with his own—and yet he was always very watchful and objective." That evening at Frinton, he did not share the audience's enthusiastic response to her performance, for he found her somewhat shrill, trying too hard in a role that required no histrionics—but he saw a significant talent that could be tempered and burnished.

Michael insisted that Vanessa lose weight, and so he sent her off to a dietician, who at once prescribed no more than four ounces of protein daily, a quart of liquid, a serving of lemon juice, some sliced tomatoes and a few diuretic pills. This was more than severe; it was downright dangerous, but as Vanessa recalled, "My father was obstinate, and I was determined not to let him down. Rightly or wrongly, he insisted that I take weight off—which I seriously did."

Her weight dropped from 156 pounds to 119 by the time he successfully campaigned for her to appear with him in the medical melodrama *Behind the Mask,* in which she played his daughter. In the picture, Vanessa had little to do but react shyly to the romantic attention of her father's rival, but reviewers took notice and her photograph appeared on the cover of *Picture Show* magazine. "Saw Vanessa's scenes with Tony Britton in rough cut and wept for joy," Michael noted in his diary that autumn.

—m—

HE WAS PROUD of her motion picture debut, but Vanessa refused all film offers for the next eight years. Not only did she regard herself on the screen as "stupid and ungainly," but she also disliked the insipid movie roles sent for her consideration; instead, she concentrated on the theater.

As it happened, a good play for Vanessa's West End debut came along immediately—again, through her father's intercession. For his return to the London stage after two and a half years, Michael chose N. C. Hunter's family drama *A Touch of the Sun,* about the contaminating effect of extravagant wealth on the family of an idealistic teacher, who must also confront his own failed career and miserable marriage. Hunter, Redgrave and producer Binkie Beaumont unanimously agreed that Vanessa was perfect for the role of the teacher's daughter, and director Frith Banbury agreed: "How exciting it was when Vanessa walked on stage, and we saw that particular quality of vulnerability, power and beauty. She read three or four lines at an audition, and I turned to Binkie and said, 'We obviously won't get anybody better, and I can really, truthfully, say that. There will be no charge of nepotism.'" Rehearsals began in October for a tour before the London premiere in January. But there were complications all along the route.

For one thing, Vanessa fell in love with Dinsdale Landen, the actor playing her brother in *A Touch of the Sun,* and they enjoyed what she called "wonderful times"—until she learned that he was committed to the actress Jennifer Daniel, whom he subsequently married. This disappointment Vanessa took with equanimity, but then another problem arose. She was stymied by the sudden change in her father's behavior. He was having problems with Fred, who still had no means of support; and Michael's alcohol consumption was now occasionally affecting his ability to memorize dialogue.

Frith wanted to raise the issue of Michael's drinking when he accepted an invitation to lunch one Sunday at Hans Crescent. He arrived to find his host pacing nervously, for Margaret was about to arrive, and

Michael said he hoped that Frith, who had known her for years, would succeed in tempering her drinking that day. Before Frith could discuss his concerns about Michael, Margaret arrived—"pretty far gone with gin already," as Frith recalled—and she asked for a gin and tonic. After one sip, she shouted, "More gin!" and then began a loud, unpleasant invective against her son: he had lost his way, she said; he was ruining his career; he was simply no good. "She was just dreadful," according to Frith, "and he was in agony in her presence. I wasn't surprised when that sent him back for gin refills, too."

—᷈—

AS REHEARSALS FOR *A Touch of the Sun* continued, Michael offered Vanessa suggestions on how to play her role—"but only when she asked," he recalled. But that was not her recollection: "My dad gave me very harsh criticism—it was like a nonstop master class, and sometimes I was very frightened working with him because he was very demanding. That was tough, and sometimes I wished the master class would stop." Corin was present for the last rehearsals, and he recalled that his sister "had a very difficult time acting with Michael, who was a severe critic. Working with him was invaluable but also torture for her—what a harsh and unsparing taskmaster he was, and it must have been quite painful for her. He was forever handing her notes on how to improve her performance"—which, of course, he was not officially directing—"and she found the experience agonizing. He had high hopes for her, and he was not going to let up at all. He told her everything she was doing wrong. He had a very acute eye, and it can be painful to be watched by an acute eye. Most people would have been broken by this, but not Vanessa."

But there was an important, even career-transforming, moment in their collaboration one evening as they left the theater together, when she told her father that she was disappointed in herself. "Yes, and you let everyone know it," he replied. Vanessa explained that her discomfort derived from the feeling that Caroline, her character in the play, would not do such and such a thing or speak some words written for her dialogue.

"And why not?" her father asked.

"Well, if I were in that situation," Vanessa continued, "I wouldn't do and say that."

"But you are not Caroline," Michael said. "Your job is to play *her*—not yourself!"

This was perhaps worth all the difficulties in their relationship that year, all the harshness of his tutelage and the discomfort she felt over his imperious attitude during preparations for her West End debut. Years later, Vanessa was able to articulate what had happened that winter evening in 1957. "We are so conditioned to start from ourselves that all too often, when we consider a character in a play, we proceed from a word here or a phrase there, and instead of considering the character and the given circumstances that make them act the way they do, we are in reality considering only ourselves." With those words, Vanessa identified the source of what goes wrong in very many performances onstage and in films.

—⁂—

WITH THE CHRISTMAS greetings that year came the announcement that Corin had won a scholarship to Cambridge, for he had graduated near the top of his class at Westminster, where he acquitted himself especially well in literature and languages. He had also performed in Latin a major role in the school's presentation of the ancient Roman comedy *Miles Gloriosus,* by Plautus. "The great joy of Christmas has been C's scholarship," Michael wrote in his diary on December 23, adding less happily, "I retire disconsolate after trying to pacify both Rachel and Fred." On New Year's Eve, Rachel went down to Wilks Water with Glen Byam Shaw, while (Michael added) "darling Fred stays the night with me."

After playing to audiences in Blackpool and Brighton, *A Touch of the Sun* opened in London at the Saville on January 31, 1958—one day after Vanessa's twenty-first birthday. "Vanessa a distinct hit, an enormous success," wrote Michael, accurately summarizing the critical consensus about her performance. He, too, was very well reviewed, and when the *Evening Standard* Theatre Awards were announced at the end of that year, he was cited as the best actor of 1958. The play continued for eight months, but Michael left the cast after three: he was committed to rehearsals and then a long season at Stratford, and he was in the midst of a literary project he longed to complete.

The previous year, while walking alone in the country, Michael began to wonder, "What makes an actor *tick*?" and it occurred to him at once that this question might be the basis for a story. Now, in the spring of 1958, he began work on his only published work of fiction, a novella titled *The Mountebank's Tale,* the strange and haunting account of an actor and his understudy that is the most revealing insight he provided into his divided self. Written in a structure reminiscent of Henry James, the *Tale* became a story within a story within yet another story—a kind of allegory of Michael's lifelong dilemma, the split in his own nature; it is also a meditation on the actor's simultaneous awareness and forgetfulness of self.

"I am a ghost, haunting my life," says one of the protagonists of the *Tale.* "What drives me is a flight from myself." The narrator and the subject of the story within the story are, in the words of the text, and like its author, "fascinated, obsessed even, by the problem of the acting temperament. He wanted to know what made an actor an actor."

That this should have been Michael's obsession is not surprising, for he was aware that his public self was a pretense, a triumph of showmanship. In a recurring nightmare he had, he regarded his own reflection in a mirror after applying heavy makeup in his dressing room. He then gazed helplessly as the cosmetics slid down his face onto his chest, and then he beheld no face at all in the mirror—but only a blank where his face had been.

This is precisely what lies at the center of the story—the double's dream:

"It was hot, unbearably hot, in my dressing room [at the theater]. My hands trembled as I applied my make-up, and the greasepaint would not stay in place, but would slide around my face and into my ears and hair like drops of oil on a pond . . . I looked in dismay at the mirror, and there I could see the make-up slowly start to drain down my face, over my chin, down my neck and onto my chest . . . and there, on my chest, was the greasepaint portrait of my face." The false face was something he had to lose—but what remained would perhaps be nothing at all.

The Mountebank's Tale is dedicated "To my daughter Vanessa," and in the book, the character's daughter takes stage center at the end of the tale—just as Vanessa's recent accomplishments in school and onstage augured well for her future. "Acting isn't private theatricals in front of the family," says the actor at the end of the tale. "It's 'out there,' in front of all 'those faces' . . . Try to make her see sense!" That last sentence summarized his relationship as father and mentor to his daughter, whom he regarded as the primary heir of any talent he had to bequeath.

—⚏—

AT THE AGE of fifty, Michael was preparing to appear as Hamlet at Stratford (for £10 a week), when he received a card from Bob Michell, who had recently married. "I don't suppose I will be hearing from you anymore," Bob wrote, "except for greeting cards at Christmas. I only wanted to tell you that I wish you success for the season [at Stratford] and I hope you are happy with F[red]." Three years later, there was more personal news from Bob: "Were you pleased that I named my son after you? I had to have a Michael around to always remind me of you."

As he had for Bob, Michael found work for Fred. That same season, thanks to Redgrave's intercession, Fred was employed as assistant to Glen Byam Shaw for the production of *Hamlet*. This situation resulted in the curious arrangement, like a variation on *La Ronde,* of a director (Glen) aided by an assistant (Fred) whose lover (Michael) knew that his wife (Rachel) was the mistress of the director. The entire company at Stratford seems to have known who was involved with whom; most of all they resented not the sexual high jinks, but the fact that Michael's assistant was an American. As for Rachel, she assumed three roles that season: Lady Capulet in *Romeo and Juliet,* Dionyza in *Pericles* and Ursula in *Much Ado About Nothing*.

Meanwhile, Vanessa was appearing in minor roles at the Royal

Court, while fifteen-year-old Lynn spent most of the summer in Stratford with her parents. "If being a Redgrave child had its problems," Lynn recalled, "the big plus was our exposure to great theater." That season, her father patiently explained the plot of *Hamlet,* and then she saw him perform it several times.

Richer in detail and more haunting than his earlier portrayal, Michael's slightly mad young prince was terrifying, and the consensus was that he had achieved one of the great highlights of his career. According to Vanessa, he listened to the ghost's opening speech with agony pouring out of him: "My fate cries out!" was shouted full voice, she recalled—"as if his lungs and heart were strained to breaking point." That he performed this role in repertory for six months at Stratford (concurrent with his Benedick in *Much Ado*) may be counted as nothing less than heroic, doubtless due to his reduced alcohol intake that season. In December and January, the Stratford company then shoehorned the entire season into a three-week tour to Leningrad and Moscow, where audiences—their tickets subsidized by the Soviet government—responded zealously to Shakespeare in English.

There was one significant interruption that season, when Michael's mother died in a nursing home on October 6, at the age of seventy-four. "Drink destroyed her personality and character," Corin wrote without exaggeration. The last decade of her life, after Andy's death, was a sad and self-destructive downward spiral in which she alienated everyone and became bitter, lonely and incapable of any human connection. "I am ashamed I could not help her more," Michael wrote in his diary; "really ashamed and dreadfully pained and depressed. Of course she was partly out of her mind," but he also remembered the early times, when her life seemed so full of gaiety and promise. "He was sobbing, absolutely sobbing," Lynn said of the day Margaret died. "But that night he went out [onto the stage at Stratford] and gave one of his greatest performances, as Hamlet."

That experience, and her memory of it, left Lynn "spellbound," as she said, and during the season, as she watched her parents on- and offstage, she began to wonder if there might be a place for her in the theater, too. The decisive moment came several days after she saw the gold-and-pastel, Regency-inspired Stratford production of *Twelfth Night,* with a historic performance by Dorothy Tutin as Viola. "Shakespeare's immaculate play of mistaken identity transformed me," Lynn recalled. "But could I act?" She had performed only at school, in a Christmas pageant and in scenes from *A Midsummer Night's Dream,* which her father had missed. "Nothing was expected of me—unlike Vanessa and Corin," Lynn recalled. "This was both immensely unflattering and very freeing. My parents were deeply shocked when I eventually said I wanted to go to drama school."

Rachel replied that Lynn had to want the theater as much as life itself, a creed echoed by Michael, who said publicly and perhaps brutally, "You can't really be at your best as an actor unless you want to act more than anything else, and that really means to the exclusion of everything—even your home and your family. You've got to get to the point where the day only really begins when the curtain goes up."

—⁂—

FOLLOWING THE FAMILY tradition was not Corin's first ambition during most of his time at Cambridge. Tall, blond, athletic and blue-eyed, he was bookish and idealistic, personable and self-confident; in fact, for a time it seemed as if he would become a classical pianist (for which, even more than his father, he had a marked talent).

"He didn't laugh at silly things as much as the rest of us did," recalled his classmate Ian McKellen, "but he could tell a story well, with killer punch lines. If his eyes sometimes looked beyond you coldly, the argument was hot." Years later, McKellen recalled a day when Vanessa came to Cambridge for a visit and joined them for a stroll along the river. McKellen asked the genus of a certain tree, and Corin replied that it was an oak. McKellen knew he was wrong and showed him the evidence of a fallen leaf that was not oak-shaped. "Ah," said Corin, "that's because it's an unusual type of oak—one you haven't seen before." McKellen protested while Redgrave persisted—until Vanessa took Ian's arm and whispered ironically, "Corin is always right, you know."

Right or not, Corin was regarded as one of the most studious men at college. While classmates hosted parties, sipped champagne, had affairs and punted on the Cam, Corin read; his only other activity, it seemed to many, was acting in or directing student productions. In the spring of 1959, before his twentieth birthday, Corin cowrote, sang and danced in a musical based on Shakespeare's *Love's Labour's Lost,* which ran at the ADC and then transferred for a week to the Lyric, Hammersmith. McKellen, also in the cast, recalled that Corin had "brilliant theatrical insights"—one of which was a piece of advice McKellen applied from that time forward: "Only ever pause before an interesting word."

Vanessa took Corin's counsel to heart, too—but at first, she had little opportunity to practice it. After her first film and her West End debut, her roles were unexceptional, and work at Stratford did little to challenge her. From early April through mid-autumn, she appeared in the crowd scenes of Tony Richardson's production of *Othello* and Tyrone Guthrie's staging of *All's Well That Ends Well*; as Helena, she was somewhat lost in the stage business of Peter Hall's *A Midsummer Night's Dream;* and there was no great reaction to her as the gentlewoman Valeria, in Hall's *Coriolanus,* with Laurence Olivier. None of these productions showed her to best advantage, although Richardson remembered that, among the crowd, "she set a record for getting back and forth across the stage with pots and pans on her head—twice as many as anyone else." One of her few reviews took note of her Helena as having "an engaging freshness, almost a piece of clowning."

During 1959, Michael was mostly occupied with supporting film roles (in *Shake Hands with the Devil* and *The Wreck of the Mary Deare*), with promotional activities for *The Mountebank's Tale,* and with preparations, at last, for his production of *The Aspern Papers*. There was one gratifying interruption when, on June 13, it was announced that he was to be knighted. Ralph Richardson, Laurence Olivier, John Gielgud and Alec Guinness had already received that honor, and now, at fifty-one, Redgrave followed.

In the absence of the queen, Queen Elizabeth the Queen Mother officiated at the ceremonies on July 7 at Buckingham Palace. That day, Vanessa was opening at Stratford in *Coriolanus* and could not attend, but she came up to London the following weekend to celebrate: "Ours is a family that rejoices in each other," she told the press, and that was certainly true. For a week, London newspapers published photos of Sir Michael and Lady Redgrave with their three children.

The general feeling in London theatrical circles—an impression Rachel shared—was that Michael's unorthodox sexual life had delayed his knighthood until he was past fifty; for years there had been widespread but quiet talk about his promiscuity, although it was never so much as hinted at in the press. But theater people were aware. Strolling across Leicester Square with a friend, Noël Coward saw the marquee of the Odeon: "Dirk Bogarde and Michael Redgrave in *The Sea Shall Not Have Them,*" whereupon Coward said, "I don't see why not—everyone else has." More recently, there had been stories about Redgrave dabbling in sadomasochistic bondage at grimy private clubs—talk that John Gielgud, at his naughtiest, could not help exploiting when he happened to meet Redgrave in Sloane Street later that summer: "Ah, Sir Michael," said Sir John, extending his hand, "I'll be bound!"

Years later, the actor and writer Simon Callow referred to the "darker and darker" sexual realms into which Redgrave descended, "usually fueled by large quantities of alcohol. This is something that goes well beyond bisexuality or promiscuity. It is an irresistible compulsion, driven by unshakeable guilt and the constant need for endorsement." Ironically, Michael may have alluded to this himself when he said oddly, "I like attempting parts of men in invisible chains."

—⁓—

WORKING AT STRATFORD and always eager for Michael's approval, Vanessa wrote to him, "I wish I could have seen more of you. In London, you are completely occupied, and there are so many people. I feel it is such a long time since I was really *with* you. When we write to each other, we communicate, and when we were in 'A Touch of the Sun'—but here I am, going on about feeling out of touch with you. It has suddenly occurred to me that family life is very deceptive, whether everyone is living together or taken apart by work . . . Well, my dearest, I know you are busy and I don't expect a letter back right away. But I long to know what you think about this. With all my love, your daughter."

Sir Michael Redgrave was in high spirits after his investiture. *The Aspern Papers* (with Fred credited as coproducer) opened in Newcastle-upon-Tyne on July 27, continued to Manchester on August 3 and then had its London premiere at the Queen's on the twelfth. "It feels like a hit," Michael wrote in his diary, and he was on the mark, as critics praised his "signal achievement" as a playwright as well as his performance and those of Flora Robson and Beatrix Lehmann.

Leon Edel, then the reigning Henry James biographer and scholar, wrote to Michael, praising "a very beautiful rendering of a story I have always considered one of James's best. You and your actors have caught the fine nuances and the beautiful pathos of your play"—which ran for more than eight months, until late April 1960. Subsequently performed in a dozen countries, it opened on Broadway in 1962 (with Maurice Evans replacing Michael), and the reviews were rhapsodic: "As rare as it is rewarding, *The Aspern Papers* is a mystery with a heart . . . Michael Redgrave has retained the flowing grace of the literary style, the undercurrent of gentle irony and the detached yet affectionate regard for character." With that, he had achieved distinction as a stage and screen actor, a producer, director, poet, essayist, lecturer, critic, novelist and playwright. Years later, Vanessa appeared with Christopher Reeve in a highly praised West End revival of her father's play.

—⟋⟍⟍—

THE REDGRAVES WERE predictably proud, even as they were coping with their own lives, problems and aspirations—Lynn, perhaps most poignantly, with a lack of immediate purpose and a surfeit of weight. At sixteen, she quit Queen's Gate and enrolled in cooking classes at the Regent Street Polytechnic, perhaps not the wisest choice, for, as she remembered, "we stirred up soups and hors d'oeuvres, meat and fish entrées with potatoes and vegetables, and delicious desserts—and then we ate the lot for lunch, everything. I arrived home hot and sticky, but full and happy," only to hear Rachel say sympathetically, "You poor darling, you've worked so hard—I've got a beautiful dinner ready when you've had your bath."

Eager to be slim, attractive and eligible for romantic leading roles,

Lynn by early 1960 had developed the unfortunate and dangerous habit of alternately bingeing and starving, even after she received the good news that she had been accepted at her sister's alma mater, the Central School of Speech and Drama. (Neither Lynn's brief memoir nor another relevant document identifies her audition selections or her performances at CSSD.)

Vanessa, meanwhile, took on a stage role that was particularly daring for the time. Joan Henry's play *Look on Tempests* dealt explicitly with the subject of homosexuality; until recently, the Lord Chamberlain strongly enforced laws banning anything "perverted" as unsuitable for general audiences. Such plays could, however, be performed at private-membership clubs that were not subject to censorship— and where, His Lordship presumed, people had no concern for their own righteousness. (Stage censorship was not completely withdrawn until 1968.)

One such enterprise was The New Watergate Club, which from 1956 took the risk of staging doubtful plays at the Comedy Theatre, in Panton Street, the quite respectable and historic venue of the London premieres of Arthur Miller's *A View from the Bridge,* Robert Anderson's *Tea and Sympathy* and *Cat on a Hot Tin Roof,* by Tennessee Williams. In April 1960 the great Gladys Cooper, at the age of seventy-one, agreed to star in *Look on Tempests*; Vanessa signed on, and a bit of theater history was made.

The two actresses played the mother and wife of a gay man engaged in a double life. He does not appear onstage, and all the dialogue and action feature the two women, who represent the attitudes of their generations toward homosexuality. The mother, outraged, disowns her son; the wife, on the other hand, admits that when she married the man, she knew about him, but insists that she loved him, loves him still, and hopes that a good marriage can alter his nature—more the fool she.

Except for the role of the enraged mother, the play addressed precisely the situation of Sir Michael and Lady Redgrave; in this regard, it is reasonable to suppose that Vanessa, highly sensitive, alert, liberal and close to her father, knew the confluence of life with art even without discussing it with him. Corin claims to have known about Michael during his teen years, and it could hardly have been a subject left unaddressed in conversations with his sister; Lynn, on the other hand, insisted she was in the dark until her twenties. Perhaps the play was too close a stencil of their own family secrets, for Vanessa and everyone in the family never mentioned *Look on Tempests* following its run—although it was a significant theatrical event that year and marked a major moment in the swiftly advancing career of its star. "Vanessa Redgrave moves at one stride into the front rank of our younger actresses [in this play]," wrote a senior London drama critic. "She has shown good promise before, but this performance is promise fulfilled."

—⁓—

ALL DURING THAT season, Lynn was dealing with the weight problem that would plague her for years to come—and which she later attributed at least partly to the family tensions concerning Michael's secret life. In June the Redgraves faced another crisis, when Vanessa announced that she had again fallen in love—this time so seriously that she planned to marry. She had already moved from Hans Crescent into her own apartment in Kensington. "I'm a very family person," she told a reporter, "but one has to get away."

Vanessa had met a forty-year-old businessman who was divorced and had a four-year-old son. "I am going to marry a sweet, darling man named Gavin Welby," she wrote to her father. "I expect this will come as quite a shock to you. He isn't in the theatre. He is in one of Lloyd's insurance syndicates and has shares and that sort of thing, but rest very assured, darling, I am going to go on acting for dear life, and he understands and is willing that this should be so. I love Gavin very much and am so happy." She planned to be married on a date close to her parents' silver wedding anniversary that July.

Rachel, who heard the news after returning from a visit to Corin at Cambridge, was immediately anxious, not to say suspicious that Welby, who had a colorful social life as a man-about-town, would indeed force her daughter to abandon her career. Soon after, Vanessa brought Gavin to Hans Crescent. "I am in a very distressed state of mind," Rachel wrote afterward to Michael, who was then on a holiday in Greece with Fred. "God knows what sort of background he has. He is very attractive physically, and Vanessa is completely infatuated. I only pray we can prevent this marriage." Lynn contributed her reaction, too, calling the proposed marriage "wrong and disastrous."

Rather than expressing outrage or even mild disapproval—which would, he correctly reasoned, have pushed Vanessa more tightly into her beloved's arms—Michael prudently took the opposite approach, trusting Vanessa's passion for the theater to change her mind. "My dear, dear girl," he wrote, "Thank you for your beautiful letter. Your happiness is as close to my heart as anything in this wide world. Be happy, and give my love to Gavin."

But very soon, Vanessa discovered that her career ambitions did not go down well with Welby. "For various reasons, I know it wouldn't work," Vanessa wrote to Michael later that summer. "I feel relieved, but also sad, because he does love me, and in many ways I love him and have had some very happy days with him. I had a talk with Mum this evening."*

—⁂—

WHATEVER HER KEENEST feelings at the time, Vanessa had reason to prize her independence that summer: once again, she assumed a role as her father's daughter, this time in another controversial work, Robert Bolt's *The Tiger and the Horse.* Michael had read it as early as February 1959 and called it "my play, for I truly love it." He portrayed a university professor with a wife and two grown daughters. As a candidate for an important position, he compromises his conscience by refusing to sign an unpopular but important petition to ban nuclear weapons. His wife, unappreciated and unloved, blames herself for her husband's

---

* Gavin Welby died in 1976 at fifty-seven. His son, Justin Welby, attended Cambridge, was ordained an Anglican priest, became a highly respected theologian and ethicist and in 2007 (at age fifty-one) was named dean of Liverpool Cathedral. He kept fond memories of his brief childhood friendship with the Redgraves and recalled that Vanessa once took him for an outing in a rowboat. Unaware that his father had almost married her, he said in 2009 that he found it "quite exciting to think that Vanessa Redgrave could have been my stepmother."

weakness and suffers a complete emotional breakdown after one of the daughters, played by Vanessa, becomes pregnant by the author of the petition.

Here was a play that the two Redgraves regarded as timely and powerful—a work that none too subtly took the position that a lack of involvement in the great issues of the day destroys lives. *The Tiger and the Horse* was inspired by Robert Bolt's lifelong commitment to the cause of nuclear disarmament, and this topic exercised the playwright during long conversations with Vanessa at rehearsals early that summer. "She has a conscience, like her mother's, the size of Grand Central Station," as Michael said.

"*The Tiger and the Horse,* and Robert Bolt himself, influenced me immensely," Vanessa recalled. "He attended all the rehearsals, never intervening in the direction [by Frith Banbury] but talking seriously and deliberately about its ideas. I started reading the newspaper again and saw that everything indicated an increasing threat of nuclear war."

Whereas Vanessa was becoming more involved, Michael was not. During rehearsals, and then while the play ran in Brighton, Manchester and Leeds before the London opening on August 24, he was again drinking heavily, forgetting his lines when hungover and performing more slowly and perfunctorily. "When he'd had a few, Michael was capable of putting a quarter of an hour on the running time [of the play]," according to Banbury. In addition, Michael suddenly disliked playing an unsympathetic role and wanted to be loved by everyone in the company and in the audience. To that end, he repeatedly asked Bolt for rewrites, to make his character more appealing. "I could not believe that an artist of Michael's character could so twist a part in order to get what he erroneously believes is the sympathy of the audience," Banbury added.

"He went off the tracks because of the drives in him that he just could not seem to control," said Robert Bolt. "I don't know how Rachel put up with it. He seemed to want everything—some of it for his reputation, much of it for his own satisfaction. He wanted his wife, his lovers at home, his boyfriends here and there, and also, by this time, rough trade. He was the most tortured man I ever knew. But when he was good at his work, he was brilliant."

The Tiger and the Horse received superlative notices. One critic described Vanessa's performance as "stunningly perfect, resounding in depth—and what a play, what a play!" Another praised her "truly remarkable performance. There is no question of the daughter of a famous father getting a part for which she is no match. On the contrary, on the strength of this performance alone, Miss Redgrave has a great career before her." Michael, on the other hand, was described as "bristling with technical accomplishment that rarely comes to life."

The play prevented Michael from attending the rehearsals and performances of another work that he produced anonymously and for which he gave Fred sole credit and responsibility: a staging of William Fairchild's thriller *The Sound of Murder.* This, alas, barely covered its costs. Nor was the next venture more successful, despite the attachment of Michael's name as producer: Noël Coward's fiftieth work for the stage, *Waiting in the Wings,* whose premiere coincided with Bolt's play. The inclusion of an all-star cast under Margaret Webster's direction did not mitigate the critics' displeasure, but the public flocked for six months to see a group of venerable players (Sybil Thorndike, Mary Clare and Marie Lohr) in a new Coward vehicle.

"Sadoff delighted in the company of these senior actors," recalled Peter Eyre, "and he proved himself both an excellent diplomat and impresario since, as well as battling with fading memories and difficulties with lines, some of the old stars were also battling with each other, off and onstage." Another conflict occurred when Noël complained to Michael that Fred had demanded too high a salary and an unreasonable percentage of the box office receipts. "Michael was upset," recalled Rachel in a triumph of understatement. "He hated rows of any sort, and this was anathema to him." Because of Fred's insistence, a permanent fissure opened in the Coward-Redgrave friendship, a cool if polite distance henceforth separating them after more than twenty years of variations on a friendship.

Fred continued to produce or manage several additional projects over the following two years: he still had no permit to work as an actor, but he could manage FES, and he was, perhaps quixotically, determined to establish himself as a director. With Michael contributing partial funding, Fred went to New York in the spring of 1961 to help prepare for Michael MacLiammoir's one-man play *The Importance of Being Oscar,* and then Fred returned to London. In 1963 and 1964 he finally realized his ambition to direct; the project was a trio of O'Neill one-act plays, indifferently received and quickly pulled from a small theater.

Undeterred, Fred then decided to write, produce, direct and star in a double bill of two plays in London, as if he were deliberately taking a page from Michael. The failure of this undertaking eventually convinced him to return to America. "He knew he had made a fool of himself," according to Peter Eyre.

To pay the expenses and ultimately the debts of Fred and FES, Michael supplemented theater performances with work in movies and on television from 1959 to 1964. He dispatched minor supporting roles in the films *The Wreck of the Mary Deare*; *No, My Darling Daughter*; *The Innocents*; *The Loneliness of the Long Distance Runner* and *Young Cassidy,* and more important parts in *Hedda Gabler* and *Uncle Vanya*. Despite all this exposure and perhaps to his surprise, Michael was, by 1961, far less frequently in the press than Vanessa.

Eleven

FAT FOR COMEDY, THIN FOR TRAGEDY

(1961–1963)

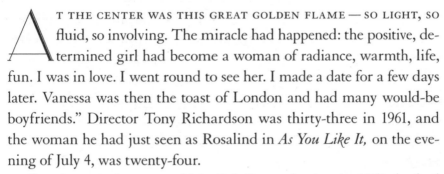

T THE CENTER WAS THIS GREAT GOLDEN FLAME — SO LIGHT, SO fluid, so involving. The miracle had happened: the positive, determined girl had become a woman of radiance, warmth, life, fun. I was in love. I went round to see her. I made a date for a few days later. Vanessa was then the toast of London and had many would-be boyfriends." Director Tony Richardson was thirty-three in 1961, and the woman he had just seen as Rosalind in *As You Like It,* on the evening of July 4, was twenty-four.

For the crowd scenes of his *Othello* production in 1959, he had moved her about the stage along with other nonspeaking players, but at that time, Tony and Vanessa had nothing more than a brief introduction. Now he was in the audience, and he could not contain the extravagance of his praise. "Even before he met her," recalled Corin, "Tony thought Vanessa was the greatest actress alive. He was smitten by her and by her enormous talent."

At Oxford on scholarship, Tony had quickly refined his theatrical talents; he worked at the BBC and was then invited to direct at the Royal Court—John Osborne's groundbreaking plays *Look Back in Anger* and *The Entertainer* were among the controversial works he staged. Director and playwright then formed a film-producing partnership, with Richardson directing the screen versions of the Osborne plays. By 1961 Tony was regarded as one of the most inventive and daring forces in theater and film, for he introduced a new tone and style into English movies and dealt with issues of social change, individual rights and class distinctions. It was no exaggeration to say that with Richardson, Osborne, playwright Arnold Wesker and the team at ESC, the British theater horizons were forever widened. "We are in the midst of a new movement," said Wesker. "Ideas are stirring, and the artist is beginning to realize that the man in the street affects his life, so he must affect theirs." That was a doctrine endorsed by everyone at the Royal Court.

—⚬—

THE GREAT LEAP forward in Vanessa's career, and what must be called the loving admiration felt for her by the press and the theatergoing public, had actually begun the previous March, when she assumed the role of Boletta, the awkward but wiser elder daughter in Ibsen's *The Lady from the Sea.* "If there is better acting than this in London, I should like to hear of it," wrote Kenneth Tynan, who was not easily impressed. Other critics offered similar praise: Vanessa was described as "glowing . . . shining . . . beaming . . . unaffected," and when the *Evening Standard* Theatre Awards were announced later that year, she was named the best actress of 1961. Her crowded schedule continued with multiple readings in *The Hollow Crown,* an entertaining anthology offering thumbnail sketches of British monarchs from William the Conqueror to Victoria.

Her father, however, expressed some concern that Vanessa's habit of heavy smoking, indulged since her teens, was compromising the quality of her voice. Well, she replied, she had continually dieted, she exercised, and she routinely denied herself social events and holidays for the sake of her career—but she was not prepared to abandon cigarettes. Her vocal tone became a permanently wistful, remote contralto, but her diction was invariably flawless, and her articulation of texts always suited the role perfectly.

But hours before the premiere of *As You Like It,* her success was actually in grave doubt. "Our director, Michael Elliott, took me aside and said, 'Vanessa, this entire production is going to fail because of you, if you don't perform this with all your heart and soul. You are just not giving yourself up to it—you are holding back, just as you have all during rehearsals. If you don't give everything of yourself to this play tonight, and to the actors and the audience, we will all completely fail. That's all I have to say. If you can't do that, there's no meaning to the play.'"

For a few moments, Vanessa was paralyzed with terror. But precisely because of Elliott's shock tactic, she realized that she had nothing to lose and everything to gain if she stopped trying to control her performance by overworking, by intellectualizing in order to get everything just right, as she had done since the first day she began to memorize Rosalind, the longest female role in the Shakespeare canon. Now, with only moments to spare, she dismissed all thoughts of how this ought to be said and how that ought to be done and instead found an "alertness and immediacy" that remained with her for the rest of her career. "I threw myself into the moment of Rosalind's life."

The result was a performance that literally made theater history. Vanessa leaped onto the stage barefoot: she was curt, even rough and aggressive when disguised as Ganymede—eager in her long, quick-witted speeches and, with Orlando, glowing in the pastoral heart of the play. At that point, a mysterious transmutation occurred, and Vanessa seemed transported: quite simply, said historians, critics and audiences, she offered one of the great Shakespearean performances of all time.

"Acting isn't mysterious," she said later, "but in acting there can be moments of mystery that illuminate the human condition. My goal is to imagine totally another life from the inside out. When I achieve that, I know it's why I'm in this business. I'm trying to capture the rhythms and temperatures of real life."

In his extravagant praise of Vanessa, Tony was not alone: next day, virtually all the major British drama reviewers, and those visiting from abroad, were ransacking their vocabularies for superlatives. "She wins your heart," wrote one critic. "This was not acting at all," commented another. "It was living, breathing, loving." From July 5, 1961, Vanessa Redgrave was indeed the toast of the English theater world, if not of all London society. Nor was her Rosalind merely an achievement of the moment: she followed this, at Stratford, with highly praised portrayals of Katharina in *The Taming of the Shrew* ("fiery, lovely, right and true") and Imogen in *Cymbeline* ("she speaks the poetry clearly and unaffectedly, the slight huskiness of her voice caressing the ear").

—ᵚᵚ—

VANESSA WAS ALSO making non-theatrical news. In February, without telling colleagues or family members, she joined Bertrand Russell and others in the Committee of 100, an antiwar group committed to peaceful acts of civil disobedience. The Committee scheduled sit-down demonstrations, at which participants were strictly required to abstain from violence: "We ask you not to shout slogans and to avoid provocation of any sort," the Committee's instructions stipulated. "The demonstrations must be carried out in a quiet, orderly way. Although we want massive support for these demonstrations, we ask you to come only if you are willing to accept this non-violent discipline."

That winter and spring, Vanessa (among five thousand others) joined the playwrights Robert Bolt, Shelagh Delaney, John Osborne and Arnold Wesker in acts of civil disobedience at the U.S. embassy and at the Ministry of Defense, protests planned to coincide with the expected arrival of an American ballistic missile submarine on the River Clyde. Then, on September 17, she came up from Stratford to London to join the Committee and more than fifteen thousand people protesting war and nuclear stockpiling.

Along with more than fourteen hundred others, Vanessa was arrested, taken to a police station in Ealing and locked up for a night before being taken to court. Robert Bolt, whose plays *The Tiger and the Horse* (with a new cast) and *A Man for All Seasons* were running concurrently in the West End, was imprisoned for a longer time and was denied access to his typewriter, which caused a considerable delay in his submitting the screenplay for *Lawrence of Arabia*. Before the magistrate, Vanessa was cited "for inciting to commit a breach of the peace," the only statute a public prosecutor could use to justify a small fine and a formal warning. She was, of course, undeterred by this scolding, and for the rest of her life, Vanessa was committed to nonviolent protest, not only as a tactic but also as a principle in working against nuclear arms, war and social injustice.

That month, her father was in New York, preparing for his next Broadway appearance. As she had anticipated, word of her public actions reached him, and she wrote Michael a long letter: "Anything we create or work for in our ordinary lives can only be done for each other in the present. The only thing we can do for the future is to do all we can to make sure there *is* a future . . . and the only hope we have is disarmament."

But Michael, recalling his wartime experience with the People's Convention, was certain that his daughter was being used. "I could see nothing wrong in being used," Vanessa countered, "provided I understood and believed in the cause for which one was used, which I did." Finally, however, her parents did nothing to turn Vanessa from her commitment against war and nuclear proliferation: "Michael and I supported Vanessa's stance on nuclear weapons," according to Rachel, who performed in a short antiwar play on the steps of St. Paul's Cathedral.

These concerns exercised the Redgraves while Michael was appearing on Broadway in Graham Greene's play *The Complaisant Lover,* which opened on November 1, 1961, and had a three-month run until January 27, 1962. The story is worth noting: a dentist (played by Michael) is married to a woman who has taken a lover. So that neither man will lose her, all agree that she may spend long holidays with the lover as long as she remains with her husband for the rest of the year. The lover, in other words, must be as complaisant as the husband—just as Michael had chosen (of all people) Glen Byam Shaw to direct the play. In a civilized confluence of art and life, Rachel came over for the premiere, and she, Glen and Michael dined and socialized *à trois*. It was all very civilized and tepid, just as the *New York Times* drama critic described the play.

The commercial failure of *The Complaisant Lover,* according to producer Irene Mayer Selznick, was primarily due to her error in casting Michael—"who was not a good, stout fellow who happened to be a dentist," as she recalled. The play had enjoyed a yearlong run in

London in 1959 (with a different cast), but there was another reason
for the disappointing Broadway production: the sad behind-the-scenes
spectacle of Michael, more and more unable and unwilling to control
his drinking. Fred had been paid and credited as an associate producer,
but his real function was to keep Michael sober, a task for which he
was ill suited.

—⁂—

AFTER HER DEBUT as Rosalind, Vanessa was invited to dinner by Bernard Levin, drama critic of the *Daily Express*. Of her performance, he
had written, "Nothing more beautiful and more accomplished has ever
met my sight," which may have indicated that he had more in mind
than the restaurant's specialty. Indeed, Levin repeated his invitation
several times, spicing the meals with intense declarations of undying
love. Vanessa politely defused the situation, for she was already involved with Tony Richardson—who, after calling backstage a second
time, drove her off to dinner in his red Ford Thunderbird.

At first she was hesitant about Tony. "I knew that he had fallen in
love with me because of my Rosalind, and I also knew the difference
between watching someone in a play and being with them in real life.
I wasn't confident at all—I felt illiterate, stupid. But with guidance, I
could act. And then of course Tony and I did fall in love."

To Vanessa, he seemed exciting, passionate, mercurial, unpredictable, witty and intelligent. She found that his political views coincided
with her own; his scorn for hypocrisy matched hers; and his artistic
vision, while full of fresh ideas, always took her into account.

But they were determined not to marry and chose instead to live
together because, as free spirits, they wanted to avoid the traditional
legal sanctions. Perhaps she also had some reservations about his other
(not so secret) sexual life with a variety of men. And so they shared a
succession of London flats before finally buying a three-story house at
30 St. Peter's Square, which boasted a large garden, a lily pool and a
variety of trees and flowers. Tony, who loved birds, installed an avi-
ary, a conservatory and an extensive tropical sanctuary in the former

garage. Soon the couple became known as the quintessence of cool, hip London in the early Swinging Sixties.

—⚏—

AMONG THE FAMILY, Corin was always Vanessa's outspoken ally and confidant. She had visited him at Cambridge when he directed performances of Shakespeare and Sheridan and was remembered as "passionate and alert, a super-intelligent intellectual, a worker." Even before his graduation, he had traveled to London more than once on a special assignment: in October 1960, for example, George Devine urged Rex Harrison to engage Corin as vocal and line coach during Harrison's taxing preparations for a rarely performed Chekhov play.

After receiving his university degree with the highest honors, twenty-two-year-old Corin returned to London, where Devine invited him to join the team of assistant directors at the Royal Court. That December, as if he had years of experience behind him, he successfully staged Derek Marlow's *The Scarecrow,* an adaptation of a Russian drama.

But Corin—and everyone else at the ESC—received a harsh drubbing in January 1962, when he played Lysander in Tony Richardson's production of *A Midsummer Night's Dream,* which the critics damned as "an absolute disaster." Earlier, there was outrage over the so-called kitchen sink crudeness of *Look Back in Anger*; now it was considered much worse for the ESC to dare Shakespeare. The general reaction was that the play had been "badly spoken, badly acted, badly lit and badly set"—and that was the least harsh notice.

Another Redgrave was included in the critical offensive that winter. Lynn, then eighteen, had not yet completed her studies at the Central School of Speech and Drama when Corin told her about auditions for the Shakespeare comedy. After the principal of CSSD and Lynn's advisers denied her permission to try for the role of Helena, Rachel urged her daughter to telephone her father in New York for advice. Michael urged her to remain in school: there would be other auditions soon enough, he said—and with that, Lynn hastened to Sloane

Square, read for the part, and was hired at once. She was pilloried along with all the other actors in the Shakespeare production—a cast that included Nicol Williamson, Rita Tushingham, David Warner, Colin Blakely and Samantha Eggar, all of them on the brink of major careers.

"She seemed to be a very warm, if shy, person," Tushingham said of Lynn. "We had a fantastic time appearing in the play, partly because Tony Richardson made everything such fun. Of course, I knew her father was the great Sir Michael Redgrave, and that her mother was Rachel Kempson, but I wasn't fazed by any of that because no one stands on ceremony with anyone else in our business. We hit it off straight-away." Lynn was not discouraged by the reviews and quickly landed three roles on tour in repertory. When she returned in late spring, she left Hans Crescent and moved to a modest flat at the top of a house in Eccleston Square, near Victoria Station.

The following year, Tushingham endorsed Lynn's audition for a costarring role with her in the film *The Girl with Green Eyes.* "I don't know whether I was chubby to fit the part [of Baba, Tushingham's best friend], or if the part was made chubby to fit me," Lynn recalled. "I do know that I was constantly trying to get casting directors to think of me as thin and attractive, and to this end, when I was out looking for work, I made every attempt to lose the weight."

—◦—

ONE PERSON IN the audience at Sloane Square was "struck by the sheer force of Corin Redgrave's physical presence . . . by his lithe grace and eyes so blue they glittered in the lights." Her name was Deirdre Hamilton-Hill, and she had been dating Jonathan Benson, a former schoolmate of Corin. Benson had invited her to the play and to meet Corin after the performance for a late supper at a casual eatery in the King's Road. Corin smoked constantly, drank very little and, at six feet two inches, seemed awkward in a way he had not been onstage, which Deirdre found amusing and appealing. Within days, Jonathan had faded into the background, and Deirdre took stage center in Corin's affections.

Six months older than he, spectacularly pretty with the wide-eyed and slender look of a model, Deirdre was outspoken and even rebellious. Born in Hampshire, she had spent her childhood on the island of Malta, where her father directed a broadcasting company. She was then shipped off to a convent school in France. By the time she was nineteen and living in London, she was, by her own description, "wildly irresponsible, scatty, forgetful, untidy and liberal." Weary of young men with fine pedigrees, one of whom her parents hoped she would marry, Deirdre was attracted by Corin's self-confidence, erudition and authority. Recently she had taken up with a series of bearded bikers and, like them, dressed mostly in black leather. Corin was attracted by her wildness and worldliness, and they both seemed ready for something serious.

So was Vanessa, who—despite any hesitations she may have had about his continuing gay escapades—married Tony at the Hammersmith Registrar's Office on Saturday morning, April 28. She may have thought that in agreeing to marry Tony, she might succeed where her mother had not. "How long do you give them?" Michael asked Rachel some months later. "Oh, five years, at a guess," his wife replied.

In addition to the films based on Osborne's plays, Tony had directed Albert Finney in *Saturday Night and Sunday Morning,* Lee Remick in *Sanctuary* and Rita Tushingham in *A Taste of Honey*—and, in March, he directed Michael's brief but significant appearance as an aloof administrator in *The Loneliness of the Long Distance Runner.* In this grim story of reform school boys, Tony put to good use Michael's ability to portray an apparently cold man but one with essentially goodwill.

"We both wanted children," Tony said of his marriage, "and so we decided it would be more comfortable for their sake if we had a legal union." The morning after the wedding, the Richardsons departed for Athens and Corfu, but the honeymoon was limited to five days: Vanessa was still performing as Rosalind and had to be back onstage the following Friday at the Aldwych, where the play had transferred from Stratford. She and Tony arrived early at the Athens airport for the return trip, only to be told that the plane to London had been overbooked and they had been rebooked on a later flight. In a triumphantly deceptive bit of playacting, Tony informed the airline that his wife had to give a royal command performance in London that evening, and that her absence would cause a diplomatic crisis between Britain and Greece. At once there was much scurrying to and fro among airline personnel.

An hour later, a plane arrived from Karachi with two weary tourists from Kansas who were forthwith told by Greek authorities that they could not continue on their scheduled flight to London: their seats had to be given up for reasons of international diplomacy. Unaware of this little drama, Vanessa believed that the travelers had generously turned over their seats to her and Tony, and she rushed over to the inconvenienced Americans, embracing and thanking them. With confusion reigning supreme, the Richardsons quickly boarded the plane and arrived in London in time for her non-royal command performance that evening.

Next morning, Vanessa was standing on a platform in Hyde Park, holding a megaphone and demanding that Britain and America give up their nuclear arsenals. Michael stood at a distance "so as not to be seen by her," he recalled, "and I remember thinking that she was perhaps more persuasive as an actress than as a public speaker." Years later, he responded to the suggestion that political involvement would attenuate her professional skills. "Just the opposite—each commitment strengthens the other, and both are nourished by her sense of purpose. Vanessa's life has become a study in purpose, and how many parents can say that of their children?"

The following week, after her final performance as Rosalind, Vanessa went to see her brother in Arnold Wesker's *Chips with Everything,* which had opened at the Royal Court while she was in Greece. The play used class distinctions within the Royal Air Force to explore the same divisions in wider British society, and Corin had the major role of a young pilot who elaborates the case for the ruling class with chilly, almost demonic cruelty. To the astonishment of the playwright and the ESC administration, the play was so successful that it was moved to the West End; when it finally closed after 318 performances, negotiations enabled Corin to go with the play to Broadway. There it ran four months, and so Corin was the first Redgrave after his father to establish his credentials in the United States.

—⁓—

THAT SUMMER AND autumn brought a whirlwind of activity for the family. Ingrid Bergman was preparing to play the title role in *Hedda Gabler* onstage in Paris later that year, and as part of her preparation, she and her husband, the producer Lars Schmidt, arranged for an abridged television version to be filmed in advance and marketed worldwide. For the role of Hedda's husband, the dull but dependable George Tesman, they requested Michael, who instantly agreed.

During the first three weeks of May, the cast rehearsed in a gloomy, windowless army drill hall near Buckingham Palace; then, from May 27 to June 3, the play was filmed at the BBC (which released it internationally for television the following year). As the dreaded Hedda, Bergman projected a glacial severity and poisonous elegance—qualities neatly countered by Michael's low-key portrayal of the maddeningly ineffective yet honest and fair Tesman. "Who would not enjoy working with Michael Redgrave?" Ingrid asked rhetorically years later. "He is the perfect leading man, and when the day's work is done, he is a lot of fun, too. Lars and I dined more than once with Michael and Rachel during that time."

Meanwhile, Deirdre and Corin moved into Vanessa's former flat in Grenville Place, which she had not yet sold after her marriage and which she insisted they use without paying. This was a welcome offer, for Corin's Royal Court salary was next to nothing and Deirdre was working as a waitress. She often helped Vanessa prepare antiwar and antinuclear pamphlets. On Sundays, Deirdre and Corin went either to Hans Crescent or Wilks Water for a lavish family dinner prepared by Rachel, who had immediately befriended Deirdre. Just as often, Vanessa was the cook, whipping up enormous meals for a dozen guests at St. Peter's Square. Refusing to engage servants, she assumed all the household tasks while Tony was occupied with planning various film and stage productions. Nor did she slacken after she became pregnant late that summer. "Vanessa's energy was boundless," according to Deirdre, "and she loved her role as Tony's wife."

But Michael was not always easy to get along with, as Deirdre soon discovered. He invariably set the tone for a family gathering: when he was charming and witty, the mood was festive; if he was withdrawn and aloof, the conversation was awkward and the atmosphere clouded with anxiety. But Michael rose warmly to the moment one Sunday afternoon, when Corin and Deirdre announced their engagement, and he was a generous host at their wedding on July 29, at St. Paul's, Covent Garden. For that event, Michael hurried up from the Chichester Festival, where he was playing Chekhov's *Uncle Vanya*. The Festival was precursor to the long-awaited establishment of a National Theatre in London, under Laurence Olivier's management.

Olivier directed the Chekhov and took the role of Astrov; the Vanya (at Larry's insistence) was Michael, who remembered the season as one of the happiest times of his life. He had occasional difficulties with lines, but he had reduced his alcohol consumption, and created one of the defining portraits of his career. "Sir Michael Redgrave's characterization is one of the finest pieces of creative acting to be seen in the English theatre these thirty years," ran a typical review. "The character's dawning sense of uselessness, the endearing buffoonish good nature—it is all quite heartbreakingly well done, without the slightest self-indulgence."

Seen decades later in the preserved television taping of a live performance, Michael's Vanya justifies the extraordinary notices that buoyed him for the rest of the year. This was (as another critic wrote) "the highest level of acting the contemporary theatre has to offer." He used his own height and voice, and the slightly opaque expression he wore in everyday life, and these he combined with the kind of childlike bemusement he brought years earlier to his portrayals of Tusenbach and Aguecheek. When the production was repeated at the Old Vic in 1963, during the inaugural season of the National Theatre, the critical and popular response was even more enthusiastic.

—⚏—

THAT SAME SEASON, Vanessa and her friends on the Committee of 100 were planning a civil disobedience action northeast of London, at the U.S. Air Force base at Wethersfield. As part of their preparation and summons to the general public to join them, the organizers printed a map of the base and the surrounding access roads and motorways. Returning home, Vanessa was met by two police intelligence officers charged with matters of national security. Questioned for two hours about her activities and her knowledge of the air force base, she replied to everything fully and truthfully, convinced she had done no wrong. When she and several colleagues from the Committee were subsequently hauled to the Old Bailey, most of the charges were dismissed and all but three of the members freed; one of those imprisoned, spuriously convicted of an offense against the Official Secrets Act, committed suicide three months later. Shortly after that, Vanessa announced that she was more than an antiwar protestor: she was now a committed pacifist.

—⚏—

RACHEL WAS STILL spending weekends whenever possible with Glen Byam Shaw, mostly at Wilks Water. "Our relationship had remained strong and was a great support to both of us," she said. Michael, the complaisant husband, preferred London even when he was between theater engagements. For once, now that Fred was out of the picture, he had no in-house or long-term companion, but he took what comfort he could from brief liaisons. This was to be the pattern of his future, sometimes with embarrassing and even perilous risks.

Michael and Rachel were concerned when it became clear that separate schedules kept Vanessa and Tony apart for long periods. During the summer and fall of 1962, Tony was in Dorset, directing the film *Tom Jones,* in which he gave Rachel and Lynn small roles. "I wanted to get away from the rainy, industrial cities of the North," he said, referring to the location of his recent films. "I wanted something full of color and fun, and it suddenly hit me that the book *Tom Jones,* which I've loved since childhood, was it." (Released in 1963, the picture earned Tony two Oscars, for directing and for producing the best picture of the year; John Osborne also won, for his screenplay based on the Fielding novel.)

Vanessa, pregnant, visited Dorset on free weekends, but Tony had so many responsibilities and social distractions that the couple had little private time. "I often resent the time he has to spend on his directorial work," Vanessa said. "But not for one moment do I want him to give it up—I'm fascinated by it. All that Tony thinks and feels is expressed in his films." That was an exaggeration, but her mother was on the mark when she said, years later, "Difficulties started at that time, when—perhaps because of the separations—Tony not always discreetly took up with this or that member of the crew or actress or actor. Vanessa told me this later; if she was aware of it at that time, she kept still about it."

According to her own statements, Lynn was in the dark about the extra-domestic lives of her family; in any case, she had other concerns. On November 29 she made her first appearance in the West End, in *The Tulip Tree,* by N. C. Hunter (the author of *A Touch of the Sun,* in which Vanessa had made her London debut). Lynn's director was Glen Byam Shaw, whose presence gave the entire season a tangled, secretive nexus. Gently but firmly, he told her that her role as a ballet student required her to lose weight. With the help of a doctor, who provided amphetamines along with a diet, she quickly dropped the pounds that just as swiftly returned when the pills were gone and the play was taken off after 140 performances.

Although the prescription medication sometimes rendered her high-strung and tense, Lynn never missed a performance and impressed her director and costars with inventive bits of business. At one point in *The Tulip Tree,* for example, the actress playing her mother had to reprimand her, and Lynn padded off the stage, shrugging her shoulders in the precise manner of an annoyed daughter. At five feet ten inches, she was the shortest of the Redgrave offspring—Vanessa was five-eleven and Corin six-two—but like her siblings, she knew when to exploit and when to detract attention from her height by gestures and by collaborating with directors on the right onstage poses.

During the run of the play, Lynn spent many Sundays with Deirdre. Corin was on tour, playing a supporting role in Michael Bradley Dyne's comedy of sexual hypocrisy, *The Right Honourable Gentleman,* before its successful seventeen-month engagement at Her Majesty's Theatre; it, too, was staged by Glen Byam Shaw, who was not, in fact, the only director in town but may have seemed so to many people. Vanessa and Tony were in New York early in 1963, where he was directing William Inge's new play *Natural Affection.*

Deirdre remembered nineteen-year-old Lynn as invariably good-humored, quick to poke fun at herself and utterly without affectation. "Lynn is better at giving of herself in social situations," Vanessa added. "I'm afraid I'm not too good with groups of people. I have a bad habit of not giving as much of myself—of saving myself up for my work." But there was also a certain sadness about Lynn, as if, when she was about to go home after a performance, she dreaded the loneliness.

Lynn and Rachel were enormously attentive to Vanessa, who returned from New York alone during the latter part of her pregnancy, while Tony remained to consider other American productions. But when the time came for the birth, he rushed home: "Tony was with me the whole time [in the maternity hospital], giving me encouragement and telling me I looked like [the Italian movie star] Monica Vitti, which was wonderful. Monica Vitti was the one person in the world I wanted to look like, and I knew I didn't!" On May 11, 1963, Vanessa gave birth to a girl she and Tony named Natasha, after the young countess in *War and Peace,* which her parents enjoyed reading aloud to each other.

—⁊⁊⁊—

WILLIAM GASKILL, ONE of the directors engaged for the fledgling National Theatre, saw Lynn in *The Tulip Tree* and recommended her for membership in the new company of actors set for the 1963/1964 season at the Old Vic.* The National was to be managed as a repertory company, with half a dozen plays presented seasonally, in cycles. This required players to rehearse one show in the morning, perhaps perform another at a matinee and then present a third in the evening. Costume and wig fittings, voice workshops, exercise and fencing classes also had to be scheduled for each actor. Wages were low, excitement was high and no one had any free time.

Lynn appeared in eight plays during the National's first three seasons—superb ongoing training in her craft, even though not all her assignments were major roles. She began as a court lady in *Hamlet* (in which Michael was Claudius), and then she appeared to best effect as the comic figure Rose in *The Recruiting Officer*, as the demented Barblin in *Andorra*, as the scatterbrained flapper Jackie in *Hay Fever* and as the silly Miss Prue in *Love for Love*.

All this activity at the National advanced Lynn's career, but it did not establish her as anything like a star player: she was the typical young working actress in supporting character or comic roles, and she was sometimes just an understudy rather than a leading lady. But she was also quick to disappear into a role that completely altered her appearance. As Rose in *The Recruiting Officer,* for example, she played a buxom country girl—a role she alternated with her performances in *Andorra* as a traumatized, half-starved rape victim. "Fat for comedy, thin for tragedy," as Lynn said of the two characters. "I found I could gain or lose ten pounds between performances, utilizing alternate programs of starving and stuffing."

At the time, neither Lynn nor any of her colleagues thought this habit was anything other than part of her complete dedication to her career. Eventually she tried a grapefruit and egg diet, the so-called drinking man's diet, the banana diet, the rice diet, the fruit juice diet and even the fish-and-chips diet. One doctor gave her injections; another forced her to drink quarts of oxtail soup.

---

* Among the others: Laurence Olivier, Peter O'Toole, Albert Finney, Edith Evans and Maggie Smith. Franco Zeffirelli, Lindsay Anderson, John Dexter and Peter Wood were among the directors.

—m—

MICHAEL'S VANYA, REPEATED that inaugural season of the National at the Old Vic, continued to glow, and for it he received the *Evening Standard* Theatre Award as the best actor of 1963. This honor did not entirely please Olivier, who as always saw every established actor as a potential threat to his primacy—especially one such as Sir Michael.

Since his appointment as the first director of the National Theatre in 1963, Olivier jealously guarded his position as its most public figure. Popular by virtue of constant media exposure and the mantle of glamour he had so long worn—international movie star and classical stage actor, knight errant on behalf of the empire and now also a man of the contemporary theater—he was a highly documented public commodity. As such, Olivier was determined simultaneously to justify his preeminence and to earn continuing approval by creating a world-famous repertory company composed largely of rising young talent who would appeal to a broad new audience and yet remain outside his orbit of fame and beneath him in their records of achievement. Essentially, he preferred those who surrounded him to be acolytes to his fame. "He resented any success that came too near his own," as Corin saw for himself.*

But for that inaugural season, Laurence Olivier needed Michael Redgrave for box office appeal and the cachet he brought to the company. Opening night of the National Theatre at the Old Vic (October 22, 1963) augured well, although the heavily decorated and designed production of *Hamlet* displeased critics and confused many in the audience, and the stage machines failed to operate. Michael was praised for his Claudius, and Rosemary Harris (luminous in *Uncle Vanya*) for her Ophelia. But Peter O'Toole, a star since the release of *Lawrence of Arabia,* was generally considered too rebellious and angry in the title role. Olivier took the production out of repertory after nine

---

* John Gielgud never performed with Olivier at the National and was not invited to play there in any production until 1967, while Ralph Richardson was not at the National during Olivier's tenure. A few of the great actresses (Edith Evans, Sybil Thorndike and Peggy Ashcroft) were on the roster, but they made only infrequent appearances.

weeks but saved the season financially by adding performances of *Uncle Vanya.*

The real problems for Michael emerged on several fronts. Stage heights were always upsetting for him, and for his entrance, he had to descend a steep flight of stairs and then sit. During rehearsals, he frequently missed the last step, and at the first performance, he came down with extreme caution. Next day, Olivier tapped at Michael's dressing room door. "When you came on as Macbeth years ago, dear boy, it was as if you were saying to the audience, 'Fuck you—I *am* Macbeth.' Now, as Claudius, you are just *dim.* Why don't you shine?"

Michael, shocked and hurt, went home to Rachel in tears. The rest of his performances as Claudius were dispatched with "a great feeling of tiredness," as he recalled, and he frequently noticed that he had been staring rather too long at some object. "I began to think I was ill," he said later.

Then came Michael's *Evening Standard* Theatre Award, which elicited Olivier's comment, "I don't really approve of all these awards for actors—unless I'm receiving them." Michael, who was present when Olivier spoke, was not alone in understanding the truth beneath the jest.

Things became worse. Michael's next assignment was in the venerable Lancashire comedy *Hobson's Choice,* but he had great difficulty with the regional accent, and this (so his colleagues believed) caused him to drop some lines and fish for others. "I didn't satisfy myself in that role," he said, "and I didn't satisfy anybody else."

The crisis soon came, with Michael's performances as Solness in *The Master Builder.* Onstage, entire chunks of dialogue eluded him, as Lynn recalled. "All of us in the company watched aghast as, again and again, Dad called 'Line . . . Line . . . Line!'" Aware that he was the object of company whispers, he withdrew into silence backstage and was taken for aloof, uncooperative and alcoholic.

Approaching the theater each evening, he began to tremble uncontrollably, and finally the situation reached critical mass when Olivier announced to Redgrave that he would take over the role of Solness himself. This was equivalent to firing Michael from the National

Theatre. "He said I was 'rather dim' as Claudius, and I just wasn't used to that kind of criticism from him. Then [*The Master Builder*] went wrong, and a general nervousness took hold of me. I couldn't wait to leave the National Theatre at the end of the year."

Olivier's reputation for rudeness and frank unkindness toward colleagues has been as well documented as his decades of grand achievements, his signal contributions to the theater and his valor during the many years of his own physical decline years later. But perhaps his virtual dismissal of Redgrave ought not to be interpreted as rank callousness. Olivier was certainly perplexed and concerned by Michael's problems, but he knew that any attempt to reach out and help would aggravate Michael's growing insecurity. In addition, Olivier had an overarching responsibility to the National Theatre, especially in its first difficult, demanding and expensive seasons.

Amid this knot of mutual confusions and fears, Michael withdrew from the National in 1964, preserving his dignity by telling colleagues that the part of Solness was too demanding and he had decided to retire. "I admire Larry so much," he told Rachel, "so it's agony for me when he thinks I'm no good and he wants to play my part himself." Not long after this, Laurence Olivier experienced a long period of stage fright that nearly ended his career.

Twelve
GEORGY AND GUENEVERE
(1964-1966)

I N EARLY 1964 VANESSA AND TONY TRAVELED TO HAVANA, WHERE HE had been invited to address the Instituto Cubano del Arte e Industria Cinematográficos (ICAIC). This government-sponsored organization supported and developed a new cinema in Cuba and, like all cultural programs there, was dedicated to advancing Castro's revolution. The Richardsons watched Cuban feature films and documentaries and met directors and students who were using movies as part of a literacy campaign. Tony then spoke to a group about the disenfranchisement of the working poor in Britain, summarized his endorsement of a more socially conscious new wave of English directors and expressed his contempt for class divisions. This, of course, was just what his hosts wanted to hear.

Although the Richardsons were sympathetic to the goals of a social revolution that was anti-imperialistic and against any foreign (especially American) control, they also recognized that, in Vanessa's words, the "bureaucratic dictatorship of Castro's regime prevented that revolution from advancing." But she was sometimes inconsistent to the point of self-contradiction: "This visit to Cuba fundamentally transformed my political outlook. Now I realized why Castro had asked for missiles to protect Cuba from [American] invasion. Otherwise the 'Yanquis' would certainly send destroyers and bombers to impose a regime of wealthy Cuban jet-set exiles and torturers . . . Cuba showed how the rest of the Caribbean and Latin American might liberate millions from the starvation and poverty of the 'free market' system, controlled and policed from the giant skyscrapers of Wall Street, the domes of Washington and the sprawling military bases." This was passionate but poorly reasoned solidarity, mingled with the grandly stated but sometimes lost ideals of the Cuban Revolution. In time, however, Vanessa restricted her political statements to calling for an end to the American blockade of Cuba and for the normalization of diplomatic relations between the two countries.

—⚏—

RETURNING TO LONDON, the Richardsons prepared for their first important collaboration: his direction of her as Nina in *The Seagull,* which opened on March 12 for a limited eight-week season at the Queen's. "She struggled with the fiendish last act," Tony recalled, but finally Vanessa brought to life "the battered, grubby, haunted provincial actress and her painful love for Trigorin." The critics were beguiled by her portrait of a woman destroyed by love and on the verge of madness—"a struggle [said one typical critic] made poignant and heartrending precisely because it avoids the temptation to sentimentality and mawkishness." Every performance was sold out.

In this production, Rachel portrayed the minor character of Polina, a lovesick woman rejected by a philandering doctor. "We were so happy in the production that we looked forward to every performance, which we found more enjoyable than our own home lives," said Rachel, referring to her most recent preoccupation, her mother's grave illness. Her relationship with Beatrice "was not always an easy one," but she prepared a daily meal for her as she suffered from terminal tuberculosis. Beatrice died later that year, on the eve of her eightieth birthday.

Rachel's dressing room at the theater adjoined that of her daughter, who one evening told her mother that she was again pregnant. Two days later, Rachel learned that Deirdre was pregnant, too. Because he was working long hours in several television series such as *The Avengers* that year, Corin often delivered his wife to Hans Crescent, where she enjoyed Michael's company. "We shared a passion for playing cards," she remembered. "Rachel was never there, and I began to find it odd how little time she and Michael spent together—they had a completely different circle of friends." Unaware of the various Redgrave liaisons at the time, Deirdre wondered why, when the entire family gathered for a meal, Michael inevitably rose at the end of the evening to announce that he had an appointment and must leave them. "He was always mysterious about where exactly he was going." Her growing friendships with Rachel, Vanessa and Lynn did not clarify things, and Corin provided no explanation. Everyone was smilingly discreet.

The Seagull might have continued its remarkably successful engagement, but Tony, Vanessa and Rachel had another commitment: a production of Brecht's *St. Joan of the Stockyards,* a Marxist parable with music, requiring a huge cast of actors, trained singers and long and complicated rehearsal hours. Tony was convinced that the title character, a Salvation Army girl (as in Shaw's *Major Barbara*) was "a part Vanessa was born to play. She alone could find the coolness and comedy combined with passionate inner strength." But after ten days of intense rehearsals that May, Vanessa collapsed, and there were fears she would miscarry; forced to withdraw from the show, she was confined to bed until the crisis passed. (The role was assumed by Siobhán McKenna, who had played Shaw's Joan in Dublin and New York.)

At the end of July 1964, Vanessa was well enough to accompany Tony to Hollywood. He had directed one previous American feature, *Sanctuary,* which he hated and claimed never to have seen in its final form; now, however, he had high hopes for the film version of Evelyn Waugh's *The Loved One,* which he had been hired to direct. Unfortunately, it turned out to be a chaotic experience for everyone involved and a thoroughly messy finished picture for audiences—"twenty movies instead of one," as Tony accurately said.

Life for him at the studio, and for them both at home, led to a strain in the Richardson marriage. Tony had rented a house in Brentwood, a Los Angeles neighborhood between two other wealthy communities, Bel-Air and Pacific Palisades. Vanessa, Natasha and a staff consisting of nanny, cook, chauffeur, secretary and housekeeper were installed in a sprawling, luxurious compound, to which Tony invited, around the clock, a swarm of partygoers, craftsmen, journalists, producers and the usual complement of Hollywood interlopers and social climbers.

Masseurs arrived at odd hours of the night to help Tony relax, and a physical therapist was engaged to help Vanessa with the proper exercises during her pregnancy.

At that time, Vanessa was all but unknown in the United States. She had appeared six years earlier in a British movie (*Behind the Mask*) that had not been released in America, and all her stage acting had been in England. Hence in a town mostly interested in established stars, she was simply the pregnant Mrs. Richardson. The lack of fame did not bother her, but forced inactivity and Tony's increasing absence did. "I was away from the house all day," he admitted later, "and often stayed out late or arrived back with a crowd from the set, rehashing the past day or planning the next. Vanessa was alone, she didn't drive, and though she did her best, it was very hard for her. And I was neglectful and careless of her feelings. She saw little of me, and it was an awful time for her. She was really alone."

But she was also resourceful, and so she decided to enroll in a political science course that summer, at the University of California at Los Angeles. Older than her classmates, she found them bright but narrowly conservative—especially after the second so-called Gulf of Tonkin incident that August. The spurious reports from the U.S. government and press about North Vietnamese aggression were widely and uncritically accepted by the American public, and soon an act of Congress gave President Johnson limitless authority to pursue the war in Vietnam.* At that time, Vanessa suspected that all was not as the American people were being told—and she frankly expressed her doubts in class. From that time, she was an ardent opponent of the Vietnam War, a position that did nothing to advance her popularity in the United States and that later contributed to a general resentment against almost everything Vanessa Redgrave said and did for years to come. At the end of the summer, she wrote a paper on the ambitions of major powers to pursue war.

---

* In 2005 the National Security Archives of the United States declassified documents confirming that Hanoi's naval operation did not attack American forces on August 4, 1964: in fact, the North Vietnamese were attempting to salvage their own two vessels, damaged by the American ship the *Maddox* on August 2. See the note.

Without success, she tried to have her short thesis published in America; it was, however, accepted by the writer, feminist and pacifist Vera Brittain, head of the Peace Pledge Union and editor of *Peace News* in England. (After Brittain met Vanessa the following year, she described her as "a charming, unspoilt girl ... and doubtless very good-looking, but like most young actresses today, [she] seemed bent on looking as ugly as possible with large, coloured glasses and long ropes of flaxen hair.")

In time for Christmas, the Richardsons returned to London, where Vanessa gave birth to their second girl on January 9, 1965. At first Tony wanted to name her Kim, after the American actress Kim Stanley, whom he had directed and much admired—but Vanessa thought that was a harsh name. A Los Angeles acquaintance had called her own baby "Jolie"—French for "pretty"—although most people mispronounced it as "Joely" with a hard *J*. Vanessa and Tony compromised, and their daughter was named Joely Kim Richardson. During the early hours of January 14, Deirdre also bore a girl, whom she and Corin called Jemima Rebecca—"Jemma" virtually from day one.

—ന—

INSISTING THAT HE required only a long rest after his crises at the National, Michael had few engagements on his calendar immediately after he withdrew from the roster. Instead, he accepted two movie roles, performing with cool intensity the part of the apparently unconcerned medical officer at a British military prison in Sidney Lumet's harrowing film *The Hill*. At first his character seems indifferent to the sadistic treatment meted out by officers to their own wayward countrymen, but finally the doctor's better instincts emerge, and he defends the abused prisoners. Michael also filmed a few scenes for *The Heroes of Telemark*, playing a benevolent Norwegian working for the anti-Nazi underground before dying heroically.

In 1965 he was invited to act and direct for the opening of the Yvonne Arnaud Theatre in Guildford. In light of his recent problems with new scripts, he chose *A Month in the Country* as the showcase of his three productions; it was, after all, still in his memory bank from his many performances of it in 1943 and 1949, and his direction of it in 1956. Because he had enjoyed a cordial collaboration with Ingrid Bergman during the filming of *Hedda Gabler,* he invited her to play the bored and forlorn Natalia in the Turgenev play.

"She was not at her best in the Turgenev play," Michael said later, "but it just didn't matter. She had a wonderfully good nature, and it came through in everything she did. Ingrid made the summer season a great success, and because of her, we were able to move to the Cambridge Theatre [in London]," where the play ran from late September through the early spring of 1966.

"I wasn't ready," Ingrid said with typical candor about her early performances in the play. "We had four weeks of rehearsal, and it just wasn't enough time for me. English is not my language, and I knew my lines but not deeply, not with their deepest meaning and sense."

There were problems other than Ingrid's struggle with the English translation. Privately, she complained to Rachel that she found it difficult to work with Michael, who sometimes did not appear for rehearsals, who never praised her or the other cast members, and who seemed indifferent to the entire production. Rachel was sympathetic to Ingrid's concerns, for she, too, was acting at Guildford that season (not under Michael's direction), singing in French and swooning pretentiously, as her character required, in the eighteenth-century light opera *Lionel and Clarissa.*

Despite these thorny moments, Ingrid as usual rose to the occasion, and by the time the play reopened in London, there was great ardor in her acting, and a layer of ruefulness suffused her characterization. "Miss Bergman's performance now has a comic edge which throws the overwritten pathos of her part into more proportionate relief," reported one critic. "It is by her Natalia that she will live in our minds from now on," sighed another. By contrast, Michael's reviews were merely polite and respectful. For the next six years, he did not appear onstage anywhere.

Lynn, who was performing at the National as the tragic daughter in *Mother Courage* and with Olivier in *Love for Love,* always maintained that she learned as much from her several visits watching

Ingrid onstage as she had from her drama classes or her apprenticeship at the ESC. "Lynn had graduated from walk-on parts to leading roles at the National," recalled Vanessa, who noted that, offstage, her sister was now more relaxed and amusing than in the past—perhaps at least partly because Lynn had fallen in love with a young artist. That liaison was short-lived, but apparently it worked wonders for the girl's confidence. "She had a devastating mind and ear for a theatrical sketch and improvised brilliantly," Vanessa added, "embellishing real anecdotes with flights of her own observation and imagination."

Lynn and Deirdre noticed that Vanessa often seemed weary and impatient that spring. Frequently, Tony insisted on inviting friends, colleagues and business contacts to large parties at St. Peter's Square, and Vanessa was expected to supervise all the arrangements and to be a tireless and amusing hostess. She preferred more involvement in social and political issues: the plight of black people in South Africa; the increasing support Britain gave to the American presence in Vietnam, to which she fiercely objected; and her disaffection with the dominant Labour Party. At least once, she was invited by a Vietnamese journalist to travel there "to see the destruction caused by the U.S. bombing and to report back to the people and the press in Britain." She rejected the invitation—not only because (as she admitted) she was afraid of such a journey, but also because she thought that such a visit would badly impact her career, "and if that were to happen, I should be of no use to [anyone] at all."

And so she did what she could at home in London, making the occasional speech, joining this or that protest in Trafalgar Square and writing letters to newspapers. "She would really much rather have a bunch of pirates and outlaws around her dinner table engaged in passionate conversation about changing the world," remembered Deirdre, "than she would have the staid, the famous and the rich guests whom Tony chose to entertain." By that time, Richardson had abandoned some of his rebellious sociopolitical attitudes as his career became more involved with and dependent on wealthy producers, international movie moguls and mainstream stars.

In May Tony began to direct the first of two films with the French actress Jeanne Moreau. Already a veteran of three dozen pictures for major directors (among them Luis Buñuel, Orson Welles, Jean-Luc Godard and Louis Malle), she had now reached a new level of worldwide acclaim in François Truffaut's *Jules et Jim.* Soon after she joined the cast of Tony's *Mademoiselle,* a major development occurred off-screen. "I had fallen in love with Jeanne," Tony admitted, "and almost from the first days of shooting, we knew what was going to happen. I had never met a woman like Jeanne before—sophisticated, skilled, mature . . . It was as if I'd never grown up before, but my feelings led me to rush into what was to be a complete disaster."

And so it was. After three years of marriage, two children and considerable achievements despite occasional separations, the Richardson marriage was irreparably damaged. Vanessa was able to understand Tony's passion for Jeanne, but she could not accept that he no longer loved her. "It's a tragedy!" she cried between sobs one evening. "It's not a tragedy, dear," Tony replied. "It's life." She did not see things quite that simply, and then he complicated everything by offering Vanessa a part in his second film with Moreau, *The Sailor from Gibraltar,* which began production in Rome almost immediately after the completion of *Mademoiselle.* In an effort to save her marriage, Vanessa accepted the role, and the two leading ladies behaved with impeccable professionalism. Privately, Vanessa tearfully begged Tony for a reconciliation; he refused. Vanessa urged him to think of their children; he replied that the girls would be happier if the parents lived apart.

And then there were developments worthy of soap opera.

Jeanne Moreau had divorced the actor-director Jean-Louis Richard, the father of her son, Jérôme. Now, while filming in Italy with Tony, she met Theodoros Roubanis, a penniless young Greek merchant seaman much her junior. Afire with ambition to produce and act in movies, Theo sang melancholy Greek songs at Jeanne's feet or beneath her window each night, accompanying himself on the guitar. This had the desired effect, and Jeanne, who seems to have run out of patience with Tony, was soon crooning duets with the romantic Theo.

Things became doubly complicated when Vanessa took advantage of a hiatus in her filming schedule to accept an invitation to the first international gathering of artists and writers in China. Armed with her Leica, a tape recorder and a Mandarin phrase book, she boarded a Czech airliner from Rome to Moscow, there to connect with a flight to Peking. But she had no transit visa and was forced to remain overnight while Chinese authorities in Moscow sorted out her situation. During this delay, however, Vanessa had serious second thoughts about her onward journey: "My marriage is over if I don't go back to Tony," she thought. "If he believes I love him, then he'll love me. I must save our marriage."

Thus fortified by her most romantic convictions, back she went to Rome. "It would have been much better if you'd gone on to China," Tony said coolly by way of welcome, rejecting any notion of reconciliation. "I'm going on a holiday with John Osborne, on a yacht to Greece." By the time he returned, he had lost both Jeanne and Vanessa.

"The thing is, Vanessa," Tony told her not long after, "you're simply wonderful in an emergency, but life in between, with all the small humdrum details, is just as important. If you could only be reliable in small things, you would be amazing. But that's exactly what you don't care about." His precise meaning remains difficult to parse; in any case, they respected each other's talents despite separating, and they subsequently collaborated on three plays and two films. "Tony was so good at making decisions," Vanessa said, perhaps with double intent. "He told me what to do and how to do it. He has the kind of strength I admire." He asked for a divorce at once, but she temporized.

—⁂—

"SHE ARRIVED BACK home very unhappy," Rachel recalled. "She had tried her best to patch things up, but Tony moved out of St. Peter's Square. More than once, Vanessa said to me, 'Oh, the if-onlys. If only I had gone about things in a different way.' " Whatever she might have done, Vanessa could not—as her mother could not—alter her husband's sexual life.

Corin and Deirdre were closer than Vanessa to the streetwise younger generation and its social apparatus in the so-called Swinging Sixties, and they began to introduce her to the flamboyant denizens of nightclubs in Soho and the East End. Vanessa felt disconnected from this new scene—"detached," according to Deirdre, "and never a part of it. She remained entirely herself." In the autumn of that year, Vanessa accepted her first film role in eight years. She felt simultaneously that she was a member of a respected family with a serious, traditional career that required her to be at a remove from society, and yet she was convinced that she was called to be "entirely herself" within a radical new wave. This was precisely the tension felt by the character she was about to portray.

The role was that of Leonie Delt, in *Morgan: A Suitable Case for Treatment,* a comedy of bad manners directed by Karel Reisz. As the daughter of a wealthy London family, Leonie cannot abide her marriage to the impossibly difficult and eccentric Morgan (David Warner), who is besotted with her, Karl Marx and African gorillas. But she does not entirely wish to leave him, and she is not convinced that she ought to marry her boyfriend, an art dealer: she is, in other words, a young woman torn between two worlds. Her performance was a triumph of improvisation, which was just what Reisz wanted when he set up his camera in an actual house in Kensington and in the crowded streets of Mayfair.

Accustomed to the rigors of sustained concentration during stage performances, Vanessa now demonstrated a real talent for inventing bits of business, and she delivered a polished performance that was touching, redolent with romantic confusion and in almost every sequence surprising in what she found in Leonie. "This is the first time I've ever played a part purely on instinct," she told a reporter. "Leonie has no clearly worked-out ideas, no worked-out principles, and this is what enchanted me about her." The sedate film critic for the *New York Times* abandoned his usual diffidence toward neophyte movie actresses, proclaiming Vanessa as "positively smashing" and her Leonie as "appealingly beautiful, pliant, voracious, childlike and immature."

For her efforts, she was nominated for an Oscar, a Golden Globe and a BAFTA as best actress of 1966, and she won the Cannes Film Festival prize in that category. For the first time, the worldwide media lionized her as one of the great new beauties of the screen. Tall and

lithe, with balletic elegance, she was also the delight of wardrobe su-
pervisors, for whom her long torso and graceful legs showed off costumes to best advantage.

"I had felt so unconfident for so long," she said of her sudden fame
after *Morgan,* "that at first it went to my head to be photographed for
fashion magazines. But life and people soon pulled me back to some kind
of sanity." Deirdre recalled that the movie "boosted her self-confidence
at a time when she badly needed it. She had always felt that she was
too large, too tall and too overpowering to men. Now her image was
that of a sensuous woman." Vanessa was soon fitted for contact lenses,
and after that no one complained about her "coloured glasses" or blank
gaze; instead, her large, clear blue eyes highlighted her strong features.

—✸—

VANESSA WAS STILL busy with *Morgan* at the end of the year when she
was offered another role, but it was one she considered better suited
to her sister's talents—which is how Lynn Redgrave landed the part
that changed her career from walk-on stage player to international
movie star.* After a rehearsal period at Shepperton Studios with director Silvio Narizzano, Lynn began filming—none too confidently at
first, but then with understanding and sympathy for the title character.
Georgy Girl is a bittersweet picture about a plump, ungainly girl in
Mod London. Generally remembered the way it was advertised—as
a joyful, mad whirl of a screwball comedy—*Georgy Girl* is in fact a
disturbing story about completely unprincipled people, both young and
middle-aged.

Lynn was delighted that she did not have to lose weight for her role:
to the contrary, Narizzano insisted that she add pounds, and for Lynn
this was somewhat bothersome. "There were scenes I could empathize
with completely," Lynn wrote years later. "Georgy's awkwardness with
her body and her sexuality was very much mine, too. I was overweight,
and the touch of a man's hands was almost unbearable, since it would

---

* Lynn had a nonspeaking bit part in Michael Winner's 1960 film *Shoot to Kill,* but she considered her moment in *Tom Jones* as her first screen role, *The Girl with Green Eyes* her second and
Georgy Girl her breakthrough starring role.

give me such a feeling of self-loathing that romance always seemed out of the question."

But during production, Lynn used this tension the way Vanessa used her divided self in *Morgan,* and the result was a brash and unconventional characterization unlike any other seen in the 1960s. The critics were astonished, audiences loved her immediately and her awards and nominations soon equaled Vanessa's. That same year, Lynn was also a candidate for both the best actress Oscar and the BAFTA award, and she received the Golden Globe as best actress in a comedy and the New York Film Critics Circle award as best actress. She was, as she said later, off and running.

Her father, who, she presumed, thought little of her achievement, was actually very proud of her. "He greatly admired her comic ability," Corin said, "and he even felt that it went beyond his own talent for comedy. He worshipped Vanessa's talent, yet he was always very watchful and objective about her. Lynn . . . grew up to astonish him in a way neither Vanessa nor I ever could." On seeing *Georgy Girl,* Michael noted in his diary that Lynn's performance "makes me weep with laughter and affection. I love that girl."

Rachel was of course delighted with her children's successes, as she wrote to them from Monaco after completing a few scenes in the racing thriller *Grand Prix.* (She had a very brief role in *Georgy Girl* and was now busy mostly with television work.) After a holiday in Venice with Glen Byam Shaw, Rachel returned to London, where Glen wrote to her, "My darling girl, you can bewitch me. I think we have found an even greater depth of loving since you acquired E.M. [Rachel had found and purchased a snug cottage at 42 Ebury Mews, Belgravia.] Isn't it completely and absolutely for *us*? . . . Have you given me a thought? Have you wanted to be as close and as exquisitely intimate with me as I with you? I think of you naked, lying in my arms—I, your lover"—and so his letters and their affair continued.

―⁂―

IN EARLY 1966, Sidney Lumet, who had directed Michael in *The Hill,* cast Corin and Lynn in minor but effective roles in *The Deadly*

Affair, a taut movie version of John le Carré's first novel. The siblings appeared in a tangential but amusing sequence—Corin as the director of an egregiously untalented drama company, and Lynn as his befuddled stage manager. Their scene was played in absolute earnest and thus provided welcome comic relief in an intense thriller.

At the same time, Vanessa was preparing for a major stage role that also brought on the most terrifying crisis of her life. On May 5 at Wyndhams, she began performing the title role in *The Prime of Miss Jean Brodie.* Director Peter Wood found Vanessa thoroughly prepared, warm, collegial and without any star complex: "She has no esteem of herself, no vanity, no circumlocution. She is so critically self-aware it is astonishing." The premiere was enthusiastically reviewed, and everything seemed to augur a long and trouble-free engagement. "Vanessa really played a driven woman," recalled the film historian Bernard Dick. "She played Jean Brodie as a fascist—not just eccentric, but scary, the embodiment of the tyranny of the left."

In fact, Vanessa derived so much energy from the role that she agreed to go to Tony's assistance in the South of France. He had prepared a thirty-five-minute musical movie called *Red and Blue,* part of an anthology, in which Jeanne Moreau was to play an aging nightclub singer telling her story through cabaret songs. But Jeanne withdrew, and over four weekends in June, Vanessa hurried early every Sunday morning to Saint-Tropez, where she learned the songs, performed the scenes and then, on Monday afternoon, rushed back to London for her evening performance.

That same month, director Michelangelo Antonioni was in London filming the first scenes of *Blow-Up.* He required an actress to play the cool, enigmatic, nameless woman who may or may not have been involved in a broad-daylight murder witnessed by a jaded, amoral photographer (played by David Hemmings). Robin Fox, Vanessa's agent, gave Antonioni a ticket for *Miss Jean Brodie* and then sent a stack of her photos to his production office. Antonioni needed no further convincing, but he feared that Vanessa would reject the part: "After all [as he said], it wasn't a very big role in my movie, and she would have to strip down to the waist. I had not met her before, but when I did, she didn't have the slightest hesitation about the undressing part." She was also somewhat in awe of Antonioni, whose recent films she very much admired.

As she later said, Vanessa thoroughly appreciated the experience of working for Antonioni that spring. She learned how to react without seeming to do so—how to bring everything down, so that she seemed not to act at all, which was the fundamental difference between performing on stage and screen. In the finished picture, she is like a sensual sprite: glimpsed then gone, present and perhaps dangerous; seductive but unavailable and vulnerable. Finally, she is but one piece of a typical Antonioni cinematic puzzle—a movie that, years later, seems distressingly pretentious, although Vanessa is not. (Michael was not a fan of the picture, but he noted accurately in his diary that Vanessa was "staggeringly beautiful and very, very good.")

Working simultaneously on three demanding projects—eight performances a week in *The Prime of Miss Jean Brodie,* every weekend on *Red and Blue* and every day on *Blow-Up*—made for an extraordinarily demanding and exhausting schedule. Vanessa was collected early each morning at St. Peter's Square, when a car came to transport her to Antonioni's shooting locations in Notting Hill, Greenwich, Regent Street and Maryon Park. After a full day's work, she was then delivered to the theater for her evening performances, and on weekends she worked for Tony in France.

A crisis was perhaps inevitable, and it occurred one evening, several weeks into the run of the play. Just when she was about to make her first-act entrance, Vanessa was seized by nearly paralyzing stage fright. She got through the performance in "a wave of panic . . . with a shaking stomach and a trembling spine" that endured over the next several days, as she recalled.

For counsel, she wanted to turn to her father (who had endured a similar crisis at Stratford), but Michael was directing the opera *Werther* at Glyndebourne, and she hesitated to burden him. (That production was so successful that Michael was invited to return the following year to stage *La Bohème*.) More terrified by the hour, Vanessa rang her two other trusted professional advisers, Tony and Corin. The former told her to improvise or sing a song onstage if she froze; the latter advised that she think of the sense of the scene and what she was after in it, not the actual dialogue.

As it happened, Corin was learning about the relationship of a particular movie scene to the whole from director Fred Zinnemann during those same weeks, when he was acting the part of Will Roper in the film of Robert Bolt's play *A Man for All Seasons.* That movie became a major hit worldwide, won six Oscars and seven BAFTA awards, and benefited Corin's career as *Morgan* and *Georgy Girl* had advanced the fortunes of his sisters.* "Corin very good," Michael wrote in his diary after seeing the picture. "Strong. But his eyes are a little close together, I notice for the first time."

Vanessa's panic attacks during performances of *Jean Brodie* continued excruciatingly and were accompanied by the fear that she would "go berserk," as she said—that she would collapse onstage. A doctor gave her vitamin injections and mild tranquilizing capsules, but it took time to free her from this fearful experience.

—⁓—

BY MID-SEPTEMBER, *Red and Blue* and *Blow-Up* were completed, and Vanessa was for the first time able to enjoy acting as the redoubtable Scots teacher in her prime. Robin Fox then swung into action once again, when the American stage and screen director Joshua Logan came to London to consider actresses for the role of Guenevere in his production of the movie musical *Camelot.* Logan, who had a long list of Broadway credits, was best known in Hollywood for his successful productions of *Picnic, Bus Stop, Sayonara* and *South Pacific.* After he saw Vanessa onstage, he quickly offered a handsome salary of $200,000—which she just as quickly accepted. Before the end of October, she had left the play and had taken Natasha, Joely, a nanny and a secretary with her to Los Angeles, where they all settled into a rustic

---

* Vanessa's friend Robert Bolt invited her to visit Shepperton during the production of the Zinnemann film. On the spot, a brief scene was created for her: she appears wordlessly as a slightly tipsy Anne Boleyn on the day of her wedding to Henry VIII.

rented house on Napoli Drive in Pacific Palisades. She did not appear onstage again for three years.

From her new residence, she was driven daily over the Santa Monica Mountains and into the San Fernando Valley, to the Warner Bros. lot in Burbank. She stepped from the car in her usual carefree attire: jeans or polka-dotted bell-bottoms, a shirt that often clashed with the trousers, sandals, a plain band around her hair and no makeup. "People sometimes look at me a second time somewhere," she told a reporter. "But then they decide, 'No, she looks a sight—she couldn't be an actress.'"

Vanessa's two leading men, Richard Harris and Franco Nero, soon arrived. Harris, the Irish actor playing King Arthur to her Guenevere, was immediately impressed by Vanessa, who tempered his manners during production and gently scolded his frequently boozy behavior. Nero, the Italian actor cast as Lancelot, was unenthusiastic when he first met her. "Why have I got this ugly, shortsighted Englishwoman for my Guenevere?" he asked Logan after seeing Vanessa across the soundstage, out of makeup and costume. "Are you sure you made the right choice?"

Next day, Franco felt obliged to accept Vanessa's invitation (written in perfect Italian) to dine with her and her children at her house in the Palisades, to discuss their scenes. "A beautiful lady opened the door, and I told her I had been invited by Miss Vanessa Redgrave. And the beautiful lady said, 'I am she.'" The evening was evidently a great success, for very soon Vanessa and Franco were (according to the Hollywood argot) an item. "He was quite uncomplicated," she recalled, "which I loved because I am such a complicated person myself." The affair proceeded with no promises made and no indication of an imminent marriage. Indeed, she was still the wife of Tony Richardson, whom she invited to spend Christmas with her and the children in Los Angeles.

Vanessa was formally introduced to the press at a lavish studio reception. After several hours in the makeup and wardrobe departments, she was brought in looking like a fairy-tale queen, majestic in silk and furs, bejeweled, coiffed and crowned. The vast crew and the legion of publicists expected an English actress of cool remoteness; instead they met an amiable colleague somewhat bemused by all the attention—but a woman with very definite ideas about her function in the picture, and just how Guenevere should sing ("in my own voice, of course").

She was also quite frank in her criticism of the Vietnam situation. "I don't know how she does it," said David Hemmings, her costar in *Blow-Up* and *Camelot*. "I've now seen her as a queen [in *Camelot*], a posh bird having a bit on the side [in *Morgan*] and a Swinging Sixties dolly bird [in *Blow-Up*]—and still she finds time to save the whole fucking world and not have a single hair out of place."

The $13 million cost of *Camelot* could not save the three-hour-long finished movie, and in the opinion of most critics and audiences, it was a bloated failure. For Vanessa, the sole reward of those months was Franco Nero. "A long phone call from Hollywood," Michael wrote in his diary. "V sounded happier than ever and begged us to come over."

Thirteen
HIDEAWAYS
(1967–1975)

O N THE FIRST AND LAST PAGES OF HIS DIARY FOR 1967, Michael Redgrave wrote, "Time cannot be remedied, and we cannot alter the past." That could have been both a family motto and an admonition for his entire year's activities.

The previous November, Lynn had acted in a British television comedy called *What's Wrong with Humpty Dumpty?* She played the owner of an antiques shop, and John Clark, who had once been a popular child actor on British radio, played the part of her gay assistant with comic flamboyance. He had recently returned to his native England from abroad, where he had pursued a career on Canadian television, had married the actress Kay Hawtrey and then went with her to New York, where their son was born in 1963. But despite study and effort, John had managed to land only the job of an understudy in one Broadway play. Returning to London after filing for divorce, he was hired for the role in *Humpty Dumpty* and began to court Lynn Redgrave.

In early January 1967, John returned to New York, where he was hired for *MacBird!,* an Off-Broadway political satire comparing President Lyndon Johnson to Macbeth. Lynn followed John, and then events unfolded quickly. She auditioned for and won a part in Peter Shaffer's inventive and successful farce *Black Comedy* and began rehearsing for the Broadway premiere in February. Lynn then accepted John's proposal of marriage, which they planned as soon as his divorce was final.

On January 16 she outlined these matters in a letter to her parents, but as Michael noted in a diary entry, she failed to give John's surname or occupation, and he and Rachel were somewhat alarmed at the rush to the altar of a couple who had met only six weeks earlier. "He seems brash and unattractive to me," Michael observed after meeting John in New York the day before the wedding. Deirdre was in the last days of her second pregnancy, so she and Corin did not travel to America, but Vanessa gathered up Natasha and Joely and hurried from Los Angeles to New York to attend her sister.* The wedding was held on Sunday afternoon, April 2, at the home of Sidney Lumet.

By this time, John had left the cast of *MacBird!* to prepare for his wedding and, he hoped, a better career. Lynn gave her last performance in *Black Comedy* on April 9, the day Deirdre bore a son she and Corin named Luke Jordan Michael Redgrave. Next morning, the Clarks, along with Rachel, Vanessa and her two little girls, boarded an early flight from New York to Los Angeles for the Academy Awards, for which both sisters had been nominated as best actress of 1966. They seemed unfazed when Elizabeth Taylor took home the statuette for *Who's Afraid of Virginia Woolf?*.

The comings and goings of the Redgrave clan continued beyond the media's ability to keep pace. The morning after Hollywood's rite of spring, Rachel departed for London and the waiting arms of Glen Byam Shaw. The same day, Lynn and John returned to New York to pack up their belongings, for they had decided to live in England, where Lynn had a movie offer and they planned to start a family. Vanessa and her daughters, meanwhile, headed for Italy with Franco Nero, who had fastened on her wrist a gold bracelet inscribed *Francesco e Vanessa—per sempre.*

Her romance was now making news, and so Vanessa decided that it would be prudent to file for divorce at last. Her uncontested petition, made on the grounds of Tony's adulterous affair with Jeanne Moreau, was granted in London on April 28—exactly five years after her marriage, as Rachel, with uncanny accuracy, had predicted. When a friend asked her the real reason for the divorce, Vanessa replied, "The official

---

* In her memoir, Vanessa mentioned John's surname only in conjunction with her sister's marriage. Corin, too, was taciturn, citing once Lynn's "husband John Clark."

grounds? Oh, they're never the real reasons, are they? We've just made each other very unhappy." Years later she was more expansive: "I was given so much by Tony, through our marriage and children and all I learned from him. Everything else [about him] dwindled into insignificance."

The "everything else," as she later told her daughters, concerned not only the Moreau affair but also Tony's liaisons with men. "When I was about ten or eleven," Natasha recalled, "I asked my mother if he was gay. She said yes. It was so given it wasn't discussed. Yet at the same time it was a completely closed door—something he never talked about."

Once the divorce was settled, Vanessa retreated quietly with Franco to the hills outside Parma, far from the paparazzi. In May they met director Elio Petri and decided to coproduce and costar in a movie later titled (for its English-language release) *A Quiet Place in the Country.* This was no vanity project for two lovebirds but rather a scrupulously prepared psychological thriller about an artist's descent into madness—a disturbing, oblique, beautifully rendered, sometimes terrifying and occasionally profound film.

—⁂—

MICHAEL HAD RETURNED to London the day after Lynn's wedding because (as he wrote in his diary) he wanted to consult his doctor without delay: "Press cuttings contain a bad notice of the tremor in my voice, and this is not the first adverse comment." But the tremor came and went, and there was no clear diagnosis of anything serious. On most occasions, he now drank moderately, although there was the occasional bender that put him to bed for a day; and as his memory was unreliable, he rejected several offers of major roles in plays and films, preferring the occasional small movie part with a big payment.

In April Michael fainted while attending a play with Rachel, who had to bundle him home before reporters arrived with their cameras. His doctor said that Michael's blood pressure was low, that he should drink less and exercise more. Rachel and Corin recalled that when Michael came to visit Deirdre and to see his newborn grandson at the maternity clinic in Hammersmith, he seemed proud and pleased but said hardly a word to anyone.

His silence may have been related to an important moment in his relationship with his son. During the evening of April 11, the two were alone at Hans Crescent, reminiscing, listening to music, talking of the theater and gossiping. "I think I ought to tell you," Michael said after a long pause and relative to nothing, "that I am, to say the least of it, bisexual." As Corin remembered, "it took him an age to say it . . . and then his grief and rage came out in a great, terrible, heaving cascade." Corin put his arms around his father's neck and said quietly, "I know," and that was the end of the conversation. Later, Michael assured Corin that he would deal with the subject in his autobiography, but he did not. The only oblique reference was a citation he included from his 1940 diary, in which he referred to "the other side of my nature"—a phrase left without clarification.

The decriminalization of homosexual acts was much in the English press in 1967, when the long traditions of harsh laws and brutal punishment against same-sex relationships was about to crumble in light of the Wolfenden Report and a complete revision of the so-called Sexual Offences Act. Sir Michael Redgrave's affairs, therefore, which had always been conducted privately, would no longer be subject to censure under the law. "I believe," Corin wrote later, "that my father wanted me to know what he had never been able to bring himself to say before and would never talk about again. Society had forced him to live a life of concealment, and the prejudice and repression of his time had forced him to live two lives."

In the years to come, Corin poured money, time and energy into many important social, political and humanitarian causes, among them the expansion of the rights of gay men and women to live openly without censure or penalty, to work and travel without fear, to raise children and to enjoy every protection under the law routinely accorded to heterosexuals. Vanessa and Lynn, doubtless because of Rachel's lifelong tolerance, never shared the prejudices of the time, but neither did they have their father's confidence in this matter, and on the subject of his lovers they were silent during his lifetime and, for the most part, after his death.

—⚬⚬—

THAT SPRING, CORIN continued to appear in the occasional television series and the odd feature, although he never had a leading role or top billing. This seemed not to disappoint him inordinately, for he was then devoting much of his time to the antiwar movement and the plight of the poor and unemployed; the remedy for social ills, he began to believe, was the rigorous application of Marxist principles.

Later that year, he traveled to Palma de Mallorca, where he appeared briefly (speaking only two lines) as an army officer in Guy Green's film *The Magus,* based on the novel by John Fowles. The director's son, Michael Green, was also in the cast and remembered Corin as "a bit strange"—perhaps because he would much rather have been back home on the political front lines than amid the comforts of the Balearic Islands. Following that assignment, Corin traveled to Turkey, where he made a brief appearance in Tony's film *The Charge of the Light Brigade,* in which neither he nor Vanessa was challenged or necessary; at Tony's invitation, Natasha, Joely and Rachel also scampered quickly across the screen in this revisionist take on the Crimean War.

Before he left for the location shooting, Corin was able, with his cumulative salaries, to move Deirdre, Jemma, Luke and a full-time nanny into a large flat in Coleherne Court, Old Brompton Road. With her new freedom from round-the-clock child care duties, Deirdre, then twenty-eight, began to associate with a "dope-smoking, acid-dropping" crowd, as she said. "I was always more reckless than Corin, and I had so little motivation."

Soon she was a fully launched member of the sixties counterculture, staying out until dawn, taking hashish, drinking indiscriminately, downing a variety of pills and generally comporting herself on the edge of disaster. Deirdre then learned, after Corin's return from Turkey, that he had taken a lover during his four-month work tour, and that the woman in question (to his horrified surprise) expected to be financially supported in London. The affair did not endure, but the impact matched the effect of her new habits: thus began a painful spiral of this Redgrave marriage.

Deirdre confided her troubles in Lynn, envying her sister-in-law's happy marriage; her successful career; her charming home in Barnes Common, southwest London; and her apparent good health, now so obvious in her glamorous, slim figure. But Lynn's secret regime to maintain her weight loss was profoundly dangerous: "It was amazingly easy. I started throwing up. John knew what I was doing. He laughed and said no big deal, that's what the Romans did." So began a long cycle of bulimia and anorexia, interrupted only when she became pregnant with their first child, born in London on May 7, 1968, and named Benjamin. Lynn's perilous dieting habits took almost a decade to overcome; meanwhile, she found to her dismay that forced vomiting caused "little broken blood vessels around the eyes, and swollen eyelids." (She wanted to appear glamorous for her audition to play Sally Bowles in the London production of the musical *Cabaret*. Vanessa was also invited to try for the role, but the show's producers finally chose Judi Dench.)

Vanessa made a quick trip to London in June 1967 to collect the CBE announced in the queen's birthday list of honors. "I had to find a good excuse to accept it," she said later, for at the time there was no more vocal a critic of the British government than Vanessa, primarily because of its strong support of America in Vietnam. "I finally told myself that it would make the things I was doing more defiant if I had the CBE—that it would make people take more notice. But I was kidding myself, of course. What I really wanted was the recognition, and I feel ashamed of that because I gave in."

But she rarely gave in to Franco, with whom she had an intensely passionate relationship that included "thunderous rows [that] blew up from nowhere like a storm in the Adriatic . . . and some wonderfully happy days with the children," especially that summer. Almost five years younger than Vanessa, he had been born Francesco Sparanero in northern Italy. When he met her in Hollywood, he had already appeared, as Franco Nero, in many Italian films and left behind a trail of broken female hearts.

"Vanessa is an extremely independent and strong-minded woman," said Rachel, "and she was used to making her own decisions before she met Franco. He, on the other hand, wanted her to be like his wonderful mother, a splendid, stay-at-home cook and a typical Italian housewife. She decided against marrying him, and this caused a great deal of friction. Franco often came to me and said, 'I want to marry her—she is my woman,'" to which Rachel replied, "Oh, shut up, Franco, and have a whiskey."

That summer, Vanessa piled her luggage and daughters into a car and drove to the South of France, where she began long rehearsals and a protracted shooting schedule on the Riviera and in Yugoslavia for *Isadora,* the story of the American dance pioneer who had been born a Miss Duncan. Corin visited the production and recalled that Vanessa might suddenly have a blankness in her expression, as though some kind of light had been extinguished. "She just switches off," he said. "It's a very strange thing—she's done it as long as I can remember." Vanessa had a response: "I give myself up to my roles as to a lover, and so I save myself up for work, to lose myself in a role. It's the only way." This time, the blankness may well have been due to sheer exhaustion at the end of every sequence: no role ever required more physical energy.

Karel Reisz again directed Vanessa, and her performance was fiercely intense. As a sad, unkempt and alcoholic egomaniac at the end of her life, this Isadora is first seen dictating her memoirs. Flashbacks then tell of her checkered, sexually unorthodox life and her inspired career. Almost half a century later, *Isadora* still looks remarkably handsome, for the production spared no expense, and Vanessa's unquenchable energy for the many wild dance sequences was astonishing—but there was too much of *Isadora*'s muchness. (The picture also suffers from the fault of most "biopics," as they are called: historical characters are introduced with lines such as "Hello—my name is Edward Gordon Craig, and I am a stage designer . . . You must meet the famous American dancer, Miss Isadora Duncan . . .") Vanessa's performance again earned her, among other accolades, the Cannes Film Festival best actress award and Oscar and Golden Globe nominations as best actress of 1968.

—⁂—

INEVITABLY, VANESSA AND her brother became ever more active in the campaign against the Vietnam War; they also joined the socialist and Marxist movements then flourishing in England. During their busy movie schedules from 1968 to 1970, when they appeared collectively in more than a dozen pictures, Vanessa and Corin made time for protest marches in London, to address crowds and to add their names to newspaper ads denouncing American imperialism. Much of their salaries was in fact donated to the causes for which they fought.

The British government took note of their activities beginning in 1968, when the Home Office covered the Trafalgar Square protest of March 17. "Speakers included Vanessa Redgrave, Members of Parliament and leading activists against the Vietnam War," ran the report. The enormous crowd was described as "mainly peaceful and orderly." Vanessa then took her program of nonviolent but vocal protest to Manchester in 1969, when she appeared onstage for the first time since *The Prime of Miss Jean Brodie*—in an adaptation of George Eliot's novel *Daniel Deronda*. Living in a large apartment with other members of the troupe, she cooked dinner for them each evening after the performance during the five-week run of the play.

In 1970 Corin joined the Socialist Labour League (later called the Workers Revolutionary Party), and for them he coproduced an open-air musical satirizing two centuries of Labour history. A serious student of Marxist and Troskyite theory, he then drew Vanessa into the movement, providing a theoretical background for activities that were never violent or seditious and were always within the boundaries of the laws protecting free speech. In addition, those in these movements needed the kind of academic support Corin provided, for their life experience had never included any serious contact with the struggles of ordinary workers. As one colleague said, "Vanessa was always content to rely on her intuition, to draw on her inexhaustible supply of dramatic gestures.

But Corin was almost the precise opposite. A shy and reserved man, he spoke quietly, with long pauses as he searched for the proper words, drawing deeply on a cigarette."

In America as in England, these activities precipitated a virtual blacklist against both Vanessa and Corin. In 1971, for example, she was denied entrance to the United States because of her antiwar position. Openly accused of being a registered Communist, she was properly outraged: "I wouldn't be a Communist for the world. If there was a decent Communist Party, I'd be in it—but there isn't one."

In late 1974 she was again denied a visa to the United States until Charlton Heston intervened on her behalf and enabled her to travel to Los Angeles to appear onstage at the Ahmanson, from January 28 to March 8, 1975, as his Lady Macbeth. Heston later insisted that Vanessa be engaged to play Alice More in his production of *A Man for All Seasons*. He held conservative views that were completely opposed to hers on virtually every political issue, but they had great respect for each other and collaborated warmly, without a moment of rancor.

Tony Richardson and the producers at the Circle in the Square were able to obtain a work visa for her to appear on Broadway for several weeks in 1976, but otherwise, Vanessa did not receive a multiple-entry visa to America until 1985. Even when she arrived in New York for Natasha's wedding, she was detained because her record showed that she had protested the Vietnam War. And for twenty-five years, from 1970 to 1995, Corin was hired for fewer than a dozen movies and television dramas. "The theatre got a bit of a backlash for employing people like me," he recalled; added Vanessa, "There was a period when both Corin and I were blacklisted. It's very frustrating if you can't get work. How do you pay your bills?"

—⁓—

VANESSA'S PUBLIC POLITICAL life, even more than her career as an actress, took a toll on her most important relationships. She and her daughters had a memorably pleasant time in Sweden during the summer of 1968, when Sidney Lumet directed her, Simone Signoret, James Mason and others in a film of *The Seagull* (inexplicably rechristened

The Sea Gull). But when she went to Italy for a brief holiday with Franco that autumn, her lover was blunt: "I told her, 'You are a fanatic in your politics—you are ruining your life!'" She listened but altered neither her views nor her plans.

"I don't think I shared the whole of myself and my life with Franco," Vanessa admitted years later. "I kept everything—my questions, my inquiries—in a separate compartment." As Rachel said, Vanessa repeatedly refused Franco's offer of marriage—"much to his disappointment." But the couple wanted children, and on September 16, 1969, Vanessa bore a son they named Carlo Gabriel Nero. She published the news in *The Times* ("Vanessa Redgrave and Franco Nero are happy to announce the birth of a boy . . ."), and the following Sunday, *The Observer* openly denounced her (not Franco) for immoral conduct. Their situation was considered even more scandalous because they cohabited.

After Tony sold the house in St. Peter's Square for £17,000, Vanessa moved into a smaller residence nearby, which Franco purchased for £20,000 and placed in Vanessa's name for her and the three children. They hoped for a larger family together, but this was not advised after she miscarried their second child the following year. "I would have liked more children," she said. "Five was my dream."

Perhaps it was better that her dream was not realized. For almost a year after Carlo's birth, she did not work as an actress and was usually away from home, campaigning intensively for this cause or against that one—and, like Franco, her children soon began to exist in a separate realm of her life. When Natasha and Joely were of school age, Tony wanted them to have fluency in a second language, and so they were enrolled first at the Lycée Français in Cromwell Road; later, they attended St. Paul's in Hammersmith, a prestigious independent academy for girls. Natasha and Joely spent school holidays with Tony at his home in France, where they had ample opportunity to improve their French.

"My children suffered from the amount of time I had to spend away from them," Vanessa recalled. "Natasha appealed to me to spend more time with her. I tried to explain that our political struggle was for her future, and that of all the children of her generation. She looked at me with a serious, sweet smile [and said], 'But I need you now. I won't need you so much then.' It was true. She and Joely needed me. They naturally did not understand when I told them that many children could not live a happy life with their parents because of the injustice and cruelty of our society. Or rather, they did understand, but understanding did not lessen the loss they felt." Perhaps to compensate for her guilty feelings, Vanessa put her entire income from movie roles for three years into a charitable trust for disadvantaged children, and in 1973 she underwrote the construction and furnishing of a nursery school in one of the poorest of London's neighborhoods.

Years later, Natasha recalled thinking, during her childhood, that if she saved up her pocket money, she could afford to send her mother red roses as if they were a present from Tony: she hoped that this subterfuge would effect her parents' reunion. She also assumed great responsibilities at home, even before adolescence. "I was a caretaker for other people, and so I probably grew up too soon—I was very boring and almost middle-aged as a teenager." Joely added that she and Natasha "reacted against [Vanessa's] politics, because she had the idea of changing the world but not being present for those around her."

—⁂—

AT THE SAME TIME, Vanessa was concerned for her father's health. She and Franco always invited the senior Redgraves to their home in Italy during the summers, and one evening after dinner, Michael rose from a sofa and collapsed to the floor. Refusing to go to a local clinic for evaluation, he blamed the fall on overindulgence at the table. Rachel had noticed symptoms that led her to suspect something far more serious: his hand often shook; occasionally he stumbled; and sometimes he seemed to gaze fixedly at something, without focus, as if in a trance.

A confirmed diagnosis of Parkinson's disease was not made until several years later, but the signs of it were accumulating. His short time on-screen in Joseph Losey's *The Go-Between* was memorable for the heartbreaking sense of an elderly man's detachment from life—but the performance (as the director and crew recognized) was at least partly due to his affectless, almost masklike gaze. Because the tremor in his voice affected his recitation, he was compelled to rerecord his few lines in the studio.

As so often with this progressive malady that attacks the central nervous system, Michael's symptoms were capricious—sometimes almost completely debilitating, then recessive to the point that he could reasonably consider a return to the theater, from which he had been absent since 1965. "Plays had been sent to me, but I didn't want to go back to work in something that might not be worthwhile or that was beyond my scope. I thought all those years had cured me of the absolute horror of having to face an audience feeling insecure."

In 1971 he accepted an invitation to appear in William Trevor's *The Old Boys* at the Mermaid in London. Because of memory problems during rehearsals, he was fitted with an earpiece that looked like a hearing aid but was connected to an offstage prompter who fed him lines. Alas, the device, which had functioned erratically even during dress rehearsal, turned positively malevolent at the first public performance on July 29, alternately emitting a high-pitched whistle or a loud hiss. The audience, aware of trouble, became notably anxious—as did the other actors onstage. And then "a wall of fear" pitched Michael into panic: "I couldn't act—I just wanted to get off the stage and hide. At the end of the second act, I felt I had sunk the show."

He had not. With the innate resilience he so often summoned, he tossed aside the prompting device the next morning, read and reread his lines with Rachel's help and from the next performance was (thus one critic) "giving a performance as rich and deep as those we remember from his earlier days." By April the following year, he was once again sufficiently confident to assume the leading role in John Mortimer's trenchant, touching play *A Voyage Round My Father,* which he also took on tour in Canada and Australia in 1972.

—⁂—

THE VANESSA-FRANCO LIAISON, meanwhile, passed through phases as erratic as her father's illness. The couple doted on Carlo and frequently shared holidays with him and the girls, but there continued to be long separations. These, along with Vanessa's refusal to accept the permanent role of Italian housewife, caused inevitable discord; eventually Franco became critical of everything she represented.

"Look over there, Vanessa," he said one evening at a restaurant when they were dining with Corin and Deirdre. "Take a good look. There is a really beautiful woman, a *real* woman. Look at how she smiles at her man, how she is dressed. She knows how to please a man. She knows what a man wants in a woman—not like you." Vanessa Redgrave, so outspoken on the podium of politics, remained silent: her feminist voice was yet to come. "That Maggie Smith is a real actress," Franco said on another occasion, referring to the Oscar Smith had won for her performance in the film of *The Prime of Miss Jean Brodie.* "She doesn't waste her time on politics like you, Vanessa. She works hard. It is quite right that she should get an Oscar. You never will."

At Easter 1971 things reached an impasse. As usual, Vanessa wanted to include Carlo in a holiday with the girls at Tony's house in France. Arrangements had been made, but Franco insisted that they come to Italy or there would be a rupture in the relationship. "I went to France," Vanessa recalled, "knowing that this meant I would not see Franco again for a long time." However unhappy she may have been, she was not alone for more than a few weeks. That June, Vanessa began work on her first English-language picture in three years—playing the title role in *Mary, Queen of Scots,* with Glenda Jackson as Queen Elizabeth. In the role of Lord Darnley was Timothy Dalton, who soon became, as Vanessa said, one of "the three men I have really loved."

A darkly handsome, brooding Welshman nine years her junior, Tim Dalton was at the start of a long movie career. That year, he and Vanessa began a fourteen-year romance frequently interrupted by occupational demands and temperamental upsets; indeed, it was a tempestuous affair, at least partly because both of them had a keen intelligence and could be intransigent. (One of their early discussions turned into a six-hour harangue about the meaning of Hamlet's "To be or not to be . . .") With Vanessa, Tim appeared in a second picture, the underrated *Agatha,* and they acted together three times onstage (in *The Taming of the Shrew, Antony and Cleopatra* and *A Touch of the Poet*).

She valued his criticism and had a high regard for his talents—but, as she said, "we could agree on only one thing consistently, and that was fishing." Over the years, their happiest times were not in this studio or on that stage, but along the riverbanks of Derbyshire, Suffolk and Kent; in Ireland; and along the shores of Antigua.

—⁂—

VANESSA'S DIVORCE FROM Tony notwithstanding, she gladly acted under his direction several times. In February 1972 she stepped in at the last moment and gave star power to his staging of *The Threepenny Opera,* in which she was (thus Tony) "quite wonderful. She dominated the show with an incandescence that made the technical mishaps unnoticeable—a true star." That comment also summarized the critical consensus of Vanessa's richly varied performances in *Twelfth Night, Antony and Cleopatra* and Noël Coward's *Design for Living,* a trio she mastered in 1973 before returning to work in four feature films. She also pursued her usual activities with the Workers Revolutionary Party, to the point that she quixotically ran for a parliamentary seat on a platform that aimed to free oppressed workers from the ruling classes. She could not have been entirely surprised when she lost her bid by a very wide margin. "I see no conflict between acting and my political life," she said, "though I sometimes wish I could have more time for the latter."

Meanwhile, Lynn and John Clark were far removed from the political fray, living what they hoped would be an idyll in a stone cottage on the Irish coast. With the birth of their second child, daughter Kelly, on February 26, 1970, and later of Annabel, on July 5, 1981, they needed substantial income, and so Lynn accepted virtually everything on offer: thirteen movies, eight plays, ten television dramas and dozens of radio programs, commercials and book recordings. (Among the thirty-five feature films in which she had major roles after *Georgy Girl,* the most memorable were perhaps in *Shine* and *Gods and Monsters.*) The Clarks left for America permanently in 1974, when Lynn returned to star for more than eight months in the Broadway comedy *My Fat Friend.* Following that, she had considerable success on American television, and

John became her producer, director and sometime writer; in fact, his career was the management of hers.

During a quiescent time of his illness, Michael appeared as a gruesome hired assassin in an episode of a controversial television series called *The Man Outside*. To keep his franchise as a knight working at his art (and to guarantee some income), he also accepted—to the consternation of Rachel and the doctors—small, undemanding parts in no fewer than twenty movies and television plays between 1965 and 1972.

For as long as his health permitted, he then became a touring actor, just as his parents had been. His memory was too unreliable for new plays, but he still had the Shakespearean roles, and for over five years (from the summer of 1973 to the autumn of 1978), he traveled worldwide with four colleagues, reading and reciting the anthologies *The Hollow Crown* and *Shakespeare's People*. His voice was quiet but still expressive, and his gait often unsteady, but audiences seemed to provide him with a shot of adrenalin, and spectators were invariably impressed by the presence of Sir Michael Redgrave, still tall and commanding the stage—even when, as occasionally, he had to ask his fellow actors to join him sitting at a table for the performance. Sleeping on trains and buses by day but alert by evening, he also managed to attend a party or reception in his honor. "I like touring," Michael said. "One is never troubled by letters, never interrupted by telephone calls, never bothered by messages. It's all very agreeable—but it is also very lonely." In addition to his appearances in many American cities, he toured in Canada, South America, South Africa, Bermuda, and across Europe, at a total of 126 theatres in 115 towns across four continents.

His loneliness certainly felt more poignant after he made a detour during the Nevada portion of the tour—to visit Bob Michell, dying of throat cancer in a Reno hospital. Unrecognizable and unable to speak, Bob managed a smile and held Michael's hand for a moment. Nothing more was possible, or perhaps even necessary. After Fred Sadoff's departure from London, there was no contact with Michael; in 1994, at the age of sixty-seven, Fred died of AIDS in Los Angeles.

An interval at home in May 1974 coincided with the reopening of the Castle Theatre in Farnham, Surrey, which the trustees wanted to rename the Michael Redgrave Theatre. He wished to acknowledge the increasing achievements of his offspring, however, and so he asked that it be called simply The Redgrave Theatre.

—⁓—

RACHEL RETURNED TO the Royal Court in John Osborne's provocative play *A Sense of Detachment.* Then in her sixties, Lady Redgrave was up to some astonishing new tricks. "I played a woman in her eighties who receives pornographic literature in the mail and reads it out loud without understanding much of what it means. John [Osborne] had planted actors in the audience to shout out comments approving or disapproving, and I found this distracting. One evening, I had had enough, and when two young men in the front row cried out something or other, I jumped off the stage and told them to shut up or leave the theatre. After all, a stage play isn't a television program one sees in private at home. I didn't like the play very much, but I wanted to get back into the theatre." She did not fare much better in the National Theatre's production of *The Freeway,* by Peter Nichols—another play straining for contemporary cool. Set in a mobile home stranded on a motorway, the play presented a fictional family arguing about moral and political issues. Rachel seemed lost, displaced.

Much more to her pleasure was a seven-month run at the Apollo, in 1975, as Blanche Gaveston, the distracted wife of a cruel Edwardian paterfamilias (played by Alec Guinness) in *A Family and a Fortune,* Julian Mitchell's adaption of the Ivy Compton-Burnett novel.* Rachel's memorably poignant deathbed scene was unanimously praised for her painful revelation of family facts of which Blanche was thought to be unaware. At sixty-five she created a finely detailed character composed of small bits of business and variations of tone that earned her loud applause after every performance.

---

* With two minor alterations, Rachel took Compton-Burnett's title for her own autobiography—*A Family and Its Fortunes,* ghostwritten by Corin and published in England in 1986 (and in America as *Life Among the Redgraves*).

Guinness insisted that Rachel perform with him again in September 1977, in Alan Bennett's bittersweet comedy *The Old Country,* the story of an English spy who has defected to Russia. "It was certainly one of the best West End roles I ever had," she recalled of her part, a homesick wife loyal to a difficult husband (which, some might have said, was art imitating life). She stayed with the play for its yearlong run.

With their three children grown and gone, Michael and Rachel had no reason to retain the sprawling rooms of Hans Crescent. In 1972 they paid £31,500 for a long lease on 35 Lower Belgrave Street, an old but charming two-story coach house with cozy rooms. Rachel and Glen continued to use the cottage in Ebury Mews as a hideaway, and in 1976, life was once again simplified by financial constraint when they sold the coach house. Angela Baddeley died that year, and the widowed Glen Byam Shaw began to withdraw from almost everyone, Rachel included; thereafter, the Redgraves used the cottage in Ebury Mews as a pied-à-terre and Wilks Water for their main residence.

"I was intrigued by what really broke up the relationship [between Rachel and Glen]," Lynn said. "What did he say to her? Why did he do what he did?" Years later her curiosity inspired her to write the play *Rachel and Juliet,* which she prepared by putting hard questions to her mother. Lynn learned that Glen had demanded absolute silence from Rachel about their long affair, even after Angela's death, and had insisted that this extreme discretion endure forever. But Rachel could not agree to this subterfuge: for years, she had given more of herself to him than to anyone, and she was stricken by his blunt termination of their relationship. Rachel poured her anguish into long letters to Glen that went unanswered, and this pitched her into a protracted depression.

—⁓—

IN APRIL 1976, during a touring stop in New York, Michael felt particularly unwell. Lynn was with him for his performance at the Brooklyn Academy of Music, when before the curtain rose he stood shaking offstage, but as she recalled, " 'Doctor Theatre' then came to his aid.

The shaking stopped, he straightened up, his voice grew strong, and out he went onto the stage. Once again that night—magic!" But after the performance, his indisposition returned. Lynn found a team of specialists and took her father to St. Barnabas Hospital. After a battery of tests, Michael was told he had a rapidly advancing case of Parkinson's disease, news that came as no surprise to him. He was placed on a protocol of medications that temporarily slowed the progress of the illness but caused disorienting and unpleasant side effects.

When his world tour was complete—an admirable achievement that would certainly have been beyond the capacity of anyone else his age or in his condition—Michael returned to London, only to find his finances again in disarray. His pretax income of £32,000 from late 1975 to early 1978 was insufficient to pay for the new medicines and the physical therapies he needed, and for the first time in their lives, the Redgraves had to apply for public assistance from the King George's Pension Fund. "For Rachel as well as for Michael, this is a tragic situation," wrote his secretary, Joan Hirst, to producer Michael Codron.

His public appearances became less frequent as the tremors and other symptoms of the disease compromised every aspect of his life. He did, however, travel to Stratford to participate in a fund-raiser, at which he recited King Lear's awakening to Cordelia: "I fear I am not in my perfect mind . . . I am mainly ignorant what place this is . . . I know not where I did lodge last night . . . Do not laugh at me . . ." Michael's illness was known in theater circles, and his recitation that day brought many to tears—among them Peter Hall, who wrote in his diary, "Michael, weak with Parkinson's Disease . . . was simple, direct and very moving. I cried."

In a long interview conducted for his seventieth birthday, Michael spoke on the record about his illness. "I'm not going to pretend that this is easy or an especially happy time for me. For a long time, nobody understood the Parkinson's condition, and directors thought I was just forgetful or drunk—and even now, the work isn't easy. The difficulty is not just remembering lines but getting from place to place."

—⚏—

FOR THE MOST part over many years, Corin replaced acting with an intense commitment to the Marxist causes that, years later, he finally abandoned. After his highly praised performances in three major roles with the Royal Shakespeare Company in the 1972/1973 season, he devoted himself almost exclusively to political action. His outspoken involvement with the Socialist Labour League and then the Workers Revolutionary Party rendered him virtually unacceptable for employment by many companies, by the BBC and by important producers.* Nor did his challenges to the policies of the actors' union Equity endear him to many colleagues. But one who knew him personally found "a genuinely courteous, caring man of passionate convictions"—which was not an uncommon description.

His activism was also a factor in the collapse of his marriage. By late 1974, as she recalled, Deirdre could no longer endure "all those people in the Party invading my home and taking my husband away. All the socialist principles in the world can't stop a child's crying at night because he's missing a father, and can't stop a woman from feeling cold because the place in the bed beside her is empty." Deirdre complained that Corin wanted her to be Mrs. Lenin, and that he would not permit French wine and food in their home: such items he considered signs of bourgeois indulgence.

There was another side to the story, and it had to do with Deirdre's behavior. Among her romantic attachments was one to the rock musician Speedy Keen, and then there followed many casual liaisons. "She certainly did have a lot of affairs," said her daughter, Jemma, "and I did tell her that I didn't always see what she saw in someone." Deirdre was in fact so irresponsible that her daughter had to take control of normal household routines. "There was a total lack of structure, and I longed for structure, so I set about trying to create it. I tried to show

---

* Just when his finances were particularly perilous and his bank account had slid into heavy debt, Corin was agreeably surprised to learn that a bequest had been long overlooked. J. P. "Andy" Anderson, his stepgrandfather, had left him a sum that had grown to £10,000.

my Mum that certain people were hanging around who weren't particularly nice. Mum used to call me the Attitude Squad. There were always lodgers, and one of them stole, and she and her boyfriend had this awful, violent relationship, and I'd break it up sometimes. I probably missed not being mothered." In early 1975, Corin moved out of their flat in Coleherne Court.

Fourteen

HOODLUMS

(1976–1985)

I N ENGLAND AND IRELAND, LYNN HAD TRIUMPHED IN A NUMBER OF finely tuned comic performances—most notably, in plays by Coward and Congreve, and as the apparently dumb blonde in *Born Yesterday*. After the success of *My Fat Friend* on Broadway, she earned high critical marks in a wide range of works by Shakespeare, Shaw and (Neil) Simon, staged across the United States over a period of two years. She then accepted a lucrative offer as host of a television chat program before beginning a three-year stint in 1979 as the star of *House Calls,* a popular weekly comedy series in which she played a hospital administrator.

But after more than two years with that show, Lynn encountered corporate trouble. Despite several warnings from the executives at Universal Television, she continued to bring to the studio her newborn baby Annabel, whom she breast-fed in her private dressing room. In 1981 this was considered inappropriate and offensive, and Lynn was forthwith dismissed from *House Calls*. She then filed a lawsuit that took thirteen years and all her money before it was adjudicated against her, and by 1993 she had to declare bankruptcy.

She was saved in several ways when Weight Watchers hired her as their spokeswoman for commercials, a role she assumed from 1983 to 1991. With that, in addition to the very welcome income, she found at last both the solution to her eating disorder and a plan to control her weight for the rest of her life. At the end of every television advertisement for the company's program and their prepared diet foods, Lynn faced the camera, saying happily, "This is living!" which she took as the title of her brief memoir and collection of Weight Watchers recipes.

—⁓—

NINE YEARS AFTER Lynn's first New York stage appearance, Vanessa finally made her own Broadway debut, as Ellida in Ibsen's *The Lady from the Sea*—the last New York production directed by Tony Richardson; there were seventy-seven performances, from March 18 to May 23, at the Circle in the Square. Natasha and Joely remained at school in London, where they lodged with Deirdre for three months—an experiment in even greater self-sufficiency by the children than when Vanessa was at home, for Deirdre's life after Corin's departure spun almost completely out of control.

In her ceaseless efforts to spread the gospel of Marxist principles and the cause of the Workers Revolutionary Party, Vanessa collared cast members offstage during rehearsals and tapped on their dressing room doors during the run of the play, distributing leaflets and booklets and canvassing for contributions. The actors responded politely, although they found the little sermons tiresome. This kind of proselytizing occurred on every stage and film production during the 1970s and '80s.

Vanessa and Tony had together decided on *The Lady from the Sea,* but it is a difficult drama, and despite their unruffled collaboration, the experience was a disappointment for both. She felt that the play was essentially a tract on the harm inflicted on married women "by the hypocritical morality and laws of bourgeois society" (one of her favorite phrases). As she said, she identified with Ellida's yearning to regain the freedom she had before her marriage, when she was a lighthouse keeper's daughter living on a windswept seashore.

Notwithstanding her empathy with this character, Vanessa was perplexed: "I found many areas of the play very difficult to grasp." With Tony's approval, Timothy Dalton tried to help her by parsing the text. Now firmly restored to her romantic life after a long interval, he, too, found the play appealing but problematic. During this entente, Tim and Vanessa agreed to act together in a film called *Agatha,* an imaginative reconstruction of Christie's brief, mysterious disappearance in 1926. The film was produced that autumn, released in 1979 and remains one of Vanessa's most disturbing and multilevel film performances.

Despite the play's difficulties, Tony believed that Vanessa "gave one of her greatest performances" in *The Lady from the Sea*—even though his earlier enthusiasm for Ibsen wavered during rehearsals. "I became disillusioned because of the clumsiness of its construction and because the key scene—when the husband has to persuade Ellida to abandon her real or phantom lover—is underwritten to the point of extinction." Vanessa's reviews, somewhat to her surprise, were uniformly positive, and she later repeated the role in Manchester and London. Peter Hall judged that audiences could see "right through the skin to the motions, the thoughts, the hopes and the fears underneath" the character's exterior. For her performances in Britain in 1979, Vanessa again won the *Evening Standard* Theatre Award as best actress of the year.

A more rewarding task was on Vanessa's agenda that autumn of 1976: costarring with her political ally and friend Jane Fonda in Fred Zinnemann's film *Julia,* based in part of a story by Lillian Hellman.* The movie narrates the alleged lifelong friendship between Hellman (Fonda) and an ardent antifascist (the title character, played by Redgrave). The picture was partly an espionage thriller and partly a celebration of Hellman, who was still living and had the right to approve the project; it was also the story of her lover, the novelist Dashiell Hammett (played by Jason Robards); and finally, it told of the life and heroic death of Julia. At its heart, the movie turned out to be an adventure story set in 1934, as Lillian is asked to smuggle money into Nazi Germany, where Julia's resistance team works to free those in fascist captivity.

The movie was produced mostly in Paris during the autumn of 1976. "Vanessa is not the kind of actor who withdraws into some

---

* *Story* is the proper word. Hellman wrote "Julia," a fifty-page chapter in her memoir *Pentimento,* as if it had been drawn from the facts of her own life and her friendship with the title character. But in fact "Julia" was based on the life of the anti-Nazi heroine Muriel Gardiner, who never met Hellman but whose experiences Hellman had learned of from a mutual friend and then blithely appropriated for her book. See the note.

mystic trance and wanders off looking for inspiration before a scene," said Zinnemann, who had directed her cameo as Anne Boleyn in *A Man for All Seasons*. "She simply comes onto the set when the camera is ready and plays the scene, and you don't even know she is acting—she is simply *being* this other person. I have rarely worked with anyone so gifted."

All of Vanessa's scenes included Jane Fonda, and under Zinnemann's quietly ordered direction the two women created characters with complex layers of recognizable, unsentimental emotions in a picture memorable for their intense but natural performances. "There is a quality about Vanessa," Fonda recalled, "that makes me feel as if she resides in a world of mystery that eludes the rest of us mortals. Her voice seems to come from some deep place that knows all sufferings and all secrets. Watching her work is like seeing through layers of glass [to] another reality."

Vanessa spoke more plainly: "My method is to start with the script. I penetrate that script with the knowledge I have about that period of history and its social circumstances. Then I start to think it out, and then, as soon as possible, to rehearse with other people. Rehearsal is very important, because by working with others, you bring new and changed knowledge to the script . . . I don't plan. I let the character, the situation, the room and the actual circumstances of that particular moment tell me what I should do. I let the invention come without thinking about it."

Her achievement in *Julia* was considerable, although her salary was not: Vanessa received $50,000, one-fifth of the fee paid to Jane, who had already won a best actress Oscar for *Klute*. After payments to agents, managers and the Inland Revenue, Vanessa was left with the equivalent of £7,000. She could have avoided the heavy British tax burden by living outside England—the strategy of Richard Burton and others at that time who established residency in Switzerland, Monaco or the Caribbean—but Vanessa rejected every such suggestion.

—〰—

WHILE WORKING IN Paris on *Julia,* Vanessa was introduced to a Palestinian family and some of their friends who had fled from a Lebanese refugee camp after right-wing militias killed more than 3,500 people who dared to leave camp in search of water. "What had happened was so hideous that I immediately wanted to do something to assist the situation of these Palestinian refugees"—and so Vanessa decided to go to Lebanon with a camera crew to make a documentary about the plight of homeless Palestinians. To finance the film, she sold her home in St. Peter's Square and moved into a much smaller house in Ravenscourt Road. In the spring of 1977 she arrived in Lebanon; her completed documentary, which she narrated, was screened that November at the London Film Festival.

So began a hysterical outcry in the United States, as Vanessa's endorsement of a Palestinian homeland was wrongly interpreted as anti-Semitic and aimed at the destruction of Israel. "Vanessa Redgrave has financed and narrated a documentary film sympathetic to the Palestinian Liberation Organization," screamed the press, "and has vowed to destroy the Jewish homeland of Israel." In fact, Vanessa took no such position; nor did she ever endorse any program against the State of Israel. Her antifascist sentiments and lifelong fight against anti-Semitism were widely known, but the lie stuck and affected her career in America for years to come—even after she repeatedly clarified her conviction (later shared by many governments, including the United States) that the Palestinian people deserved a homeland.

"I made this film," she said that year, "because I believe the Palestinian people have been denied the right to be heard. Their views become even more important since world opinion is now turning toward the establishment of a just and lasting peace in the region. I have consistently championed the rights of the Jewish people. No one can challenge the stand I have taken against Fascism and anti-Semitism. I believe that the rights of the Jewish people in Israel can only be guaranteed by the establishment of a democratic secular state of Palestine, in which Jews and Arabs can live and work in peace together." These are neither the sentiments nor the words of an anti-Semite.

But her critics continued to ignore her signal efforts against anti-Semitism everywhere. When Vanessa organized a benefit concert in London that raised $100,000 for refugee children everywhere in the Middle East, the American press failed to report it. She then organized an international conference calling for an end to anti-Semitism worldwide; she had chosen Moscow for this meeting because of the Soviet history of anti-Semitic pogroms. The struggle against anti-Semitism, she insisted, could not be divorced from the struggle for a Palestinian homeland—for the Palestinians, after all, are a Semitic people. And so it went: when Vanessa financed the visit of the Moscow State Jewish Theatre's visit to London, no American newspaper picked up the story.

From the end of 1977, the nine-year-old Jewish Defense League launched and sustained a campaign against Vanessa Redgrave in the United States—especially after the announcement, early in 1978, that the Academy of Motion Picture Arts and Sciences had nominated her as a candidate for the best supporting actress Oscar for her performance in *Julia* (as a Jewish and anti-Nazi freedom fighter, no less). Described by the U.S. Federal Bureau of Investigation as "a violent extremist Jewish organization" and "a right-wing terrorist group," the JDL was (according to law enforcement agencies) directly involved in planning terrorist attacks against Arab and Soviet properties in America and elsewhere.

Established Jewish groups have long rejected the principles and activities of the JDL. The Anti-Defamation League, for one important example, has been since 1913 the world's leading organization fighting anti-Semitism through educational programs and services that counter hatred, prejudice and bigotry. The ADL criticized the JDL's founder, Rabbi Meir Kahane, "for preaching a radical form of Jewish nationalism which reflected racism, violence and political extremism" and consisted only of "thugs and hooligans." Rabbi Kahane later moved to Israel, where he founded the Kach Party, which was subsequently outlawed by the Israeli government as racist. In 1972 two JDL members pleaded guilty to a charge of conspiring to bomb the Soviet Mission to the United Nations. That same year, the JDL detonated a grenade at the Manhattan office of the Jewish impresario Sol Hurok, who had arranged tours in America for visiting Soviet artists and performers; one of Hurok's secretaries died of smoke inhalation.

When she arrived at the Dorothy Chandler Pavilion in downtown Los Angeles for the Oscar ceremonies on April 3, 1978, members of the JDL were massing outside, shouting and waving signs condemning Vanessa Redgrave. In New York, Lynn—who had just completed a tour as Shaw's martyred St. Joan—turned on her television and saw the ironic and frightening image of her sister burned in effigy ("Arafat's Whore" proclaimed the placard) along with a number of Palestinian leaders.

Julia was nominated for awards in eleven categories. After the statuettes were presented to Alvin Sargent (for his screenplay for *Julia*) and to Jason Robards (as best supporting actor, in the role of Dashiell Hammett), John Travolta announced that Vanessa Redgrave was the winner of the Academy Award for best supporting actress. To enthusiastic applause, she came to the stage, accepted the Oscar and addressed the audience:

"My dear colleagues, I thank you very, very much for this tribute to my work. I think that Jane Fonda and I have done the best work of our lives, and I think this was in part due to our director, Fred Zinnemann. I also think it's in part because we believed in what we were expressing—two women, out of the millions who gave their lives and were prepared to sacrifice everything in the fight against fascist and racist Nazi Germany. And I salute you and I pay tribute to you, and I think you should be very proud that in the last few weeks you have stood firm and refused to be intimidated by the threats of a small bunch of Zionist hoodlums . . ."

At this point, her speech was overwhelmed by loud shouts of protest from the audience—but she continued, raising her voice over the din.

". . . a small bunch of Zionist hoodlums whose behavior is an insult to the stature of Jews all over the world, and to their great and heroic record of struggle against Fascism and oppression.

"And I salute that record, and I salute all of you for having stood firm and dealt a final blow against that period when Nixon and McCarthy launched a worldwide witch-hunt against those who tried to express in their lives and their work a truth that they believed.* I salute you and I thank you, and I pledge to you that I will continue to fight against anti-Semitism and fascism. Thank you." And with that, she withdrew backstage, as the jeers and boos continued.

From that evening, the media completely misrepresented her: television and radio reports conveniently cut the last part of Vanessa's speech, so that listeners heard nothing after "a small bunch of Zionist hoodlums," and commentators routinely complained that Vanessa considered all Jews hoodlums. Nor was the complete text of her remarks ever fully printed in American newspapers or magazines.

Vanessa never reneged on the words she uttered that evening. "I only regret that I wasn't able to clarify calmly enough, but I don't regret saying what I did in the best way I could at the moment . . . and when I referred to the 'Zionist hoodlums,' I meant, of course, the Jewish Defense League and their death threats"—specifically, those people who had gathered outside the Dorothy Chandler Pavilion. In fact, her remarks that evening summarized the view of none other than the Anti-Defamation League. Moshe Mizrahi, the Israeli director whose film *Madame Rosa* was named best foreign film that evening, shook Vanessa's hand backstage and turned to a reporter, saying, "She's right!"

"Hollywood turned its back on her," said Meryl Streep, who made her film debut in a small role in *Julia*. "And the repercussions to her career were catastrophic." Indeed, from that April evening, Vanessa was continually and unjustly pilloried by many in America, described as an unregenerate anti-Semite and effectively blacklisted from American movies (but not from television dramas) because, it was further reported, she had denied Israel's right to exist—which she had not. Charlton Heston, for one, sprang to her defense: "Vanessa is openly

---

* This was a sincere but gilded reference to Lillian Hellman, who in 1952 had been summoned before the House Un-American Activities Committee, where she was asked to defend a charge that she had associated with alleged American Communists. Both Redgrave and Fonda regarded Hellmann with reverential awe.

blacklisted because of her anti-Zionist convictions. The film and theatre communities should be ashamed of that."

The ostracism then extended to the theater and concert hall. In 1982
the Boston Symphony Orchestra announced that Vanessa had been engaged to narrate six performances of Stravinsky's opera-oratorio *Oedipus Rex*. Pandemonium then arose: there were promises of disruptions
during the appointed evenings, complaints from a few musicians and
threats of diminished financial support from some Jewish patrons.
The BSO then cancelled the production, and Vanessa promptly sued
for breach of contract and loss of income. The litigation dragged on
for years and cost her many times the compensation she was finally
awarded for a temporary loss of income.

Because of the BSO fracas, she also lost the opportunity to act with
Lynn in an Off-Broadway production of the play *Skirmishes,* whose
backers could not find a single venue that would welcome her. The
Broadway producer Jerome Minskoff frankly admitted, "I don't think
anyone would take her on Broadway—good as she is." She felt compelled to file a grievance when the producers of Peter Shaffer's play
Lettice and Lovage cancelled her contract to appear in the nationwide
tour, insisting that "her anti-American statements [!] would keep audiences away." An arbitrator ruled in favor of the producers.

As late as the spring of 2004 she was still victimized by an epidemic
of hysteria. When she won the Tony Award for her performance in the
2003 revival of Eugene O'Neill's play *Long Day's Journey into Night,*
the CBS television journalist Mike Wallace, who is Jewish, wanted to
do an update on an earlier critical profile of Vanessa that he had conducted in 1979 on the program *60 Minutes*. After a preliminary meeting with her, Wallace reported, "I had discovered another, warmer
side to Vanessa [and found her] kind, thoughtful and quite charming.
Somewhat to my surprise, I truly liked her."

Wallace's proposal for a new interview twenty-four years after the
first was rejected by his superiors at CBS, "on the grounds that an update on Redgrave 'wasn't right' for our audience," as Wallace recalled.
"I replied, with some irritation, that I found it hard to imagine an audience that would not be interested in seeing a story on how one of

the most accomplished actresses of our time chose to play a classic role in what is widely considered to be the greatest play ever written by an American dramatist. My earnest plea fell on deaf ears. I thought [the] negative reaction [by CBS executives] was wrong at the time, and for whatever it's worth, I still think [in 2005] it was a mistake."

—⁓—

THE ENGLISH DIRECTOR John Schlesinger, proud of his Jewish heritage and always alert for any whisper of anti-Semitism, knew that Vanessa was nothing like the person touted in the American press. Soon after Oscar night, he offered her an important role in his next picture, *Yanks,* scheduled to begin production early that summer near Manchester. A story of American troops billeted in Northern England prior to D-day, the picture focused on three Yanks and three Englishwomen—one of them (Vanessa) a doctor's wife who plays the cello in a local nonprofessional orchestra. There was nothing amateur about Vanessa's preparation: although an expert musician would record the music, she studied with three cellists in order to learn precisely how her fingers and wrists should be positioned while she played the instrument. She also conveyed the depth and humor in a character both underwritten and lacking those qualities.

Returning to London that autumn, Vanessa brought fifteen-year-old Natasha and thirteen-year-old Joely back to Ravenscourt Road from their sojourn with Deirdre. Soon the conditions at home were no better than those they had endured at Coleherne Court. "All those scruffy people [were] marching around our house as though it was their home and not mine," said Joely soon after. "They come in and plot," said Jemma, who also knew about the habits of party members (and others) arriving unannounced at all hours. "They don't care what any of us is doing. They just turn off the television if I'm watching something. They treat me as if I wasn't even there." On the subject of her parents' divorce, Jemma later spoke frankly: "There was some bitterness at that point, and I didn't want to know about it. I stuffed myself with sweets and chocolates instead," rather like her aunt Lynn. "My mother was taking me to see punk bands when I was thirteen, but it was my father I went to for advice."

After his contentious divorce, Corin had fallen in love with the actress Kika Markham, daughter of David Markham, Michael's old friend and costar in *The Stars Look Down.* Kika's mother was Olive Dehn, sister of writer Paul Dehn, who wrote the superb screenplay for *Murder on the Orient Express,* produced in 1974, in which Vanessa acted with witty seductiveness opposite Sean Connery. The Markhams and the Redgraves were, therefore, no strangers to one another when Kika (a nickname for Erika) acted in *Twelfth Night* at the Royal Court with Corin in 1962; it was she who had introduced Corin to the Socialist Labour League. In 1977 he moved into Kika's house in South London, and by 1978 she was in the last stage of pregnancy; early in 1979 she gave birth to a son they named Harvey. Late in 1983 they had a second son, called Arden. Corin and Kika were married in October 1985.

Michael, meanwhile, was increasingly frail, and by early 1979 he could no longer sustain the demands of appearing even in a cameo on film or television. But then Harold Pinter rang with an invitation Michael could not reject.

Pinter had directed Michael's brief appearance in the film of *The Go-Between,* and he knew that Michael could neither move onstage nor memorize lines. But in his new drama, *Close of Play,* Simon Gray had written expressly for Redgrave the role of Jasper, once a distinguished academic now rendered catatonic by a stroke. He sits in a chair onstage, immobile and silent, for the duration of the play's two acts—the ailing head of a bickering clan, incapable of responding to their angry outbursts or offering consolation or counsel.

"The curtain rises on the stage in darkness," wrote Gray. "There is the sound of organ music, at first faint, then swelling until it fills the theatre. As it does so, a faint pool of light spreads over Jasper in his armchair. He appears to be asleep. The music stops mid-chord. Jasper opens his eyes as the rest of the lights come up steadily, until the room is filled with bright summer sunshine." Then, just before the end of the play, Jasper stirs and manages to cry out, "The door is open!" There is a pause, and the stage lights are slowly dimmed "until only Jasper in his chair is lit. That light remains for a few seconds and then, as it goes down, the sound of organ music, distantly, then swelling to fill the theatre until the curtain falls."

Peter Hall attended the first rehearsal that February. "I was moved to see Michael Redgrave there," he wrote in his diary, "Crocker Harris to the life [the character Michael had played in *The Browning Version*], listening attentively to the other actors and gazing quizzically over his half glasses. This was one of my favourite actors in his prime. Now he is slow and gentle and ravaged by Parkinson's Disease. It's a miracle this part exists to get him back onto the stage."

The play opened at the National on May 24. "Sir Michael Redgrave is the monolithic centre [of the play]," wrote critic Felix Barker. "With only [four] words to speak, one dreadful sigh and constant agony behind the eyes, he carries us into the pit of hell." A reviewer from America agreed: "Without words, Sir Michael Redgrave manages to project disdain as well as guilt for his responsibility in the downfall of his offspring." Peter Hall was present again, for the final performance on October 22: "I went round to see the cast. Michael Redgrave [was] in tears. I think he feels that this was his last time on the stage. He said to me, 'Do remember that I can learn more than four words.' His illness has resulted in such a loss to us all."

Michael knew that the course of his disease was irreversible, and that *Close of Play* was an ironic, apt title: his career ended that autumn of 1979. But he did not withdraw from life: "I don't feel old," he said with a certain wistfulness. "I just feel slow." He saw old friends and made a few new ones, in whom he confided not only freshly summoned details of his film career but also candid comments about his life and his family's. He could no longer memorize new material, but his recollections of the past remained clear.[*]

---

[*] This author found him a cheerful, articulate and a genial host quick to refill glasses of afternoon refreshments. There were occasional hesitations typical of a Parkinson's patient, but he never lost the thread of our conversations.

—※—

FOR SEVERAL YEARS, after complaining that she had been raised in a household of bourgeois morality, Vanessa had virtually no communication with her father, who felt deeply offended. Rachel wrote a long letter to Vanessa, expressing her belief that her daughter's high-toned denunciation was part of the legacy of her marriage to Tony Richardson, who "was no good to you as a husband, for you deeply suffered with him. Suffering does make one revengeful towards one's family—*I* know that very well."

The rupture between Michael and Vanessa had another unfortunate consequence. When appointments were confirmed for the infrequent interviews Michael granted, his secretary, Joan Hirst, informed visitors in advance that Vanessa's name was "not to be mentioned during conversations with Sir Michael"—a stipulation he sometimes made directly: "I never discuss Vanessa. I am sorry," he told one journalist.

"As often happens," Vanessa admitted, "my marriage, family and career had taken me away from my parents, and then my intense involvement in political work in the seventies distanced me from them"—just as there were prolonged absences from her children. The rapprochement with her father was ultimately bridged when he agreed to recite Lear's awakening scene, with Vanessa as Cordelia, as part of a filmed documentary produced at Wilks Water for the Kuwait Cinema Club in the spring of 1980. Michael had never before performed any Shakespearean role on film. Despite increasing frailty, he appeared in the same scene with her again, at the Roundhouse Theatre, North London, in October 1982, a benefit for the Young Socialists' youth training center. It was his final public appearance.

"I was honestly proud that Vanessa and Corin had the courage to fight for their convictions," said Rachel when the family wound was healed. "They didn't do any political work for their own personal gain, and I was very happy when they asked me to appear at a fundraiser to benefit one of their causes—which I gladly did."

Remarkably, Michael's intimate life was never interrupted until the last few years of his life. There were romantic trysts at Ebury Mews with at least one younger man—a genial forty-year-old, married and from North London. He began as Michael's adoring fan and then, for over a year, became (as Michael confided to Corin) "my lover." The man also acted as a caregiver when there was the occasional minor accident at Ebury Mews.

This aspect of Michael's life went unaddressed in his memoirs, contracted thirty years earlier but still unwritten. For reasons understood by everyone close to him, he had avoided the task: "He wanted to write about his bisexuality, but never managed to," according to Corin, and that nagging issue alone caused the long delay. Now, with the expenses of his illness, of nurses, of physical therapists whenever he traveled and the pocket money he spent on his new companion, Michael needed more income. In June 1981 his agents successfully cancelled the long outstanding publishing contract without financial detriment and then negotiated a new deal wherein he received $70,000 for a forthcoming British publication by Weidenfeld and Nicolson, and an American edition by Viking. Because of Michael's illness, it was understood that Corin would write the text—and quickly.

"There is something of me in [Michael's book] *In My Mind's Eye,*" Corin said of the Shakespeare-inspired title, adding that "whole chapters fell to me to complete and even to write entirely, [and] I invented the sound of his voice." In fact, only the final two pages of the book came directly from Michael—"a kind of after-dinner dozing dream," as Corin called the phrases and half sentences about Scudamores and Redgraves that he quickly jotted as his father rambled. (Even a quick comparison of Michael's book with Corin's, Rachel's and Vanessa's reveals beyond any doubt that Corin was the author of all these volumes.)

"It was April 1983 when we finished my father's autobiography," Corin continued. Michael insisted that the dedication page bear two words: "To Corin," just as he had signed *Mask or Face* "To My Wife Rachel"; *The Mountebank's Tale* "To My Daughter Vanessa"; and *The Aspern Papers* "To Flora Robson and Beatrix Lehman," his costars in that play. Had there been another literary work forthcoming, he would certainly have dedicated it to Lynn, whose achievements he much praised in his last years.

In My Mind's Eye was rushed into print, and Michael was honored at a literary luncheon at the Dorchester Hotel, which was attended by Rachel, Vanessa and Corin; Lynn was occupied in Hollywood with three television projects.

Michael paid no attention to the book reviews, which was a prudent decision, for they were unfavorable. According to one critic whose disappointment summarized the consensus, the book "failed to bring him into focus [as an actor] . . . nor is there a very profound portrait of Michael Redgrave the man."

He was not expected to speak at the luncheon, but he insisted on taking the microphone. "When I was a child . . ." he began. Then, after a long pause, his voice shaking and faint, he slowly said, "I think I'd better sit down, don't you?"

—⁂—

IN THE SUMMER of 1979, CBS announced that Vanessa was to star in *Playing for Time,* a three-hour television drama based on the memoirs of Fania Fénelon, a singer, musician and member of the French Resistance who had survived Auschwitz by organizing a woman's orchestra for the entertainment of Nazi officials. Some Jewish groups swung into action, furious that a supporter of the Palestinian cause was to portray a concentration camp inmate. From her home in Paris, Fénelon (born Fania Goldstein to a Jewish father and a Catholic mother) joined the chorus of naysayers demanding that Redgrave be forthwith fired from the production.

Apparently no one dared suggest that a dramatization of Fénelon's experience (no matter the cast) would honor all Holocaust victims and strike a loud blow against the outrage of Nazi genocide. After all, if the Shoah was never to be forgotten, there could be nothing better to remind a new generation about it than a television movie, broadcast over a major network and seen by millions. And if Redgrave *was* anti-Semitic (an assertion no one bothered to say was patently untrue and even libelous), then what better way for her to reverse and repent of her prejudice than in a production condemning such a horrific ideology?

This absurd attempt to stymie an actress—an objection based on once again misrepresenting her as an enemy of Israel—was loudly countered by no less an authority than the Jewish playwright Arthur Miller, who had written the teleplay of *Playing for Time*:

"Having been blacklisted myself, I have fought against the prac- tice abroad as well as here," Miller said, "and I cannot participate in it now—but something more needs to be said. No actress can possibly play Fania without generating the profoundest sympathy for the Jewish people, as well as a deeper understanding of some of the experiences that cried out for the creation of the State of Is- rael. Anti-Jewish, anti-Israeli fanaticism will take no heart from this film . . . which can only lift the sufferings of the Jews, and especially of Jewish women, to a new ground of understanding." Which, as Vanessa said, was precisely her intention in asking to play the role after Barbra Streisand turned it down.

There were ongoing calls for the firing of Vanessa, and Fénelon, on a speaking tour across America, insisted with absolute seriousness that Liza Minnelli would be the best one to play her. "I didn't think it was important that Fania Fénelon didn't want me to play the role," said Vanessa. "I thought her life was important, and that people needed to know about it, and that it would endure. Whatever she said about me wouldn't endure."

When she arrived at the New York rehearsal rooms that autumn of 1979, Vanessa found armed guards posted outside. The office of the producer, Linda Yellen, had already been vandalized, and pickets were marching at the home of William S. Paley, chief executive of CBS. Yel- len and Paley, both Jewish, stood firm in Vanessa's support. Because of ongoing threats of violence, the security surrounding the production was even tighter during the six weeks of filming in Fort Indiantown Gap, an army post near Harrisburg, Pennsylvania. The filming was completed in early January without incident.

Playing for Time was broadcast nationwide on September 30, 1980;

the next morning, Fénelon threatened to sue CBS "on moral grounds" for presenting Redgrave as the exponent of her life. At the same time, however, Vanessa received overwhelmingly positive reviews and was eventually awarded the Emmy as best actress in a television movie for a performance that could have matched Eleanora Duse's for intensity. That comparison is no overstatement, for in the nineteenth century the Italian actress had developed techniques for what she called "the elimination of self," the art of suppressing one's own character in order to create another through muted expressions and a profound silence. In crucial scenes, Vanessa's fingers tremble as Fania approaches her audition to play in the camp orchestra, and again later, as she reaches for a piece of sausage she would rather not eat despite her hunger. With her head shaved, her large blue eyes full of outrage, and her ghostly pallor, Vanessa gave "the most extraordinary performance of her illustrious career," as the *New York Times* put it.

The same level of praise, without any concomitant charges of inappropriate casting, surrounded Vanessa following her performance in the 1986 television broadcast *Second Serve,* based on the true story of a man who, after years of struggle, underwent transgender surgery and, as a woman, became the professional tennis champion Renée Richards. Portraying a man who becomes a woman, Vanessa was not only entirely credible in every scene: she also communicated vulnerability through her height, not despite it, and there was something like a mystic unity of male and female contraries in a performance that critics and television audiences found "extraordinary" and "astonishingly convincing."

During her preparations for the role, as Vanessa said, "I realized how many of my notions of what is normal or healthy were based on ignorance and fear, and I was alarmed. If I, who thought myself an unprejudiced person, could have been guilty of such stereotyped thinking, how much more so [would] someone whose ignorance was regularly played upon by politicians, judges and the press?"

With these intense performances behind her, she was glad to act in a madcap, low-budget British comedy, *Consuming Passions.* As an eccentric, tattooed kind of Earth Mother transplanted to London, she

did a riff on someone resembling an aging sexpot, mad for men to replace a husband who, as her character says, "went back to his old sailor
ways—if you get my meaning."

—⁓—

JUST BEFORE SHE began *Playing for Time,* Vanessa had received an invitation to attend the Moscow Film Festival. She accepted, but only
on condition that the organizers allow her, during the visit, to state
openly her belief that Soviet Jews had the absolute right to emigrate
anywhere, including to Israel. To that stipulation Moscow made no
reply, and so Vanessa told the press that for this reason she would not
travel to the festival. The matter was never mentioned in American
newspapers.

As Vanessa became better known in the United States—and sometimes appreciated, too—Rachel was gaining a new generation of ad-
mirers abroad as she appeared in several prestigious productions. In
1980 she earned enthusiastic reviews for her complex and profoundly
touching performance as a lonely old spinster in the television drama
Kate the Good Neighbour, and in early 1984 she and Peggy Ashcroft
joined a large cast for the fourteen-part *Jewel in the Crown*—one of
several productions in the early 1980s (*Gandhi, Heat and Dust, The Far
Pavilions* and *A Passage to India* were others) that capitalized on Britain's curious contemporary preoccupation with India and empire. At
seventy-four, Rachel had a stately beauty and undiminished energy: off
she went to various inhospitable locations in the excruciating heat of
India, where she acted in many difficult scenes as Lady Manners, a
bravely unconventional character.

She returned to London to find Michael incapable of being left
alone, even for short periods. Corin had prudently arranged for nurses
alternating in constant attendance at Wilks Water, but now Michael's
muscles no longer obeyed his brain, the medications for Parkinson's
were causing frequent bouts of mental confusion and he required frequent catheterization of his bladder. After a time in St. Bartholomew's
Hospital, London, doctors advised that it was necessary to provide permanent care, and in the autumn of 1984 he moved into a nursing home

in Denham. "I never heard him complain," Corin recalled. "In all the discomfort of his long-drawn-out illness, he never once uttered a syllable of self-pity. Parkinson's inflicts countless small humiliations on its patients, but he bore them all with stoic dignity. And he made others feel at ease. He was able not only to prepare himself for death, but to prepare other people, too."

A crisis at Christmastime passed, and early in 1985, doctors said that Michael was sufficiently stabilized, and that Rachel (who wished to supplement the family's bank account) could travel to Nairobi, where she had been offered a part in *Out of Africa,* a lavish movie epic starring Meryl Streep and Robert Redford. Her brief role, less than a minute in the final cut of the film, was that of the kind and aristocratic Lady Belfield, transplanted from the comforts of home to the wilds of Kenya in 1913. Rachel was accompanied by twenty-year-old Jemma, who had now firmly decided on an acting career and was completing her studies at the London Academy of Music and Dramatic Art. Rachel's scenes were quickly dispatched, and she and Jemma were back in London after ten days.

―᠁―

"I'VE DONE A few good plays and pictures I'm not ashamed of," Michael said in 1981. "From now on, whatever happens to me doesn't really matter terribly much, does it? It's strange: the curious thing about death is that one worries more about other people's passing than one's own." He had, of course, accomplished far more than "a few good plays and pictures." His versatility had been remarkable, from Shakespeare to Restoration comedy, from musicals to dark thrillers—an astonishing body of work that included more than 260 plays and movies, plus television and radio appearances and recordings almost past counting. All these credits were achieved despite (in the words of Simon Callow) "the unremitting intensity of his private experience."

Working from a deep interior understanding of emotional complexity, Michael Redgrave disclosed in his art the changes and chances of life, passing them through the prism of a capacious talent. He was rarely miscast; instead, he created a vast album of colorful, original but always recognizable men forced to confront unexpected tangles in their own hearts and in those of others—hence he offered audiences not only specific characters but also reflections of themselves. A true intellectual of astounding scholarship, he had mastered the crafts of acting, teaching, writing fiction and nonfiction, translating, producing and directing, and these he complemented with related activities such as staging grand opera. He could certainly be favorably compared with Laurence Olivier, John Gielgud, Ralph Richardson and Alec Guinness, and no one could have reasonably denied that he was worthy of his knighthood.

About his children he was frank after breaking his silence on the subject of Vanessa: "I always knew she was going to be an actress. Sometimes her politics drives me mad, but I see her touch real greatness in her work, and I am immensely proud. Corin has given up his career for his politics, but perhaps one day he will be a fine actor, too. Lynn avoids politics altogether and focuses on her work and her children. I have every reason to be a happy father." And, as he soon discovered, a happy grandfather, too. In early March, he insisted on going up to London for Natasha's memorable performance as Ophelia with the Young Vic. Returning home, he turned to his family and said of Natasha, "She's a true actress."

Michael was effusive in his praise of Rachel, with whom, in 1985, he marked a marriage that had somehow endured for half a century. There was no doubt that the relationship was often bitter and stormy because of instincts he would not or could not control. But it must be stressed that no one in his family ever abandoned him. Rachel, Vanessa, Corin and Lynn discovered something intensely admirable and even lovable in his complicated nature: he was not, in other words, an unsympathetic man to those who knew him best.

—⁓—

BY LATE WINTER 1985, Vanessa and Lynn had visited their father but had to return to work in America, Lynn for the Broadway revival of *Aren't We All?* with Claudette Colbert and Rex Harrison, and Vanessa for the filming of *Three Sovereigns for Sarah,* a television miniseries about the Salem witch trials. Rachel was at the nursing home on Michael's seventy-seventh birthday, but the following morning, March 21, 1985, she was close to collapse from fatigue, and Corin insisted that she rest at Wilks Water.

That afternoon, Corin stepped quietly into the sickroom and sat by his father's bedside. Michael's breathing became shallow and labored, and then Corin thought that he was about to speak. But there was only one deep sigh, and then another, and then silence.

fifteen

THINGS HAPPEN

(1985–2012)

"My mother sacrificed so much of her career to my father's," Corin recalled after Michael's death—"and she sacrificed so much for us as children." When she learned that her husband had left no assets but only books, boxes of disorganized professional papers and some personal effects, Rachel knew that practically her only recourse for solvency was work. "It's so important for me to earn money," she said. "Work is essential to me—for my feeling of well-being and for financial security."* For a starter, she appeared in a West End production of Eliot's *The Cocktail Party*—not a well-paying job, but psychologically enriching and good professional exposure.

In April 1986, Rachel ignored all advice to the contrary and visited Glen Byam Shaw in a London hospital. She asked no questions and demanded no explanations for his mysterious, decade-long silence; she simply sat at his bedside and held his hand. For one moment, he awakened, smiled and then whispered, "You look so pretty, Rachel." Two days later he died. Soon after, his son returned to Rachel the many letters she had written to Glen after he terminated their relationship in 1976; he also informed her that another member of the family had intercepted every letter she had sent, and that Glen had never seen any of them. "Her lover adored her for over thirty years, until he died,"

---

* Several of this author's books were optioned for film and television during the last years of Rachel's life. "If you could get me a part in a production of yours, it would be perfect," she wrote in one of her letters.

according to Vanessa. "All the same, she has never believed she has beauty, nor that she was a very special actress."

Work was Rachel's refuge from these separations and the necessary absences of her children. In 1989 she was invited, at Corin's suggestion, to play Volumnia to his Coriolanus at the Young Vic. At seventy-nine, she gave a performance that won her better reviews than those received by her son, who was "baffled and angry" by the critics' personal attacks.

He ought not to have been surprised, for his early attempts to reestablish himself as a serious actor were invariably rebuffed. "I was simply excluded because of my politics," he said, and that was not a paranoid reaction: the year before, he had been appointed general secretary of the newly formed Marxist Party. It took the passing of another three years before the press fairly assessed Corin's significant talents, in Ibsen's *Rosmersholm*—"Redgrave is the production's best feature," ran a typical notice, and from that event Corin dated his theatrical renascence.

At the Young Vic, he was immensely impressive as John Proctor in *The Crucible,* as Angelo in *Measure for Measure,* and as Brutus in *Julius Caesar.* But for more than very minor movie appearances, he had to wait for *In the Name of the Father,* in which he expertly played a mesmerically cruel and mendacious police inspector, and for *Four Weddings and a Funeral,* in which his comic talent was evident as an amusing, kilted Scotsman.

—⁂—

VANESSA EVENTUALLY HAD consistently better offers to work in films, although only four of her forty-six features between 1985 and 2011 were made in the United States. Among her finest performances was that of Olive Chancellor, the forlorn feminist in James Ivory's film of the Henry James novel *The Bostonians.* Filmed in New England in the summer and autumn of 1983 and released in 1984, the picture was the first project Vanessa was offered after the Boston Symphony uproar. To her role she brought a haunting, painful passion as a woman coping with both society's prejudices and her urgent, frustrated love for a female protégée. Although the movie was made in enemy territory (her lawsuit against the BSO was still unsettled) and despite the fact that Vanessa's work was often interrupted by calls from attorneys, she was nothing like a diva with her colleagues or the public.

"She was always visible and accessible in a way that Christopher Reeve could not be," said Ivory, speaking of Vanessa's costar, who had already achieved international fame in three *Superman* movies. "She carried requests for autographs in to him and when he'd signed, she brought them out again to distribute. She did not try to push her political views on her co-workers, as we had been told in England she might try to do . . . [and] she did a lot of the cooking for us." The movie was a critical triumph for Vanessa, who received an Oscar nomination as best actress of the year.* No such success attended *The White Countess,* another James Ivory picture, featuring Vanessa, Lynn and, in the leading roles, Natasha Richardson and Ralph Fiennes. Lacking both emotional impact and narrative focus, that unfortunate movie, produced in Shanghai in 2004, was remarkable only for the subtle array of Natasha's finely tuned reactions and her expert assumption of a Russian-inflected accent.

David Hare, who wrote and directed *Wetherby* in 1985, the year after *The Bostonians* was released, gave perhaps the fullest account of working with Vanessa. At first, he recalled, it was "hell to get to the starting point. She says she's going to do your project, and then when you ask around, you find she's got five others she's planning to do. All around London there are directors expecting to work with Vanessa in six weeks' time. It's as if it takes her a very long time to focus. Her bad eyesight physically heightens the impression that she is someone wandering around in a fog.† Rehearsals are therefore pointless. Or more accurately, they are pointless to you. But then, when she does focus, the effect is more intense than with anyone else." In this film—about a

---

* Vanessa had been nominated as best actress for *Morgan, Isadora* and *Mary, Queen of Scots*; she had won the supporting actress award for *Julia* and was nominated again in that category for *Howards End.* But she received no further Academy statuette after *Julia.*
† Disturbed by what she called the "bags" under her eyes, Vanessa had cosmetic surgery in 1985.

mysterious stranger who kills himself in the home of a woman played by Vanessa—Hare thought that sometimes it was difficult to know just what she was doing:

"She has a very direct access to her own feelings and to the camera. She likes to talk a part through with you, but these discussions have very little bearing on what she will actually do. Most actors strain to find an emotion. They have to hunt around for it and some actors, mostly Americans, make great play in their search for it. Vanessa seems to have some sort of plumb line that takes her straight to the one she wants. It comes up pure. This is why she is the most admired actor among her peers."

In the flashbacks of *Wetherby,* Joely Richardson (then nineteen) portrayed Vanessa's character when much younger. "Of course it's helpful to be a member of a prominent theatrical family," Joely said, "but obviously you're up against a measuring stick. You not only have to be as good as they are to be taken seriously—you almost have to be better." Natasha agreed and added another perspective: "I know how it is to be the daughter of a great actress, and how very hard it is to make your own way, to be compared to someone of such great talent and beauty—and to feel, when am I ever going to make it on my own and be judged on my own merit? I only have to go back to England for five minutes to feel I've been put in my place—worthy of notice only because I happen to be a Redgrave." But that was not exactly the case. When Natasha later returned to London to appear onstage—for example, in *The Seagull* and *The Lady from the Sea*—she received consistently good reviews that said nothing about her ancestry.

At the time *Wetherby* was being filmed, the Richardson sisters were still living with Vanessa in a flat in Chiswick. "My mother's politics were such that she gave everything away," Joely recalled. "We had a rota on the fridge for Tash [Natasha], me and my half-brother Carlo—one of us did the shopping, one did the cooking, and one did the washing-up." (Among their occasional supper companions was the girls' half sister Katherine Grimond, born to Tony Richardson and Grizelda Grimond during their liaison after his divorce from Vanessa.)

While she was working with her mother in *Wetherby,* Joely was attending classes at RADA, where she had begun studies in 1983 and graduated two years later. "I shied away from acting during my teens. I did it occasionally, but if someone asked me if I was actually going to become an actress, I would say absolutely not, not in a thousand years."

At five feet ten inches by the time of her mid-teens, Joely was such an expert tennis player that in 1979 she earned a scholarship to the Harry Hopman Tennis Academy in Florida. But Tony intervened, giving her a bit part in his picture *The Hotel New Hampshire* ("I've never loved any movie more," he said of it), and insisted that Joely make an attempt at serious acting. "I think that because Mum is so famous, people assume that she was the main influence. But in those early years, it was more my father. He was really passionate about me and Tash being actresses."

Natasha, who graduated from the Central School of Speech and Drama without ever telling anyone she was a Redgrave, agreed. (Corin's daughter, Jemma Redgrave, could obviously not keep the same silence at LAMDA or at the Lyric Theatre, Belfast, where she bore the family name and subsequently performed in repertory.) According to Natasha, "The first time my father saw me act, he said, 'I'm pleased to see you've got talent, and I'm pleased to see you move very well—but that's not all there is to it.' And then he proceeded to tell me, for about two hours, what I'd done wrong—which upset me very much at the time. But then I realized how good it was that he did that. You learn from people you respect, and from them telling you objectively what they think."

Natasha made her movie debut in a small role in *Every Picture Tells a Story,* based on the true account of an orphaned boy whose art school education was financed by his dead father's neighbors. Soon she accepted a great number of movie and television roles, some of which were worthy of her talent. In a production of *The Seagull,* for example, Natasha played Nina opposite the Arkadina of Vanessa (who won her third *Evening Standard* Theatre Award as best actress, and a fourth after that, when she again portrayed Isadora Duncan—this time on-stage, in *Where She Danced*). For her efforts, Natasha received high marks even from Tony, her severest critic. She then moved in with

Robert Fox, the producer of *The Seagull,* an established theater and film impresario eleven years her senior and the son of Vanessa's former agent, Robin Fox.

With that, the press tried to stir up indelicate rumors of shocking antics in the lives of the Richardson sisters. "It was a big joke between us," recalled Joely, "because all they could say [apart from Natasha's cohabitation with Fox, which was hardly scandalous in 1986] was that these girls are not into sex, drugs and rock 'n' roll. Quite right—our life really couldn't have been farther from all that." In fact, they worked—and then worked some more. Joely took on no less a ferocious part than that of *Miss Julie*; she was a touching Emily in *Our Town*; and she later appeared with her mother in *Lady Windermere's Fan,* a production they both enjoyed enormously.

In matters relating to her family, Vanessa ignored gossip as much as she discounted praise. From the 1980s she very rarely gave interviews, and if she was contractually obliged to meet with a journalist to promote a film or play, certain strict conditions were established in advance: her politics and private life were off-limits, and she had the right to approve the final draft of an article.

—⚹—

THE TABLOIDS MAY have been dismayed to find such purpose in the lives of Natasha and Joely, but in the 1980s, Lynn could have provided a whisper of scandal. "I had successfully turned around thirty years of food addiction," she recalled, "but it was too soon to have a go at changing my desire to drink. When I was honest with myself, I had to admit that I was placing myself at the mercy of the grape in exactly the same way I had allowed myself to be ruled by food. I was drinking much more than I'd been advised by Weight Watchers." Finally she was able to control this problem, too, but she always felt somehow at the mercy of what she called her "anxious heart."

All the Redgrave women had romantic anxieties even as their careers flourished. Vanessa finally separated from Timothy Dalton—"because I told him I was going to a big rally for trade unionists in Manchester one Sunday afternoon when he wanted me to stay with him." Natasha married Robert Fox and, at twenty-seven, became stepmother to his three children. "I was so young to be taking on so much," she said later, "but I was in love with Robert and we made each other laugh." The merriment endured for only two years before they were divorced, for the marriage could not sustain the long distances and absences required by separate careers. "At that time, because my parents had split up, I didn't feel marriage was necessarily something for life—nor, because they remained friends, did I see divorce as necessarily failure and misery. I thought it was perfectly normal and okay for people to be married for a few years and then to break up if it wasn't working out."

Her second marriage, to the Irish actor Liam Neeson, endured. In January 1993 they performed together on Broadway in O'Neill's *Anna Christie,* and after the play closed in March, Natasha followed him to Poland for the filming of *Schindler's List.* (Vanessa publicly praised the Spielberg movie and urged the public to see it for its stark portrayal of Nazi barbarity—and to consider what one courageous person can do to save the lives of many in horrific circumstances.) Natasha and Liam were married on July 3, 1994, at a farmhouse they bought and renovated in Millbrook, New York, a two-hour drive north of Manhattan. Their two sons, Michael and Daniel, were born in 1995 and 1996.

Joely, meanwhile, had met and fallen in love with Archibald Stirling, husband of the formidable actress Diana Rigg. He eventually ended the extramarital affair and returned to his wife, but his contrition could not save the marriage, which was soon on the divorce docket. Then, in 1992, Joely married the producer Tim Bevan, and they had a daughter they named Daisy, after the child's great-great-grandmother. The Bevans were married for nine years, and then (as she described it), "My marriage collapsed, and it was a pretty low time for me. I had to sell the home, the cottage in the country, this whole little life I'd created over a decade. I questioned everything." But after a time, Joely and Tim Bevan salvaged a friendship from their broken marriage. "He was a fabulous husband and he's a fabulous ex-husband," she said, adding that, as late as 2010, she remained on good terms with him and his second wife, the artist Amy Gadney.

There followed Joely's more or less intense relationships with the talk show host Jamie Theakston; with the American actor John Hensley; and with Evgeny Lebedev, a billionaire Russian entrepreneur. Simultaneously, she received an avalanche of film offers and acted in various productions with Mel Gibson, Glenn Close, Hugh Laurie and Emma Thompson. She also won a Theatre World Award for her role in the Off-Broadway play *Madame Melville*—and then she spent half of each year in Hollywood, where she starred in more than one hundred episodes of the television series *Nip/Tuck*. Even as their careers advanced and their achievements became more noteworthy, Joely and Natasha invariably retained in public an admirable lack of pretense and vanity, and their occasional conversations with journalists were, as one said, "frantically self-effacing." Like their parents, the sisters had no sense of humbug.

In September 1990 Tony Richardson was the host, at his Los Angeles home, for a celebration of Carlo Nero's twenty-first birthday. Franco joined the entire family at the party, which was somewhat muted because Tony was ill and feverish. During the following year, his health failed rapidly and alarmingly, and by October it was known that he was dying of AIDS. Vanessa, Natasha and Robert Fox, Joely, Katherine Grimond and her mother, Grizelda, all hastened to be with him.

Tony Richardson died on the afternoon of November 14, 1991, at the age of sixty-three. That evening, in the clutter of a closet at his house, Natasha found a lengthy unedited manuscript, full of mistakes, discursive and incomplete, but with trenchant, witty observations on parts of his career; it contained few personal details and nothing about his bisexuality. Natasha published the text two years later under the title *The Long-Distance Runner*. "I doubt his book will solve many of the myriad mysteries he carried with him," said his friend and former colleague John Osborne.*

In 1992 Jemma Redgrave married a lawyer named Tim Owen, whom reporters sometimes confused with Tim Bevan (or even Tim Dalton). Jemma and her husband subsequently dallied with others,

---

* With Corin as amanuensis, Vanessa published her autobiography in England the year Tony died; three years later, a much revised and expanded edition appeared in the United States.

separated, were later reconciled and had two sons, Gabriel and Alfie. She and her brother Luke, then beginning his career as a camera operator on feature films, helped to care for their mother, Deirdre, during her struggle with cancer. "Every time she had bad news," according to Jemma, "she said, 'I will beat this—don't worry, I'm fine.'" But the disease ravaged her, and Deirdre finally succumbed in 1997 at the age of fifty-seven. Jemma then resumed full-time work on British television in more than fifty productions—most notably in twenty-six episodes of the critically acclaimed series *Bramwell* (in which she played the eponymous Victorian doctor) and as the fey but good-natured Lady Bertram in a worthy production of Austen's *Mansfield Park*.

Only Lynn's marriage appeared stable and secure. By 1993 she had been Mrs. John Clark for twenty-six years. In an effort to understand the conundrum of what she called her father's emotional distance, she wrote and performed a one-woman play called *Shakespeare for My Father,* a presentation of scenes from the Redgrave family's life, which her husband directed and which enjoyed enormous success in twenty-seven American cities before opening on Broadway, where it ran for almost a year. "I needed to forgive myself for feeling guilty for the bad thoughts I had about him," Lynn said of her play. "He was what he was, for better or worse—a difficult, tortured man who could be the joy of people's hearts or the nightmare of your life." From this time, Lynn spoke of Michael as openly as Vanessa did of her politics. Rachel, ever the supportive mother, came to every Saturday evening performance when Lynn took her play to London, and Vanessa said, "You have given me a window into your soul and into Dad's."

Lynn followed *Shakespeare for My Father* with three more plays about her family, each more fanciful and fictitious, and far less appealing to audiences: *The Mandrake Root* (about her mother), *Nightingale* (about her grandmother Beatrice) and *Rachel and Juliet* (about her mother's lifelong quest for a real-life Romeo). She then continued her busy schedule with repertory performances across America and in feature films—most famously, as the wife of a brilliant but psychologically damaged pianist in *Shine*; and as the amusingly grumpy but loyal housekeeper to an aging movie director in *Gods and Monsters,* for which she received an Oscar nomination as best supporting actress. She also acted with Vanessa and Jemma in a West End production of *The Three Sisters*. "It was challenging and really quite frightening for me," Jemma said of this collaboration, "because neither Vanessa nor Lynn had seen any of my work before that. But in the end it was really the best professional experience of my life."

"The pressures on students and young performers today are well nigh intolerable and without precedent," Vanessa commented after this production. "The same pressures exist for us older ones—the lack of work, the lack of time to do work well if there is work, the pressure to deliver the required 'effect' and so on. Yet they are not the same, for the young have higher aspirations and are made to feel that they have very little time in which to prove themselves before they may be cast aside."

Over the years, Lynn was regarded as the only family member in a happy marriage. But its steadfastness proved illusory. As she prepared Thanksgiving dinner at her home in Los Angeles in 1998, John informed her that, seven years earlier, he had had an affair with Lynn's personal assistant, a young woman named Nicolette Hannah. The result of this liaison was a baby—now a seven-year-old boy named Zachary.

John and Nicolette had kept the identity of their child's paternity a secret, even after Nicolette married John and Lynn's son, Benjamin Clark, who took on the single mother and her son. ("No one was supposed to know," as John said.) But when Nicolette and Ben separated, she told him that his stepson was actually his half brother, and the recriminations began: the family now resembled one from the pages of Eugene O'Neill, if not Aeschylus. John did not quite understand Lynn's outrage. After she spoke to the press, he told a magazine reporter that he "felt betrayed—and my response is, 'Lighten up, Lynn!' She's dumping me for no good reason." Lynn filed for a divorce, which was granted in 2000.

This unhappy situation flooded newspapers and magazines in America and England just as Natasha was receiving the Tony Award for her performance as Sally Bowles in a revival of *Cabaret*—"an electrifying triumph," according to the *New York Times*. By this time, she was living permanently in the United States and, like her mother, had no comment when asked about the Clark family shenanigans in California.

—∿—

DURING THE 1991 Gulf War, which she loudly condemned, Vanessa organized a fund-raiser at the Royal Albert Hall for the orphaned and homeless children of Iraq. During a break in the production of *Howards End* (in which Jemma played her daughter), she traveled to that country for five days, taking a cameraman and a staff from UNICEF, to make a short film about the plight of children in war-torn locations. She then accepted the organization's request that she become their special representative from 1993 to 1995.

Following that term, UNICEF executives invited her to be a Goodwill Ambassador. By this time, Vanessa had unofficially but clearly abandoned her strident Marxist ideology—but not her passionate involvement in humanitarian causes. Of this time, she later said, "I wouldn't call myself a Marxist. My main concern has not been any political party for a long time, since I first became a UNICEF ambassador." Vanessa and her son, Carlo, then produced, at their own expense, a compelling documentary about the sixty-year history of UNICEF, and she began a cycle of frequent travels, on behalf of deprived children, to hot spots around the world. "To be non-political—in other words, to put first the needs of children, their mothers, their parents, their families, before any politics whatsoever—I've become convinced that this is what's needed." She brought this conviction to college forums, too, as when she inaugurated a four-week program, the International Diploma in Humanitarian Assistance, at Fordham University in New York City.

About the same time as she began her work with UNICEF, Vanessa received a letter from 10 Downing Street, inquiring if she would accept the high honor of being named a Dame of the British Empire. She replied that she would not. More important to her was her involvement with the Office of the UN High Commissioner for Refugees and with the UN Relief and Works Agency for Palestinian Refugees in

Gaza, the West Bank and Lebanon. She and her colleagues at UNI-
CEF then drafted a schedule that included visits to refugee camps in
Albania, Kosovo, Afghanistan and the former Yugoslavian Republic of
Macedonia, and she established conferences in Uganda, Central America and elsewhere, all of which she attended. Later, Carlo directed his
mother, Joely and Michael Moore in a film called *The Fever,* about the
confusions of a middle-class matron, caught in a dangerous war-torn
country, whose values are chastened by reality.*

In addition to all these activities abroad, Vanessa quietly assumed
responsibilities at home. After selling Wilks Water and 42 Ebury
Mews, Rachel lived for several years in a duplex apartment in Flood
Street, Chelsea. Clear of mind and in good health into her eighties,
she nevertheless found stairs an increasing challenge. Vanessa then insisted that Rachel come to live with her in Chiswick: she engaged a
companion when she was acting in the West End, and if she had to
travel in America, her mother gladly came along and stayed in Millbrook with Natasha and Liam, who found Granny's presence a treat.
"I cannot tell you what it means to me—to feel so welcome in Natasha's home," Rachel told a friend. "She is really the most loving, most
caring young woman—completely without airs and graces. She hasn't
a thing to do with being a star, she wants only to be a very good actress.
Natasha and Liam have a wonderful marriage—one can sense that
straightaway—and there is the most wonderful, peaceful atmosphere
in their home."

In 1997 Rachel and Corin performed a radio reading of *Whole
Days in the Trees* by Marguerite Duras, and then Rachel played Vanessa's mother in a brief, touching scene in the romantic movie *Déjà Vu.*
That was her one hundredth movie and television role, and it turned
out to be her last. The following spring, just when she marked her
eighty-eighth birthday, Rachel joined Vanessa onstage, reading Chekhov short stories at an arts festival in Massachusetts and then at a Manhattan theater. One journalist compared the event to "an evening in
the Redgraves' parlor" and noted the "frail and beautiful [Rachel] . . . a

---

* Carlo also directed Vanessa and Franco in an Italian thriller called *Uninvited.*

distinguished guest." But soon that frailty caught up with the Redgrave matriarch, and she began, gently, to decline.

—⁂—

DURING THOSE YEARS, several acclaimed productions occupied Vanessa during her visits to America. She returned to Broadway after a thirteen-year absence, in Peter Hall's staging of *Orpheus Descending,* by Tennessee Williams—a performance marred only by her erratic, faux Sicilian American accent. With Corin and Kika, she then founded the loosely organized Moving Theater Company, performing plays classic and modern wherever they might find a welcome mat. Corin had enjoyed an astonishing comeback, earning high marks in a chilling performance as the alcoholic actor in *The Country Girl* (earlier rendered by Michael when it was called *Winter Journey*) and dispatching a number of roles in television series and feature films. Corin and Vanessa then took their troupe to Houston's Alley Theatre, where she directed and played the Egyptian queen in *Antony and Cleopatra,* and he directed and took the title role in *Julius Caesar.*

"The only living actress to whom theatrical luminosity comes so naturally," according to one critic, "she projects a mounting, burnished radiance that mixes girlish breathlessness with a ripe, all-consuming passion." Corin played Caesar as "splenetic, sadistic and ailing, a man asking to be assassinated," which was certainly a controversial interpretation in an awkwardly staged production. But both Redgraves were praised as directors. She brought her *Antony and Cleopatra* to New York's Public Theater the following year, where the same critic—reminding his readers that Vanessa was "arguably the greatest living actress of the English-speaking theatre"—concluded a lengthy review by describing her as "transcendent . . . magnificent. Here at last is a Cleopatra of hypnotic majesty and passion."

While the Redgraves were in Texas, they visited the University of Texas at Austin, which had purchased the Tennessee Williams papers. They had heard of his hitherto unproduced 1938 play *Not About Nightingales,* a realistically violent drama based on an incident in which many men died hideously in a Pennsylvania prison, scalded to death in a torture shed where the radiator temperature was raised to 150 degrees, an event that triggered a national scandal and provoked a federal investigation. Vanessa coproduced the play to great effect in London, where Corin won the Olivier Award for his portrayal of the sadistic warden; in New York, he was nominated for the Tony as the best actor of 1999.* "Mr. Redgrave has never been more mesmeric," proclaimed one British critic in a review that summarized the majority on both sides of the Atlantic. The following season, brother and sister played brother and sister—the fussy Gayev and the aristocratic Ranevskaya—in *The Cherry Orchard*. Audiences at last appreciated them as gifted actors, not as reformed revolutionaries. Vanessa received her usual glowing notices, and Corin was equally praised: "He was always a very sound actor," said Peter Hall. "Now he has become a great one. He seems to have inherited the mantle of his father in a major way."

—⚏—

AMONG VANESSA'S MANY television roles, she played a lesbian pitched into grief by the sudden death of her lifetime partner in *If These Walls Could Talk 2*. Written and directed by Jane Anderson, it was produced during the summer of 1999 as part of an anthology and remains remarkable for Vanessa's performance and that of her costar: she accepted the part not only because she admired the script and what it said about bigotry, but also for the opportunity to work with the celebrated American actress Marian Seldes, as the devoted companion who suddenly dies, leaving her bereft but not weak. During the filming, as Seldes recalled, "Vanessa led us all, treating everyone with care." Critics praised the "eloquence" of Marian's performance and the "exquisitely understated performance" of Vanessa's (for which she won the Emmy for the outstanding performance by a leading actress in a television movie). Cinematographer Paul Elliott rendered each sequence with his usual artistry, from the harsh light of a hospital corridor to the penumbral, twilight sadness of an empty home.

---

* According to the London agent Laurence Evans, Vanessa had first learned about the play after she read this author's book *The Kindness of Strangers: The Life of Tennessee Williams* in 1985, which immediately aroused her interest in *Not About Nightingales*.

Vanessa also made two of her rare excursions into comedy that same year: in *Cradle Will Rock,* about the 1937 production of a Marc Blitzstein musical (which originally had a definite article before the first word of the title). Part social satire and part political invective, the picture featured Vanessa as if she were a latter-day Isadora Duncan—the daffy, dancing countess who joins a protest movement in favor of artistic freedom, against the police and contrary to the principles of her staid husband.

She then hurried to London, where she again played a marvelously dotty free spirit, joining Corin (playing her old flame) and Kika (as his wife) in a revival of Noël Coward's bittersweet comedy *Song at Twilight.* For a few journalists and perhaps some in the audience, the special attraction was the appearance of sibling actors playing ex-lovers—with the added fascination that she discloses his homosexuality. "The play is a comedy about repression," Corin said, "and people who are oppressed often become the worst oppressors."

The critic Sheridan Morley, who directed *Song at Twilight,* liked working with Corin and Kika—but he had only harsh words for Vanessa, calling her "incredibly boring, fatuous and pretentious [with her] terminally antiquated and irrelevant political views [and giving] a performance of marathon self-indulgence and hysteria." She found Morley moody and uninspiring, but her response was polite. "If I have ever been rude to you, I am sorry," Vanessa told him. "It's no excuse, but I get upset and fussed and can't work properly if things are not calm and thoughtful. I will certainly try my best to make them so." And then she made her point: "Sometimes *you* don't know how to make them so, for lack of experience."

Soon after the play closed, Corin was diagnosed with prostate cancer, which was routed with surgery and a course of aggressive chemotherapy. He could not work for almost a year, a time he used for earnest, quiet study and preparation for roles he still hoped to perform and which he often discussed at length with Kika and Vanessa.

—⁀⁀—

"WHEN SORROWS COME, they come not single spies, but in battalions," as Shakespeare wrote. So it was for the Redgrave family. By 2002 Rachel had slipped into virtually permanent dementia, and although she remained docile and was not confined to bed, she required constant care and attention—which Vanessa, Lynn and Natasha provided.

Then, at Christmastime that same year, Lynn felt a lump in her right breast, and in January 2003, after receiving a diagnosis of cancer, she underwent a radical mastectomy in New York—insisting, immediately after she awoke from anesthesia, that she would honor her commitment to perform in a play three months later. That season, her daughter Annabel Clark was completing studies in photography at the Parsons School of Design in New York, and she and her mother documented in word and images the course of Lynn's treatment and recovery. The photographs, along with Lynn's journal entries, were subsequently published as a book that reveals, as Annabel said, Lynn's "incredible will to overcome this disease with both strength and grace."

In addition to her rental apartment in Manhattan, Lynn had purchased a country house in Kent, Connecticut, and there she retreated for weekends during her convalescence. During months of chemotherapy, she was buoyed by long transatlantic calls from Corin, who tempered empathy with leavening humor, and by Vanessa, who (as Lynn wrote) "keeps turning up like an angel just when I need her most—like the day I was at MSK [Memorial Sloan-Kettering Cancer Center, New York], running around having bone scans . . . Much of my recovery was thanks to Vanessa." She sat quietly with Lynn when that was appropriate, took her to lunch on good days, attended her without fuss or intrusion—and then returned to her own tasks and to the care of their mother.

As she had promised, Lynn, despite intermittent bouts of weakness and severe nausea, was present that winter for the first New York rehearsals of Alan Bennett's anthology *Talking Heads,* for which critics praised what they considered one of the best comic performances New York had seen in years; for it, she won the Drama Desk Award as best featured actress. At the time, no one outside the family knew of her condition. In March Natasha and Liam joined Lynn's children at a party honoring her sixtieth birthday. Annabel completed her degree at Parsons and began a successful career as a photographer; Kelly, who had changed her name to Pema and studied Buddhism, soon bore a son and later became a pop singer with a band; and Ben was a flight captain for Delta Airlines, now remarried and with children of his own. Lynn had joined a Congregational Church in Connecticut—"a wonderful haven for me [with] the comfort of shared prayer."

By late spring 2003, Rachel was living permanently with Natasha and Liam at their country house in Millbrook. "Darling Mum," Lynn noted after a visit. "She held out her hands, and her mouth was open in an 'Oh!' and her eyes were wide as I hugged and kissed her. I cried, and she was teary, too, and darling Vanessa was so sweet . . . " During a visit some weeks later, "Mum for an instant didn't know it was me. Then she said, 'It's my Lynn!' and we had tea and she dozed."

Lynn was optimistic about her full recovery from cancer—until one of her doctors said that she was at high risk for a spread of the disease within the next five to six years. "I fell apart and called my sis—who got in a taxi and came right over." Vanessa had just begun performances in *Long Day's Journey into Night* on Broadway, which sent reviewers scurrying for superlatives and which won her the Tony as best actress of the year.

"I think my Mummy is fading away," Lynn wrote in her diary on May 12. A few days later, Rachel suffered a major stroke, and then a milder one. Lynn and the children alternated at her bedside, and Lynn brought a recording of Rachel's favorite music, selections by Vaughan Williams. "When 'Greensleeves' first began playing, I said, 'Do you remember this?' And Mum nodded twice and smiled."

"In the early morning," Rachel had said a few years earlier, "I sometimes feel that I just can't carry on any longer. But of course somehow I do. I still don't believe very much in myself, and I haven't much confidence in what I do—but my children are so encouraging. Imagine—I still need encouragement at my age!" As Lynn said, there were aspects of Rachel's life "that filled her with 'if only's . . . if only I had done this . . . or that . . . '"

Corin arrived from London, and by May 20 their mother was drifting in and out of deep sleep. Among the photos at her bedside were pictures of her parents and brothers, of Michael and their children. Very late on Friday, May 23, her breathing became labored, but she was unconscious and free of pain. During the early hours of Saturday morning, Rachel Kempson Redgrave died peacefully. She was interred in the nearby cemetery of St. Peter's Church on May 29, the day after her ninety-third birthday.

Lynn felt that her last weeks with Rachel were "a privilege, full of tears and yet happiness, too." The church cemetery was "beautiful—in a field overlooking more fields. I will want to be buried near her." For years to come, whenever she could find them, Vanessa brought into her own home pots of blue hyacinths, her mother's favorite blossoms. "I don't feel lonely," she said. "I still feel that my mother is here. I can smell the hyacinths."

—⁓—

WHILE NATASHA, LYNN and Vanessa traveled to Hong Kong the following year, for *The White Countess,* Corin acted in a wide variety of successful stage appearances—among them *King Lear* at Stratford and *The Entertainer* in Liverpool. He and Vanessa had recently formed the Peace and Progress Party, which had no leftist political ties but that condemned the British and American presence in Iraq and called for a cancellation of debts owed by third world countries. "Human rights can become an organizing principle for opposition to war," he said.

When Vanessa returned from Asia, she planned to go at once into Stratford's production of the Greek tragedy *Hecuba,* but this was delayed when she had to submit to surgery for a painful attack of kidney stones, which was followed by a hip replacement. Then, one evening in June 2005, while Vanessa was recuperating, Joely told her mother the worrying news that her daughter, Daisy, then thirteen, had to be treated for a rare vascular condition affecting the circulation in her legs: this was not a morbid diagnosis, but it was serious, and Joely at once rearranged her schedule to be at home with Daisy.

That same month, Corin was addressing a group in London about the problems and rights of refugees and foreign travelers in England. Immediately after he told a group of councilors, "You have the power of life and death—to do a great deal of good or the power to do harm," he suddenly collapsed. Emergency medical personnel arrived and raced him to the hospital, where it was determined that he had suffered a massive heart attack from which he might not recover. Jemma rushed home from Ireland (where she and Peter O'Toole were among the cast in a remake of *Lassie*), and Corin's other children quickly joined her for a long vigil; in fact, he was critically ill for months, and when the crisis had passed, his memory was severely impaired. "It affected everything I did for quite a while," he said, explaining why he was forbidden to plan any performances.

A year passed before Corin could accept a small movie role, and two years before he stepped onstage with Oscar Wilde's *De Profundis,* which he was forced to read "because he could no longer memorize," as Jemma said. But like Wilde during his incarceration at Reading Gaol, Corin was completely in the moment, and, as Jemma added, "his own sense of imprisonment came through" while he read the text with calm passion.

There was one remarkable moment, as director David Thacker recalled. In late 2006 Kika invited David to their London home when Corin was attempting to reboot his memory. They asked Jemma to join them in reading the reunion scene between father and daughter from the final act of *Pericles,* the character Corin was playing at The Globe when he had his heart attack. At first Corin could recall neither the production nor his part in it. But as he read the scene—with Jemma assuming the voice of Marina—Corin suddenly smiled. He recognized the text, and he knew the great joy of being with his own daughter. "It was," said Thacker, "an extraordinary privilege to watch this synthesis of great art and real life."

That same season, Vanessa brought a similarly controlled emotion to her performance as a dying mother in the disappointing soap opera *Evening,* filmed mostly near New England seashores. Natasha played one of her daughters, and both she and her mother were clearly superior to their material. Meanwhile, Joely was in Vancouver, appearing, calmly and beautifully, as the anxious mother of two children visited by benevolent otherworldlings in *The Last Mimzy.*

On the last day of December, Vanessa invited family and friends to her London home for her wedding to Franco Nero. They had met forty-one years earlier, and he had been an occasional presence in her life after their subsequent separation; since that time, there had been "all sorts of other people involved" in their lives, as Vanessa said. "The worst times were when we were not speaking to each other or were shouting at each other." She was about to turn seventy and he sixty-six, and they both wanted something "with the greatest possible commitment and love." Franco had been with Vanessa (or in constant communication with her) throughout the happy and sad events of recent years, and during times of loss, illness and death, and so he would be in the years to come.

Determined to avoid what they considered the financial complexities of a legally binding marriage, the couple decided instead to have a private, nonlegal ceremony. "The games are done," said Franco. "All of our tears now will be the bond that makes us stronger." Later, art (or at least popular entertainment) mimicked life: Vanessa and Franco starred in a pleasantly harmless, beautifully scenic movie called *Letters to Juliet,* filmed in the Tuscan countryside. They played a couple separated for many years before they are reunited and invite all the locals to their festive wedding.

—⁂—

BECAUSE SHE HAD regained most of her energy after radiation and chemotherapy treatments and was pronounced cancer-free, Lynn resumed an astonishingly rigorous work schedule onstage. From 2005 to 2008 she appeared in two more Broadway plays; picked up nominations for her performance in Maugham's *The Constant Wife,* rewrote and performed her own plays and accepted roles large and small in the works of others. Her portrayal of Lady Bracknell was a particular success in Los Angeles and New York, and there were others. "She had a lot to battle," as Ian McKellen said: "her family history, her weight, a difficult marriage"—and then the prospect of a fatal illness. Six years after her mastectomy, it seemed that the battles had been won. Lynn had faced her own mortality, had written about it and had watched as her daughter documented her illness in the remarkably frank photographs they later published, hoping to help other women. Lynn cheered her sister's solo performance in *The Year of Magical Thinking,* Joan Didion's account of coming to terms with the deaths of her husband and daughter and of somehow surviving—"the finest portrayal of controlled grief I ever saw," as Bernard Dick recalled.

Corin also came to New York to see Vanessa's performance, and during his visit he gave a benefit reading of the one-man show *Tynan,* about the controversial, often dyspeptic critic. He also joined his sisters and a team of journalists, military officials and academics who gathered for discussions on the topic "A Question of Impeachment," which explored the case against President Bush and Vice President Cheney. At another event, the three Redgraves recited "Poems from Guantánamo," a collection by political detainees.

But in early 2009 Lynn's illness returned. Despite the stage-four cancer—the indicator that the disease had spread and was unlikely to be cured—she continued to perform, even when, ultimately, she had to sit at a desk and read the text of *Nightingale.* "I could be dead, but I'm not," she told a reporter with deliberate whimsy. "Here I am. I just go on working. After all, I've lived with cancer for years now."

—∞—

BUT THE BATTALIONS of sorrows continued to advance.

In March, while Liam was in Toronto acting in the movie thriller *Chloe,* Natasha went to the Mont Tremblant ski resort in the snowy Laurentian Hills, a two-hour drive from Montreal and seven hours from Toronto. Not proficient on skis, she was accompanied by an instructor on the morning of March 16, when she approached the gentle slope of a beginner's run. Suddenly, she fell. "She didn't hit anyone or anything," according to Lyne Lortie, a spokeswoman for Mont Tremblant. For just a moment, she seemed to faint or become disoriented, but then Natasha picked herself up and laughed at her own awkwardness, showing no signs of injury and refusing medical assistance. Her ski instructor, however, thought it best for her to return to the resort and rest, and he left her in her room. An hour later, she complained of a severe headache, dizziness and nausea. Paramedics were called, and she was taken to a local hospital, where she slipped into a deep coma.

Liam was summoned at his production site in Toronto and hurried to her bedside. By this time, his wife was unresponsive, and a scan revealed intracranial swelling caused by severe bleeding; soon no brain activity registered at all. Liam arranged for her to be transferred by air-ambulance to Lenox Hill Hospital in Manhattan; the immediate family was summoned; and after further tests and consultations, the hard decision was made to remove the futile life support. On March 18, 2009, Natasha Jane Richardson Neeson was pronounced dead at the age of forty-five. She was buried near Rachel in the cemetery at Millbrook.

Medical experts familiar with Natasha's case disagreed on the precise cause of the fatal bleeding in her brain. She may have had a stroke or a small aneurysm that moved or burst and caused her to stumble—or the fall may have precipitated a stroke. "Blunt force" was mentioned in the official New York autopsy, but that seems to have been a hypothesis more than a final explanation: there was no sign of injury to her skull, much less a fracture, nor was there anything nearby to have caused "blunt force" where she fell. (This is not to suggest any indication of a suspicious death, which there was never any medical or moral reason to insinuate, imply or suggest.) Natasha never took so-called recreational drugs, and tests in Canada and New York showed no signs of any psychotropic medication in her system. But she had been a heavy smoker since her teenage years, and that could not be ruled out as a contributing factor in a stroke: her age was no guarantee of immunity in that regard. It is also possible that she had a congenital cerebral weakness, a condition impossible to diagnose in anyone before a medical emergency occurs.

Soon after the funeral, Liam returned to Toronto and honored his obligation to complete the interrupted film, which he did in two days. He and his two young sons then withdrew from the public, and Vanessa, Joely and the rest of the family also maintained a dignified silence during their time of private mourning, refusing all requests from reporters to tell the world "what it feels like when a loved one dies." Later, Vanessa simply said that losing an adored child was of course unimaginable. That summer, Jemma effectively spoke for the family, recalling how much Natasha loved to gather a crowd, set a table and cook lavishly for all of them. "Tasha embraced every second of every day. She celebrated family and friends. She was a centrifugal force, keeping us all in contact. Relationships and friendships happened because of her. It was the way she lived her life, rather than the manner of her death, that taught me so much."

—⁓—

THE REDGRAVE SIBLINGS drew ever closer to one another. "Ten years ago," said Vanessa during a joint television interview with her sister, "Lynn and I were at odds for a short time [over my political manifestoes]—but not since then. Lynn is an immensely giving and generous person. I'm very lucky to have her as a sister." Replied Lynn: "My illness brought us so much closer together. Sisters aren't always so close—at any time in their lives, let alone at this later point."

Their shared devotion was all the more necessary and appreciated when, after Natasha's death, Lynn's illness became more limiting and painful for her. Nevertheless, in July she traveled to Wisconsin, where she conducted a master class in acting at Ten Chimneys, the former home of Alfred Lunt and Lynn Fontanne. After reciting from *Hamlet* onstage with her students ("Speak the speech, I pray you . . . "), she received thunderous applause and all but broke down in tears. With that, Lynn Redgrave had closed the circle honoring the woman after whom she was named. For the rest of that year, she continued to perform *Nightingale*; despite its different denotations in their respective projects, the word had become like a talisman for her and Corin. Even with severe pain, Lynn insisted on honoring her commitment to read *Rachel and Juliet* in Tucson in January 2010. That same month, she was inducted into the Theater Hall of Fame at ceremonies in New York.

In February, Vanessa traveled to London, where she received BAFTA's Academy Fellowship in honor of her significant contributions to British cinema. Her agents then announced that she had been cast in four pictures to be made during 2010. Early that spring, she was in Serbia, beginning work as Volumnia in a modern film version of *Coriolanus,* with Ralph Fiennes directing and in the title role. When the picture was released the following year, Vanessa was described as "quite tremendous . . . both implacable and hugely moving. She grasps the part with fire in her soul."

On April 6 a call from England was put through to her in Serbia. At home, Corin had died, suddenly and peacefully, that morning, after suffering heart failure; he was seventy years old. Vanessa and Lynn at once spoke by telephone and arranged to meet in London, where the funeral was held for Corin William Redgrave at the actors' church, St. Paul's, Covent Garden, on April 12. Lynn, now very frail, had been urged not to make the trip to London, but she insisted. "She rewrote the rules about 'too-sick-to-travel,' " as Jemma said.

Kika, Vanessa and Corin's four children offered readings at the memorial, and then Lynn—almost unrecognizable and relying on others for support—slowly stepped up to speak. As she approached the microphone, she accidentally knocked over a candle. "Well, things happen!" she said lightly, turning to the congregation, and there was a burst of welcome laughter. Lynn then told some touching anecdotes about her brother, concluding with the memory that, when they were children, Corin taught her how to climb a tree—"but he didn't teach me how to climb down!" More laughter.

"He was my North Star," Jemma said later of her father, "a man of fixed principle and astonishing breadth of artistry and intellect." That was a description that could not be denied by anyone who had even a passing acquaintance with Corin Redgrave. "And to me," Jemma continued, "he was in every way the most influential and inspirational person in my life. I feel rudderless without him."

Vanessa returned to work and Lynn to her home in Connecticut, where the three Clark children came to visit; finally, as complete lethargy overtook her, they moved in. On May 2, 2010—three weeks after Corin's death—Lynn quietly slipped away. Six days later, after a service at the Congregational Community Church in Kent, she was laid to rest near her mother and her niece in the churchyard cemetery at Millbrook. Within fourteen months, Vanessa had endured three great bereavements.

—ɷ—

FOR MANY YEARS, the entire extended family of Redgraves was collectively called a dynasty, but that is not the appropriate word to describe them.

There was certainly something grand about them. They took themselves with utter seriousness, and most often they chose spouses within the ranks of theater folk, marrying actors, producers and directors: Daisy Scudamore married Roy Redgrave; Michael Redgrave married Rachel Kempson; Vanessa Redgrave married Tony Richardson and later Franco Nero; Corin Redgrave married Kika Markham; Lynn Redgrave married John Clark; Natasha Richardson married Robert Fox and later Liam Neeson; Joely Richardson married Tim Bevan; Carlo Nero married the actress Jennifer Wiltsie.

They are not alone, of course, in their experiences of life's reversals. But they have always somehow managed to transmute the sine curve of triumph and failure, ascent and decline, into something recognizably authentic for tens of thousands in theater audiences and for many millions of moviegoers. The most commonly used word critics have employed to describe the collective art of the Redgraves is *true.*

Theirs was no claustrophobic, self-absorbed lineage, hell-bent on preserving a mystique. "Most people go into the theatre for what they can get out of it," Michael's mother had told him. "And not enough people think about what they can put into it." That was not a charge that could be leveled against anyone in the clan. There is something refreshingly anomalous about the Redgraves that cannot be said of, for example, the Barrymores, whose self-destructive impulses destroyed one or more of them in every generation. Roy Redgrave was certainly a type of the Western world's playboy, but he never stopped working, and the record shows that he entertained audiences on two continents with fiery glee. His wife, Michael's mother, tried mightily to reach beyond her talents, and her story was finally an unhappy tale of descent into alcoholism. But as Rachel and Michael saw for many years, she represented a particular kind of theatrical madness—usually the sort that infuriates others, but often the type that beguiles. Margaret was like the perpetual apprentice who rashly snatches a colorful plumed hat and dashes onstage, only to find herself without a script and in the wrong play.

"We're on the shoulders of the generations that came before us," Vanessa said. "They gave us the courage to meet our own challenges in a way that the four-minute mile became a spur to athletic excellence. Of course we all come to the theatre with baggage—the baggage of our daily lives, the baggage of our problems, the baggage of our tragedies, the baggage of being tired. It doesn't matter what age you are. But if our hearts get opened and released—well, that's what theatre can do, and sometimes does, and everyone is thankful when it happens." She paused. "For me, it's about getting my arms around a character who is a stranger to me. That's purely personal. What can it mean to anybody else? Maybe nothing—but that is how I feel."

That metaphor of embrace and intimacy may go far toward an understanding of the family's profound connection, throughout their careers, to characters who suffer; it is also relevant toward an understanding of the deep humanitarianism of Vanessa and Corin, chastened and annealed as it was over a lifetime so that it finally became free of caustic ideology.

No fancy, formal fund-raising dinners for Vanessa Redgrave: she has burrowed into the most dangerous corners of the world, dodging bombs and spurning criticism in order to rescue the victims of war—and always bringing to people the crazy, necessary graces of art, which has often evoked unfair sneers from adversaries but has never seemed dispensable to any Redgrave. "I've come to realize all that the theatre can mean to people. I always felt it was important, but I didn't realize that it was absolutely vital to civilization until about 1992 or 1993"—when she took the performing arts to the besieged city of Sarajevo. "I think theatre is as essential to civilization as safe, pure water."

Just as she has a direct connection to the souls of playwrights, so they have a special appreciation of her. Arthur Miller once said about

Vanessa, "I don't think she really listens to anything except some genie deep inside her." That sprite revealed to her, as playwright David Hare reflected, "the great abstract nouns she believes in, with capital letters—like Youth and Enthusiasm and Wickedness and Art. These nouns are real to her, and inform all her acting. Her exceptional gift is for knowing what people feel, and having absolutely no sense of a dividing line between having a feeling and showing it."

—⁓—

UNLIKE SO MANY in their profession, past and present, the Redgraves over time became indifferent to the cultivation of a public image. Limited by convention and forced to wear the mask to which he so often referred to as the most powerful symbol of the actor's craft, Michael, paradoxically, never attempted to justify himself, never sought approval or endorsement, never consorted with the media or the Right People: he had the kind of humility that he saw constantly and consistently in Rachel, a quality of realism that was inherited by the next generation, and the next. His three children and their families lacked completely the impulse to sue for the public's love and approval. The Redgraves never courted fans, never appeared on talk shows to celebrate their wonderful selves, or to apologize, or to strike a pose of professional or moral grandeur or to affect an attitude of noblesse oblige. They never tried to appear as if they were Just Folks—not because they held themselves as better, but because they always felt different. "All families are peculiar in some way," Lynn said, "but ours was extraordinary—a volatile, emotional and passionate mix, which probably helped us to be good actors." Like all the Redgraves, she never endorsed the blandishments of mere familial celebrity. Fame, in fact, was something they all held in a kind of downright, uneasy contempt.

Much of this had to do with a certain sense of dignity. One never saw or heard of a Redgrave drunk or disorderly, or manipulating the press—just as they could never be found at advantageous social events, or striving to be fashionable. "What can we do for one another?" Vanessa has asked so often that it has become something of a mantra. "What can *I* do?"

In October 2010, Vanessa once again came to Broadway, in *Driving Miss Daisy*; the name of her grandmother and granddaughter seemed to follow her everywhere. Her performance was so successful that the closing notice had to be pushed back twice; she brought the play to London the following year, again to high critical praise. In November 2011, the Academy of Motion Picture Arts and Sciences honored Vanessa for her "consistently brilliant career." No fewer than six film roles were on her agenda as of 2012. "I don't picture myself acting forever and ever. But I sense that I have always been searching for something and have never found it. Whatever it is, I always think I will find it in acting—but maybe not."

By 2012 the Redgraves had marked seven generations of life in and of the theater. There is no indication that audiences have seen the last of them, their achievements or their involvement in the world.

Interviewers continue to ask about the Redgrave dynasty. "But we are not a dynasty," Vanessa replies quietly. "We are a family."

Notes

The following abbreviations are used:

THM Victoria and Albert Museum: Theatre Collections (London), Sir Michael Redgrave Archive. The archive, containing materials relevant to the entire family, has been designated THM 31 by the museum and consists of 204 boxes, 1,411 files and more than 135,000 items. In these notes, the specific location of an item is indicated by the number of the box in the archive, followed by the file, folder and item number within that box. When a note, for example, refers to "THM 31/3/9/6/1," the source in the Redgrave Archive is Box 3, file 9, folder 6, item 1.

The context clearly indicates when the following abbreviations refer either to an interview or to a volume in the bibliography that bears the individual's name as author:

CR   Corin Redgrave
LR   Lynn Redgrave
MR   Michael Redgrave
MSR   Margaret (née Daisy) Scudamore, later Redgrave
RKR   Rachel Kempson Redgrave
RR   Roy Redgrave
VR   Vanessa Redgrave

Chapter One: Their Wedding Days (1894–1921)

1   **"Mother looked across":** MR, in the *Western Daily Press* (Bristol, England), Nov. 14, 1952.

2   **"a poor unfortunate child":** Mrs. Patrick Campbell, 33.

4   **"If you are not my daughter":** Recorded by MSR in her notebook dated 1955: THM 31/4/2/22. The incident and F. A. Scudamore's words were also much repeated by, for example, CR, *Michael Redgrave, My Father*, 37. See also Warren Skidmore, "Fortunatus Augustus Davis Scudamore (1846–1904), Playwright," *Occasional Papers* 2 (n.d.).

4   **"a pleasing representation":** *South London Press* (Deptford), n.d.: THM 31/1/2/1.

4   **"her grace and buoyancy":** *The Era* (Surrey), April 1901: THM 31/1/2/1.

4   **"a charmed circle":** CR, *Michael Redgrave, My Father*, 49.

5   **"nearly as dear to me":** Ellen Sheridan Gillet Davis Scudamore to MSR: THM 31/4/2/22.

5   **For more than a millennium, there have been Redgraves:** On the origin of the name Redgrave, see Reaney, and Reaney and Wilson.

6   **"He was one of the first":** Quoted in the *Bristol Evening World*, Nov. 14, 1952.

6   **"took to the stage":** Roy Redgrave, in *The Theatre* (Australia), July 1, 1913.

7   **she married the actor William Arthur Parrett:** Esther Cooke's marriage to William Parrett was noted in *South Africa* magazine, Nov. 28, 1903.

8   **"an excellent drama . . . He played the part . . . a dashing sailor hero":** The *Stage* (London), 1903.

8   **And what of Ellen Maud Pratt:** On the divorce of Ellen Maud Redgrave and George Elsworthy Redgrave, see Item J 77/854/5968 in the Records of the Supreme Court of Judicature/Court for Divorce and Matrimonial Causes, Catalogue of the National Archives (UK) at Kew.

8   **"He preferred to be a big fish":** Recorded by MSR in her notebook dated 1955: THM 31/4/2/22.

8   **"He is already a leading":** *Player* (Australia), Aug. 15, 1904, 10.

9   **"my first duty":** Undated letter from RR to MSR: THM 31/3/9/8.

9   **"If you say you will have me":** Ibid.

10   **"I am going to bed":** THM 31/3/9/14.

10   **Roy and Daisy were married:** The marriage of Roy and Daisy was considered bigamous and therefore invalid by both MR and CR (see MR, *In My Mind's Eye,* 5–6, and CR, *Michael Redgrave, My Father,* 155–56). Their unwarranted assumptions were interpretations of a letter from Roy to Daisy before their wedding in Glasgow, in which he

wrote that he "need not necessarily produce papers" confirming his divorce, "which will take trouble and money and time to get." This was interpreted as subterfuge—i.e., that he was not divorced, but in fact, he and Ellen/Judith were divorced in 1905 (see page 312).

10   **"My father was illegitimate":** Mary Riddell, "A Twist in the Redgrave Tale," London *Daily Mail,* Mar. 12, 2005.

10   **"Mr. Roy Redgrave is magnificent":** *The Thanet Advertiser* (Kent, UK), Aug. 22, 1908.

11   **"That's where the real money":** Findlater, 9.

11   **"My mother was determined":** London *Evening Standard,* Apr. 14, 1972.

12   **"Australian landladies":** *John Bull* magazine, Sept. 20, 1952.

12   **"flotsam and jetsam":** CR, *Michael Redgrave, My Father,* 46.

13   **"She gave up":** Ibid., 35.

13   **"desperately unhappy":** *Evening Standard,* Apr. 14, 1972.

14   **"I don't remember [my mother] being":** London *Evening Standard,* Apr. 14, 1972; and MR's letter to F. T. Smith, managing director of Collins Publishers, London (April 1, 1954): THM 31/3/1/31.

14   **"When I was very young":** Quoted in the *Toronto Star,* Oct. 30, 1972.

15   **"I didn't know what a home was":** "Michael Redgrave," in Ross and Ross, 334.

15   **"At the age of five":** *John Bull* magazine, Sept. 20, 1952.

15   **"Miss Scudamore . . . has a clever small son":** From an undated and unsourced newspaper article, preserved in MR's earliest scrapbook: THM 31/1/1/1.

15   **"My dear Michael":** J. M. Barrie's letter is preserved in THM 31/3/19/1–22.

15   **"Being a writer":** Findlater, 7.

16   **"I got best marks":** THM 31/3/9/1/2.

16   **"The first place":** Findlater, 11.

16   **"When deeply interested":** MR, *In My Mind's Eye,* 1.

18   **"she managed to implant":** Ibid., 3.

Chapter Two: Ghosts and Guilt (1921–1935)

20   **"Whenever it was possible":** Ross and Ross, 335.

21   **"One of the best":** "Roy Redgrave's Retrospect—Dead Actor's Last Lines," Sydney *Morning Herald,* May 27, 1922.

22 **"remarkable":** *The Cliftonian* (summer 1923).

22 **"It was no surprise":** MR's performances at Clifton were reviewed in Bristol newspapers in June 1924 and June 1925. Without identifying the sources, Michael and Margaret saved these clippings in scrapbooks—frequently along with her comments: THM 31/1/1/1.

23 **"uncommonly good":** "A. M. L." in *The Lady* magazine, n.d. [probably December 1923].

23 **"Mummy overacted a little":** THM 31/1/1/1.

23 **"You and I don't talk":** Ross and Ross, 335.

24 **"I dedicate this volume":** All MR's diary entries from August 1925 to March 1927 are contained in a handwritten notebook: THM 31/4/1/1.

26 **"What followed":** MR, *In My Mind's Eye,* 53. In his memoir, MR changed Margaret Chute's name to Margot Dempster.

27 **"intelligence, grace of movement":** *The Cambridge Review* (summer 1926).

27 **"My mother and stepfather":** *John Bull* magazine, Sept. 20, 1952.

29 **"At the time":** MR to the author, Jan. 20, 1981.

29 **"I wrote stories":** Ross and Ross, 336.

30 **"Burgess was one":** MR, *In My Mind's Eye,* 76.

31 **"tall and slim":** Lehmann, 150–51.

31 **"flower-like":** Haffenden, 164.

31 **"I was very highly":** Burton, 100.

31 **"with an exquisite":** Francis Birrell, in *The Nation* (UK)

31 **"I replied":** MR, *In My Mind's Eye,* 73.

32 **"one of the best teachers":** Burton, 99.

32 **"The two years":** MR's diary for 1929: THM 31/4/1/2.

33 **"I love you more than anything":** THM 31/3/5/3/6.

33 **"The two of us":** MR, *In My Mind's Eye,* 72.

33 **"he just didn't want me to go":** MR to the author, Jan. 1981.

33 **"You are too tall":** E.g., Burton, 99.

34 **"The only commercial asset":** Ibid., 100.

34 **"I never intended to become":** MR, in the Timaru (New Zealand) *Herald,* May 23, 1977.

34 **Michael was quickly engaged to teach:** MR discussed his work at Cranleigh in Carleton (see the bibliography).

35 **"I suddenly became fired":** Ibid.

35 **"When I first performed":** MR, *Mask or Face,* 72.

35 **"compelling":** A clipping of the review survives, without bibliographi-

cal details: THM 31/12/1/10. It is quoted more extensively in Findlater, 20.

36   **"Teaching provided me"**: R. Quilter Vincent, "An Interview with Michael Redgrave," *The ABC Film Review* (1954); see also *The Times* (London), Feb. 3, 1961.

36   **"I thought I could do"**: Burton, 101.

36   **"I can't see anything"**: MR to the author, Jan. 1981; see also Findlater, 22.

37   **"We'd like to have you"**: E.g., Findlater, 22–23; CR, 53.

37   **"but you are almost certain"**: William Armstrong to MR, letter dated May 21, 1934: THM 31/3/5/12/1.

38   **"It was a very lovely theatre"**: MR to the author; see also Burton, 101, and MR, 84–85.

38   **"a promising member"**: Quoted in Findlater, 25.

38   **"an ambitious, arrogant"**: Ross and Ross, 335.

39   **"Oh, dear"**: MR, *In My Mind's Eye,* 87–88.

Chapter Three: Faithful, in a Fashion (1935–1937)

40   **"Oh, good—you're tall"**: RKR to the author, Nov. 1, 1989. See also RKR, 91, 87.

40   **"never quite belonged"**: RKR, 87.

40   **"I do not believe"**: Eric William Kempson, quoted in RKR, 87.

41   **"like most young women"**: RKR to the author, Jan. 15, 1990; also RKR, 3–4.

41   **"I'm afraid I have to"**: LR, "Finding My Grandmother," on Oprah .com, Jan. 25, 2010; and at an American Theatre Wing symposium for the City University of New York, Graduate School of Journalism, July 15, 2005.

41   **"She had a habit"**: Rachel's comments on her mother were confided to her daughter Lynn, who spoke them in the July 15, 2005, American Theatre Wing symposium after her mother's death.

42   **"they were in an impasse"**: RKR, 23.

43   **"Only Rachel Kempson"**: W. A. Darlington, in the London *Daily Telegraph,* Mar. 9, 1933; the second review, without attribution, was included in RKR's notebook for 1931–1934: THM 31/1/3/1.

43   **"Miss Rachel Kempson"**: *The Times* (London), July 16, 1933.

43   **"a triumph"**: The Birmingham *Mail,* July 14, 1933.

44   **"golden and handsome":** RKR, 76, 86.

44   **"I believed myself":** RKR to the author, Jan. 27, 1990.

45   **"I fell more in love":** RKR to the author, Jan. 16, 1990.

45   **"She was the most romantic":** Lynn Redgrave, interview, Folger Shakespeare Library, Washington, D.C., April 2009, www.folger.edu/template.cfm?cid/3109.

45   **"Rehearse Act II":** MR's diary for 1935: THM 31/4/1/3.

45   **"It's wonderful":** RKR, 92; similarly, to the author, Jan. 19, 1990.

46   **"I was very fearful":** RKR, 95.

46   **"were so real to me":** Ibid., 92.

46   **"So I left":** MR, 88; in RKR's version (93–94), she had to turn off the lamp.

46   **"Miss Kempson, who gave":** The reviews of *Flowers of the Forest* were preserved in RKR's scrapbooks but without source details: THM 31/1/3/1.

47   **"Couldn't we":** RKR, 95.

47   **"It was his":** RKR to the author, Jan. 25, 1990.

47   **"the truth was":** RKR, 96–97.

47   **"R. reassures me":** THM 31/4/1/3.

48   **"It folded after":** "To Ann and Nicholas Monsarrat, the Sea Is Never Cruel," *People* 12, no. 1, July 2, 1979.

48   **"There were moments":** MR, *In My Mind's Eye,* 89.

48   **"He was far from happy":** RKR, 105.

48   **"I was feeling pretty carefree":** Ibid., 110.

49   **"Rachel seemed rather nervous":** MR, *In My Mind's Eye,* 90.

49   **"My father":** LR, Folger Shakespeare Library interview.

50   **"I had seen Larry":** John Gielgud to the author, Nov. 4, 1989.

50   **"A fine clear statement":** THM 31/4/1/4.

50   **"He felt that I":** John Gielgud to the author, Nov. 4, 1989. Additional quotations from Gielgud are from the same date unless otherwise noted.

51   **"knock their bloody eyes":** Olivier, 34.

51   **"I will show them":** Burton, 13.

51   **"inexpert . . . gabbling":** *The Sunday Times,* Oct. 20, 1935.

51   **"temperamentally ill at ease":** *The Times* (London), Oct. 18, 1935.

51   **"He was deeply hurt":** Gielgud to the author.

51   **"A very important facet":** RKR, 112.

51   **"I went to the Turkish baths":** THM 31/4/1/3; similar excursions are cited in THM 31/4/1/4.

52   **"Michael Redgrave possessed":** *The Liverpolitan,* April 1936.

53   **"He had all the graces":** Duff, 48.

53   **"I don't suppose":** Quoted in MR, *In My Mind's Eye,* 94.

53   **"He offered us":** Burton, 101.

54   **"entirely new entertainment":** "A Brief History of the Old Vic," from the theater's website (oldvictheatre.com/history.php).

54   **"In my life":** Ibid.

54   **"a licensed pit of darkness":** Ibid.

54   **"a cheap and decent place":** "The Old Vic: A Short History," in the playbill for the Old Vic Theatre, autumn 1989.

55   **"What's a raid":** From the company's website.

55   **"She was an extraordinary person":** John Gielgud to the author.

55   **"ran the place":** Sybil Thorndike, quoted on the audiocassette *The Old Vic: Story of a Theatre,* London: Soundfact Series no. WHC007.

55   **the Vic's centenary gala:** On the atmosphere of the Old Vic, see Peter Roberts, ed., *Lilian Baylis Centenary Festival,* Old Vic souvenir program, 1974, 29.

57   **"Michael always had":** RKR to the author, Jan. 19, 1990; see also RKR, 116.

57   **"neither old enough":** James Agate, cited in Findlater, 30.

58   **"I should have played it":** Burton, 102; Findlater, 30.

58   **"I remember her saying":** Burton, 102, and Findlater, 31.

58   **"Guthrie made me very nervous":** Ibid.

Chapter Four: Lost Ladies (1937–1939)

60   **"Edith Evans helped me":** Burton, 101.

60   **"Find the life":** Ibid., 129.

60   **"There was no doubt":** John Gielgud to the author.

60   **"runs up and down":** Burton, 131.

61   **"the highly distinguished":** John Mason Brown, in the *New York Evening Post,* Dec. 21, 1934.

61   **"She played a guileful":** Brooks Atkinson, in the *New York Times,* Dec. 21, 1934.

61   **"a great artist":** James Agate, quoted in Morley, 119.

61   **"What sort of actor"**: MR, 106; similarly, to the author, Mar. 1, 1981.

61   **"that she was suggesting"**: MR, 106; also to the author, Mar. 3, 1981.

61   **"You don't want to go"**: Forbes, 182; also MR, *In My Mind's Eye,* 100–101; Ross and Ross, 337.

62   **"I fell head over heels"**: MR, *In My Mind's Eye,* 104.

62   **"Acting with Edith Evans"**: Ross and Ross, 338.

62   **"At first"**: RKR, 124; similarly, to the author, Mar. 4, 1990.

62   **"Michael and Edith became lovers"**: Forbes, 184.

62   **"I hope we can love each other"**: The letters exchanged between Edith Evans and MR, mostly undated but obviously written between 1937 and 1939, are preserved in THM 31/3/5/225/1–7, 16–28, 29–35.

63   **"set a standard"**: Audrey Williamson, quoted in Morley, 121.

63   **"He decided that I was"**: Findlater, 41.

63   **"as one obsessed"**: Forbes, 185.

64   **"immeasurably strengthened"**: MR, *In My Mind's Eye,* 106.

64   **"it was Edith"**: Ibid., 107.

64   **"Ladies and gentlemen"**: Ibid., 108.

64   **"Among the young actors"**: The source is unknown, but the published clipping is preserved in THM 31/1/1/3.

64   **"nuzzling her tummy"**: RKR, 124.

65   **"But I soon felt"**: RKR, 117.

65   **"She wanted to dedicate herself"**: LR, Folger Shakespeare Library interview.

65   **"But I misappropriated"**: MR to the author, Mar. 7, 1981; similarly, Burton, 107; see also George Gent, "Redgrave Frowns on 'Method' Excesses," *New York Times,* Apr. 25, 1974.

65   **"I hadn't warned"**: MR to DS, Mar. 11, 1981; similarly, MR, *In My Mind's Eye,* 128–29.

66   **"into a delirium"**: Findlater, 35.

66   **American actor Karl Malden**: Karl Malden, who knew Strasberg well, often discussed him with the author over the many years of our friendship.

67   **"I found myself"**: RKR, 129.

67   **"this was another blow"**: RKR to the author, Jan. 9, 1990; also, RKR, 129.

67   **in a letter she posted to her son:** Margaret Scudamore's notes and letters to Rachel and/or Michael dated 1938 are preserved in THM 31/3/6/53/1–9.

68   **"He was the greatest possible help":** Frequently documented (e.g., Burton, 107–8; Ross and Ross, 339–40; Findlater, 41–42; MR, *In My Mind's Eye,* 113).

69   **"Mr. Michael Redgrave, who has given . . . his very bones":** The two reviews are cited without bibliographical details in Findlater, 41.

71   **"The difference between":** Brown, 89–90; see also Gilliat's letter to *Screen International,* no. 172, Jan. 13–20, 1979, 4.

72   **The production schedule:** On the delayed production of *The Lady Vanishes,* see C. A. Lejeune, "Carrying on in London," *New York Times,* May 22, 1938.

72   **"At first, I couldn't":** MR to the author, Jan. 30, 1981.

73   **"Hitchcock wasn't really":** Ibid.

73   **"I found him most disconcerting":** Margaret Lockwood to the author, Jan. 16, 1981.

73   **"Maggie was right":** MR to the author, Jan. 30, 1981.

74   **"I learned that in films":** Ross and Ross, 339.

74   **"has a far better chance":** Hare, 161.

76   **"my presence didn't help much":** MR, *In My Mind's Eye,* 143.

77   **"I agreed to do":** MR to the author, Feb. 9, 1981; similarly, Ross and Ross, 341.

77   **"became happy at last":** RKR, 131.

77   **"wanted to go on":** *Theatre World,* no. 168, Jan. 1939.

77   **"magnificent clowning . . . uncommon freshness":** The excerpts from reviews by James Agate and Charles Morgan are preserved in THM 31/1/1/4.

78   **"The first thing":** MR, *The Actor's Ways and Means,* 40.

78   **"It was a hard struggle":** RKR, 134.

78   **"Michael was out":** Ibid., 135.

79   **"an unresolved amalgam":** *Manchester Guardian,* Mar. 22, 1939, 13.

79   **"a new flexibility":** Audrey Williamson, quoted in Morley, 321.

79   **"tears of fright":** MR, *In My Mind's Eye,* 116.

79   **"I am cowardly":** MR, diary entry for May 12, 1939: THM 31/4/1/5.

Chapter Five: The Stars Look Up and Down (1939–1941)

80   **"the most euphonious":** MR, *In My Mind's Eye,* 118.

80   **"big and fine and placid":** MR to Edith Evans, Oct. 8, 1939: THM 31/3/5/225/30.

81   **"conscious of the whole business":** McFarlane, *An Autobiography of British Cinema,* 554.

81   **"the theory of artistic":** Quoted by CR in MacKillop and Sinyard, eds., 226.

81   **at least in the movies:** For Philip French's observations on MR's screen career, see "Michael Redgrave, 1908–1985," *The Observer,* Jan. 8, 2009.

82   **"Movie-making was in his blood":** MR to the author, Feb. 9, 1981; see also his *Mask or Face,* 135.

83   **"I was terribly":** RKR to the author, Feb. 15, 1990; see also RKR, 139.

83   **"a convinced and very public socialist":** CR, 31.

83   **"left-wing cultural":** Deborah Haynes, "MI5 planned to Intern Sam Wanamaker for Communist Links, Files Show," *The Times* (London), Sept. 1, 2009.

84   **"His appearance was attractive":** Isherwood, 222.

84   **"He was pleasant-looking":** Spender, 175. In his memoir, Spender calls Tony Hyndman "Jimmy Younger," because people identified as homosexual could be imprisoned in 1951—the time of the publication of his book *World Within World*—and writers who wrote about homosexuals could be prosecuted for obscenity.

84   **"His relaxed, pleasure-loving nature":** Stephen Spender, "My Life Is Mine: It Is Not David Leavitt's," *The New York Times Book Review,* Sept. 4, 1994.

85   **"by now fathoms deep in love":** CR, *Michael Redgrave, My Father,* 95.

85   **"The knowledge that I shall certainly":** MR to Tony Hydman, Apr. 29, 1940: THM 31/4/1/5 (MR's diary for 1938–1941).

85   **"blissfully happy":** THM 31/4/1/5 (n.d.).

85   **"She asked me":** MR, diary for Apr. 30, 1940: THM 31/4/1/5.

86   **"She wanted to go to the nursery":** MR, diary for May 5, 1940: THM 31/4/1/5.

86   **"always cheerful":** MR, diary for May 14, 1940: THM 31/4/1/5.

87   **"I jumped up and down":** Ibid., 227.

87   **"For two nights":** MR, diary for May 4, 1940: THM 31/4/1/5.

87   **"This was a difficult time":** RKR to the author, Feb. 8, 1990.

88   **The theater had more than its complement of notable homosexuals:** Some of the many notable gay or bisexual people in the modern world of the arts: Max Adrian, James Agate, Frith Banbury, Cecil Beaton, Hugh "Binkie" Beaumont, Benjamin Britten, Simon Callow, Noël Coward, Clemence Dane, Anton Dolin, Denholm Elliott, William

Empson, Rupert Everett, E. M. Forster, John Gielgud, Radclyffe Hall, Nigel Hawthorne, Robert Helpmann, A. E. Housman, Derek Jacobi, Charles Laughton, Ian McKellen, Somerset Maugham, Ivor Novello, Esmé Percy, Eric Portman, Dennis Price, Elsie Randolph, Terence Rattigan, Tony Richardson, Vita Sackville-West, John Schlesinger, Lytton Strachey, Ernest Thesiger, Antony Tudor, Alan Webb, Emlyn Williams, and Sandy Wilson.

88   **"Redgrave was wonderful in this crisis":** Duff, 51.

89   **"not properly prepared":** Diary entry for Apr. 30, 1940: THM 31/4/1/5.

90   **"better played":** "The Theatre: London Hit," *Time,* Aug. 12, 1940.

90   **"probably the closest":** CR, in MacKillop and Sinyard, eds., 229.

90   **"Yesterday T. came to lunch":** MR's diary entry for June 25, 1940: THM 31/4/1/5.

90   **"an undesirable friend":** RKR, 234.

90   **"The earliest memory":** VR, *Vanessa Redgrave—An Autobiography,* 1.

91   **"We put down old mattresses":** RKR, appearing in *Intimate Portrait: Vanessa Redgrave,* produced by Joseph Feury, directed by Lee Grant, in association with Lifetime TV (USA), 1998. See also RKR, 141–43.

91   **"I saw a fierce red glow":** VR, 5.

91   **"She was mother and godmother":** RKR, 142.

92   **"Looking back":** RKR, 63–64.

92   **"Captivating and enchanting":** "Jeannie, a Captivating Comedy, Arrives at the Little Carnegie," *New York Times,* Sept. 3, 1943.

92   **"No actor is worth":** MR, *Mask or Face,* 137.

93   **"In the evenings":** Ibid., 138–39.

93   **"My father was":** VR, on *Charlie Rose* (Public Broadcasting System, U.S. television), June 20, 2007.

93   **"I am a red-hot":** Quoted by CR, *Michael Redgrave, My Father,* 62.

93   **"He embraced socialism":** Ibid., 63.

94   **"as bad as Nazi Germany":** On the wider context of the political fracas that troubled MR in 1941, I am indebted to the essay by English journalist Nick Cohen, "Eric Hobsbawm and the Hitler-Stalin Pact," in *Nick Cohen: Writing from London* (nickcohen.net/2009/03/02/eric-hobsbawn-and-the-hitler-stalin-pact/).

94   **"BBC Gives Stars":** The London *News Chronicle,* Mar. 4, 1941.

94   **"because of his pacifist views":** "BBC Bars Film Star for Peace Activities," *New York Times,* Mar. 5, 1941.

95   **"The careers of those of us":** MR, *In My Mind's Eye,* 142.

95   **"My political development"**: MR, *In My Mind's Eye,* 222.

95   **"The reasons for his silence"**: VR, *Vanessa Redgrave—An Autobiography,* 25.

96   **"There are still a few old ladies"**: Hoare, 509.

96   **he and Noël Coward began an intense romance:** MR's affair with Noël Coward has been well documented by RKR, 210; by Strachan, 244ff.; and by Coward's biographers (see, e.g., Hoare, 323, and Day, 440–43).

96   **"Noël's nickname for Michael"**: RKR, 210.

96   **"I had of course"**: RKR to the author, Feb. 20, 1990; similarly, RKR, 210.

97   **"They had a long marriage"**: Peter Marks, "For Redgrave, the Show, and Life, Must Go On," *Washington Post,* Apr. 5, 2009.

Chapter Six: A Garden of Earthly Delights (1941–1946)

98   **"very good . . . superior"**: Papers relative to MR's service in the Royal Navy: THM 31/3/5/50.

99   **"I'd always heard"**: MR to RKR, Nov. 30, 1941: THM 31/3/7/7/1–6.

99   **"I thought she was marvelous"**: Ross and Ross, 335.

99   **"a wild and wonderful dream"**: Day, 441.

99   **"I am waiting"**: MR to Noël Coward, Jan. 25, 1942, in Day, 441.

99   **"You would be of more use"**: MR, *In My Mind's Eye,* 164.

99   **"We acted in little plays"**: VR, on *Mark Lawson Talks To . . .* (BBC4), broadcast (taped) June 1, 2010. Similarly, VR on the cable television program *Downstage Center,* produced by the American Theatre Wing for the City University of New York's Graduate School of Journalism and broadcast in New York on July 6, 2007.

100   **"I really didn't know"**: VR, on *Intimate Portrait: Vanessa Redgrave.*

100   **"He observed his children fondly"**: CR, *Michael Redgrave, My Father,* 35.

100   **"It closed within"**: MR, *In My Mind's Eye,* 164.

100   **"Rachel was on tour"**: Ibid., 163.

100   **"the seedier West End"**: Quoted in Strachan, 258.

101   **"I have no doubt"**: CR, 38.

101   **"It wasn't a very good time"**: RKR to the author, Mar. 19, 1990; see also RKR, 147.

101   **"But she never persisted"**: Ibid., 37–38.

101   **"Redgrave gave"**: Cited in Morley, 321.

102 **"had orchestrated an entrancing cotillion"**: MR, "A 'Sleeper' from Russia," *New York Times,* Apr. 1, 1956.

102 **"His performance is exemplary"**: T. C. Worsley's review of MR in *A Month in the Country,* cited in Morley, 321.

103 **"It's a very good thing"**: LR, *Shakespeare for My Father,* 15.

103 **"Here . . . 1943"**: LR, *This Is Living,* 4; similarly, *Shakespeare for My Father,* 11.

103 **"Our second daughter"**: THM 31/4/1/7.

103 **"He was amusingly"**: Duff, 49.

103 **"With all its faults"**: MR, *In My Mind's Eye,* 168.

104 **"to defy the superstition"**: Findlater, 64.

104 **"thin high-mindedness"**: MR, *In My Mind's Eye,* 168.

104 **"cannot afford to appear"**: *Time,* Jan. 4, 1937.

104 **"Mr. Redgrave's production"**: *The Times* (London), Sept. 9, 1943.

104 **"She didn't play down"**: Duff, 12.

105 **"a relationship I cherished"**: Houghton, 244.

105 **"tall, broad-shouldered"**: Ibid., 180.

105 **"You're the author"**: Ibid., 137–38.

105 **"we were together . . . more than literate"**: Ibid., 138.

107 **"R[achel] comes in"**: MR's diary for 1944 is contained in THM 31/4/1/8.

108 **"He has given no better"**: *The Times* (London), Mar. 30, 1944.

108 **"greater than [in] anything"**: W. A. Darlington, critic of the London *Daily Telegraph,* in a dispatch to the *New York Times,* Apr. 30, 1944.

109 **"It was getting me down"**: Burton, 107.

109 **"By the end of the evening"**: MR to the author, Jan. 19, 1981; similarly, MR, 171. See also his *Mask or Face* (149–64) and *The Actor's Ways and Means* (68–70) for MR's treatment of the rehearsal period and the effects of *Uncle Harry* on him.

109 **"I fail myself"**: THM 31/4/1/8.

109 **"reform week"**: Diary entry for June 13: THM 31/4/1/8.

109 **"He was tired and fed up"**: RKR, 149.

110 **"whose existence . . . It hurt my vanity . . . Waking up there"**: MR's diary entry for Aug. 31, 1944: THM 31/4/1/8.

110 **"I miss N. very much"**: MR's diary entry for Sept. 2, 1944: THM 31/4/1/8.

110 **"The sad thing is"**: Diary entry for Sept. 4, 1944: ibid.

110 **"Don't let us drift":** Norris Houghton to MR, Oct. 20, 1944: THM 31/4/1/8.

111 **"What an amazing child":** Ibid.

111 **Mary needed a title for her new play:** On MR naming Mary Hayley Bell's new play *Duet for Two Hands,* see his diary for 1944: THM 31/4/1/8.

113 **"At rehearsals":** Duff, 48.

113 **"Miss Rachel Kempson":** James Agate, in *The Sunday Times,* June 10, 1945.

113 **"I remember nothing":** CR, *Michael Redgrave, My Father,* 38.

113 **"surprising in an actor":** Duff, 49.

113 **"made him both":** Ibid.

115 **"genteel reverence":** Richard Winnington, in the London *News Chronicle,* May 25, 1946.

115 **"grand, and wholly credible":** *Variety,* Dec. 31, 1946.

116 **"played immaculately":** McFarlane, *An Autobiography of the British Cinema,* 77.

116 **"We children, growing up":** CR, *Michael Redgrave, My Father,* 80.

116 **"received a mixed press":** McFarlane, *An Autobiography of the British Cinema,* 74, 78.

117 **he bought Bedford House:** For a description of Bedford House in 1946, see Powell, 273–74.

118 **"John and Mary [Mills] are":** THM 31/4/1/9 (MR's diary for 1945–1949).

118 **"looking a little mad":** Ibid.

119 **"Rachel is justifiably":** Ibid.

119 **"About this time":** CR, *Michael Redgrave, My Father,* 89.

Chapter Seven: A Term in Hollywood (1947)

120 **many Brits were delighted:** Alfred Hitchcock's statement about the English in Hollywood was part of my discussion with him on Nov. 6, 1976.

121 **"Is there much Buddhism":** MR, 181. See also his recollection of 1947 in Rena Andrews, "Sir Michael Looks Like [a] King," *Denver Post,* Aug. 13, 1973.

121 **"I have met":** MR to Norris Houghton, Feb. 10, 1947: THM 31/4/1/9.

122 **"an original mind":** MR, in an undated letter to Norris Houghton, cited in Houghton, 182.

123   **"Corin and Vanessa":** RKR to MR, Feb. 12, 1946: THM 31/3/6/4.

123   **"for which he made":** RKR to the author, Apr. 9, 1991; see also RKR, 164.

123   **"My sister and brother":** LR, *Shakespeare for My Father,* 15.

123   **"which made her breathless":** VR, *Vanessa Redgrave—An Autobiography,* 33.

123   **"Vanessa was the dream sister":** LR on National Public Radio program *All Things Considered* (USA), with Robert Siegel and Michele Norris, Dec. 20, 2005; and Kate Kellaway, "A Very Special Sisterhood," *The Observer,* Dec. 9, 1990.

124   **"a fish out of water":** VR, *Vanessa Redgrave—An Autobiography,* 33.

124   **"I was hungry for reading":** Ibid., 30.

124   **"I knew at an early age":** VR, on *All Things Considered* (USA), Dec. 20, 2005.

125   **"very generously":** MR's diary entry is noted on the page for March 18, but it continues the entry begun on the page for March 21: THM 31/4/1/9.

125   **"He had a dazzling smile":** CR, *Michael Redgrave, My Father,* 99.

125   **"Out with Bob":** THM 31/4/1/10. For additional details concerning Bob Michell, see Strachan, 299–30.

126   **"She thought I was not much good":** RKR to the author, Mar. 19, 1990.

128   **"a real Jekyll and Hyde":** Bernstein, 197.

128   he had accepted the part: On *Secret Beyond the Door,* there is a singularly fine critical essay by Moira Finnie on the Turner Classic Movies website (TCM.com). See also Kellow, 313–14.

128   **"I have never seen":** MR, *Mask or Face,* 139–40.

128   **"I knew before we finished":** R. Quilter Vincent, "An Interview with Michael Redgrave," *ABC Film Review* (UK), 1954.

128   **"Michael Redgrave was a mess":** Kellow, 312.

129   as his diaries entries confirm: For MR's diary entries for March through the end of the year 1947: THM 31/4/1/9.

129   **"He has never before":** J. Brooks Atkinson, in the *New York Times,* Oct. 27, 1931.

130   this play marked the high point: There is a fine treatment of *Mourning Becomes Electra* by Bernard F. Dick (106–16), who is a renowned classical scholar as well as a highly respected biographer and film historian.

132   **"The movie sustains":** *Life* magazine, Dec. 8, 1947.

132 **"A static and tiresome":** Bosley Crowther, in the *New York Times,* Nov. 20, 1947.

133 **"because the camera remained fixed":** MR, *In My Mind's Eye,* 178.

133 **"easy to act with":** THM 31/4/1/9.

133 **"murder, [and] Michael Redgrave":** Russell and Chase, 147.

134 **"a dark, handsome man":** For these and the subsequent comments by RKR on the Leo Genn affair: RKR to the author, Feb. 12, 1991; see also RKR, 161–62.

134 **"Rachel and I had reached":** MR, *In My Mind's Eye,* 181.

134 **"rather a dull time":** Ibid.

135 **"a great friend":** Ibid., 212.

135 **"I was accompanied":** MR, *In My Mind's Eye,* 183.

135 **"and he brought a friend":** CR, *Michael Redgrave, My Father,* 100.

136 **"Dad had taken us":** VR, *Vanessa Redgrave—An Autobiography,* 42.

136 **"I just looked":** VR, quoted in *Time* magazine, Mar. 17, 1967; also, MR, 185.

137 **"a buzz of excitement":** CR, *Michael Redgrave, My Father,* 42.

137 **"As soon as he arrived":** RKR, 162.

138 **"If you come to play Macbeth":** MR, in Garrett, ed., 139.

138 **"Now and again":** CR, *Michael Redgrave, My Father,* 40–41.

138 **"lacking poetry and tragic emotion":** *The Times* (London), Dec. 19, 1947.

138 **"Speeches and phrases":** Ivor Brown, in *The Observer,* Dec. 20, 1947.

138 **"While Macbeth is":** Harold Hobson in *The Sunday Times,* Dec. 21, 1947.

139 **"that commands our respect":** T. C. Worsley, in *New Statesman* (in Morley, 321–22).

139 **"I wasn't very good":** Burton, 107.

139 **"I do not like being called":** A pocket diary entry for 1947–48: THM 31/4/1/10.

139 **"Leo asked me":** RKR, 162.

Chapter Eight: A Thunderbolt (1948–1953)

141 **"Michael was a brilliant pianist":** VR, on *Downstage Center.*

141 **"personally vigorous":** For the *New York Times,* Brooks Atkinson wrote two lengthy reviews—on April 1 and 11, 1948.

142 **"but when it came to":** MR, *Mask or Face,* 99.

142   **"I noticed that he looked":** Ibid., 103.
142   **"quite a heavy burden of guilt":** Quoted in Read, 246.
142   **"My father was gay":** CR, in the A&E documentary biography *The Redgraves,* produced by Caroline Sommers for ABC (USA), 2004.
143   **"I didn't remember Daddy":** LR, *This Is Living,* 7–8; see also *Shakespeare for My Father,* 19–20; and the Associated Press syndicated obituary for LR, May 3, 2010.
143   **"My father must have seemed":** CR, *Michael Redgrave, My Father,* 88.
144   **"isolated, insignificant and cold":** RKR to the author, Feb. 19, 1990; see also RKR, 158.
145   **"the best dressed and best acted":** *The Times* (London), Nov. 25, 1948.
145   **"a thunderbolt":** Brooks Atkinson, in the *New York Times,* Nov. 17, 1949.
146   **"He failed to convey":** Audrey Williamson, in *The Times,* Dec. 1, 1948.
146   **"The fuse was laid":** Findlater, 81.
146   **"another half-successful assault":** Ibid., 83.
147   **"with his cello":** THM 31/4/1/9.
147   **"Ach!":** CR, *Michael Redgrave, My Father,* 41.
147   **Corin boarded the train . . . to Malvern:** Regarding Corin's time at Malvern Wells, RKR's chronology (156–57) misstates the years and CR's (41–44) conflates the events.
147   **"was a crank and a sadist":** Ibid., 43.
148   **"of the significance":** VR, *Vanessa Redgrave—An Autobiography,* 43.
148   **"In those days":** LR to the Associated Press, 1993; quoted in her AP obituary, May 3, 2010.
148   **"as though farce":** Harold Hobson, in *The Sunday Times,* May 1, 1949.
149   **"not asked to be":** An unattributed review saved in THM 31/1/3/3.
149   **"She was a great help":** RKR, 159.
149   **"She seemed quite unaware":** Deirdre Redgrave, 49.
150   **"though there was not much joy":** MR, *In My Mind's Eye,* 187.
150   **"Redgrave, perhaps more":** Philip Hoare, in *The Independent,* July 9, 2002.
151   **"He moves with a new grace":** T. C Worsley, in *New Statesman,* March 1950.
151   **"Even my mother":** RKR, 228.
151   **"He allowed audiences":** RKR to the author, June 11, 1991.
152   **Vanessa...was invited to appear in a photo shoot:** The photo of VR that appeared in Langley Moore's book was first featured in the *New York Times,* Dec. 4, 1949.

152   **"I suppose I connected"**: VR, in *Intimate Portrait: Vanessa Redgrave.*

152   **"Vanessa Redgrave already shows signs"**: *Queen* magazine, Jan. 17, 1951.

152   **"After that, the whole school"**: Quoted in *Time* magazine, Mar. 17, 1967.

153   **"Having a father"**: VR, in the *Daily Express,* Sept. 23, 1950.

154   **"I've got a headache"**: MacKillop and Sinyard, eds., 229.

155   **"a performance of extraordinary"**: T. C. Worsley, cited in Morley, 322.

155   **"It was apparent to all of us"**: RKR, 163.

156   **"never better . . . and their presence"**: MR's diary for 1951–1953: THM 31/4/1/11.

156   **"a dainty, feline"**: Findlater, 105.

156   **"It's so sad"**: RKR, 163.

156   **"Every afternoon we played"**: VR, *Vanessa Redgrave—An Autobiography,* 47.

157   **"He still has hopes"**: THM 31/4/1/11.

157   **"With Vanessa"**: Diary for Mar. 22, 1951: THM 31/4/1/11.

157   **"Homosexuals in general"**: *Hansard Parliamentary Debates,* vol. 521, Dec. 3, 1953, cited in Rebellato, 157.

158n   **"very feminine"**: See the long scholarly essay on the website www .glbtq.com/social-sciences/united_kingdom_02,7.html

159   **"Her request"**: RKR to the author, Mar. 4, 1990.

160   **"Michael Redgrave shows us"**: W. A. Darlington was critic of the London *Daily Telegraph* when he wrote "West End Wire" for the *New York Times,* Apr. 13, 1952.

160   **"the best serious performance"**: Tynan, quoted in Findlater, 115.

161   **"For the real actor"**: MR, *The Actor's Ways and Means,* 120.

Chapter Nine: Tom (1953–1956)

162   **"Our lives revolved"**: LR, *Shakespeare for My Father,* 22.

162   **"When he had a large part"**: VR, *Vanessa Redgrave—An Autobiography,* 49.

163   **"I was an equestrian"**: Michele Norris, "A Conversation with Lynn and Vanessa Redgrave," National Public Radio (USA), Dec. 20, 2005.

163   **"lived for riding"**: LR, *This Is Living,* 16–17.

163   **"She loved acting"**: VR, *Vanessa Redgrave—An Autobiography,* 48.

163   **"Some things he did"**: Tynan, cited in Morley, 322.

163   **"His speech":** VR, *Vanessa Redgrave—An Autobiography,* 50.

164   **"It's a very curious":** Burton, 103.

164   **"I saw my father stop":** CR, quoted in MacKillop and Sinyard, eds., 223.

164   **"the next night":** VR, *Vanessa Redgrave—An Autobiography,* 49.

164   **"With this performance":** Findlater, 127–28.

164   **"all urgent concern":** An unsourced clipping: THM 31/1/3/4.

164   **"Rachel Kempson is the most":** *News Chronicle* (London), July 15, 1953.

165   **"Michael Redgrave has played":** Tynan, cited in Morley, 323.

165   **"in a very large":** Jasper Rees, "Redgrave's Second Act," *Daily Telegraph,* June 15, 2004.

165   **"that other relationships would not be":** RKR, 159.

165   **"He was a great charmer":** Richardson, 128.

165   **"The relationship took place":** Rees, "Redgrave's Second Act."

166   **"If only married partners":** RKR, 45.

166   **"joyful":** Ibid., 165.

166   **"The only thing that bothered me":** VR, in *Intimate Portrait: Vanessa Redgrave.*

166   **"frightened that":** Ibid.

166   **"It was not totally fulfilling":** RKR, 165.

167   **"nearly bankrupt":** CR, in MacKillop and Sinyard, eds., 229, and CR, 57.

167   **"There is the rent":** MR, *Mask or Face,* 142.

168   **"Peggy and George":** RKR, 166–67.

169   **"enormous fun":** Ibid., 167.

169   **"I was ignorant":** VR, *Vanessa Redgrave—An Autobiography,* 53.

169   **"The 'little ancient world' became":** Ibid., 52.

170   **"an artful, romantic story":** I am indebted to John L. Darretta, Ph.D., for his erudition and assistance, and for his expert commentary on the Fogazzaro novel.

170   **"my father did not wish":** Ibid., 56–57.

170   **"Bob gives me dinner":** THM 31/4/1/12.

171   **On Aug. 24, 1954:** MR delivered a lecture at the Cameo Cinema, Edinburgh. This was revised and published as "I Am Not a Camera" in *Sight and Sound* 24, no. 3 (Jan.–Mar. 1955). It was also considerably expanded for inclusion in his 1958 book *Mask or Face,* 120–48.

171   **Judi Dench was one of her classmates:** Judi Dench's recollections of VR at CSSD are mentioned in Hare, 165.

171   **"The only class":** Ibid.

172   **"A very happy day"**: THM 31/4/1/12.

172   **anniversary of Hans Christian Andersen's birth**: MR's reading of "The Fir Tree" in Denmark on Apr. 2, 1955, is preserved on *Six Fairy Tales by Hans Christian Andersen,* Gate 2 History CD 10018 (1997). The same CD also contains readings by Laurence Olivier, Ginger Rogers, John Gielgud, Gordon Whelan and Boris Karloff.

173   **"Michael Redgrave is so intelligent"**: Clurman, 205.

173   **"This is a monumental"**: Kenneth Tynan, in *The Observer,* June 3, 1955.

173   **"What did you think of"**: Clurman, 206.

174   **"towering"**: Brooks Atkinson in the *New York Times,* Oct. 23, 1955.

174   **"He combines"**: Clurman, cited in Findlater, 137.

174   **"He is shy and easily hurt"**: Clurman, 207.

175   **"Is it likely"**: MR to the author, Feb. 9, 1990; see also MR, *In My Mind's Eye,* 143.

176   **"I was not convinced"**: VR, *Vanessa Redgrave—An Autobiography,* 65.

176   **"It may be an excellent"**: MR, *Mask or Face,* 29–30; see also Mark Shivas, "Papa Redgrave Meets 'Uncle Vanya,'" *New York Times,* Feb. 5, 1967.

176   **"Don't use your own past"**: Stella Adler to the author, Nov. 9, 1984.

177   **"Stanislavski . . . instructed"**: Adler to the author; see also MR, *Mask or Face,* 50.

177   **horrifying, brutish**: Brooks Atkinson, in the *New York Times,* Nov. 16, 1955.

177   **"self-serving, pushy"**: Strachan, 382.

177   **"a slightly sinister"**: Ibid., 449.

177   **"and he was a demanding"**: Peter Eyre, obituary for Fred Sadoff, *The Independent* (London), July 8, 1994.

179   **"charmed relationship"**: Deirdre Redgrave, 22.

179   **"I will never find"**: Ibid.

179   **"As children, none of us"**: LR, in *The Redgraves.*

180   **"a close friend of Dad's"**: VR, *Vanessa Redgrave—An Autobiography,* 65, 79.

180   **"Some people thought"**: CR, *Michael Redgrave, My Father,* 104.

180   **"Daddy never comes"**: LR, *This Is Living,* 100–101.

182   **"We all felt"**: RKR to the author, April 19, 1990.

183   **"enthralled"**: VR, *Vanessa Redgrave—An Autobiography,* 69.

183   **"a place for myself"**: RKR, 173.

184   **"I like him immensely"**: Quoted by Philip French in *The Observer,* Jan. 18, 2009.

Chapter Ten: Ghosts (1956–1960)

185   **"mucky and trivial"**: Quoted in Fairweather, 22.

186   **"Michael Redgrave squanders"**: Brooks Atkinson, in the *New York Times,* Nov. 2, 1956.

186   **"but on too much vodka"**: MR, *In My Mind's Eye,* 213.

186   **"I wrote the adaption"**: Joseph L. Mankiewicz to the author, Feb. 24, 1984.

186   **"to get a performance"**: MR, diary entry for Mar. 21, 1957: THM 31/1/4/1/12.

187   **"get back on the treadmill"**: MR to the author, May 1, 1981; see also MR, 217.

188   **"More than anything else"**: VR, *Vanessa Redgrave—An Autobiography,* 88.

188   **"For Vanessa, he was much"**: CR, *Michael Redgrave, My Father,* 154.

188   **"My father was obstinate"**: VR, *Vanessa Redgrave—An Autobiography,* 89; also *Intimate Portrait: Vanessa Redgrave.*

188   **"Saw Vanessa's scenes"**: MR, diary entry for Nov. 21, 1957: THM 31/4/1/13.

189   **"stupid and ungainly"**: VR, *Vanessa Redgrave—An Autobiography,* 89.

189   **"How exciting it was"**: Duff, 123.

189   **"wonderful times"**: VR, *Vanessa Redgrave—An Autobiography,* 93.

190   **"pretty far gone"**: Duff, 123.

190   **"She was just dreadful"**: Frith Banbury to the author, Aug. 12, 1998.

190   **"but only when she asked"**: MR, *In My Mind's Eye,* 218.

190   **"My dad gave me"**: VR on *Mark Lawson Talks To*; also, VR on *Downstage Center.*

190   **"had a very difficult time"**: *Intimate Portrait: Vanessa Redgrave*; also, CR in Jasper Rees, "It's All Relative," *The Independent* (UK), July 6, 1997.

190   **"Yes, and you let"**: Often repeated (e.g., VR, *Vanessa Redgrave—An Autobiography,* 90–91).

191   **"We are so conditioned"**: Ibid., 91.

191   **"The great joy"**: THM 31/4/1/13.

191   **"Vanessa a distinct hit"**: Diary entry, Feb. 2, 1958: THM 31/4/1/13.

192   **"What makes an actor":** MR, *In My Mind's Eye,* 205.

192   **"I am a ghost":** Ibid., 28, 62.

192   **"fascinated, obsessed even":** MR, *The Mountebank's Tale,* 6.

192   **a recurring nightmare:** See CR in MacKillop and Sinyard, eds., 223–24.

192   **"It was hot":** MR, *The Mountebank's Tale*, 98.

193   **"Acting isn't private":** Ibid., 131.

193   **"I don't suppose":** Bob Michell to MR, letter dated May 2, 1958, from North Hollywood, California: THM 31/3/5/81/3.

193   **"Were you pleased":** Bob Michell to MR, Oct. 27, 1961: THM/31/3/5/148/10.

194   **"If being a Redgrave child":** LR, 19.

194   **"as if his lungs and heart":** VR, *Vanessa Redgrave—An Autobiography,* 95.

194   **"Drink destroyed":** CR, *Michael Redgrave, My Father,* 49–50.

194   **"I am ashamed":** MR, diary entry for Jan. 13, 1967: THM 31/4/1/15.

194   **"He was sobbing":** LR, at the High Falls International Film Festival, Rochester, N.Y., May 17, 2009.

195   **"Shakespeare's immaculate play":** LR, *This Is Living,* 22.

195   **"Nothing was expected":** LR, American Theatre Wing's symposium.

195   **"You can't really be":** MR, in Robert Muller, "There Are Two of Me," *The Daily Mail* (London), Aug. 17, 1959.

195   **"He didn't laugh":** From Ian McKellen's website: mckellen.com/writings/tribute/100407cr.htm.

196   **"she set a record":** Richardson, 129.

196   **"an engaging freshness":** W. A. Darlington, in the *New York Times,* June 3, 1959.

196   **"Ours is a family":** Widely quoted—most recently, on *Mark Lawson Talks To.* Numerous newspaper articles with this comment were also included in MR's diary for July 12, 1959: THM 31/4/1/13.

197   **"I don't see why not":** Hoare, 393.

197   **"Ah, Sir Michael":** Morley, *John Gielgud,* 257.

197   **"darker and darker":** Simon Callow, in *The Guardian,* May 15, 2004. Callow was describing "territory not covered in [Alan] Strachan's book" about Redgrave.

197   **"I like attempting":** Quoted by Callow in ibid.

197   **"I wish I could have":** VR to MR, undated, summer 1959: THM 31/3/6/44/1–11.

198   **"It feels like":** MR, diary entry for Aug. 12, 1959: THM 31/4/1/13.

198   **"signal achievement"**: Peter Robert in *Plays and Players* (UK), Sept. 1959.

198   **"a very beautiful rendering"**: Leon Edel to MR, letter dated Sept. 1, 1959, preserved in THM 31/4/1/1.

198   **"As rare as it is"**: Howard Taubman, in the *New York Times,* Feb. 8, 1962.

198   **"we stirred up"**: LR, *This Is Living,* 24–25.

200   **"Vanessa Redgrave moves"**: W. A. Darlington, "Drama Along the Thames," *New York Times,* Apr. 10, 1960.

200   **"I'm a very family"**: Collie Knox, "Show Page," *Woman's Own,* Oct. 22, 1960.

200   **"I am going to marry"**: VR to MR, letter, June 1960: THM/31/3/6/45/1–5.

200   **"I am in a very distressed"**: RKR, quoted in Chris Hastings, "The Secret Fiancé Dropped by Vanessa Redgrave," *The Sunday Times,* Sept. 13, 2009. Except as noted otherwise, quotations regarding the Welby-Redgrave affair are drawn from this article.

201   **"My dear, dear girl"**: MR to VR, June 28, 1960: THM/31/3/6/45/1–5.

201   **"my play"**: Duff, 209.

202   **"She has a conscience"**: MR to Frith Banbury, cited in Turner, 158.

202   ***"The Tiger and the Horse"*:** VR, 99–100.

202   **"When he'd had a few"**: Turner, 170.

202   **"I could not believe"**: Frith Banbury to Jerome Chodorov, Dec. 2, 1960, cited in Duff, 214.

202   **"He went off the tracks"**: Robert Bolt to the author, Jan. 9, 1990; see also Duff.

203   **"stunningly perfect"**: Bernard Levin, in the *Daily Express,* Aug. 25, 1960.

203   **"truly remarkable performance"**: Peter Roberts, in *Plays and Players.*

203   **"bristling with technical"**: Ibid., Oct. 1960.

203   **"Sadoff delighted"**: Eyre, obituary for Fred Sadoff.

203   **"Michael was upset"**: RKR, 209–10.

204   **"He knew he had made a fool"**: Eyre, obituary for Fred Sadoff.

Chapter Eleven: Fat for Comedy, Thin for Tragedy (1961–1963)

205   **"At the center"**: Richardson, 154.

205   **"Even before he met her"**: CR, in *The Redgraves.*

206   **"We are in the midst"**: Barnes, 254.

206   **"Our director, Michael Elliott":** VR, 101–2; also VR on *Mark Lawson Talks To,* June 1, 2010.

207   **"alertness and immediacy":** VR, *Vanessa Redgrave—An Autobiography,* 102.

207   **"Acting isn't mysterious":** On *Mark Lawson Talks To*; also Godfrey Smith, "Vanessa, Victorious," *New York Times,* Apr. 10, 1966.

207   **"She wins":** Peter Roberts in *Plays and Players,* Sept. 1961.

207   **"This was not acting":** Bernard Levin, in the *Daily Express,* July 7, 1961.

208   **"fiery, lovely . . . she speaks the poetry":** *Time,* May 27, 1966.

209   **"Anything we create":** VR, 104–5.

209   **"I could see nothing wrong":** Ibid., 107.

209   **"Michael and I":** RKR, 189.

209   **"who was not":** Selznick, 355.

210   **"I knew that he had fallen":** VR, in *Intimate Portrait: Vanessa Redgrave.*

211   **"passionate and alert":** Ian McKellen's website.

211   **"an absolute disaster":** CR, interviewed by Ian MacKillop for the Theatre Archive Project at the British Library. No date is given for the conversation, but internal evidence suggests that it was conducted during late spring/early summer 2003.

211   **"badly spoken":** Caryl Brahms, in *Plays and Players,* Feb. 1962.

212   **"She seemed to be":** Rita Tushingham, in the Internet site devoted to her career: members.cox.net/rjd0309/tush/.

212   **"I don't know whether":** LR, *This Is Living,* 33.

212   **"struck by the sheer force":** Deirdre Redgrave, 12–13.

213   **"wildly irresponsible":** Ibid., 29.

213   **"How long do you":** *Intimate Portrait: Vanessa Redgrave.*

213   **"We both wanted children":** Richardson, 155.

214   **"so as not to be seen":** MR, *In My Mind's Eye,* 223, and to the author, Mar. 9, 1981.

214   **"Just the opposite":** MR, on *TV-AM* (UK), 1983.

215   **"Who would not enjoy":** Ingrid Bergman to the author, May 8, 1975.

216   **"Vanessa's energy":** Deirdre Redgrave, 86.

216   **"the highest level of acting":** Writing in *The Guardian,* Nov. 20, 1963, critic Philip Hope-Wallace was reviewing the Old Vic revival of *Uncle Vanya* the following year and praising it as even better than the Chichester premiere he had seen in July 1962.

217   **"Our relationship had remained":** RKR, 193.

217   **"I wanted to get away"**: James Barron, "Tony Richardson, the Director of 'Tom Jones,' Is Dead at 63," *New York Times,* Nov. 15, 1991.

218   **"I often resent"**: Smith, "Vanessa Victorious."

218   **"Difficulties started"**: RKR, 189; and to the author, Feb. 22, 1990.

219   **"Lynn is better"**: VR, in Peter Bart, "Britain's Vanessa: Regal and Reticent," *New York Times,* Dec. 18, 1966.

219   **"Tony was with me"**: *Intimate Portrait: Vanessa Redgrave.*

220   **"Fat for comedy"**: LR, *This Is Living,* 35–36.

222   **"When you came on:** MR, *In My Mind's Eye,* 227; to the author, Jan. 8, 1981; see also Jasper Rees, "It's All Relative," *The Independent* (UK), July 6, 1997.

222   **"a great feeling"**: Ibid.

222   **"I don't really approve"**: Gourlay, 72.

222   **"I didn't satisfy myself"**: Burton, 104.

222   **"All of us"**: LR, *Shakespeare for My Father,* 47.

223   **"He said I was"**: Sheridan Morley, "Michael Redgrave at Seventy," *The Times* (London), Mar. 20, 1978.

223   **"I admire Larry"**: Quoted by RKR to the author, Nov. 15, 1989.

Chapter Twelve: Georgy and Guenevere (1964–1966)

224   **"bureaucratic dictatorship"**: VR, *Vanessa Redgrave—An Autobiography,* 124–25.

225   **"She struggled"**: Richardson, 186.

225   **"a struggle . . . made poignant"**: Martin Esslin, on the BBC, Mar. 16, 1964.

225   **"We were so happy"**: RKR, 194.

225   **"was not always"**: Ibid., 177.

225   **"We shared a passion"**: Deirdre Redgrave, 133.

226   **"a part Vanessa was born"**: Richardson, 189.

226   **"twenty movies"**: Ibid., 198.

227   **"I was away from the house"**: Ibid., 201–2.

227   **so-called Gulf of Tonkin incident:** On the Gulf of Tonkin, the literature is vast. See, e.g., Robert J. Hanyok in *Cryptologic Quarterly* (Winter 2000/ Spring 2001): 177; and Edwin E. Moïse, *Tonkin Gulf and the Escalation of the Vietnam War* (Chapel Hill: University of North Carolina Press, 1996).

228   **"a charming unspoilt girl"**: Vera Brittain's diary entry, Mar. 12, 1965, quoted in Bostridge and Berry, 516.

229   **"She was not"**: MR to the author, Feb. 22, 1981.

229   **"I wasn't ready"**: Ingrid Bergman to the author, May 22, 1975; see also "Ingrid Bergman—A Stable Romantic Ideal in the Midst of Change," *The Times* (London), Dec. 6, 1965.

229   **"Miss Bergman's performance"**: *The Times* (London), Sept. 24, 1965.

229   **"It is by her Natalia"**: *The Daily Telegraph* (London), Sept. 24, 1965.

230   **"Lynn had graduated"**: Ibid., 132.

230   **"to see the destruction"**: VR, *Vanessa Redgrave—An Autobiography,* 143.

230   **"She would really much rather"**: Deirdre Redgrave, 124–26.

231   **"I had fallen in love"**: Richardson, 211.

231   **"It's a tragedy"**: VR, *Vanessa Redgrave—An Autobiography,* 144.

232   **"My marriage is over"**: Ibid., 145.

232   **"It would have been much better"**: Ibid., 146–48.

232   **"The thing is, Vanessa"**: Ibid., 147–48.

232   **"Tony was so good"**: Dominic Searle, "Vanessa Redgrave: A Born Heroine," *Woman's Mirror,* Dec. 3, 1966.

232   **"She arrived back home"**: RKR to the author, April 7, 1990; see also RKR, 196.

233   **"detached"**: Deirdre Redgrave, 126.

233   **"This is the first time"**: Smith, "Vanessa, Victorious."

233   **"positively smashing"**: Bosley Crowther, in the *New York Times,* Apr. 5, 1966.

234   **"I had felt so unconfident"**: *Intimate Portrait: Vanessa Redgrave.*

234   **"boosted her self-confidence"**: Deirdre Redgrave, 175–76.

234   **"There were scenes"**: LR, *This Is Living,* 47.

235   **"He greatly admired"**: Rees, "It's All Relative," and CR, *Michael Redgrave, My Father,* 154.

235   **"makes me weep"**: MR, diary entry for Jan. 17, 1967: THM 31/4/1/15.

235   **"My darling girl"**: Glen Byam Shaw to RKR, June 9, 1966: THM 31/3/8/9/1–7.

236   **"She has no esteem"**: Searle, "Vanessa Redgrave."

236   **"Vanessa really played"**: Bernard Dick to the author, Jan. 29, 2011.

236   **"After all [as he said]"**: Quoted in *Time,* Mar. 17, 1967.

237   **"staggeringly beautiful"**: MR, diary entry for Mar. 17, 1967: THM 31/4/1/15.

237   **"a wave of panic"**: VR, *Vanessa Redgrave—An Autobiography,* 151.

238   **"Corin very good"**: MR, diary entry for Apr. 4, 1967: THM 31/4/1/15.

239   **"People sometimes look"**: Peter Bart, "Britain's Vanessa: Regal and Reticent," *New York Times,* Dec. 18, 1966.

239   **Nero . . . was unenthusiastic:** On the first meeting of VR and Franco Nero, see, e.g., VR, *Vanessa Redgrave—An Autobiography,* 154; Alexis Chu, "Lost & Found—A Love Story," *People,* June 7, 2010; Susan King, "Vanessa Redgrave and Franco Nero Know Well the Wait for Love," *Los Angeles Times,* May 14, 2010; and their respective statements for *The Redgraves* and *Intimate Portrait: Vanessa Redgrave.*

240   **"I don't know how"**: Peter Evans, "So Why Did Redgrave the Red Bend the Knee to Royalty?" *Daily Mail* (online edition), Feb. 27, 2010.

240   **"A long phone call"**: MR, diary entry for Feb. 1, 1967: THM 31/4/1/15.

Chapter Thirteen: Hideaways (1967–1975)

241   **"Time cannot be remedied"**: THM 31/4/1/15.

242   **"He seems brash"**: MR, diary entry for Apr. 1, 1967: THM 31/4/1/15.

242   **"The official grounds"**: Evans, "So Why Did Redgrave."

243   **"I was given so much"**: *Intimate Portrait: Vanessa Redgrave.*

243   **"When I was about ten"**: Quoted in Michele Kort, "Natasha's Gay Genes," *The Advocate,* Nov. 7, 2000.

243   **"Press cuttings"**: MR, diary entry for Jan. 6, 1967: THM 31/4/1/15.

244   **"I think I ought"**: CR, *Michael Redgrave, My Father,* 108.

244   **"the other side of my nature"**: MR, *In My Mind's Eye,* 132, citing MR's diary for May 4, 1940: THM 31/4/1/5.

244   **"I believe"**: Ibid., 118.

245   **"a bit strange"**: Michael Green to the author, Feb. 12, 2011.

245   **"dope-smoking"**: Deirdre Redgrave, 149–50, 98, 102.

246   **"It was amazingly easy"**: LR, *This Is Living,* 58.

246   **"little broken blood vessels"**: Ibid., 69.

246   **"I had to find"**: Ibid.

246   **"thunderous rows"**: VR, *Vanessa Redgrave—An Autobiography,* 157.

247   **"Vanessa is an extremely"**: RKR to the author, Apr. 4, 1991; see also RKR, 198.

247   **"She just switches off"**: *Time,* Mar. 17, 1967.

248   **"Speakers included"**: The National Archives of the United Kingdom, Public record reference HO 325/89.

248   **"Vanessa was always"**: David Walsh and David North, "The Life and

Career of Corin Redgrave," in wsws.org/articles/2010/apr2010/redg-a12/shtml.

249   **"I wouldn't be a Communist":** Fred Ferretti, "Miss Redgrave Waits for Visa," *New York Times,* June 19, 1971.

249   **"The theatre got":** Matt Wolf, "A Redgrave Moves Up in the Family Business," Feb. 21, 1999.

250   **"I told her":** Franco Nero, in *Intimate Portrait: Vanessa Redgrave.*

250   **"I don't think":** Ibid.

250   **"I would have liked":** Jan Moir, "Beautiful? I'm Usually Just a Scruff," *Daily Telegraph,* Feb. 14, 2005.

250   **"My children suffered":** VR, *Vanessa Redgrave—An Autobiography,* 203; also *Intimate Portrait: Vanessa Redgrave.*

251   **"I was a caretaker":** "Natasha Richardson," *The Telegraph* (London), Mar. 19, 2009.

251   **"reacted against":** Ticky Hedley-Dent, "Joely's Journey," *Tatler* (UK), Jan. 2010.

252   **"Plays had been sent to me":** MR to Peter Lewis, in the *Daily Mail,* Aug. 16, 1971.

252   **"a wall of fear":** Ibid.

252   **"giving a performance":** Ibid.

253   **"Look over there":** Deirdre Redgrave, 180–81.

253   **"I went to France":** VR, *Vanessa Redgrave—An Autobiography,* 176.

253   **"the three men":** Ibid

254   **"we could agree":** Ibid.

254   **"quite wonderful":** Richardson, 277.

254   **"I see no conflict":** Judith Weinraub, "Two Feisty Feminists Filming Hellman's 'Pentimento,'" *New York Times,* Oct. 31, 1976.

255   **"I like touring":** MR to the author, Feb. 12, 1981.

256   **"I played a woman":** RKR to the author, Apr. 19, 1990.

257   **"I was intrigued":** LR, Folger Shakespeare Library interview.

257   **"'Doctor Theatre'":** LR, *Shakespeare for My Father,* 48.

258   **"For Rachel as well":** Joan Hirst to Michael Codron, Feb. 28, 1978.

258   **"Michael, weak with":** Diary entry for June 29, 1975, in Hall, 173.

258   **"I'm not going to pretend":** Sheridan Morley, "Michael Redgrave at Seventy," *The Times* (London), Mar. 20, 1978.

259   **"a genuinely courteous":** Alan Strachan, "Corin Redgrave: Actor Whose Involvement in Radical Politics Kept Him Away from Stage and Screen for Two Decades," *The Independent* (London), Apr. 7, 2010.

259   **"all those people in the Party":** Deirdre Redgrave, 214.

259   **"She certainly did have":** Cassandra Jardine, "I Was Terrified of Being on My Own," *The Telegraph,* Mar. 19, 2001.

259   **"There was a total lack":** Simon Hattenstone, "So Whose Daughter Are You?" *The Guardian,* Jan. 6, 1999.

Chapter Fourteen: Hoodlums (1976–1985)

262   **"by the hypocritical morality":** VR, *Vanessa Redgrave—An Autobiography,* 217.

263   **"gave one of her":** Richardson, 282.

263   **right through the skin:** Diary entry for July 1979 (n.d.), Hall, 451.

263   **alleged lifelong friendship:** Lillian Hellman never challenged Muriel Gardiner's claim to be the real "Julia." On the controversy surrounding the story in *Pentimento,* see, e.g., Gardiner; and Sutherland, 517–19. Gardiner also figures significantly in the lives of both Stephen Spender and Tony Hyndman.

263   **"Vanessa is not the kind":** Fred Zinnemann to the author, Nov. 5, 1982; see also Benedict Nightingale, "An Actress in Love with Risk," *New York Times,* Sept. 17, 1989.

264   **"There is a quality about Vanessa":** In 1968 Jane Fonda and her husband, director Roger Vadim, named their newborn daughter Vanessa not primarily (as commonly presumed) in tribute to VR but because, as Jane wrote, "I liked the alliteration. I also thought of the name because of my fascination with Vanessa Redgrave—not just because she's a transcendent actor, but because she is strong and sure of herself and was the only actress I knew who was a political activist, though I didn't know the particulars of her politics [at that time]." See Fonda, 364.

264   **"My method is":** Judy Klemesrud, "Vanessa Redgrave—'The Only Person Who Could Play Julia,'" *New York Times,* Oct. 2, 1977.

264   **"I don't plan":** Nightingale, "An Actress in Love with Risk."

265   **"Vanessa Redgrave has financed":** *San Francisco Chronicle,* Aug. 9, 1979.

265   **"I made this film":** *New York Times,* Nov. 11, 1977.

266   **"violent extremist":** See www.fbi.gov/stats-services/publications/terror/terrorism-2000-2001. See also jdl.org.

266   **Established Jewish groups:** On the opposing principles of the Jewish Defense League and the Anti-Defamation League, see their websites: jdl.org and adl.org.

266   **"for preaching a radical form":** For the Anti-Defamation League on the JDL, see www.adl.org/extremism/jdl_chron.asp. See also Bohn.

267   **JDL detonated a grenade:** On the Sol Hurok attack, see Harlow Robinson, "Sol Hurok: America's Dance Impresario," *Dance* magazine, Nov. 1994.

268   **"I only regret":** *The Telegraph* (London), Feb. 22, 2010.

268   **"and when I referred":** VR, *Vanessa Redgrave—An Autobiography,* 237.

268   **"Hollywood turned its back":** Meryl Streep in *Intimate Portrait: Vanessa Redgrave.*

268   **"Vanessa is openly":** Raymond, 305.

269   **"I don't think anyone":** Brent Lewis, "Vanessa Redgrave—A Romantic Firebrand," *Films and Filming,* Oct. 1986.

269   **"her anti-American statements":** Leslie Garis, "The Redgraves Finally Do a Sister Act," *New York Times,* May 4, 2003.

269   **"I had discovered":** Wallace, 231–32.

270   **"All those scruffy people . . . They come in and plot":** Deirdre Redgrave, 230.

270   **"There was some bitterness":** Ian Woodward, "Not So Precious Jemma," *The Daily Mail* (London), May 3, 1997.

271   **"The curtain rises":** Gray, 175, 238–39.

272   **"I was moved to see":** Diary entry for Feb. 19, 1979, Hall, 416.

272   **"Sir Michael Redgrave is":** Felix Barker, in the *Evening News,* May 25, 1979.

272   **"Without words":** Mel Gussow, "Demonstrations of the Actor's Art," *New York Times,* Aug. 12, 1979.

272   **"I went round to see":** Diary entry for Oct. 22, 1979, Hall, 469.

272   **"I don't feel old":** MR to the author, Apr. 1, 1981; similarly to CR, *Michael Redgrave, My Father,* 149.

273   **"was no good to you":** RKR to VR, undated letter drafted in 1976: THM 31/3/6/27/5.

273   **"not to be mentioned":** Joan Hirst to the author, Jan. 4, 1981.

273   **"I never discuss Vanessa":** MR, in *The Sunday Telegraph* (Australia), June 3, 1973.

273   **"As often happens":** VR, *Vanessa Redgrave—An Autobiography,* 214.

273   **"I was honestly proud":** RKR to the author, Mar. 9, 1991; see also RKR, 203.

274   **"my lover":** CR, *Michael Redgrave, My Father,* 18.

274   **"He wanted to write":** Ibid., 4, 20, 148.

274   **"There is something of me"**: Ibid., 20.

275   **"failed to bring him into focus"**: Julius Novick, in the *New York Times,* Mar. 11, 1984.

276   **"Having been blacklisted"**: Quoted in Richard F. Shepard, "Vanessa Redgrave's Casting Is Protested," *New York Times,* Aug. 8, 1979. See also Alan Richman, "Security Is Tight as CBS Begins Redgrave Film," *New York Times,* Nov. 9, 1979.

276   **"I didn't think"**: *Intimate Portrait: Vanessa Redgrave.*

277   **"on moral grounds"**: Tony Schwartz, "Names of Redgrave Film's Sponsors Guarded by CBS-TV and Ad Agencies," *New York Times,* Sept. 25, 1980.

277   **"the most extraordinary performance"**: John J. O'Connor, "TV: Vanessa Redgrave, Inmate," *New York Times,* Sept. 30, 1980.

277   **"extraordinary ... astonishingly convincing"**: John J. O'Connor, "CBS's 'Second Serve,'" *New York Times,* May 13, 1986.

277   **"I realized"**: VR, *Vanessa Redgrave—An Autobiography,* 285 ff.

279   **"I never heard him"**: CR, *Michael Redgrave, My Father,* 151; Aleks Sierz, "Unkind Reviews," *New Statesman,* Feb. 28, 2005.

279   **"I've done"**: MR to the author, Mar. 3, 1981.

279   **"the unremitting intensity"**: Simon Callow, in *The Guardian,* May 15, 2004.

280   **"She's a true actress"**: VR, *Vanessa Redgrave—An Autobiography,* 274.

Chapter Fifteen: Things Happen (1985–2019)

282   **"My mother"**: CR, *Michael Redgrave, My Father,* 152.

282   **"It's so important"**: RKR to the author, Mar. 22, 1991.

282   **"You look so pretty:** Ibid., 235.

282   **"Her lover adored her"**: VR, *Vanessa Redgrave—An Autobiography,* 380.

283   **"baffled and angry ... I was simply excluded"**: Jasper Rees, "Redgrave's Second Act," *The Telegraph,* June 15, 2004.

283   **"Redgrave is the production's best feature"**: Paul Taylor, in *The Independent,* Sept. 25, 1992.

284   **"She was always visible"**: James Ivory, "The Trouble with Olive: Divine Madness in Massachusetts," *Sight and Sound* 54 (Spring 1985).

284   **"hell to get"**: Hare, 164–65.

285   **"Of course it's helpful"**: Steven Goldman, "The Next in the Long Line of Redgraves," *New York Times,* Nov. 27, 1988.

285   **"I know how it is"**: Michele Kort, "Natasha's Gay Genes," *The Advocate,* Nov. 7, 2000.

285   **"My mother's politics"**: Ticky Hedley-Dent, "Joely's Journey," *Tatler* (UK), Jan. 2010.

286   **"I shied away"**: Steven Goldman, "The Next in the Long Line."

286   **"I've never loved"**: Richardson, 322.

286   **"I think that because"**: Hedley-Dent, "Joely's Journey."

286   **"The first time"**: Leslie Bennetts, "New Face: Natasha Richardson—Continuing Dynasty," *New York Times,* May 15, 1987.

287   **"It was a big joke"**: Hedley-Dent, "Joely's Journey."

287   **"I had successfully"**: LR, *This Is Living,* 126.

287   **"because I told him"**: VR, *Vanessa Redgrave—An Autobiography,* 203.

288   **"I was so young"**: Cassandra Jardine, "I Wake Up Every Day Feeling Lucky," *The Telegraph,* Feb. 27, 2003.

288   **"My marriage collapsed"**: Euan Ferguson, "How I Survived Divorce, the Tabloids and Jamie Theakston," *The Observer,* Dec. 30, 2001.

288   **"He was a fabulous husband"**: Hedley-Dent, "Joely's Journey."

289   **"frantically self-effacing"**: Ibid.

289   **"I doubt his book"**: John Osborne's endorsement of Tony Richardson's posthumously published memoir, printed on the back jacket of the book.

290   **"Every time she had bad news"**: Simon Hattenstone, "So Whose Daughter Are You?" *The Guardian,* Jan. 6, 1999.

290   **"I needed to forgive myself"**: Tony Vellela, "Interview with Lynn Redgrave," *The Christian Science Monitor,* May 28, 1993.

290   **"You have given me"**: Peter Marks, "For Redgrave, The Show, and Life, Must Go On," *Washington Post,* Apr. 5, 2009.

291   **"It was challenging"**: Jemma Redgrave, in the documentary *The Redgraves.*

291   **"The pressures on students"**: VR, in MR, *The Actor's Ways and Means,* ix.

291   **"No one was supposed to know"**: See Clark's website, www.johnclarkprose.com.

291   **"felt betrayed"**: Dan Jewel, "A Family Affair," *People,* Mar. 29, 1999.

291   **"an electrifying triumph"**: Ben Brantley, "Desperate Dance at Oblivion's Brink," *New York Times,* Mar. 20, 1998.

292   **"I wouldn't call myself"**: VR, on *Mark Lawson Talks To*; also, Lynn Barber, "She's Got Issues," *The Observer,* Mar. 19, 2006.

292   **"To be non-political"**: "Unite for Children," UNICEF bulletin, Dec. 7, 2006.

293   **"I cannot tell you"**: RKR to the author, Nov. 9, 1995.

293   **"an evening"**: Peter Marks, "An Acting Dynasty Recites Chekhov," *New York Times,* May 6, 1998.

294   **"The only living actress"**: Ben Brantley, "Two Redgraves Paired in Roman Shakespeare," *New York Times,* Feb. 8, 1996.

294   **"arguably the greatest living"**: Ben Brantley, "Getting Cozy If a Bit Dizzy as Cleopatra," *New York Times,* Mar. 14, 1997.

295   **"Mr. Redgrave has never"**: Charles Spencer, "First Time Out for a Gripping Prison Drama," *The Telegraph,* Mar. 14, 1998.

295   **"He was always a very sound"**: Matt Wolf, "A Redgrave Moves Up In the Family Business," *New York Times,* Feb. 21, 1999.

295   **"Vanessa led us all"**: Marian Seldes to the author, Aug. 23, 2010.

296   **"The play is a comedy"**: Mark Espiner, in *The Guardian,* Mar. 13, 2000.

296   **"incredibly boring"**: Michael Thornton, in *The Daily Mail,* Aug. 27, 2000.

297   **"incredible will"**: LR, *Journal,* 13.

297   **"keeps turning up"**: Ibid., 53.

297   **"Much of my recovery"**: Michele Norris, "A Conversation with Lynn and Vanessa Redgrave," *All Things Considered,* National Public Radio, Dec. 20, 2005.

298   **"a wonderful haven"**: LR, *Journal,* 60.

298   **"Darling Mum"**: Ibid., 64.

298   **"I think my Mummy"**: Ibid., 76.

298   **"In the early morning"**: RKR to the author, July 8, 1994.

298   **"that filled her"**: LR, in a tribute to her mother on her website, www .redgrave.com.

299   **"a privilege"**: LR, *Journal,* 81.

299   **"I don't feel lonely"**: Jan Moir, "Beautiful? I'm Usually Just a Scruff," *The Daily Telegraph,* Feb. 14, 2005.

299   **"Human rights"**: Adam Bernstein, "Behind the Scenes, Actor Corin Redgrave, 70, Played Leftist Political Role," *Washington Post,* Apr. 7, 2010.

300   **"It affected everything"**: Dominic Cavendish, "Corin Redgrave: Brilliant, Bolshie—and Back," *The Telegraph,* Mar. 12, 2009.

300   **"because he could no longer memorize"**: Kate Kellaway, "Jemma Redgrave: 'Grief Is Like a Tsunami,'" *The Observer,* July 11, 2010.

300   **"It was ... an extraordinary":** David Thacker, "Corin Redgrave, 1939–2010: A Tribute," *The Guardian,* Theatre Blog, April 7, 2010.

301   **"all sorts of other people":** Laura Roberts, "Vanessa Redgrave Speaks About Marriage to Second 'Husband' for the First Time," *The Telegraph,* June 11, 2010.

301   **"The games are done":** Alexis Chiu, "Lost & Found—A Love Story," *People,* June 7, 2010.

301   **"She had a lot":** wn.com/Sir_Ian_McKellen_remembers_Lynn_Redgrave.

302   **"I could be dead":** Felicia R. Lee, "To Lynn Redgrave, the Examined Life Is Worth Staging," *New York Times,* Nov. 1, 2009.

302   **"She didn't hit":** Bruce Weber, "Natasha Richardson, Actress, Dies at 45," *New York Times,* Mar. 19, 2009.

304   **"Tasha embraced":** Kellaway, "Jemma Redgrave: 'Grief Is Like a Tsunami.'"

304   **"Ten years ago":** VR and LR to Mike Wallace, on *60 Minutes* (CBS-TV), June 3, 2007.

305   **"quite tremendous":** advance review of *Coriolanus* in *The Telegraph,* Feb. 11, 2011.

305   **"She rewrote the rules":** Ibid.

305   **"He was my North Star":** Ibid.

307   **"We're on the shoulders":** Brent Lewis, "Vanessa Redgrave, A Romantic Firebrand," *Films and Filming,* Oct. 1986; also Patrick Healey, "A Reluctant Redgrave, on 'Daisy' and More," *New York Times,* Feb. 15, 2011.

307   **"I've come to realize":** Frank Bruni, "Under a Bare Bulb," *New York Times,* Feb. 16, 1997.

308   **"I don't think":** Nightingale, "An Actress in Love with Risk."

308   **"the great abstract nouns":** Hare, 168.

308   **"All families":** "Show Business," *Time,* Oct. 9, 1989.

308   **"What can we do":** Diana Jean Schemo, "Even in Her Own Words, a Woman of Convictions," *New York Times,* Dec. 27, 1994.

309   **"I don't picture myself":** Peter Bart, "Britain's Vanessa: Regal and Reticent," *New York Times,* Dec. 18, 1966.

309   **"But we are not":** VR, on *Mark Lawson Talks To.*

Bibliography

Andersen, H[ans]. C[hristian]. *Eventyr.* Viborg, Denmark: Gyldendal, 2005.

Barnes, Philip. *A Companion to Post-war British Theatre.* Totowa, NJ: Barnes and Noble Books, 1986.

Barr, Charles. *English Hitchcock.* Moffat, Scotland: Cameron and Hollis, 1999.

Behlmer, Rudy. *Shoot the Rehearsal! Behind the Scenes with Assistant Director Reggie Callow.* Lanham, MD: Scarecrow Press, 2010.

Bergman, Ingrid, and Alan Burgess. *Ingrid Bergman—My Story.* New York: Delacorte, 1980.

Bernstein, Matthew. *Walter Wanger, Hollywood Independent.* Berkeley: University of California Press, 1994.

Bohn, Michael K. *The Achille Lauro Hijacking: Lessons in the Politics and Prejudice of Terrorism.* Dulles, VA: Brassey's/Potomac Books, 2005.

Bostridge, Mark, and Paul Berry. *Vera Brittain: A Life.* London: Virago, 2008.

Brown, Geoff. *Launder and Gilliat.* London: The British Film Institute, 1977.

Burton, Hal, ed. *Great Acting.* New York: Bonanza Books, 1967.

Campbell, Mrs. Patrick. *My Life and Some Letters.* New York: Dodd, Mead, 1922.

Carleton, Patrick. *The Amateur Stage: A Symposium.* London: Geoffrey Bles, 1939.

Clurman, Harold. *All People Are Famous.* New York: Harcourt Brace Jovanovich, 1974.

Coldstream, John. *Dirk Bogarde: The Authorised Biography.* London: Phoenix, 2004.

Cole, Toby, and Helen Krich Chinoy, eds. *Actors on Acting: The Theories, Techniques and Practices of the Great Actors as Told in Their Own Words.* New York: Crown, 1949.

Day, Barry, ed. *The Letters of Noël Coward.* New York: Knopf, 2007.

Dick, Bernard. *Forever Mame: The Life of Rosalind Russell.* Jackson: University Press of Mississippi, 2006.

———. *Joseph L. Mankiewicz.* Boston: Twayne Publishers, 1983.

Didion, Joan. *The Year of Magical Thinking.* New York: Vintage International, 2007.

Duff, Charles. *The Lost Summer: The Heyday of the West End Theatre.* London: Nick Hern Books, 1995.

Eliot, T. S. *The Complete Poems and Plays 1909–1950.* New York: Harcourt Brace, 1952.

Fairweather, Virginia. *Cry God for Larry.* London: Boyars and Calder, 1969.

Findlater, Richard [pseud. of Kenneth Bruce Findlater Bain]. *Michael Redgrave: Actor.* New York: Theatre Arts Books, 1956.

Fonda, Jane. *My Life So Far.* New York: Random House, 2005.

Forbes, Bryan. *Dame Edith Evans: Ned's Girl.* Boston: Little, Brown, 1977.

Gardiner, Muriel. *Code Name "Mary": Memoirs of an American Woman in the Austrian Underground.* New Haven, CT: Yale University Press, 1983.

Garrett, John, ed. *Talking of Shakespeare.* London: Hodder and Stoughton, 1954.

Geist, Kenneth L. *Pictures Will Talk: The Life and Films of Joseph L. Mankiewicz.* New York: Charles Scribner's Sons, 1978.

Gourlay, Logan. *Olivier.* New York: Stein and Day, 1974.

Gray, Simon. *Key Plays: Butley, Otherwise Engaged, Close of Play, Quartermain's Terms, The Late Middle Classes.* London: Faber and Faber, 2002.

Haffenden, John. *William Empson: Among the Mandarins,* vol. 1. New York: Oxford University Press, 2005.

Hall, Peter. *Peter Hall's Diaries,* ed. John Goodwin. London: Hamish Hamilton, 1983.

Hare, David. *Writing Left-Handed.* London: Faber and Faber, 1991.

Hoare, Philip. *Noël Coward, A Biography.* London: Sinclair-Stevenson, 1995.

Houghton, Norris. *Entrances and Exits: A Life in and out of the Theatre.* New York: Limelight Editions, 1991.

Irving, Laurence. *Precarious Crust.* London: Chatto and Windus, 1971.

Isherwood, Christopher. *Christopher and His Kind.* Minneapolis: University of Minnesota Press, 2001.

Kellow, Brian. *The Bennetts: An Acting Family.* Lexington: University Press of Kentucky, 2004.

Kempson, Rachel, Lady Redgrave. *Life Among the Redgraves.* New York: E.P. Dutton, 1986.

Lehmann, John. *The Whispering Gallery: Autobiography I.* London: Longmans, Green, 1955.

McFarlane, Brian. *An Autobiography of British Cinema.* London: Methuen, 1997.

McFarlane, Brian, ed. *The Encyclopedia of British Film,* 2nd ed. London: Methuen/British Film Institute, 2003.

MacKillop, Ian, and Neil Sinyard, eds. *British Cinema of the 1950s: A Celebration.* Manchester and New York: Manchester University Press, 2009.

Morley, Sheridan. *The Great Stage Stars.* London: Angus and Robertson, 1986.

———. *John Gielgud: The Authorized Biography.* New York: Simon and Schuster, 2002.

Olivier, Laurence. *Confessions of an Actor.* New York: Simon and Schuster, 1982.

Pendergast, Tom, and Sara Pendergast. *Actors and Actresses: International Dictionary of Films and Filmmakers,* vol. 3 (4th ed.). New York: Gale/St. James Press, 2001.

Powell, Michael. *Million Dollar Movie.* London: Heinemann, 1992.

Rattigan, Terence. *The Browning Version.* London: Nick Hern Books, 1994.

Read, Piers Paul. *Alec Guinness.* London: Simon and Schuster, 2003.

Reaney, P. H. *The Origin of English Surnames* (rev. ed.). London: Routledge, 1992.

Reaney, P. H., and R.M. Wilson. *A Dictionary of English Surnames.* Oxford: Oxford University Press, 2005.

Rebellato, Dan. *1956 and All That: The Making of Modern British Drama.* London and New York: Routledge, 1999.

Redgrave, Corin. *Julius Caesar* (Actors on Shakespeare Series). London: Faber and Faber, 2002.

———. *Michael Redgrave, My Father.* London: Richard Cohen Books, 1995.

Redgrave, Deirdre, and Danaë Brook. *To Be a Redgrave: Surviving Amidst the Glamour.* New York: Linden Press, 1982.

Redgrave, Lynn, with photographs by Annabel Clark. *Journal: A Mother and Daughter's Recovery from Breast Cancer.* New York: Umbrage Editions, 2004.

———. *Shakespeare for My Father: A One-Woman Play in Two Acts.* New York: Samuel French, 1993.

————. *This Is Living*. New York: Dutton, 1991.

Redgrave, Michael. *The Actor's Ways and Means*. London: Nick Hern Books, 1995.

————. *The Aspern Papers: A Comedy of Letters* (adapted from the story by Henry James). New York: Samuel French, 1959.

————. *In My Mind's Eye—An Autobiography*. London: Weidenfeld and Nicolson, 1983.

————. *Mask or Face: Reflections in an Actor's Mirror*. London: Heinemann, 1958.

————. *The Mountebank's Tale*. New York: Harper and Brothers, 1959.

Redgrave, Vanessa. *Antony and Cleopatra* (Actors on Shakespeare Series). London: Faber and Faber, 2002.

————. *Vanessa Redgrave—An Autobiography*. New York: Random House, 1994 (revised and expanded version of the original UK edition, London: Hutchinson, 1991).

Richardson, Tony. *The Long-Distance Runner—An Autobiography*. New York: William Morrow, 1993.

Ross, Lillian, and Helen Ross. *The Player: A Profile of an Art*. New York: Simon and Schuster, 1962.

Russell, Rosalind, and Chris Chase. *Life Is a Banquet*. New York: Random House, 1977.

Saint-Denis, Michel. *Theatre: The Rediscovery of Style and Other Writings* (Jane Baldwin, ed.). New York: Routledge, 2008.

Selznick, Irene Mayer. *A Private View*. New York: Alfred A. Knopf, 1983.

Shipley, Joseph T. *The Crown Guide to the World's Best Plays, From Ancient Greece to Modern Times* (revised and updated). New York: Crown Publishers, 1984.

Spender, Stephen. *World Within World*. New York: Modern Library, 2001; first published in 1951.

Spoto, Donald. *The Art of Alfred Hitchcock*. New York: Doubleday/Anchor, 1992 (revised edition of the original—New York: Hopkinson and Blake, 1976).

————. *The Dark Side of Genius: The Life of Alfred Hitchcock*. Boston: Little, Brown, 1983.

————. *Laurence Olivier: A Biography*. New York: HarperCollins, 1992.

————. *Otherwise Engaged: The Life of Alan Bates*. London: Hutchinson, 2007.

————. *Spellbound by Beauty: Alfred Hitchcock and His Leading Ladies.* New York: Three Rivers Press, 2008.

Strachan, Alan. *Secret Dreams—A Biography of Michael Redgrave.* London: Orion, 2005.

Sutherland, John. *Stephen Spender—A Literary Life.* New York: Oxford University Press, 2005.

Turner, Adrian. *Robert Bolt: Scenes from Two Lives.* London: Hutchinson, 1998.

Wallace, Mike, with Gary Paul Gates. *Between You and Me.* New York: Hyperion, 2005.

Wapshott, Nicholas. *The Man Between: A Biography of Carol Reed.* London: Chatto and Windus, 1990.

Wearing, J. P. *The London Stage 1940–1949: A Calendar of Plays and Players.* Metuchen, NJ, and London: Scarecrow Press, 1991.

Index

About the Author

DONALD SPOTO is the author of twenty-six books, including internationally bestselling biographies of Alfred Hitchcock, Tennessee Williams, Laurence Olivier, Marlene Dietrich, Ingrid Bergman and Audrey Hepburn.